ART APPRECIATION

an organic approach to the visual arts

Paige Wideman

Kendall Hunt
publishing company

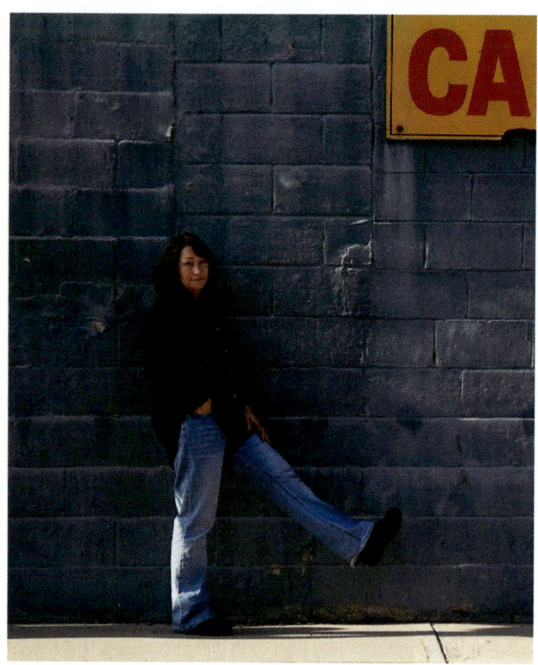

ABOUT THE AUTHOR

Paige Wideman has been in academia for almost 20 years. As coordinator of the Art Appreciation area at Northern Kentucky University, she has had a unique opportunity to develop a class that combines both art history and studio arts elements. In addition, Wideman continues to explore her own artistic and curatorial pursuits.

Kendall Hunt
publishing company
www.kendallhunt.com
Send all inquiries to:
4050 Westmark Drive
Dubuque, IA 52004-1840

ISBN: 978-1-5249-3647-1

Printed in the United States of America

CONTENTS

INTRODUCTION

Veering from the chronological approach to the arts, this book takes a more organic, thematic direction providing a different perspective to why humans create works of art. By focusing on aspects of a philosophy, a culture, or an artist's life, the purpose behind these creations puts them into a context which makes each come alive. This more humanistic approach helps to engage the reader, in particular non-art majors, allowing them to discover how significant art really is and why it should not be ignored or dismissed so easily.

Art Appreciation: an organic approach to the visual arts is divided into three sections—Body, Thought and Environment. These categories address aspects that are important to all humans and in turn help readers realize art is all around them, impacting their lives daily. Some cultures and artists appear in more than one area of the book to help convey the complexity of art as a tool of communication and form of expression.

Because of the diversity of our world and our scholarly institutions, a more global perspective is needed to illustrate the diversity of why art is created throughout the ages. For this reason, artwork from Western and non-Western cultures—from ancient times to the present day—are provided. In addition, the approach used in this book will help the reader discover or deepen their existing appreciation for art, whether for its beauty, its complexity, its simplicity or the sole purpose of its creation.

ACKNOWLEDGMENTS

From a young age, I found myself surrounded by amazing teachers who showed me there were no boundaries to what could be done. For their dedication to engaging and shaping young minds, I want to thank all of them, but especially Mrs. Miller, Ms. Wolfe, Madame Hobson, 'Chappie', Dale Eldred (1933–1993), Jim Leedy, and Richard Anderson. A special thank you goes to Patricia Renick (1932–2007), who not only was an amazing educator, but a true mentor and friend to me long after graduate school—and the first to plant the seed to write my own Art Appreciation textbook. And to Laura Chapman, a very dear friend who naturally assumed the role of mentor and who has encouraged and guided me along my path as an artist, an educator and now a writer.

To my family—my mother, Susan and my aunt, Kathy—for the time consuming dedication to proofreading my original drafts and for their unconditional love and support. To my colleagues, Thom McGovern—for replanting the seed to write a textbook and Kim Allen-Kattus—for the initial fact checking and proofreading.

Without the help of the following extraordinary artists, this book would not be complete. A heartfelt thank you to the following for donating their images to this project: Farron Allen, Joell Angel-Chumbley, Mary Barr Rhodes, Michelle Blades, Liliana Duque Piñeiro, Ana England, Stuart Fink, Saad Ghosn, Timothy Gold, Renee Harris, Celene Hawkins, Andrea Knarr, David Martin, Lisa Merida-Paytes, Kevin Muente, Cheryl Pannabecker, Carrie Pate, Kathleen Piercefield, Randel Plowman, Ellen Price, Michelle Red Elk, Matthew Reed, Merle Rosen, Randall Sackerson, Bryn Weller, and Carole Winters.

Last but not least, I want to express my appreciation towards all the dedicated people at Kendall Hunt Publishing Company for their time and commitment to helping me bring this book to fruition. A special thanks to my rep and Acquisitions Editor, Kerry Hollifield, for seeing the potential in this project, and to Sara McGovern, my initial Senior Project Coordinator who helped me get this underway. And finally, to Michelle L. Bahr, my current Senior Project Coordinator who helped me bring it home.

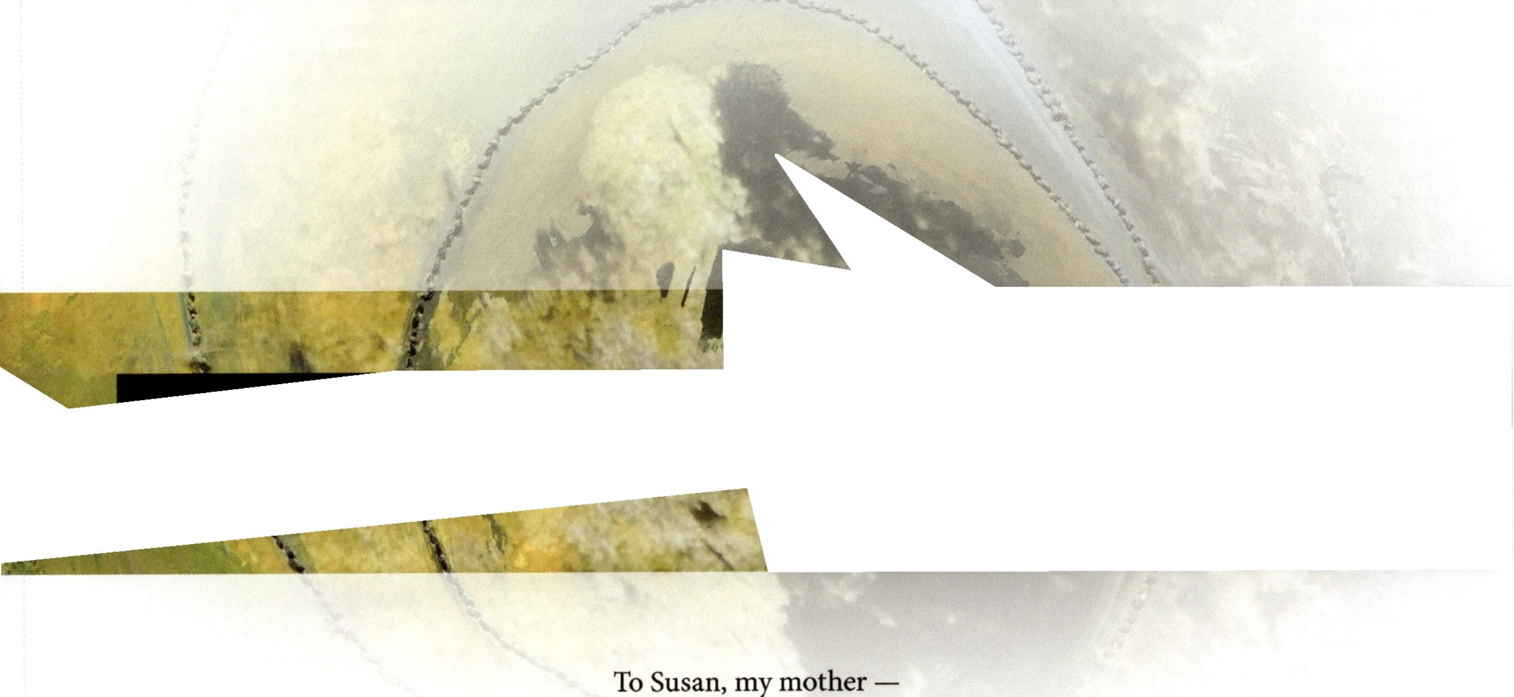

To Susan, my mother —

and all my family for their love, support and continuing encouragement to pursue my creative endeavors.

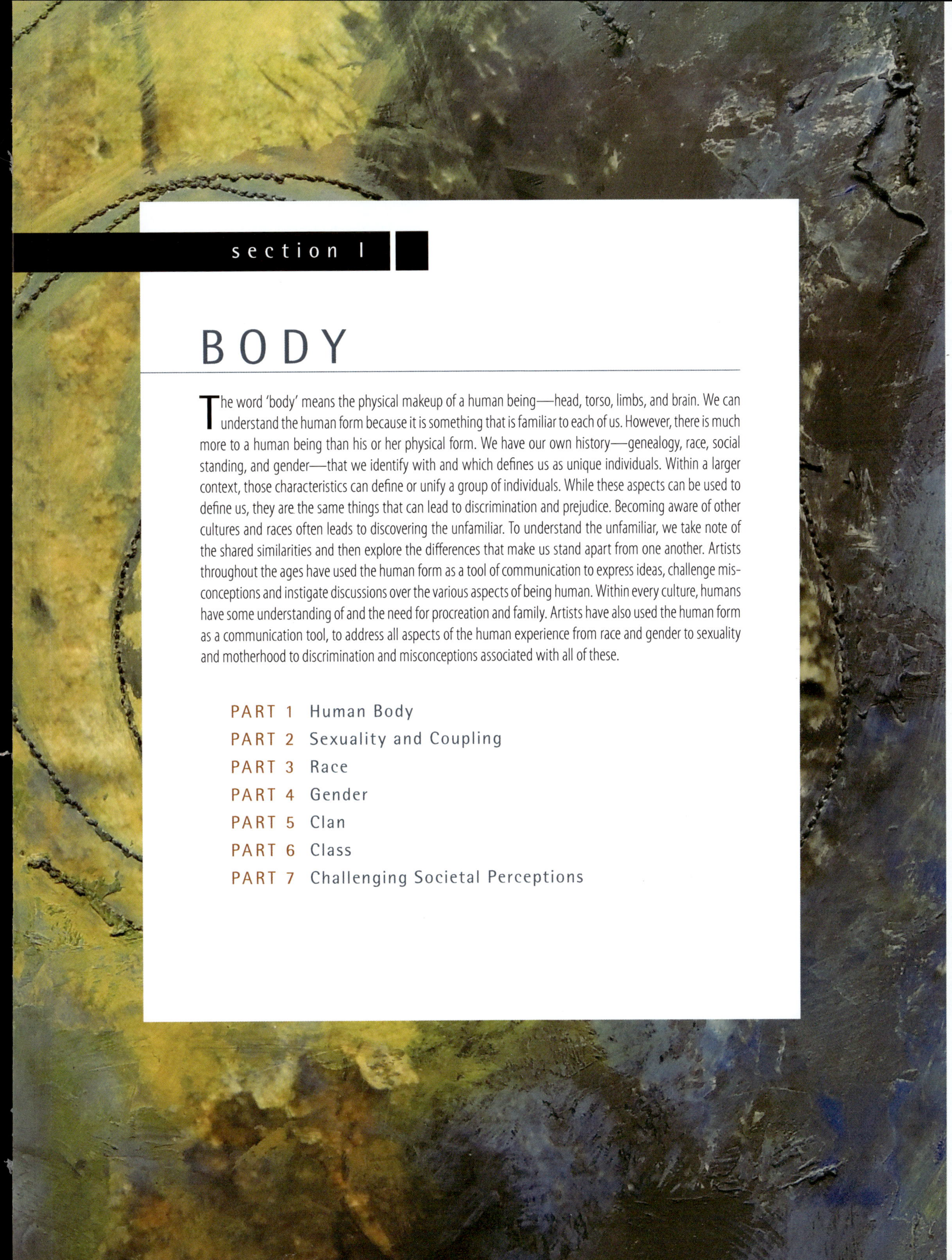

section I

BODY

The word 'body' means the physical makeup of a human being—head, torso, limbs, and brain. We can understand the human form because it is something that is familiar to each of us. However, there is much more to a human being than his or her physical form. We have our own history—genealogy, race, social standing, and gender—that we identify with and which defines us as unique individuals. Within a larger context, those characteristics can define or unify a group of individuals. While these aspects can be used to define us, they are the same things that can lead to discrimination and prejudice. Becoming aware of other cultures and races often leads to discovering the unfamiliar. To understand the unfamiliar, we take note of the shared similarities and then explore the differences that make us stand apart from one another. Artists throughout the ages have used the human form as a tool of communication to express ideas, challenge misconceptions and instigate discussions over the various aspects of being human. Within every culture, humans have some understanding of and the need for procreation and family. Artists have also used the human form as a communication tool, to address all aspects of the human experience from race and gender to sexuality and motherhood to discrimination and misconceptions associated with all of these.

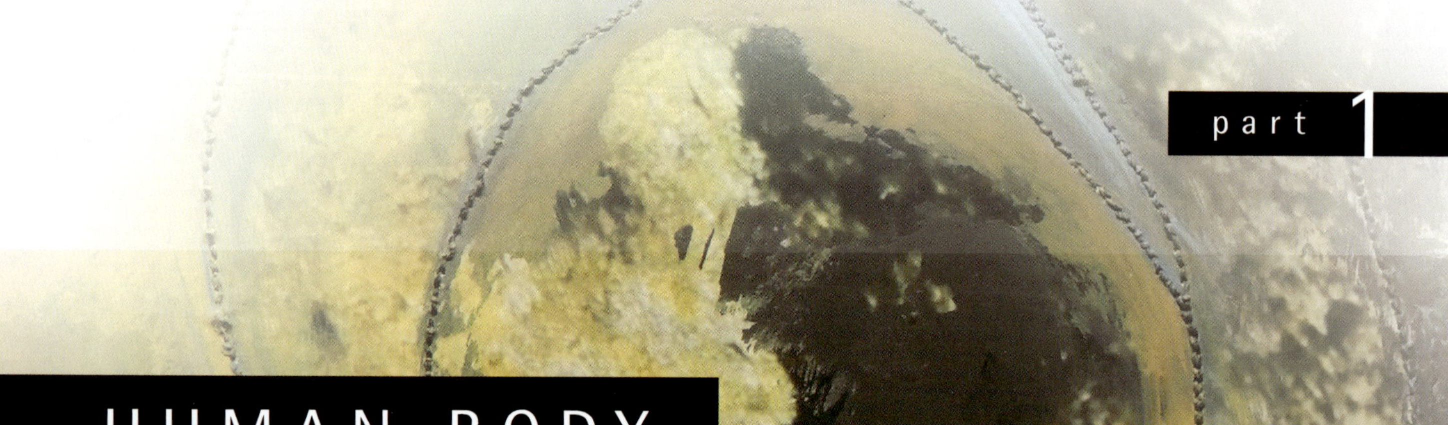

part 1

HUMAN BODY

IDENTITY

Our bodies can be a form of identity—cultural or personal—not only through our unique physical facial features or overall body stature, but also other aspects such as our hands, fingerprints, and way we dress.

Over 40,000 years ago during the Paleolithic period in Europe, our ancestors left behind their handprints or outlines of their hands on cave walls. Through recent discoveries, like the Chauvet Cave in France in the 1990s, and through extensive studies, archaeologists have noticed that the handprints are not all the same. There are unique characteristics that separate them, such as the spacing between fingers, the overall size of the hand, and the length of certain fingers. By recording the unique characteristics of each, they can then see that certain individuals have left their 'mark' or 'signature' near specific cave paintings of animals. This could signify man's earliest form of signature and desire for recognition of their works of art.

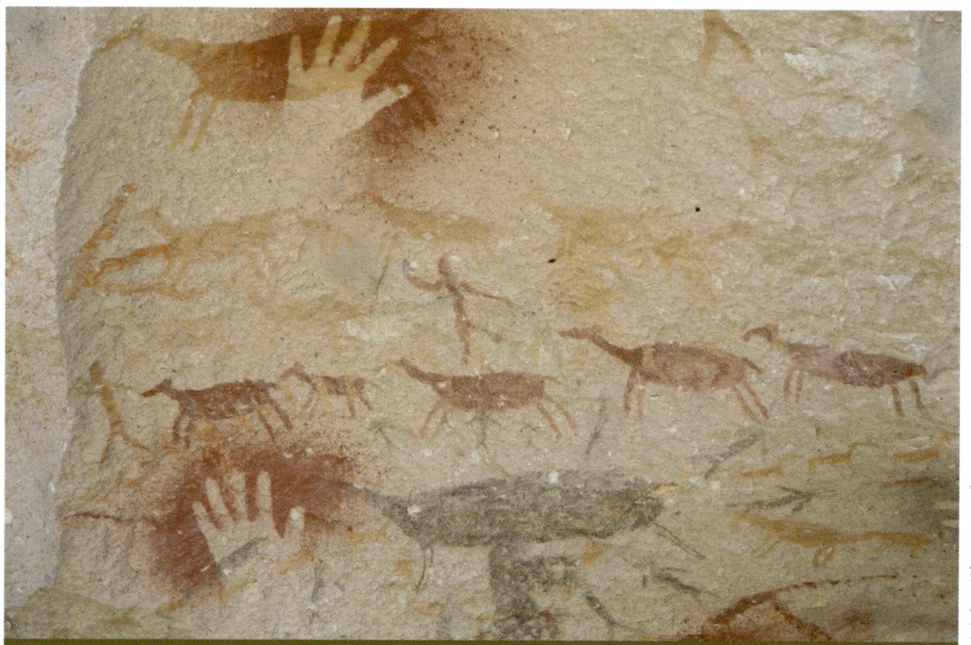

FIGURE 1.1 – Cave of the Hands. Argentina. c. 8000 BC. Pigment on rock.

The Cueva de Los Manos (Cave of Hands) located in Patagonia dates back almost 13,000 years. Extensive imagery of plants, animals, hunting scenes, and outlines of hands adorn the cave. The habitat around the cave has remained intact and still has many of the animal and plant species depicted on its walls. Due to the low humidity and stable rock strata upon which the images were created, they had been well preserved until recent tourism led to vandalism. This included graffiti and the removal of fragments of painted rock. The mouth of the cave is shielded by a large rock wall with multiple painted hand outlines (see Figure 1.1). Over the centuries, the hunter-gatherers in the region returned to the cave to continue leaving imagery upon its walls, superimposing the newer images over those from earlier periods. As seen throughout Paleolithic times, the images were painted with minerals readily found in the environment, which they then ground into a powder and mixed with some type of binder before applying to the walls.

BINDER - a liquid substance that holds color pigment and when it dries creates a paint layer.

Mesopotamia was the region located in between Tigris and Euphrates rivers, which today is Iraq and parts of Iran, Syria, and Turkey. Unlike other civilizations nearby, such as Egypt, this region throughout history was home to a variety of cultures. While the cultures shared a few commonalities, such as their deities, they differed in many ways from one another in social customs, laws, and languages. Significant inventions and developments, such as the wagon wheel, bronze, advanced weaponry, and domestication of plants and animals, led to the development of large-scale civilizations. The main source of trade—food—was used to obtain commodities such as copper, gold, and other raw materials. These in turn could be made into other tradable objects. During Mesopotamia's history, there were three cultures that rose to the top—Sumerian, Assyrian, and Babylonian.

The Babylonian culture (1900 BC) was located in a city nestled along the east bank of the Euphrates River in the southwestern part of Mesopotamia. This location was ideal for agriculture and trade, but left it vulnerable to attack. When the city was left without strong leadership to defend it, Babylon found itself easily overtaken by invaders. Its initial rise to power came through the reign of Hammurabi (1811–1750 BC), who successfully ruled for forty-two years. Following his death, the empire gradually fell into decline. It was not until Nebuchadnezzar II (634–562 BC) gained control over the area in 605 BC that the city rose again in power and wealth. Due to the success of trade, this region became the center of civilized trade for over a thousand years.

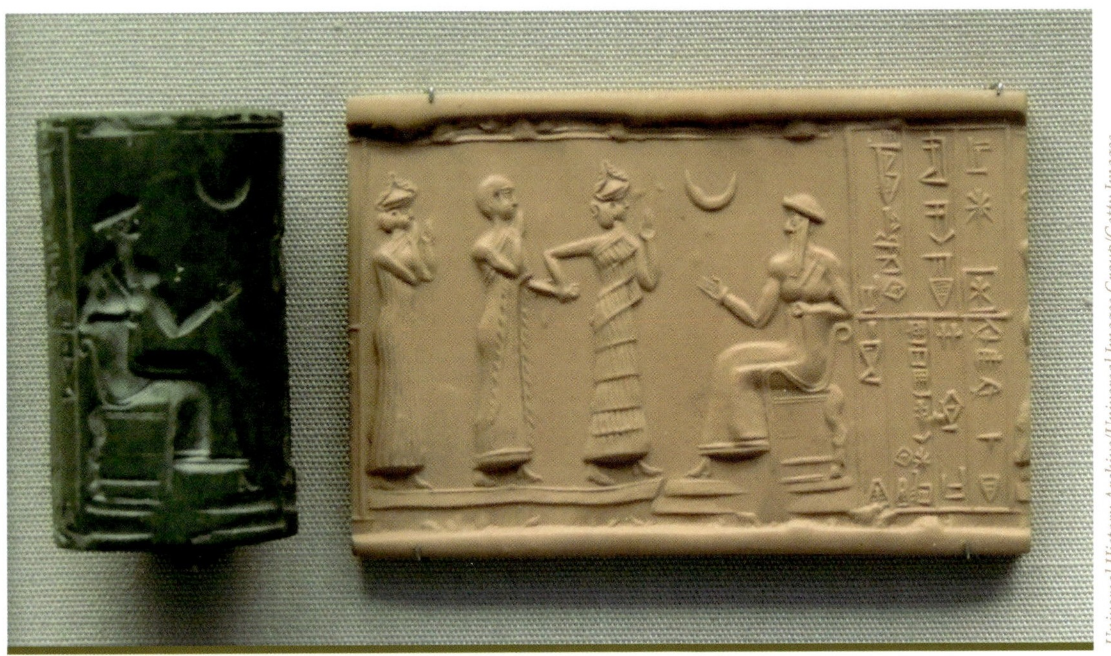

FIGURE 1.2 – Greenstone Cylinder Seal. Iran/Iraq. c. 2047–2030 BC. Engraved stone.

The creation and use of cylinder seals seems to have been a common Mesopotamian practice. Cylinder seals were usually three or four inches in height and made from a variety of materials, including ceramics and semi-precious stones, such as carnelian and lapis lazuli. Unique images, sometimes including text or patterning, were incised into the seal in order to identify a specific person. A hole was drilled through the center so that the stone seal could be worn around its owner's neck or wrist. When concluding a business transaction, the seal impressions, created on clay, from the parties involved acted as a form of receipt. Seal impressions were also used to verify the authenticity of a document or package. As each design of a seal is unique to its owner, it was seen as their personal signature. The *Greenstone Cylinder Seal* (see Figure 1.2) and its impression on the right shows the owner of the seal standing in between two goddesses. They are leading this person to the King who is shown seated on an elaborate throne. The inscription on the far right of the seal indicates that it belongs to the governor of the city of Ishkun-Sin, and he is in the service of the King.

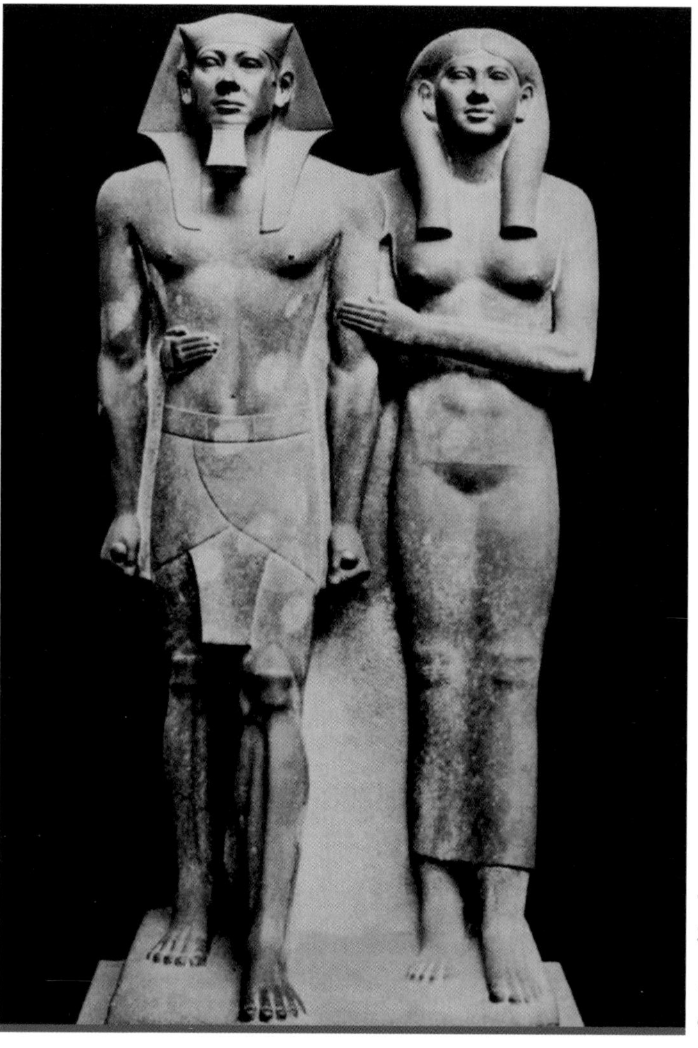
Courtesy of Corel

FIGURE 1.3 – Menkaura and Wife. Egypt. c. 2490 BC. 22.5 x 56 x 21.75 in. Graywacke.

Artists can show the status of a person through how they are depicted. This occurs in many ways, including type of clothing, personal adornment, scale, style, and the environment in which they are shown. The Egyptian sculpture of *Menkaura and Wife* (see Figure 1.3) is from the Old Kingdom Fourth Dynasty between 2548 and 2530 BC. Throughout a large part of Egyptian history, pharaohs and their spouses were depicted in a stylized manner. For the males, the body is depicted as youthful, muscular, and broad shouldered to visually convey the idea of strength and power. Menkaura is wearing a traditional kilt around his waist, a false beard, and a *nemes* (headdress) all of which are symbols of his position as ruler.

In contrast, his queen, Khamerernebty II, conveys the Egyptian ideal of feminine beauty. She is slim bodied with narrow shoulders and wearing a shear, tight-fitting dress traditional of her status. The artist creates the illusion of shear fabric by making the breasts, nipples, stomach, and knees of the queen less detailed compared to that of Menkaura. Unlike the majority of Egyptian royal art, the queen is not perfectly mimicking the pharaoh's pose. Here, she is seen wrapping one arm around his torso and placing the other on his arm in what may be seen as a sign of support or perhaps comfort.

Located in the Gulf Coast of Mexico, the Olmec culture thrived from 1200 to 400 BC. They developed large-scale complex societies, monumental architecture, and elaborate political and religious systems. Being the first major Mesoamerican civilization, the Olmecs are considered the forefathers of Pre-Columbian cultures, such as the Maya, Toltec, and Aztec. In each of those cultures, there are similarities within their writing, artwork, and religion that can be traced back to the Olmec culture. However, even with a similar writing style, the Olmec language is undecipherable to us and therefore, many specifics of their culture are gleamed from those that proceeded them. One of the few remaining forms of artwork from the Olmecs are the colossal stone heads that were salvaged before the destruction of much of this culture's remains by the oil industry in 1930s.

The Olmec Heads (see Figure 1.4) were constructed out of basalt rock that was quarried approximately sixty miles from their final resting place. Rafts, sledges, and sheer man-power were most likely used to transport the large chunks of basalt ranging from five to ten feet in height and fifteen feet in circumference. These stones weighed anywhere from eight to forty tons each. Once placed in a particular location, artisans used stone hammers and tools to carve naturalistic representations of human heads. There is still some discussion as to whom these sculptures are meant to represent. Because of the style of the helmets depicted, these sculptures could represent Olmec warriors or ball players. However, due to their size and similar figurative depictions in altars, these most likely represent specific Olmec rulers.

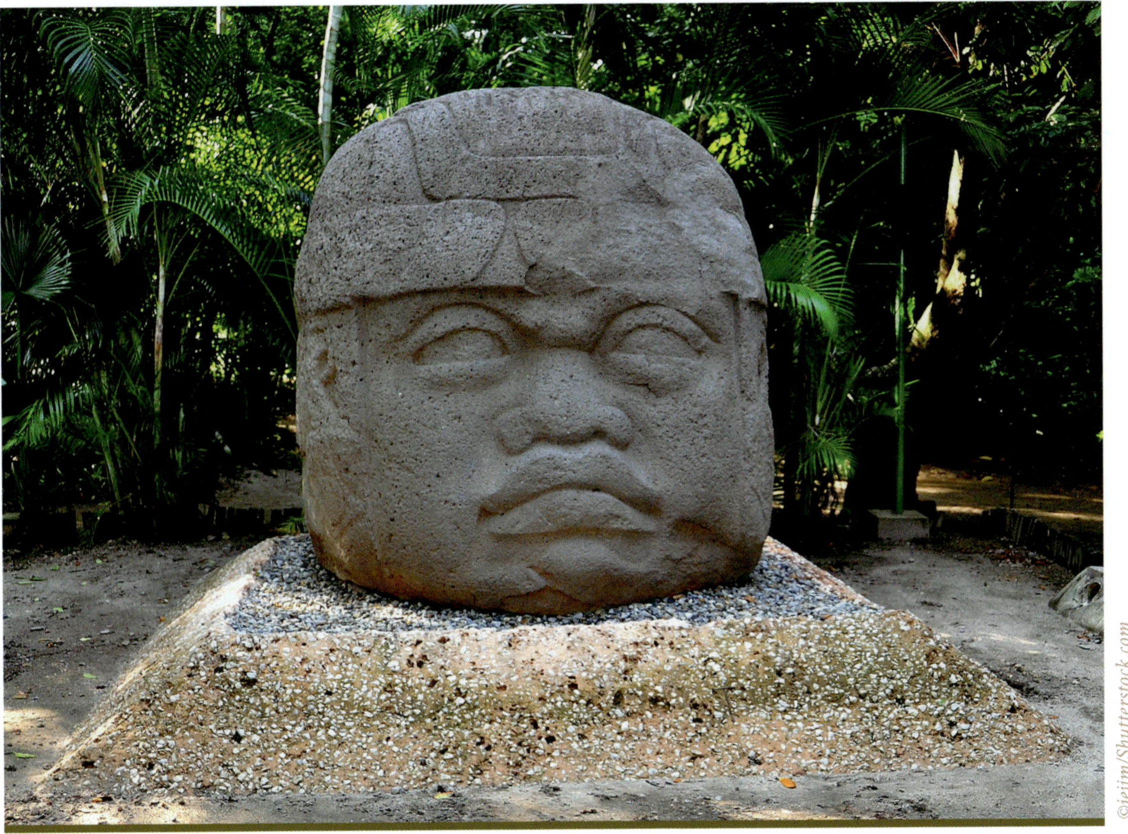

FIGURE 1.4 – Giant Olmec Head. Pre-Columbian. c. 1100 BC. Approximately 6 ft. high. Basalt rock.

While each Olmec head (see Figure 1.5) has a unique helmet design and unique facial features, there are similarities among them. These include the earplug, the broad nose, the slight downturned edges of the mouth, and the pronounced "fatty pad" between the brows creating feline-like characteristics common to a jaguar. In some helmet designs, clear references to the jaguar are seen. In later Pre-Columbian cultures, the jaguar is often associated with rulers and shamans. It is possible the Olmec rulers also associated political and religious power with the jaguar.

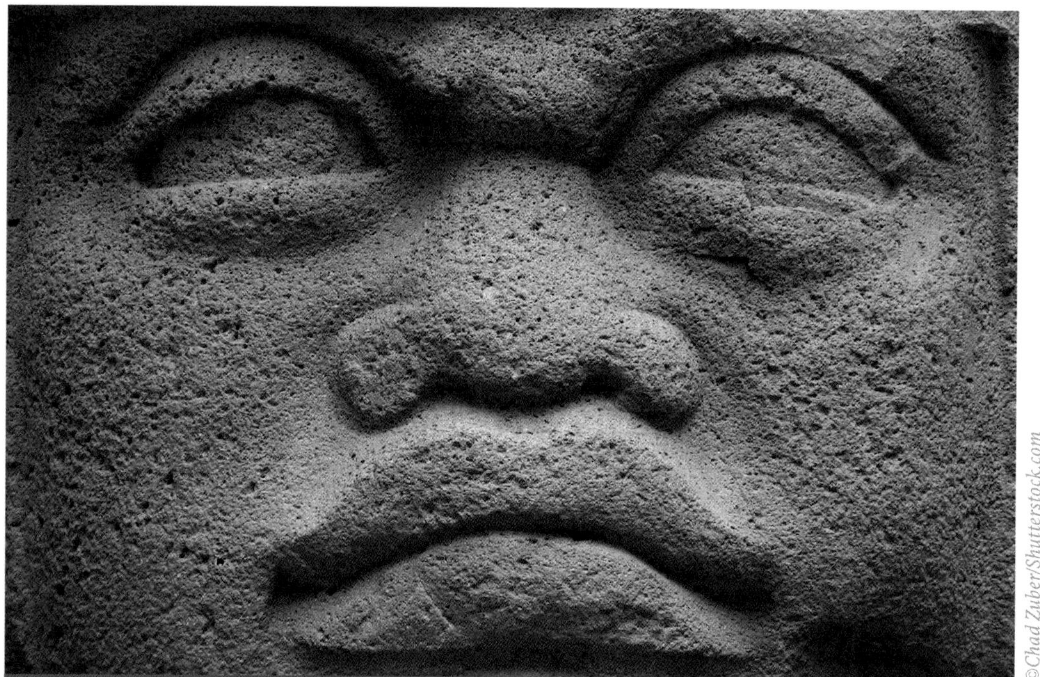

©Chad Zuber/Shutterstock.com

FIGURE 1.5 – Olmec Head (detail). Pre-Columbian. c. 1100 BC. Basalt rock.

There is much mystery and speculation surrounding these monumental works of art, why they were created and why they were placed in each location. One purpose may have been to visually mark a ruler's territory by placing them on the outer edges of the city. Another possibility is their presence reminded others of the power of the current ruler. Damage to many of these sculptures seems to have resulted during the time of their culture. This suggests that subsequent rulers had these works vandalized to neutralize any perceived lingering power of the deceased ruler or to help legitimize their own claim to the throne.

PORTRAITS

Throughout the ages, artists have created portraits of significant people within their cultures. The wealthy would have portraits painted of themselves or their families to adorn their homes, while political figures often did so to memorialize specific events and achievements in their lives. The use of the portrait has expanded over time to include sports figures, famous people, and even the everyday person.

In 1799, General Napoleon Bonaparte (1769–1821) staged a coup d'état against the existing revolutionary government. In this process, he not only made France a great power but also became the most powerful man in France, eventually declaring himself Emperor. The King of Spain, Charles IV, commissioned French artist Jacques-Louis David (1748–1825) to paint a portrait of Napoleon to hang in the royal palace gallery with those of other great military leaders.

The image that David chose to depict was of Napoleon crossing the Swiss Alps (see Figure 1.6) in May of 1800. It was a military campaign which led to the defeat of the Austrians at the Battle of Marengo. In this painting, Napoleon is shown calmly controlling a rearing stallion, demonstrating his ability as a leader to govern with composure and sound judgment.

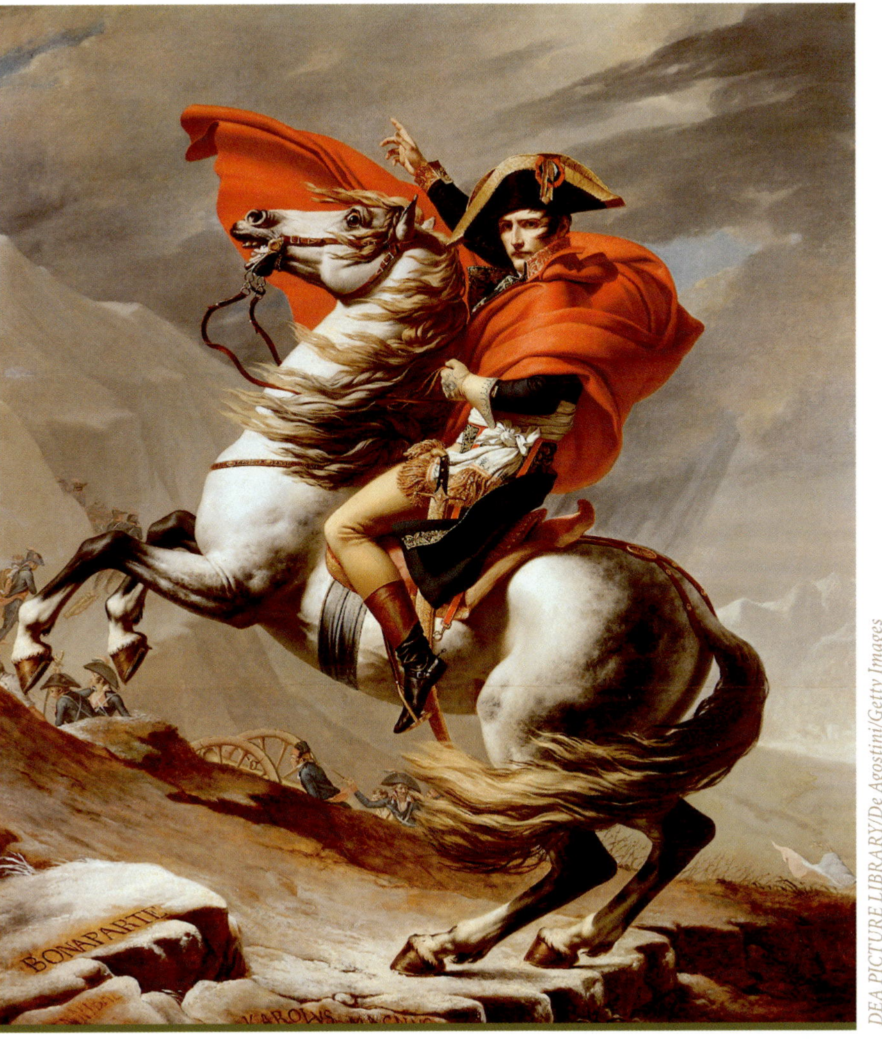

DEA PICTURE LIBRARY/De Agostini/Getty Images

FIGURE 1.6 – Bonaparte Crossing the St. Bernard Pass, Jacques-Louis David. 1800. 261 x 221 cm. Oil on canvas.

This portrait of Napoleon has inaccuracies throughout. For example, while Napoleon was only 5'7" in height, the figure appears to be much taller in stature. This is probably due to the fact that Napoleon refused to pose for the portrait, forcing David to use one of his sons as a stand in. The image also shows Napoleon's troops off in the distance implying that he is leading the charge. In actuality, he followed a day later on a mule.

Nonetheless, the portrait is dynamic in its composition. The strong diagonal lines created by Napoleon's raised arm, red cloak, and the mountain range in the background are counterbalanced by the direction of the clouds to his right. These elements draw the viewer's attention to the central figure of Napoleon. In the lower left corner of the image, Napoleon's name is carved into the rock along with other notable historical figures—Hannibal and Charlemagne—who crossed that same passage through the Alps.

Using a new technology, James Brewerton Ricketts (1817–1887) also had a portrait done. He was a native New Yorker, was a graduate of the United States Military Academy, and served his country for almost fifty years. During the Mexican War, he was an Officer of Artillery. By 1852, Ricketts was made a Captain and by the time of the Civil War, he was in command of a battery in the Union Army. He continued to be promoted throughout his career and served his country in various positions until 1869. He was buried in Arlington Cemetery in Washington, DC upon his death in September of 1887.

With the invention of photography, portraits eventually became more affordable to the masses. This image of *General and Mrs. J.B. Ricketts* (see Figure 1.7) was typical for the Civil War era. High ranking officials would be photographed alone or with members of their family—wives or children—by their side. This photographic image was created with the wet-collodion process, invented in 1851 by Englishman Frederick Scott Archer (1813–1857). The process involved coating a piece of glass with a mixture of soluble iodide and collodion, before immersing it in a solution of silver nitrate in a darkroom. The wet plate was then placed into the camera and the photograph was taken. Immediately afterward, it was processed with other chemicals to more permanently adhere the image to the glass surface. The end result produced a high level of clarity and detail.

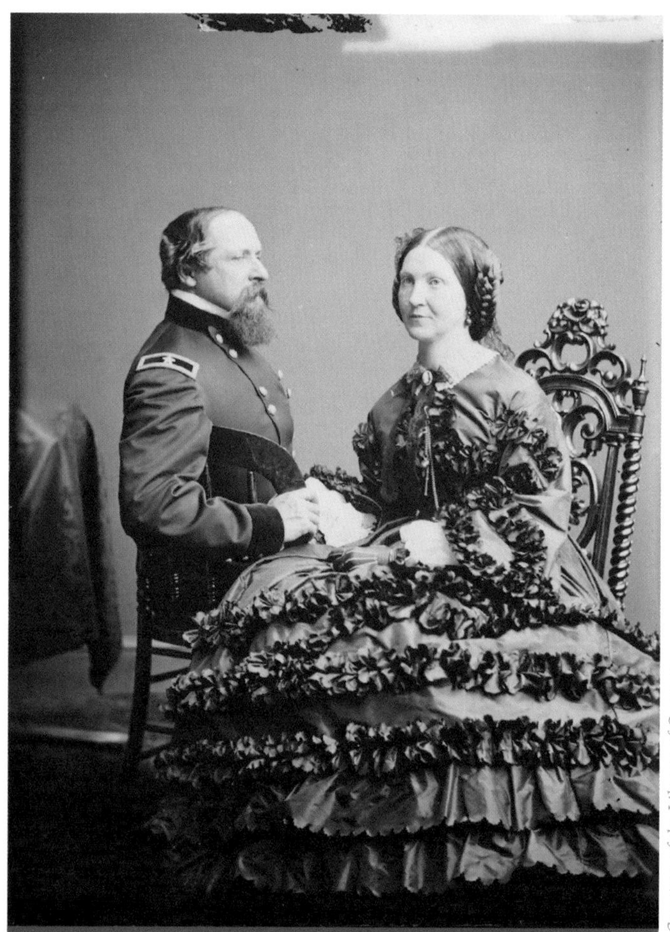
Courtesy of the Library of Congress

FIGURE 1.7 – Gen. and Mrs. J.B. Ricketts. c. 1860. 6 1/8 x 8 3/4 in. Glass, wet collodion.

Around the American Civil War (early to mid-1860s), the sport of baseball gained popularity in the United States. As teams and players became better known to the population, baseball-themed picture cards were produced. There were large versions called 'cabinet cards' that were meant to be put on display in cabinets. Miniature versions were called 'carte de viste.' While it was common to have famous players depicted on them, amateur, local, and youth teams were also the subjects of cards. These could be easily carried around and were collected as mementoes.

By the late 1860s, the creation of baseball cards was taken over by commercial companies. Peck and Snyder, a sporting good company, was first to print cards in large quantities to be given away as a form of advertising, rather than being sold with a product. The front would depict a famous baseball team, while on the back there was an advertisement for the company. These cards were known as 'trade cards' and considered the first modern baseball cards.

Between the 1870s–1890s, trade cards were a popular form of advertising for many companies that utilized a variety of imagery, including animals, comics, and images of presidents. By the mid-1880s, baseball cards for the first time were being mass produced in quantities that could be distributed nationwide. Tobacco companies were one of the main producers of these, using them not only as a way to boost their sales, but also as a 'stiffener' for their cigarette packs. While Goodwin & Co. started this trend with the creation of the *Old Judge* card, others quickly followed suit, flooding the market with other unique versions that the public soon rushed to collect. Eventually, many of the tobacco companies fell under the control of the American Tobacco Company.

The American Tobacco Company produced the T-206 and T-205 series, depicting images of both major and minor leaguers. The popularity of the white-bordered T-206 (1909–1911) cards led to the creation of the gold-bordered T-205 series in 1911 (see Figure 1.8). Remaining true to the original 'trade card' format, the image of a player was on front, while advertising for the company's product was on the back (see Figure 1.9). Although photography was a well-established art form at this point, these cards were color lithographs.

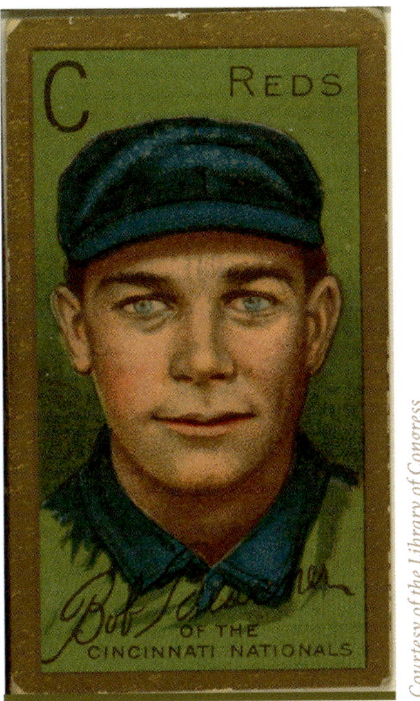

Courtesy of the Library of Congress

FIGURE 1.8 – Robert H. Bescher, Cincinnati Reds, baseball card (front), American Tobacco Company. 1911. 1 7/16 x 2 5/8 in. Lithograph.

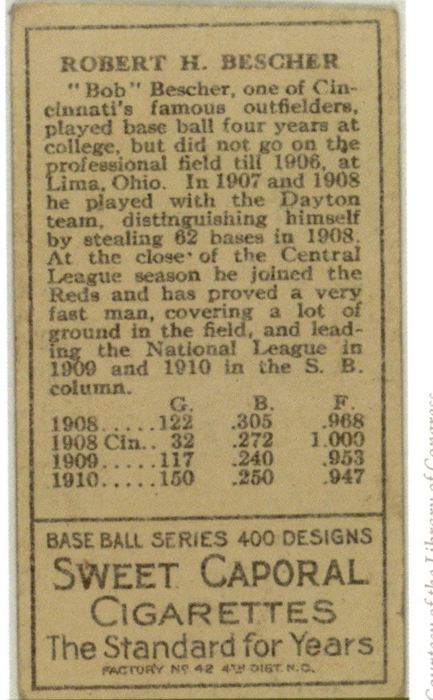

Courtesy of the Library of Congress

FIGURE 1.9 – Robert H. Bescher, Cincinnati Reds, baseball card (back), American Tobacco Company. 1911. 1 7/16 x 2 5/8 in. Lithograph.

LITHOGRAPH - a printmaking process where an image is drawn on a flat, stone surface with a greasy or oily medium, such as a crayon, prior to inking and printing.

In the early 1900s, the U.S. government sued to break up the American Tobacco Company monopoly. With its success, this reopened the market for other companies to create such advertising cards. Eventually history repeated itself, when in the 1950s Topps Chewing Gum Company monopolized the baseball card industry. The court ruled in 1980 that other companies could produce baseball cards, but Topp's remained the only company allowed to package them with gum.

Robert H. Bescher, an Ohio native, grew up to become a Cincinnati Reds player. Although only having played for eight seasons in the major leagues, he had 428 career stolen bases and for a long time held the single-season record for stolen bases—a total of 81 in 1911. His success on the field led to his being featured on a trade card that same year.

SELF-PORTRAITS

Many artists have used themselves as subject matter. Sometimes as a way to perfect their skills artistically; other times as a way to record a moment within their lives.

Albrecht Dürer was born in Nuremberg, Germany in 1471. His father was a goldsmith, known as Albrecht Dürer the Elder. Around the age of fifteen, Dürer became an apprentice to a painter and woodcut designer named Michael Wolgemut (1434–1519). Both men taught and inspired Dürer, who became a painter and printmaker.

Around 1495, Dürer traveled for the first time to Italy. His stay in Venice had a major impact on the direction of his art. The Italian tradition of capturing harmony and beauty, along with depicting the human form in a more naturalistic way, can be seen in his 1498 self-portrait (see Figure 1.10).

In this image, the 26-year-old artist is showing himself dressed in clothing that appears to be well-made and expensive. By doing so, the artist was using the current mindset in Nuremberg, where clothing and jewelry were used to distinguish one's social class from another. Here, he is suggesting that an artist like himself should occupy an elevated social position in society.

The setting in which Dürer places himself is the interior of a building, flooded with light from the window to his right. Outside the window, Dürer has created a mountainous landscape, employing the Italian tradition at that time of combining portraits with landscapes. The viewer's eye is drawn to the artist through his use of light colored clothing, which also accentuates the intricate detail of his golden hair. His posture and direct gaze visually communicate an air of self-confidence.

Just below the window sill, the artist made it clear that this is a self-portrait with the inscription that includes his full name, age, and year of the painting. Underneath this information, one can see his now famous monogram of a D placed within a larger A.

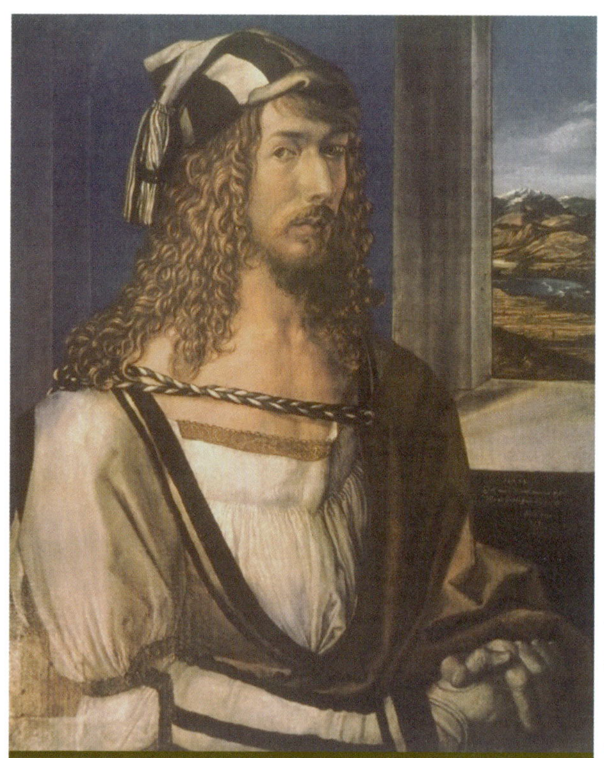

Courtesy of Corel

FIGURE 1.10 – Self-Portrait, Albrecht Dürer. 1498. 52 x 41 cm. Oil on wood panel.

Dutch artist, Vincent van Gogh (1853–1890) was a prolific artist whose real fame and notoriety came well after his death. He struggled with poverty and depression throughout his life, seeking solace in his art. Van Gogh worked with a wide range of subject matter, including nature and people. Within his short life, he created over 2100 works of art.

SUBJECT MATTER - the idea represented in a work of art.

At the age of 35, Vincent van Gogh saw his dream of starting an artist colony come to fruition. He moved to Arles in the South of France, where he felt the natural light, landscape, and people had much to offer. A year earlier, van Gogh had an encounter with Paul Gauguin, a painter he greatly respected. With the encouragement of van Gogh's brother, Theo, Gauguin eventually accepted the invitation to be the first to stay at the artist colony and work alongside van Gogh in the fall of 1888. Their time together was initially productive and showed how two painters could paint the same subject in two completely different ways.

After a time, the deterioration of van Gogh's mental health started to show through odd behavior. Gauguin, eventually concerned for his own safety, made preparations to take leave of Arles. Van Gogh was devastated at the prospect of losing his companion and pleaded for him to stay. Gauguin acquiesced, but eventually it became too difficult for him to remain. On 23 December 1888, Gauguin confirmed he was finally leaving. Later that night he left for a walk. Reportedly, he turned to find van Gogh walking after him with a razor in his hand. When Gauguin confronted him, van Gogh lowered his head and returned home. Gauguin stayed at a hotel for the night.

When he returned the next day, Gauguin found a bloody scene and the police standing near van Gogh's bed. Van Gogh had reportedly cut off his ear after Gauguin's departure and had carefully wrapped it in newspaper. He left it with a woman at a nearby brothel before returning to his home.

There is much speculation around the actual incident. It is known that Gauguin was an excellent fencer and was fearful of his safety when around van Gogh. One theory now taking hold is that Gauguin accidentally cut off van Gogh's ear during a fight and van Gogh made up the story of doing it himself in order to protect his friend. They both vowed to never speak of the actual incident, leading to the continued mystery around the event. This event led to the subsequent creation of the self-portrait *The Man with His Ear Cut Off* (see Figure 1.11) created in 1889.

Austrian artist, Egon Schiele (1890–1918) exhibited a talent for drawing in his early childhood. He attended the Academy of Fine Arts in Vienna from 1906–1909, where he encountered a well-known artist, Gustav Klimt. Klimt became a 'father' figure to the young artist and introduced him to influential collectors who became important supporters of his work.

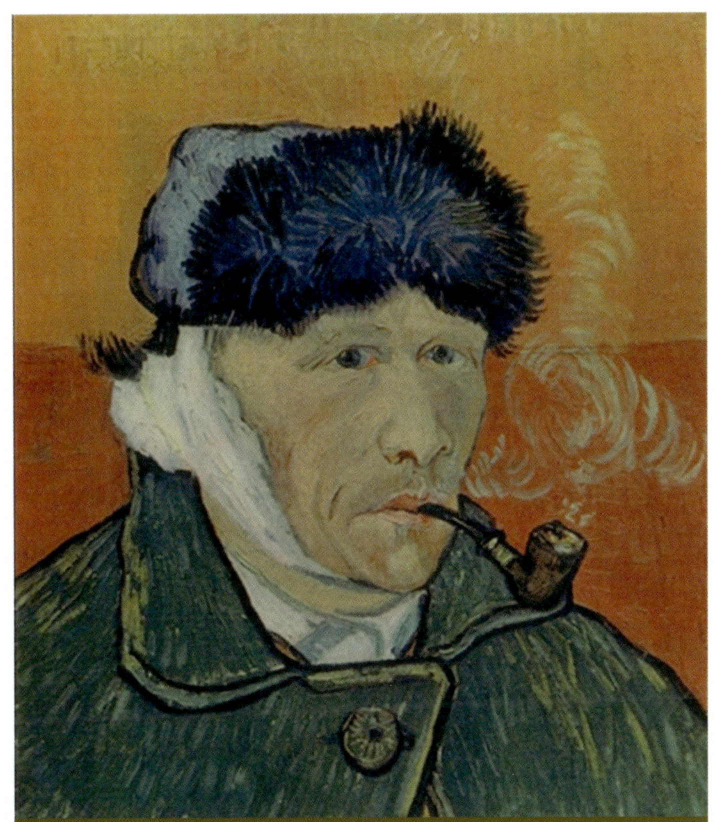

Courtesy of Corel

FIGURE 1.11 – The Man with His Ear Cut Off, Vincent van Gogh. 1889. 16 x 24 in. Oil on canvas.

At the time, Schiele's work was gaining recognition, traditional portraiture focused on the idealist aesthetics of the beautiful. However, he was pushing the boundaries of the accepted by using intimate perspectives of the nude figure, bordering on the explicit and erotic. In addition, Schiele's portraits appeared to be looking into the psyche of the individual and how it impacted their body physically. His art was considered very dramatic in contrast to the norms of the time. Schiele would stage the body in a way that also addressed ideas of sexuality. While putting another on display in such a manner may seem easier to do, he applied the same critical eye to his own portraits, as well. His focus on body language (facial expressions and bodily gestures) is the means in which the person within the painting comes alive.

In 1912, Schiele and a young woman, Valerie Wally Neuzil, moved to Neulengbach, in hopes of finding inexpensive studio space and inspirational surroundings. His studio space became a gathering place of the delinquent children of the town. Soon after he was arrested for allegedly seducing an underage girl. Schiele spent just under a month in jail awaiting trial. Although the judge found nothing to support the charges of seduction, he did find Schiele's work to be pornographic in nature and inappropriate to be viewed by children. After he was eventually released, Schiele created a body of work that reflected the difficulties and discomfort he experienced in prison.

COMPOSITION - arrangement of visual elements in a work of art.

In *Self-Portrait with Chinese Lantern Plant* (see Figure 1.12), Schiele's simple composition and sparse use of color draw the viewer's eye directly to his face. The way he applied the paint to the canvas creates the appearance of scars and other subtle deformities. While not clearly stated as one of the images created directly after his imprisonment, the image of the artist looks as though he has suffered physical injuries. Perhaps, this is his way of showing the emotional and mental impact from that experience.

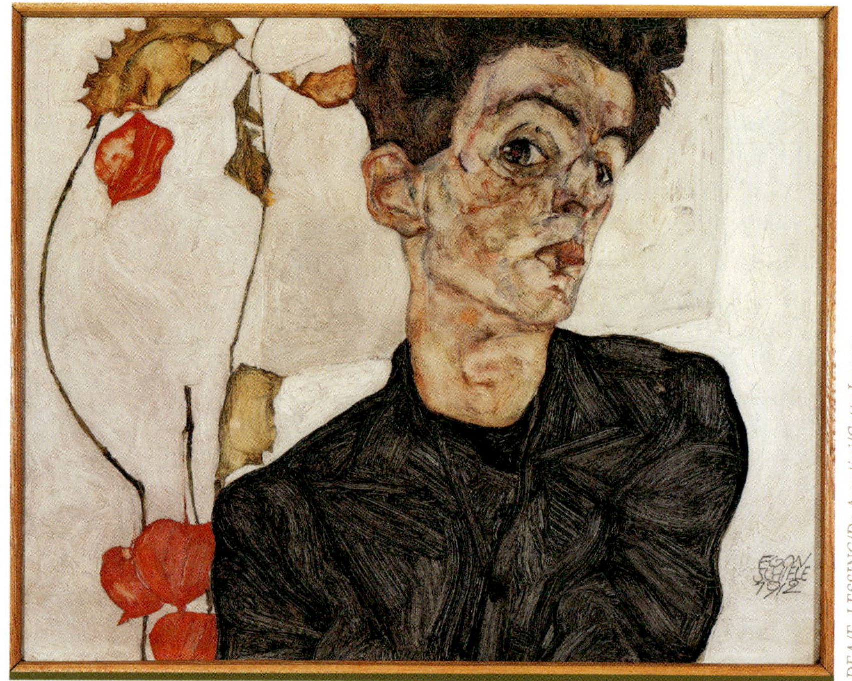

DEA/E. LESSING/De Agostini/Getty Images

FIGURE 1.12 – Self-Portrait with Chinese Lantern Plant, Egon Schiele. 1912. 32.2 x 39.8 cm. Oil on canvas.

REFLECTION

From a stick figure to the highly realistic rendering of the human form, artists use the body to communicate cultural ideals of perfection and behavior. In addition, by looking at the collective works created by an artist, the way the human figure is depicted can communicate changes in their views, perspectives, or feelings over time.

From the early Greek times, philosophers began to define what constituted perfection and proper human behavior. The artists were charged with visually capturing these ideas to communicate them to the masses. Through this process, *cannon* or rules of proportion were created. This provided any artist within the Greek culture the guidelines to use to create a perfect rendering of a human form.

Through extensive measuring of the human body, the Greeks discovered that the measurement from the top of the head to the bottom of the chin is repeated approximately eight times in the total body height of an individual. This allows an artist, whether drawing, painting, or sculpting the human form, to create a perfectly proportioned body every time.

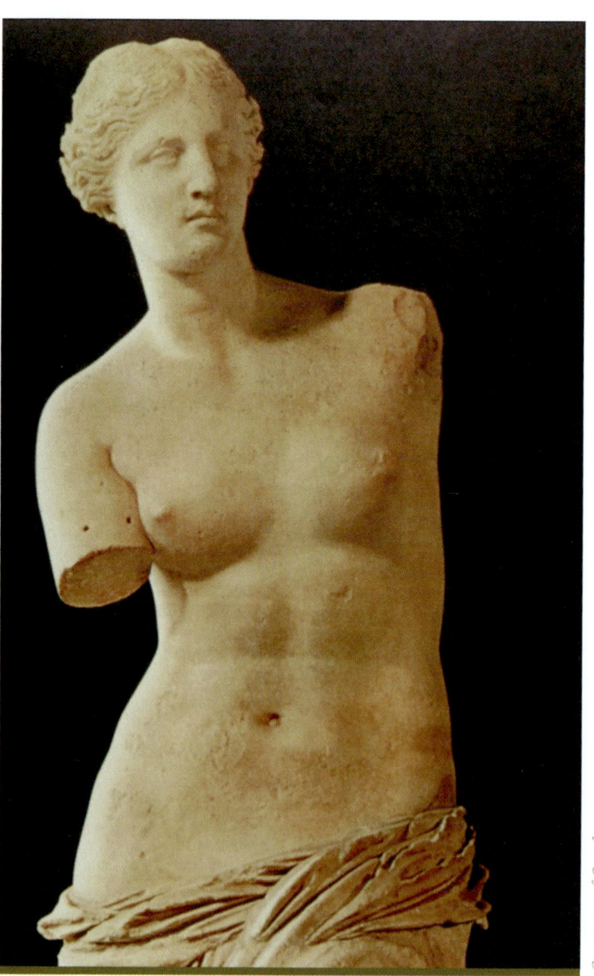

Courtesy of Corel

FIGURE 1.13 – Venus de Milo, Alexandros of Antioch. Greece. c. 130 BC. 203 cm. high. Marble.

Venus de Milo (see Figure 1.13) was created between 100 and 130 BC by Alexandros of Antioch. This sculpture is believed to represent the Greek goddess of love and beauty. Standing over six feet tall, *Venus de Milo* is representational of ideal feminine beauty at the time of its creation. In addition, it communicates the philosophy of near perfection that philosophers like Plato defined years earlier. These can be seen artistically through the body proportion and stance and the lack of emotion in her facial expression.

The sculpture is unique in that is was made in multiple sections. The main body of the sculpture is in two parts; the fold of the fabric draped at her waist cleverly hiding the separation line where the two pieces meet. The pedestal, each arm and the right foot were made from separate pieces of marble, which were then pinned to the piece.

Venus de Milo was discovered in an underground cavern near the ruins of an ancient Aegean theater in 1820 by a Greek peasant named Yourgos. It was badly damaged and found in pieces, which included a pedestal, piece of an upper left arm and left hand holding an apple. He stored all of it in a barn on his property, until it was discovered by Turkish authorities who confiscated it. Eventually, a French Ambassador to Turkey purchased the sculpture, had it repaired, and then presented it to King Louis XVIII of France in 1821. Although the King had attempted to replace the arms, he finally decided to display Venus without her arms and placed the sculpture in the Louvre Museum in Paris, where it resides today.

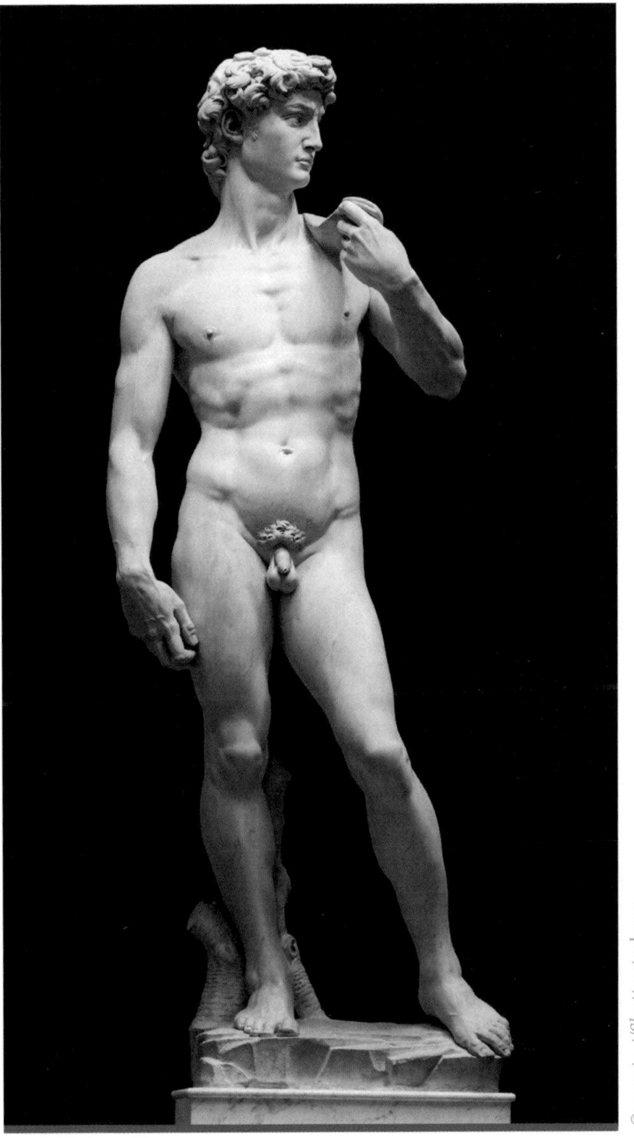

FIGURE 1.14 – David on Piazza della Signoria, Michelangelo. 1504. Appoximately 17 ft. high. Carrara marble.

For nearly thirty-five years in the courtyard of the Florence Cathedral in Italy, a large oblong chunk of Carrara marble was left abandoned by an earlier sculptor. Eventually, the young and ambitious artist, Michelangelo (1475–1564) was given the chance to create something from it. He chose to show his love for his native Florence through patriotic symbolism. As David had stood against Goliath, Florence stood against all potential threats in defense of its liberty. Thus, making David an appealing symbol of Florence itself.

Standing at almost seventeen feet tall, *David* (see Figure 1.14) by Michelangelo is a unique depiction of a biblical figure differing from two famous predecessors whose sculptures of David resided in Florence. While Donatello di Niccolò di Betto Bardi (1386–1466) and Andrea del Verrocchio (1435–1488) depicted David as an adolescent, Michelangelo chose the physical prowess and authority of someone in their early adult years. He leaned toward the Greek and Roman traditional depictions of their gods and legendary heroes, where the figure possesses something greater than mortal nobility. Often these figures are depicted in the nude, showing the ideal of perfection and eluding to man's potential grandeur. Michelangelo's *David* shows through his stance and muscular body to possess the force and wherewithal needed to conquer his enemy. Unlike the complete lack of emotion shown in *Venus de Milo*, the slightest hint of it is communicated on David's face (see

Figure 1.15) through the knitting together of his eyebrows. As was more traditional of the High Renaissance period (1492–1527) when Michelangelo created this sculpture, more attention was paid to how the figure was depicted. This can be seen through the detail in the hair, the definition in the muscles, and the depiction of the bones and veins in the backs of the feet and hands of the figure.

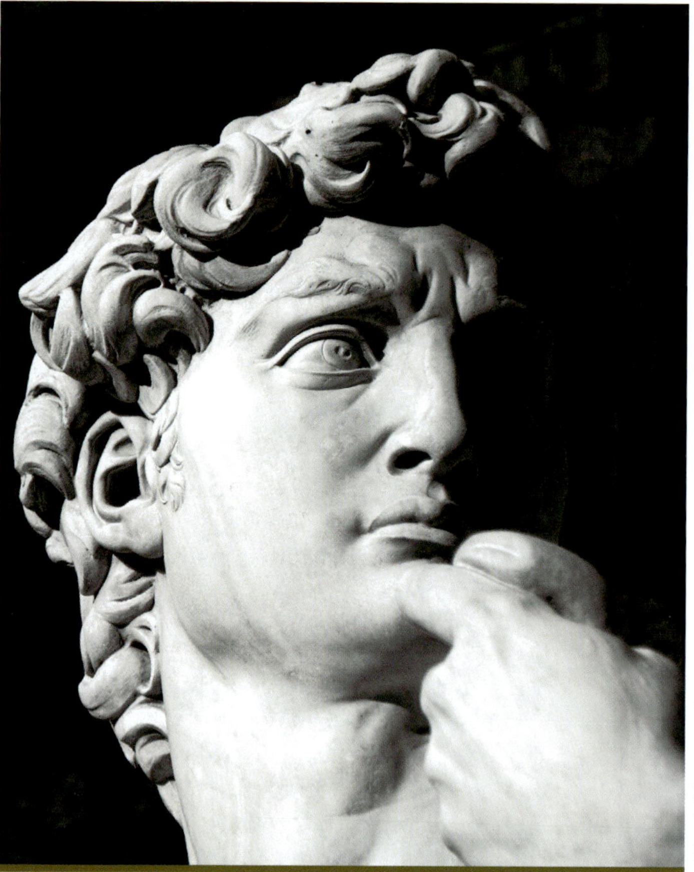

©Conde/Shutterstock.com

FIGURE 1.15 – David (detail), Michelangelo. 1504. Carrara marble.

Farron Allen (1957–) was the product of three generations of coalminers from West Virginia, where religion played a strong role in life. Throughout his childhood, Allen constantly drew and worked alongside his father as he built things around the house. Although it was clear, Allen had a penchant for the arts in those early years, he did not pursue his artistic ambitions until his late twenties. While he eventually became an educator, he pursued sculpture and painting artistically, using primarily fabricated or found metal objects in his work. The human figure is an integral part of Allen's imagery and a way to communicate ideas around sexuality, religion, moral hypocrisy, and misuse of power within society. In the 1980s, when the AIDS epidemic first emerged, Allen's work focused in part on his personal experiences around the deaths of many of his friends and lovers and on his anger at the negative societal response to the disease, which appeared to be attributed to the fact that homosexual men were predominantly affected. He coined the term 'attack of innocence' for his imagery that stemmed from this time. Beginning with full-sized figures, Allen's work over the years has simplified into using body parts, faces, hands, skulls, and bones.

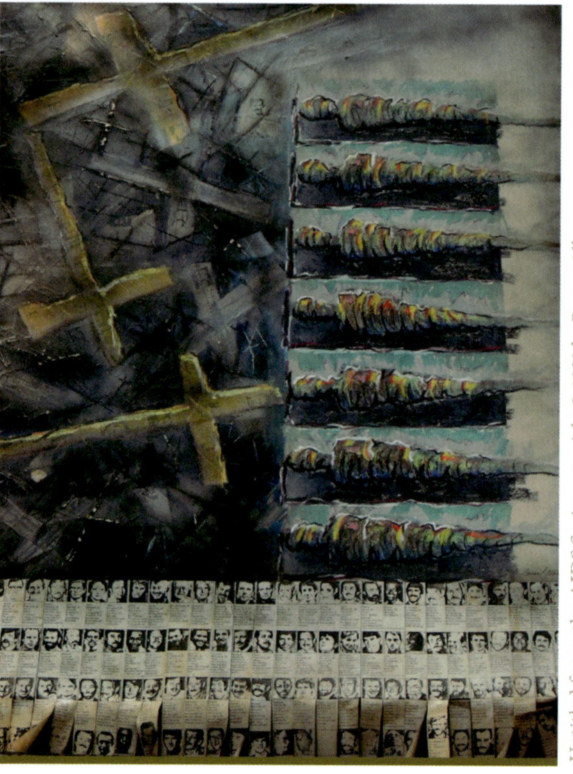

Untitled from the AIDS Series *copyright © 1989 by Farron Allen. Photo © 2016 Paige Wideman.*

FIGURE 1.16 – Untitled from the AIDS Series, Farron Allen. 1989. 31 x 46 in. Mixed media.

In *Untitled from the AIDS Series* (see Figure 1.16), Farron Allen began depicting the human figure within his work as a full-sized cocooned form. Cocooning reflected his self-preservation during the 1970s and 1980s when the Aids epidemic was emerging. His friends, and lovers, were dying around him—yet he survived. The enormity of it all was hard for this artist to deal with. Allen explains, "This was in part my way of dealing with what was going on around me. The cocoons are reminiscent of what I was feeling back then. I had to shut myself off from it in order to get through it."

Over the years, Farron Allen's figures began to open up, dark and mysterious crevices and cracks revealing the inside of the forms (see Figure 1.17). When the 'winged' figure (see Figure 1.18) first started to emerge within his work, it seemed they were more free. The artist says, "There was a sense of freedom about those figures—and whatever was there was dissipating…was gone. It was evolving and turning into something else, as was I. It became easier to deal with it." He has healed and his ideas about death have changed over the passage of time. To reflect this, Allen's imagery contains a lot of skeletal imagery, lacking the flesh that once confined them.

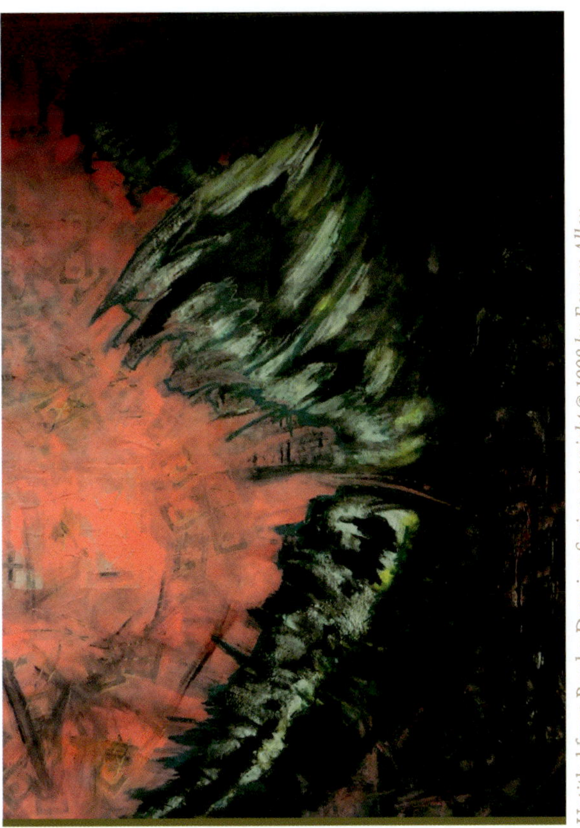

FIGURE 1.17 – Untitled from the Border Drawing Series, Farron Allen. 1998. 48 x 81 in. Mixed media.

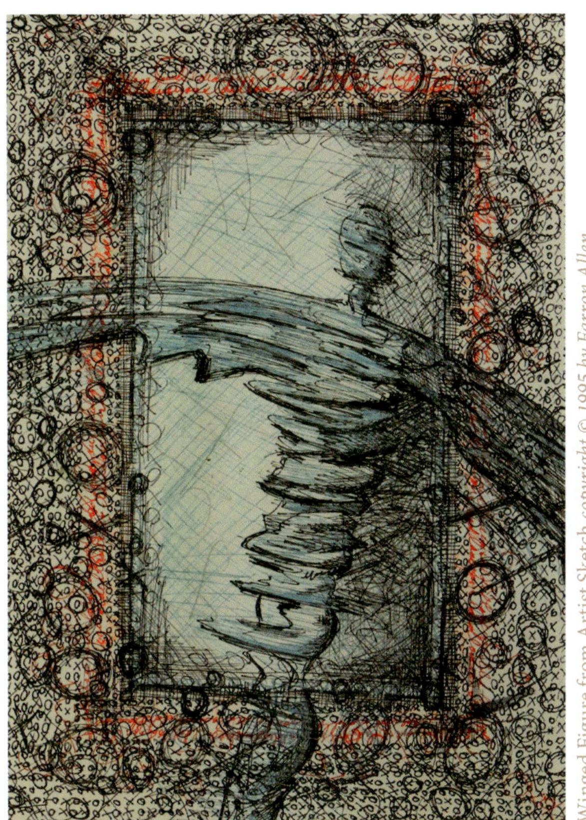

FIGURE 1.18 – Winged Figure from the Artist's Sketchbook, Farron Allen. 1995. 7 x 9 in. Pen and ink.

PSYCHOLOGICAL

Art can be a powerful tool of communication, exploration, and self-discovery. Throughout history, artists have created imagery dealing with the human psyche and condition, including providing a very personal glimpse into the artists themselves.

Merle Rosen (1949–) has worked for more than forty years in a wide variety of mediums, exploring many subjects and themes within her work. She loves the process of making art and the variety of materials and the possibilities that they hold for her as an artist. The figure is very prominent throughout Rosen's work. She taught in the university setting for many years and continues to do so in the private sector today. Rosen has completed numerous commissions in recent years, including murals, CD covers, and logo designs. She has exhibited extensively in museums and galleries nationally and internationally.

In the 1990s, Merle Rosen was in therapy exploring her relationship with her mother. Although her love for her mother was apparent, she discovered that earlier experiences had created a confused or entangled love. Rosen realized that no matter how much of herself she willingly gave to her mother it was never enough. The artist said, "If she wanted my hand and I gave her my hand, it was not enough. And then she wanted my arm and I offered my arm and that it was not enough. Then I offered the rest of my body and she took it and that was not enough. She wanted my soul." Her therapist explained that there was a hole in her mother's psyche that could not be filled by Rosen; her mother had to fill it herself. Her therapist suggested that Rosen explore these feelings through her art.

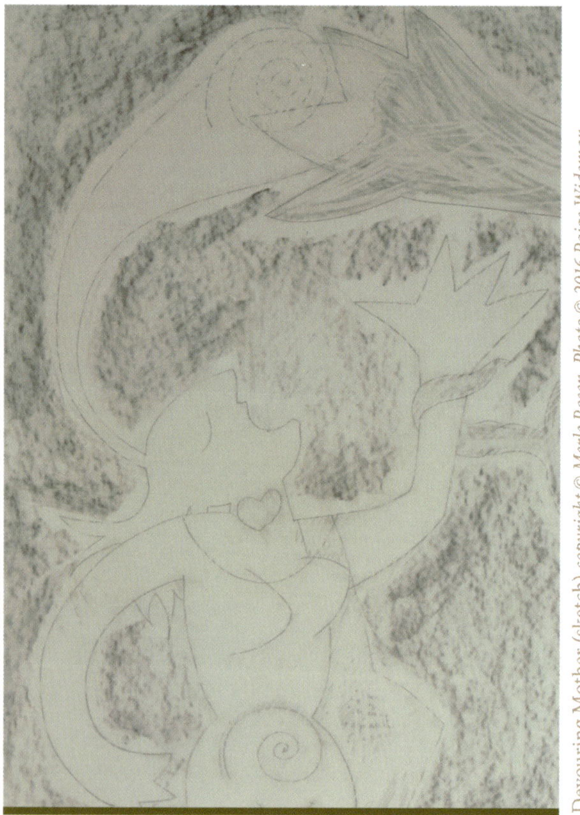

FIGURE 1.19 – All Devouring Mother (Preliminary Sketch), Merle Rosen. 1994. 30 x 44 in. Graphite on gray stonehenge paper.

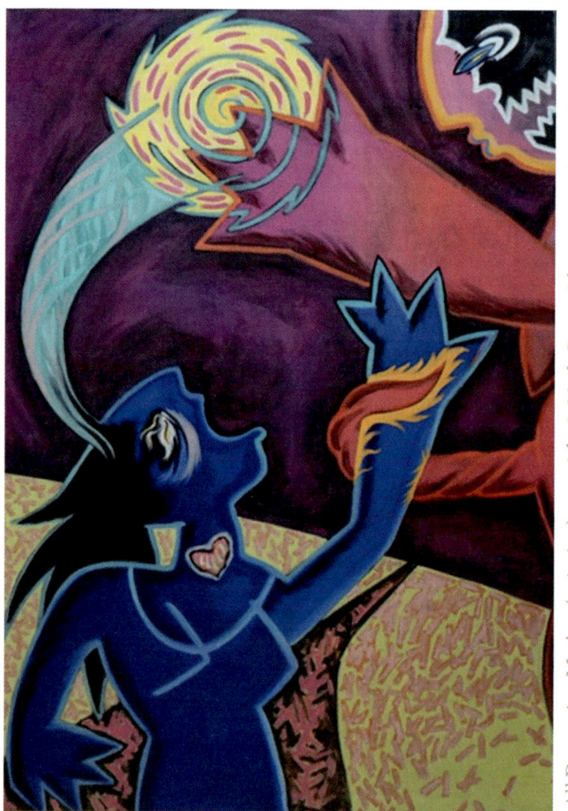

FIGURE 1.20 – All Devouring Mother (Painting), Merle Rosen. 1994. 30 x 44 in. Acrylic paint on canvas.

She was not prone to working literally or having previous success in trying to communicate dreams through her art. Therefore, Rosen was reluctant to pursue the relationship with her mother artistically. However, it was pointed out that she did not have to work literally, so she gave it a try. The result was a large pencil drawing (see Figure 1.19) that Rosen worked on in the classroom before her students arrived. She was not sure about leaving such a personal image on the wall during class, but assumed it would go unnoticed. At the end of class, the husband of one of her student's saw the image and asked Rosen if it was about her and her mother. She was stunned that he so readily understood the image and asked him about his perception. He said there were cultures, philosophies, and religions based around the 'all devouring mother' and several books written about that subject.

The drawing was then turned into a painting titled *All Devouring Mother* (see Figure 1.20). In the image, Merle Rosen shows herself depicted as the blue figure. The turquoise stream being pulled out of her through the top of her head is her 'soul energy.' Partially seen towering over her in the upper right hand corner of the image, her mother is depicted in red. The mother's hand is extended outward collecting the daughter's soul.

The mother's eyes are closed perhaps indicating her lack of understanding of the impact her actions had on her child. As the daughter's arm is raised towards her mother, an umbilical cord reaches out to entangle her, further showing that no matter what she gives it will never be enough. Yet through the process, the daughter's eternal love for her mother is symbolized by the heart shown near her throat, made from the same colors used to depict her mother.

Merle's mother suffered from Alzheimer's several years before her death. So all of the newly learned skills that Rosen developed to interact and maintain a relationship with her mother were no longer needed. All that remained for both was love.

BODY LANGUAGE

Humans are curious creatures by nature. One observes their surroundings and everything within, from the movements and behaviors of animals to the changing of seasons, the movement of the stars and other humans' behavior. One stores these observations and pulls from them throughout their lives, whether it is to attempt to understand what someone is experiencing at a given moment or a means for an artist to convey a specific emotion to the viewer.

During the Edo Period (1600–1868) in Japan, the art of Ukiyo-e was developed. This style of woodblock printing was used to depict imagery of courtesans, kabuki actors, landscapes, and more. This process involved the collaboration between a designer, an engraver, a printer, and a publisher, each contributing their unique skills in bringing about the finished product.

WOODCUT (Woodblock Printing) - a printmaking process where an image is carved onto a wood surface prior to inking and printing.

Body language is one tool artists use to communicate. This can be accomplished in a variety of ways. In *Nakmura Utaemon No Kato Masakiyo* (see Figure 1.21), the actor is portraying Kato Masakiyo, a sixteenth century Japanese general who led his warriors in the Seven Year War (1592–1598) against Korea. The artist captures the general, portrayed by Nakmura Utaemon, in a moment of frustration and/or anger. The artist used bold color and an exaggerated facial expression as a means of communicating these emotions.

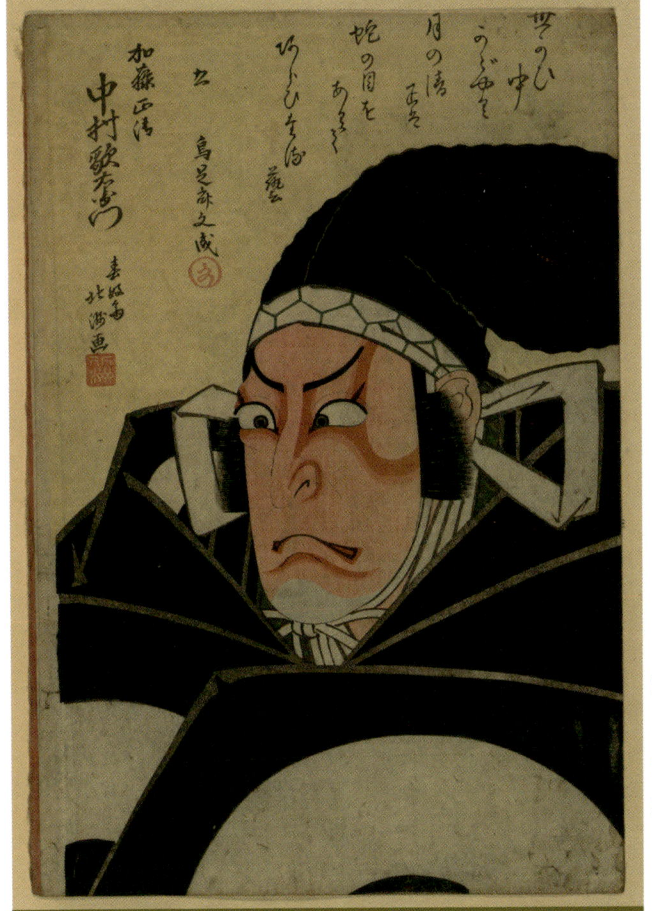

Courtesy of the Library of Congress

FIGURE 1.21 – Nakamura Utaemon No Kato Masakiyo, Katsukawa Shunsen. 1818–1830. 38.2 x 25.4 in. Color woodcut.

Less than ten years from his death, Vincent van Gogh painted *Old Man Grieving* in 1890. His health had deteriorated greatly by this point, limiting the amount of time he had to create. In those brief moments of stability, van Gogh continued to produce paintings. While this particular painting is not meant to be a self-portrait, it is believed to represent the toll van Gogh's condition had taken on him and his personal revelation that all of mankind lived with uncertainty.

In *Old Man Grieving* (see Figure 1.22), the physical position of the body clearly communicates a form of distress, in this case emotional. Although the image is closely cropped in on the old man, the lack of detail in the space around him creates a sense of isolation, as though he is sitting in an empty room. There is nothing to help support the weight of what burdens him other than his own body and the chair in which he sits. His clenched hands support a head which has become too heavy to hold upright from the emotional burden he carries...or the emotions brought on by a situation unknown to the viewer. In this case, the simplicity of the image coupled with the obvious despair of the old man elicits an emotional reaction within the viewer.

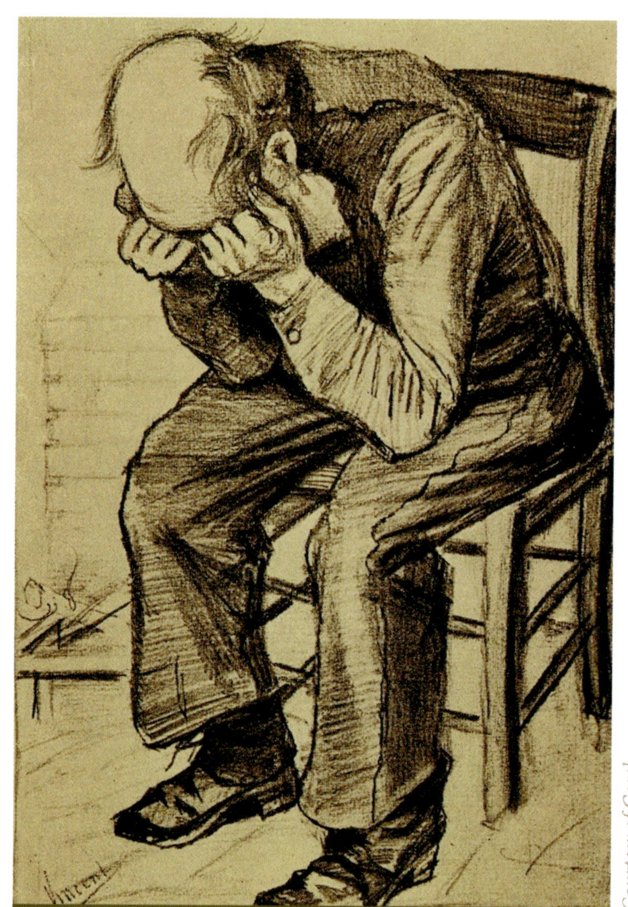

Courtesy of Corel

FIGURE 1.22 – Old Man Grieving, Vincent van Gogh. 1890. 32 x 25.5 in. Drawing on paper.

TOOL TO CREATE

Artists use their eyes, minds, and bodies throughout the creative process. When one thinks of a painter and how he/she creates a work of art, one envisions the artist sitting in front of an easel moving a paint brush between the palette of paint and the canvas. But painters use their bodies in a variety of ways during the painting process, sometimes from a creative perspective and sometimes out of necessity. This can be true of all artists regardless of their medium and process.

MEDIUM/MEDIA - the materials used to create a work of art.

American artist, Chuck Close (1940–) developed an interest in painting at an early age. He suffered from severe dyslexia and a neuromuscular condition which impacted his abilities to succeed scholastically and participate in sports. However, art was an area where he excelled. Later, Close was diagnosed with 'face' blindness. This is a condition that prevents him from seeing an individual's unique facial features that help the average person easily distinguish someone as being either a stranger or a familiar face. Close's focus during his undergraduate studies at the University of Washington was on the abstract. But during his graduate studies at Yale University, he switched to photorealism—a technique where an artist works from a photograph of a subject and tries to reproduce it as realistically as possible in another medium.

Chuck Close is a wonderful example of how an artist uses more than a paintbrush to create. During the 1980s, he created a series of large-scale realistic portraits, using the impressions of his fingerprints to create the imagery, as seen in *Phil* (2009). After taking a picture of a person, Close would mark off both the photograph and a large canvas into a grid. From there, he would use an ink pad and the impressions of his fingerprints to reproduce what he saw within each box of the grid. The end result was a highly realistic portrait of the person.

In 1988, Close suffered an injury to his spine that left him a paraplegic. Because of these physical restrictions, Close developed a new way of painting that allowed him to continue to capture realistic portraits.

The process, seen in *Self-Portrait* (see Figure 1.23), involves creating a grid in which he paints concentric circles on top of one another other in various colors. Since he is no longer able to grip a paintbrush with his hand, the paintbrush is taped to his wrist and controlled by the motion of his arm. When one steps back from the painting, the image appears to be a fairly realistic representation of the artist. Upon closer inspection, the image begins to breakdown before our eyes into a series of shapes and colors.

Janine Antoni (1964–) graduated from the Rhode Island School of Design in 1989. She developed a unique style and approach to creating her works of art, which often possess a performance component. Her work is primarily about the process of making, but also focuses on the transitions between the making and the finished product. Antoni primarily uses her body—mouth, hair, and eyelashes—as a tool, while her whole body is used to perform 'everyday' activities to create.

In 1992, Janine Antoni's first solo exhibition was *Gnaw*. This piece consisted of two 600 pound blocks—one of lard and one of chocolate (see Figure 1.24)—placed on wooden pallets. In the back of the space, a mirrored room with display cases was created. During the course of the exhibition, Antoni used her teeth to gnaw pieces of lard and chocolate off of the blocks. She created heart-shaped candy boxes from the bits of chocolate and lipsticks from the lard, placing them on display in the mirrored room. The use of these two materials speaks to ideas of desire and disgust (through taste and texture), as well as perceptions of beauty within contemporary culture. Because females tend to have more body fat in general than males, Antoni felt that lard was an appropriate material choice to further the connection to societal perceptions of femininity. During its installation, *Gnaw* was used by the media to further illustrate society's increasing concerns of the rise of eating disorders.

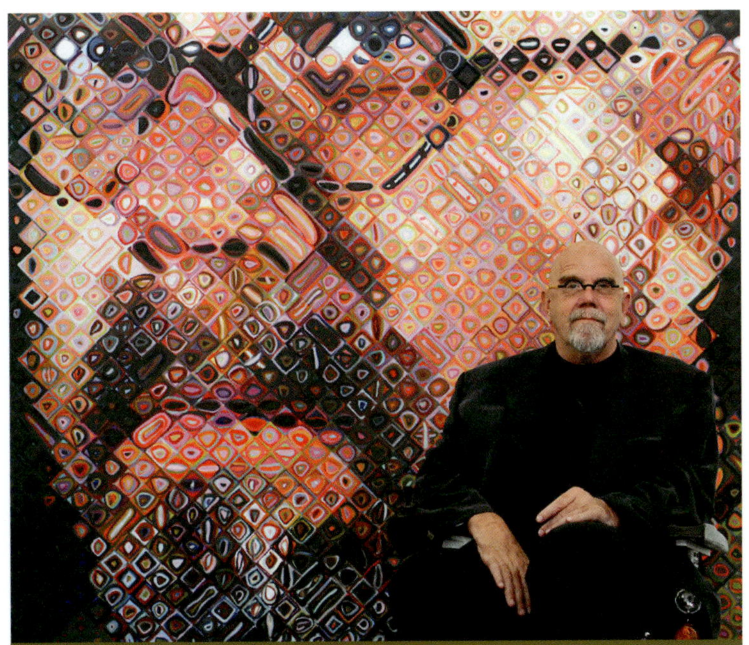

HENNING KAISER/DDP/Getty Images

FIGURE 1.23 – Chuck Close in Front of his Self-Portrait. Henning Kaiser. 2007.

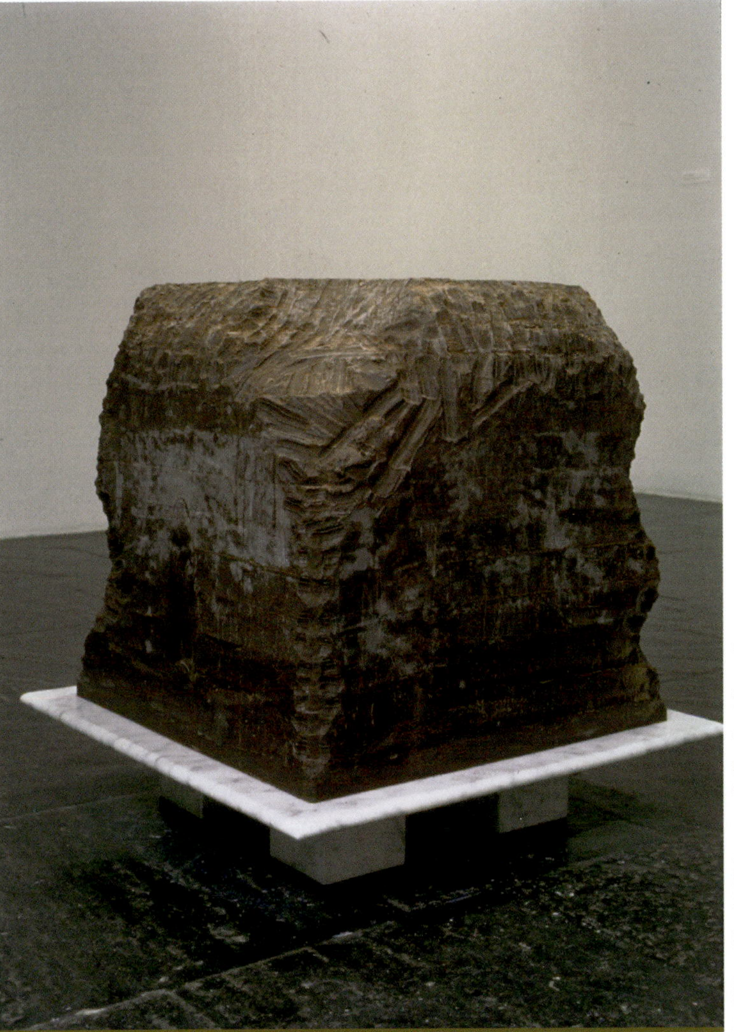

Ted Thai/The LIFE Images Collection/Getty Images

FIGURE 1.24 – Gnaw (detail), Janine Antoni. 1992. Large-scale installation.

CANVAS

In many cultures around the world, the human body becomes a canvas or a 'work of art' in and of itself. Depending upon the culture, this artistic form can communicate ideal beauty, social status, lineage, and more within the culture.

In many Polynesian cultures, the art of tattoo is a sacred tradition among its people. In the ancient Maori culture (1280) of New Zealand, both women and men could be tattooed. Every person's designs would be unique and never repeated on another person in the same way. While tattoos were usually restricted to the upper lip and chin of a female, males could be tattooed anywhere on their bodies. An individual must earn the right to be tattooed. For men, this was usually based on their success during battle. A highly decorated man is therefore considered not only fierce in battle but also an ideal mate for a woman. Maori chiefs, like Tamati Waka Nene (see Figure 1.25) would have a fully covered face. A chief's tattoo would include additional spiral designs that were perceived as 'eyes.' This was believed to give the chief the ability to see everything going on around him at all times.

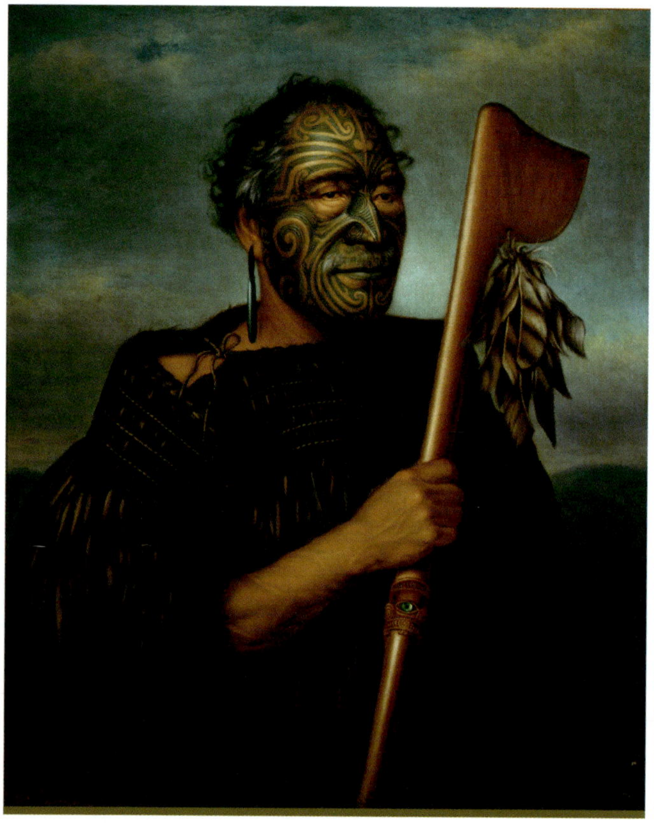

Tamati Waka Nene, 1890 (oil on canvas), Lindauer, Gottfried (1839–1926)/Auckland Art Gallery Toi o Tamaki, New Zealand/Bridgeman Images

FIGURE 1.25 – Tamati Waka Nene, Gottfried Lindauer. New Zealand. 1890. Oil on canvas.

To the Maori and many cultures around the world, the head is considered the most important part of the body. Therefore, facial tattoos carry greater cultural significance. To the Maori, they signify the individual's family lineage, social rank, marital status, and personal identity. The center of the forehead communicates the person's general rank (social status), while the area around the temples indicates marital status. The left side of the face visually communicates their father's lineage, while the right their mother's. A person having only one parent of rank (or royal lineage) will only have one side of their face tattooed. As no two tattoos are identical, the upper lip is reserved for their personal identity. During times of British occupation and land treaties, the Maori used the design on their upper lip as their personal signature, since they had no written language at the time.

In Polynesian cultures like the Maori, war dances were a significant cultural tradition which portrayed the pride and strength in their people before going into battle. This dance is more physical and violent in nature compared to other traditional Polynesian dances. Warriors, who were often heavily tattooed, had a unique presence on the battlefield against foreign enemies. They used their unique appearance along with exaggerated facial expressions, verbal sounds, and dance movements to challenge and intimidate their enemy. As seen in *Maori Men in War Dance* (see Figure 1.26), the men are performing this dance. The number of warriors, along with their features and movements, was quite impressive. Today, the tradition is carried on at the beginning of sporting events, like rugby. Although the facial expressions, movements, and body slapping are not all traditional in nature, they still serve a purpose of carrying on a cultural tradition.

Scarification is a common practice in many indigenous cultures around the world, in particular within African and western Pacific cultures. The technique and overall appearance varies depending on the culture and the purpose behind the scarification. In some cases, scarification is used as a symbol of beauty, coming of age, or an indicator of cultural belonging (one's tribe). The designs are created on various parts of the body, including the face.

Unlike the tattooing process, scarification is created by systematically damaging the skin in such a way it leaves a permanent raised mark once healed. The practitioner will cut the skin with thorns or metal blades and then rub organic sap or ash into the wound. This causes the 'wound' to heal in a raised manner. It is imperative that the person undergoing this process not show any emotional response to the pain being inflicted upon them, thereby communicating both a sense of pride and strength.

The Mursi people are one of many tribes still living in southwestern Ethiopia to practice scarification. To this tribe, a man's chest scarred in circular patterns (see Figure 1.27) symbolizes beauty and strength. To the neighboring Nuer tribe, scarification is part of transformation of a boy into a man. Scarification is still a common practice in this region because of the various cultural significance it holds among the people.

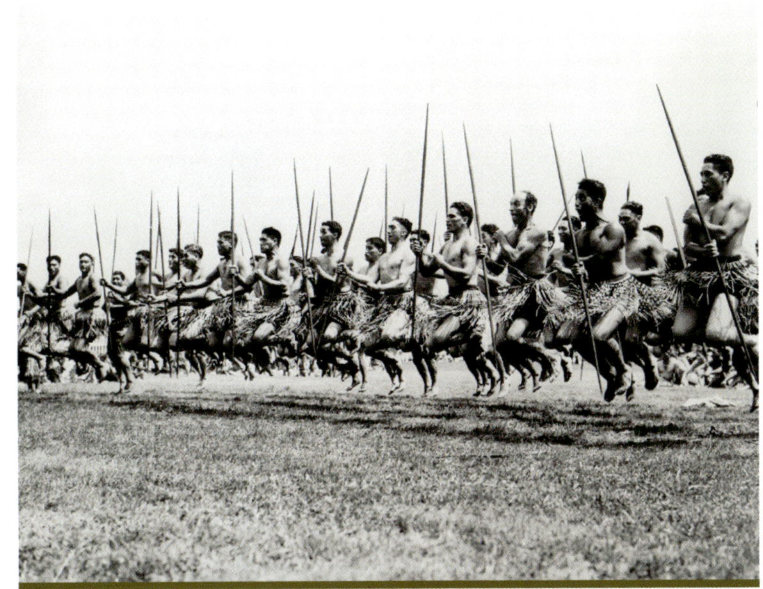

FIGURE 1.26 – Maori Men in War Dance. New Zealand. c. 1939. 10.25 x 8.01 in. Photograph

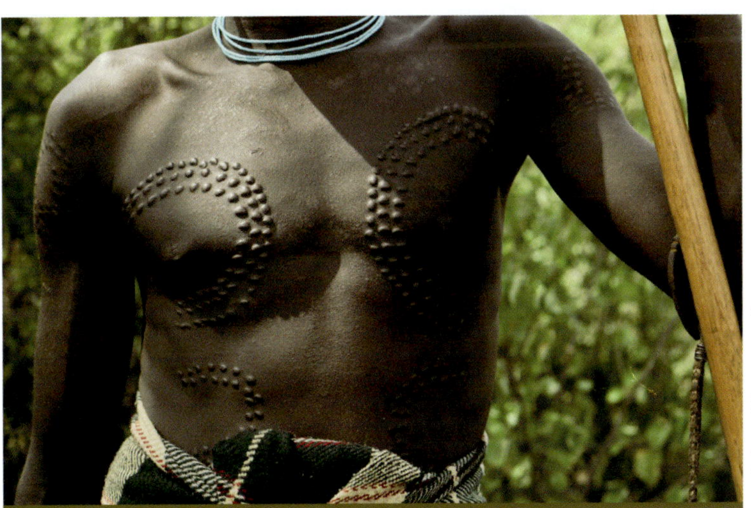

FIGURE 1.27 – Scarification of a Mursi Man (Omo Valley), Photograph. Ethiopia, Africa. c. late 20th century.

part 2

SEXUALITY AND COUPLING

Throughout the ages, artists have used various mediums, techniques, and imagery to communicate the intricacies of human sexuality, the needs to pair bond and the multi-facets and dynamics of relationships—between two lovers, a parent and child, or a family entity.

SEXUALITY AND LOVE

Concepts of love and human sexuality have interested humans in all cultures. Gods and goddesses who symbolize or exert control over these aspects have been created. Artists reflect societal, cultural, or personal views and perceptions of these aspects through their work—whether to define them for others, to create an avenue for discussion or to challenge preconceived ideas.

PERSPECTIVE - rendering the illusion of a three-dimensional space on a flat, two-dimensional surface.

Italian artist, Sandro Botticelli (1445–1510) is known for creating a wide range of artworks dealing with both secular and religious subjects. His father saw his developing artistic strengths as a painter and sent Botticelli to apprentice under one of the Florentine masters of the time, Filippo Lippi (1406–1469). Lippi helped him master linear perspective and panel and fresco painting. In addition, he influenced Botticelli's initial style of depicting the human form in a frail manner and of using the paler hues of his color palette.

FRESCO - a painting technique where pigment is applied to a plaster surface.

Eventually, Botticelli studied the sculptural works of Antonio Pollaiuolo (1429–1498) and Verrocchio. This led to a roundness and strength in how he depicted the human figure. *Birth of Venus* (see Figure 1.28) visually shows this change in style. Botticelli broke free of the traditional norm of integrating the figure into a landscape, by choosing to use nature as a backdrop instead. The central figure in this painting, Venus, represents love and sexuality. Her body is exposed yet not completely for she covers her breasts with her right arm. With her left hand, she holds the end of her long, flowing hair over her pubic region in a form of modesty. She arrives on the shores of an undistinguishable location by way of a giant shell. To her left, Zephyr—the Greek god of the west wind and a symbol of human passion—is seen holding a nymph, while using his breath to help Venus ashore. To her right, Hora—goddess of the seasons, is shown welcoming Venus. The flowers floating to her side are symbols of spring and new life and can be seen echoed in the fabric of Hora's dress. The positioning of these figures frame Venus, helping to pull the viewer's attention to her. The use of landscape in this painting is more to frame the figures than to define a specific setting.

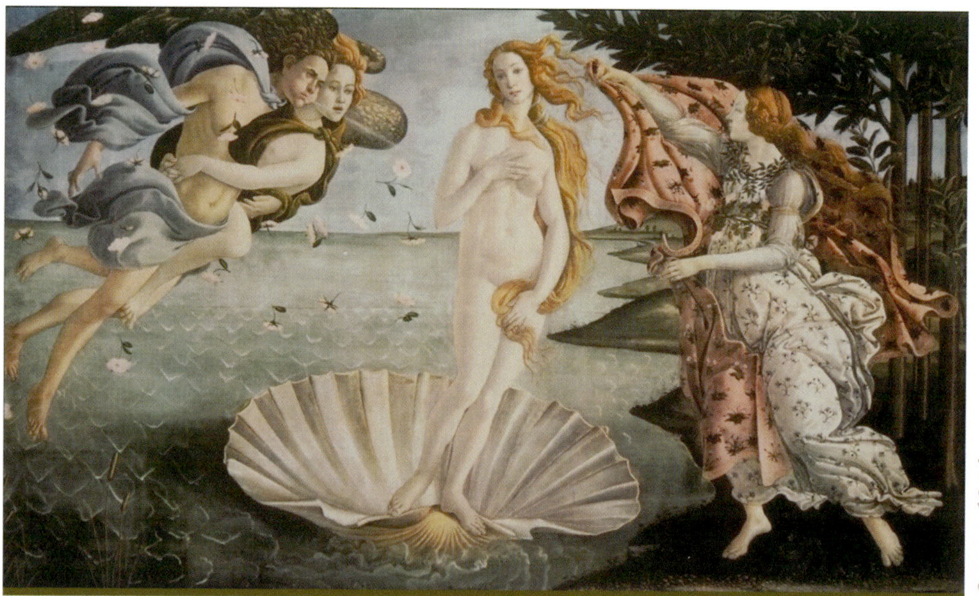

Courtesy of Corel

FIGURE 1.28 –Birth of Venus, Sandro Botticelli. 1486. 67.9 x 109.6 in. Tempera paint on canvas.

Paul Gauguin (1848–1903) was born in Paris, France. Since his interest in painting was not heavily supported by his family, he joined the French Navy for a time and then became a stockbroker. He continued to paint on his own through the years. After a decline in the economy led to his dismissal as a stockbroker, Gauguin dedicated himself fully to painting. He found inspiration in many forms throughout his career, including the writings of Edgar Allen Poe. At the age of forty-three, Gauguin began traveling to and living in Tahiti where he fell in love with the bold, lush landscape and its exotic inhabitants. During this time, he was painting both in his bold style. Before Gauguin left Tahiti to return to Paris, his friends threw him a farewell dinner where Poe's *Nevermore* was read. While Gauguin does not outwardly claim a direct reference to Poe's poem, in the painting *Nevermore* (see Figure 1.29), there are clear indications that it was a source of inspiration of this painting. In the upper left hand corner of the painting, Gauguin has written the word 'Nevermore' and sitting on the ledge of the windowsill in the background appears to be a raven. The girl's youthful appearance communicates a sense of innocence that is contradicted by her nudity and position on the bed. Her body faces away from the figures and bird behind her. Yet the direction of her gaze seems to reference that she is aware of their presence.

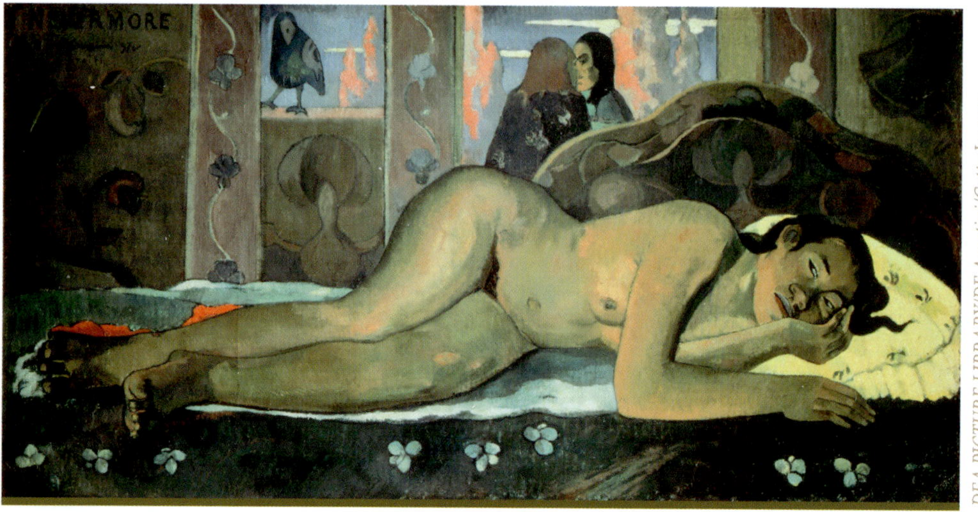

DEA PICTURE LIBRARY/DE Agostini/Getty Images

FIGURE 1.29 – Nevermore (Never Again), Paul Gauguin. 1897. 60 x 116 cm. Oil on canvas.

His figurative paintings of the Tahitians were of an exotic and mysterious people. Gauguin communicated that they were unashamed of their nakedness, since he often depicted them scantily clothed doing everyday activities outdoors. The boldness of the colors used in these paintings helped to convey the sense of an exotic people and the richness of their land.

As discussed earlier in this section, one of the central themes depicted in Japanese woodcuts from the Edo period were courtesans. These women became symbols of femininity within the Japanese culture at that time. Courtesans were considered licensed prostitutes and, therefore, elevated in status over ordinary prostitutes. The Brothel proprietors defined the courtesan's style of dress to appear expensive and worthy of an aristocratic woman. The clientele was then expected to have a certain level of style, culture, and money.

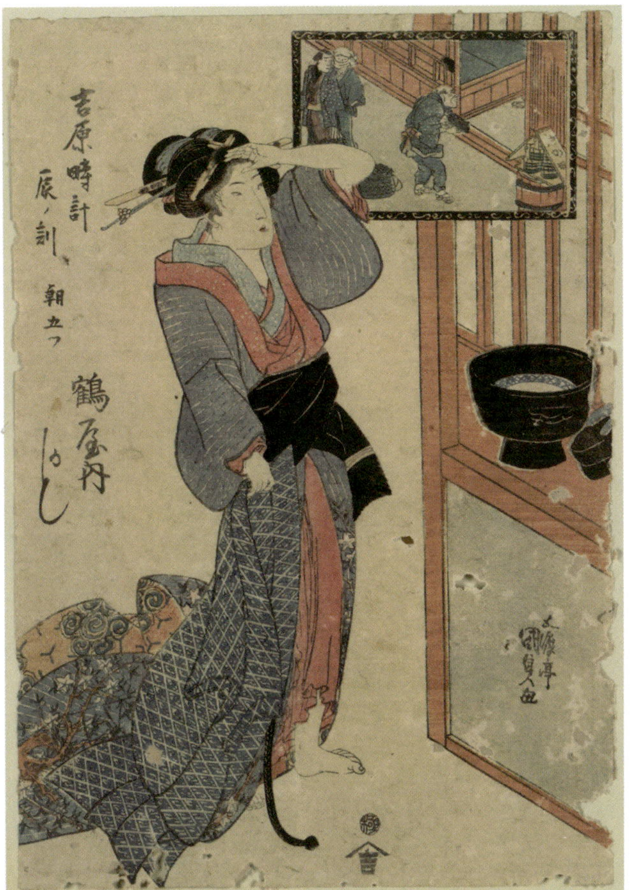

Courtesy of the Library of Congress

FIGURE 1.30 – Tatsu No Koku Asa Itsustsu Tsuruya Uchi Kashiku, Toyokuni Utagawa. c. 1818-1830. 37.5 x 25.6 cm. Color woodcut

In *Tatsu No Koku Asa Itsustsu Tsuruya Uchi Kashiku* (see Figure 1.30), the courtesan is shown in what appears to be her room. She is wearing the traditional form of dress, consisting of a heavily padded garment over a kimono and tied if front with thick brocade sash. In addition, the elaborate coiffure helps to finish off the polished look of an aristocratic woman. Within her line of sight, the image framed in black shows three men standing outside a doorway. The similar style of its wooden construction and color to that of the interior of her room suggests these men are outside the Brothel or where she resides. The image is confusing in that it overlaps the wall and a piece of furniture. It is clearly not a painting hanging as a wall decoration or a window. However, it is placed within her line of sight. The way the courtesan's right arm is raised to her forehead, coupled with her facial expression, would appear she is perhaps shocked or caught off guard by the image. Perhaps this is the artist's way to visually show the viewer that which the courtesan is thinking.

FERTILITY

Many cultures' artwork depicts aspects of fertility, coupling, and family life. Fertility and reproduction are important factors in the survival of any species, including human beings. So artwork is designed to reflect gods and goddesses associated with fertility, to assist in the process of reproduction and more.

In Paleolithic Europe around 25,000 BC, handheld fertility objects were being created. These have become known as 'venus' forms because they all depicted the female body in what appears to be varying stages of pregnancy. As seen in *Venus of Willendorf* (see Figure 1.31), each one shares the common exaggerations or enlargement of the breasts, belly, and hips—areas of a woman's body that change in size during pregnancy. Having no written record from the people of this time, it is left to speculate the true purpose or meaning of these figures. However, given their similarities and that they are all female in form would strongly suggest that they are related to fertility in some fashion.

Throughout the history of the Aegean cultures in the Mediterranean, many female statues have been discovered sharing similar attributes to one another. The earliest of these is the *Female Figurine* found in the Aegean region of the Mediterranean around 6000 BC. The sculpture is simple and shaped almost like a musical instrument. It shows a naked female figure with her arms across her torso. This may be the earliest goddess—Earth Mother—form in these cultures from which the rest of their gods and goddesses would have stemmed.

For example, the *Minoan Snake Goddess* (see Figure 1.32) is thought to represent fertility. Visual aspects of this sculpture relating to fertility include the open bodice which exposes her full breasts and the holding of snakes in each hand. Snakes are thought to be tied into agriculture, regeneration, and fertility. The observance of snakes in the fields and their consumption of rodents was viewed as a protective role, guarding people's food resources. Through the shedding of their skin, they represent regeneration seen from season to season in nature and in the growing/harvesting of crops.

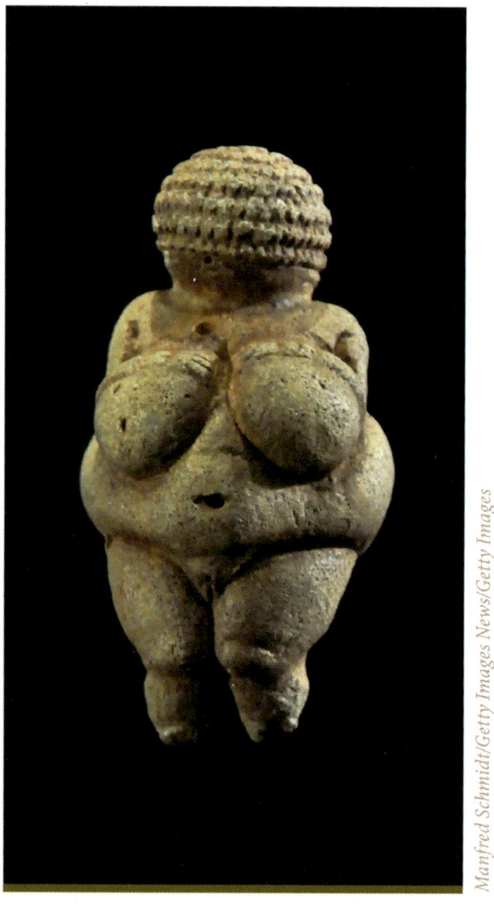

Manfred Schmidt/Getty Images News/Getty Images

FIGURE 1.31 – Venus of Willendorf. Paleolithic Europe. 11 cm high. Limestone.

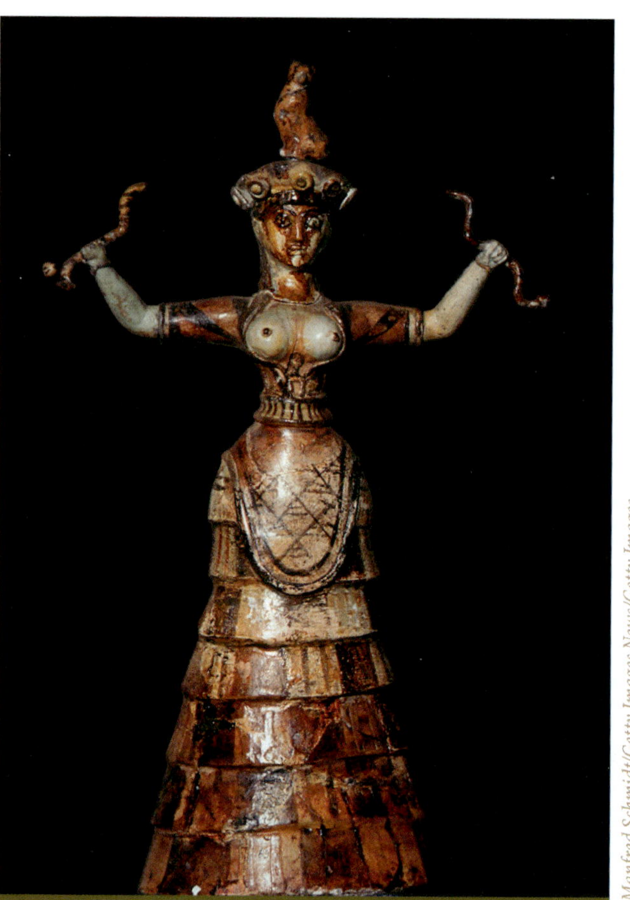

Manfred Schmidt/Getty Images News/Getty Images

FIGURE 1.32 – Minoan Snake Goddess. Crete, Greece. c. 1,700 BC. 13.5 in. high. Ivory.

The *Cerne Abbas Giant* (see Figure 1.33) was carved into the face of an English hill, exposing the chalk below. The exact dates of its creation and by whom are unknown. One theory that seems to hold some weight, based on the archaeological find of a bronze handle nearby the site, indicates it could be from the second century CE. If this is true, it most likely represents the Celtic god Nodens—associated with healing and hunting—who was worshipped by the local people at that time.

Cerne Abbas Giant depicts a naked man with testicles and an erect phallus, wielding a club. While the culture that created this did not leave any written records of the image's purpose, the image and what is shown can give us clues. One theory that relates to the 'healing' aspect of Nodens would be associated with the figure's erection. Over the centuries, stories have been told associating this piece with fertility. A woman finding it difficult to become pregnant may find her problems resolved after sleeping near the Giant.

Recent studies have indicated that the overall image may have been altered throughout the generations of people that used and/or maintained this image. There are indications that a cloak may have once been a part of the overall image, perhaps draped over his shoulder. This figure could be showing us a warrior based on the club that he is holding in his left hand. The figure's right arm is shown extended outwardly. It appears that there was once an image of a human head dangling from that hand. The fact that he is naked could be indicative of how the warriors fought. If the garment that once was part of this piece was worn loosely around their bodies, it would be something that was cumbersome or inhibiting during battle, perhaps easily discarded. The erection could also speak to the virility of the warrior.

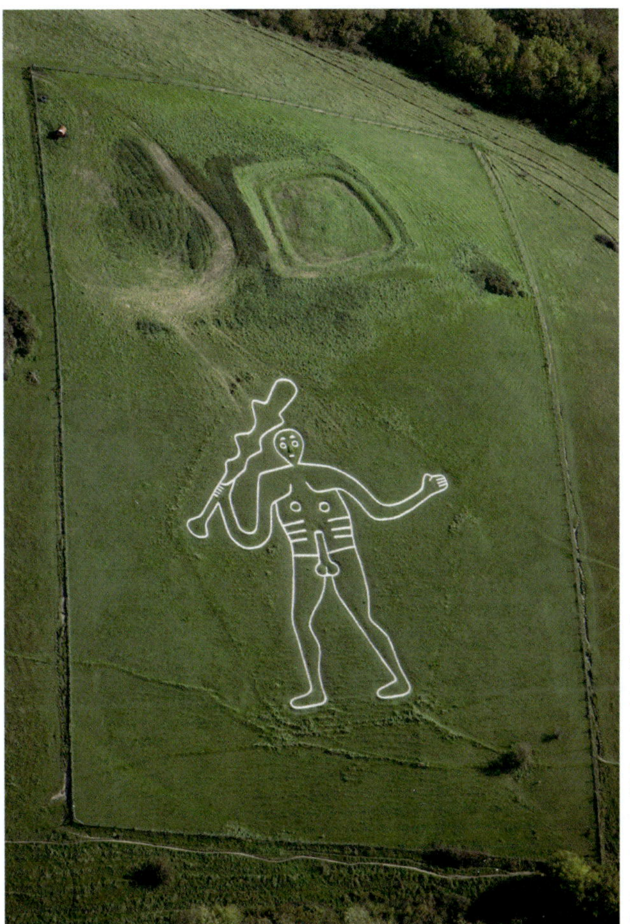

Heritage Images/Hulton Archive/Getty Images

FIGURE 1.33 – Cerne Abbas Giant. Dorset, England. c. late 17th century. 180 ft. x 120 ft. Earthwork, chalk filled outline.

PRIMORDIAL COUPLES

Throughout history, people around the world, regardless of being monotheistic or polytheistic, often believed that their culture could be traced back to two specific people or deities. The first man and woman, referred to as the 'primordial couple,' were believed to be responsible for mankind's existence.

MONOTHEISIM – a religious practice of worshipping a single deity or god.

POLYTHEISIM – a religious practice of worshipping multiple deities or gods.

The Dogon culture of Mali depicts their primordial couple as stylized figures, seated upon a circular stool supported by smaller figures. The small figures or *Nommos* represent all the forbearers of the Dogon race. The original two Nommos are enlarged and seated upon the stool, which represents the world itself. The man is shown with his right arm around the shoulder of the woman, with his hand resting on her breast and his left hand resting on his penis. This simple gesture visually communicates their sexual union. Looking more closely to their faces (see Figure 1.34), they are depicted similarly in an abstract way. That technique is used by many African artists throughout the ages to represent spiritual beings rather than specific individuals. This further reinforces that this is a depiction of their primordial couple.

STYLE - specific characteristics that are consistent within a body of work, which can be seen in an historical period, cultural tradition or an individual artist' body of work.

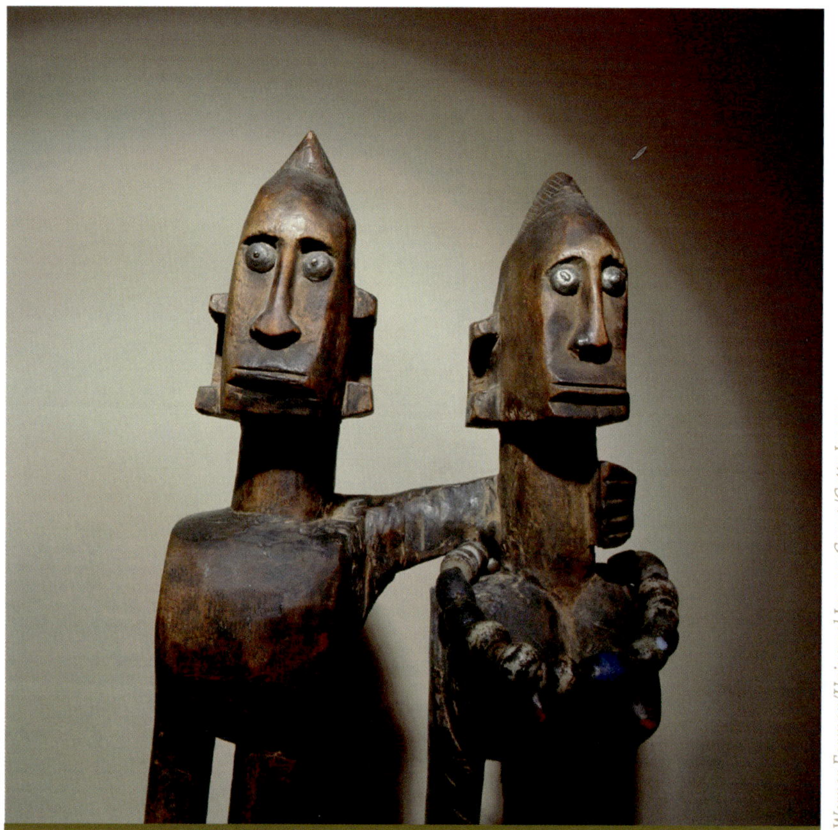

Werner Forman/Universal Images Group/Getty Images

FIGURE 1.34 – Dogon Sculpture of a Couple. Mali, Africa. c. 16th–19th century. Approximately 10 x 29 in. Carved wood.

This sculpture also depicts the roles of males and females within Dogon society. On the backs of the figures are symbols that communicate their primary roles. On the woman's back is a small infant, representing her role as mother and caregiver. On the man's back is a quiver, representing his role as the hunter and provider.

ABSTRACTION - the act of simplifying or distorting an image or object from nature or art expressed solely through non-objective forms.

In Christianity, Adam and Eve are the primordial couple. Many artists throughout the centuries have created their take on this biblical story of when mankind was banished from the Garden of Eden. Albrecht Dürer, a well-known German engraver, created a unique take on this story in his 1504 engraving, *Adam and Eve* (see Figure 1.35). Dürer's extensive study of the human body contributed to his capturing the Greek ideal of proportion when portraying Adam and Eve.

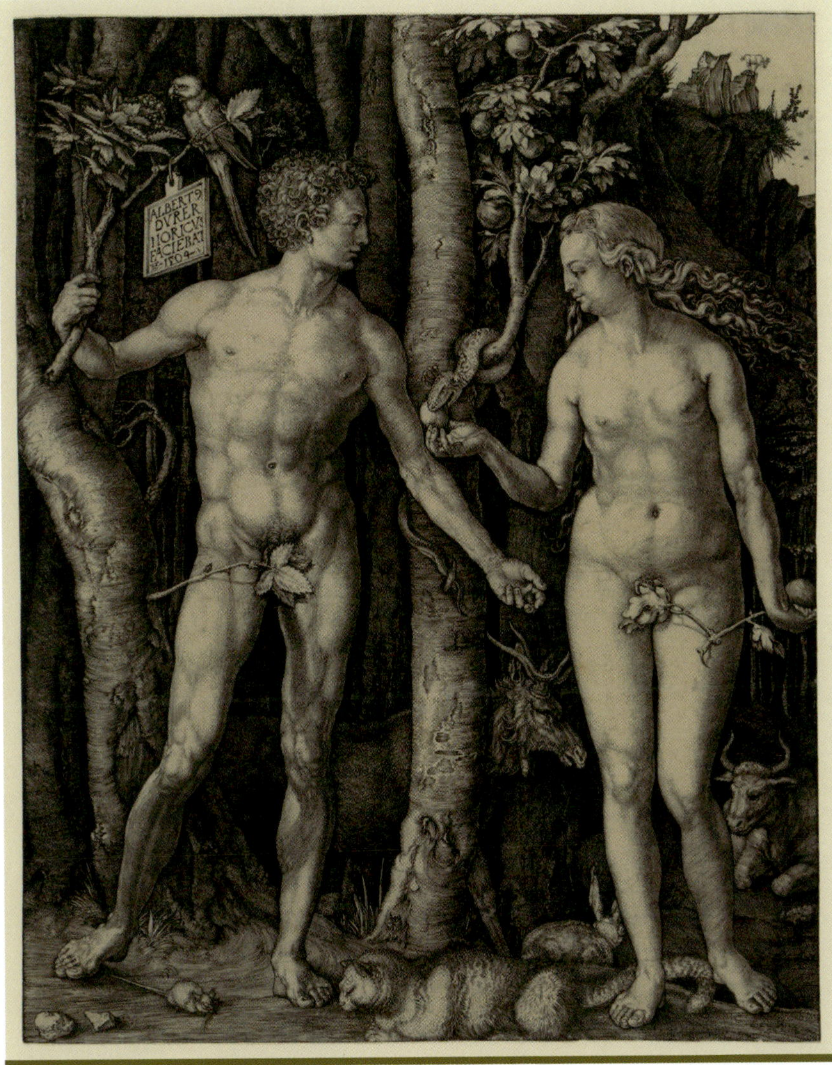

FIGURE 1.35 – Adam and Eve, Albrecht Dürer. 1504. 9 7/8 x 7 7/8 in. Engraving.

ENGRAVING - a printmaking process where an image is created by incising lines on a hard surface, such as a metal plate, prior to inking and printing.

In this rendering of *Adam and Eve*, the central figures are standing at the edge of a dense wooded area filled with a variety of plants and animals. Adam holds onto a branch of a mountain ash, symbolizing the tree of life, while he gazes over at Eve. The viewer's attention then moves to Eve, who stares down to where the seductive snake is placing a piece of forbidden fruit into her right hand. From there, following the diagonal created by Adam's extended left arm, the viewer's attention is directed to the parrot in the tree above his head. The parrot symbolizes wisdom and discernment, things that Eve seems to be lacking in this moment of temptation. In the foreground at their feet, a cat and mouse are meant to encapsulate the relationship between Adam and Eve—that of predator and prey.

Within *Adam and Eve*, Albrecht Dürer hung a tablet containing his signature from the branch upon which the parrot sits. It is believed that Dürer did this to show that he felt this was a significant artistic achievement in his career.

Minnesota-born artist, Stuart Fink (1938–) has had a distinguished artistic career spanning several decades. His large-scale public works can be found in major cities throughout Ohio. In addition, Fink has exhibited nationally in places like New York City and Washington, DC. His style of mark making and interpretation of shape and form developed out of his appreciation of the Cubist works created by Spanish artist, Pablo Picasso (1881–1973) and the abstract sculptures of American artist, David Smith (1906–1965).

In Stuart Fink's version of this biblical story, the artist pares down the image considerably in contrast to Dürer's version. *Adam and Eve* (see Figure 1.36) clearly communicate the essence of the story by focusing on the key elements. The 'tree of life' is centrally placed between Adam and Eve. Adam points toward Eve, who is raising her hand towards the snake. Unlike Dürer's version, Eve has already partaken of the forbidden fruit—as evidenced by the partially eaten apple—sealing their fate and that of mankind's. Their eyes appear to be closed, perhaps suggesting their realization of the gravity of the ensuing consequences.

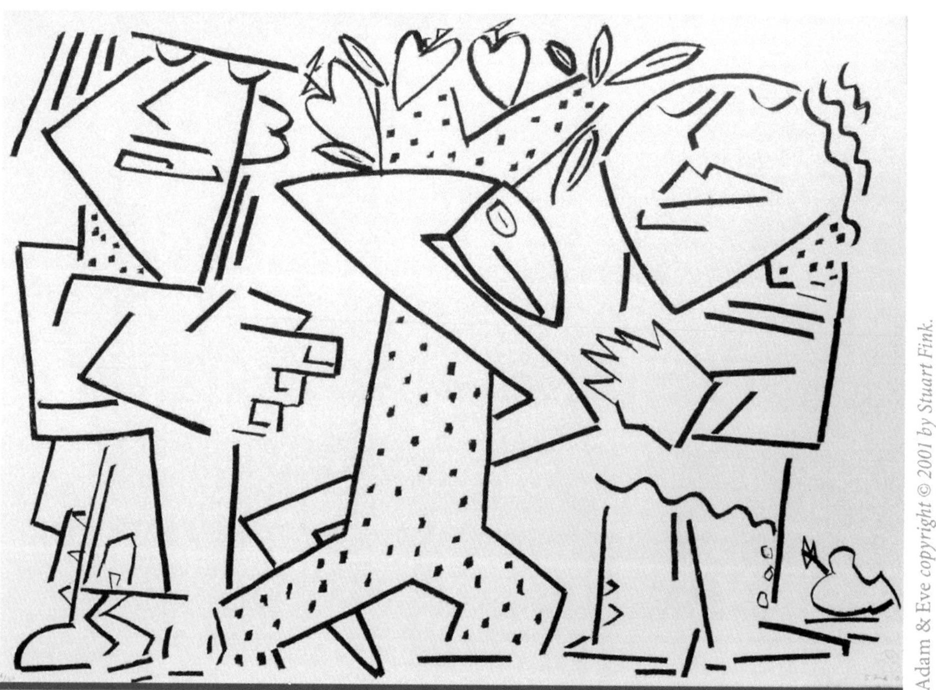

FIGURE 1.36 – Adam and Eve, Stuart Fink. 2001. 30 x 22 in. Lithograph.

COUPLING

Copulation is an inherent and essential need for the continuation of all species. In the human population, the need for this goes deeper. It can be a means to exert dominance over or to feel connected to another person or to unite with something greater than ourselves.

Tantra is one of the Hindu scriptures addressing techniques and rituals of meditative and sexual practices. In the Tantric sect, sexuality and spirituality are not in opposition of one another. Rather it is through properly channeled sexual energy that the Tantra-practitioner can unite with Shiva, one manifestation of their supreme being (Brahman). Throughout the religious architecture dedicated to Shiva, imagery of people engaging in self-pleasuring and erotic sex (see Figure 1.37) helps to remind people of this aspect of their beliefs.

ART NOUVEAU - an early twentieth-century Western art movement that included forms based on the natural world.

Austrian artist, Gustav Klimt (1862–1918) demonstrated artistic abilities early in life. At the young age of fourteen, he received a full scholarship to the Vienna School of Arts and Crafts. Although Klimt's training was typical, reflecting the classical and conservative styles of the time, a series of events and tragedies later freed him to pursue a more personal style. Eventually, he became an instructor at the Academy of Fine Arts in Vienna, where he influenced such artists as Egon Schiele and others.

ARTS AND CRAFTS - a late nineteenth-century art movement focused on the ideal of craftsmanship during an age of mass production and mechanization.

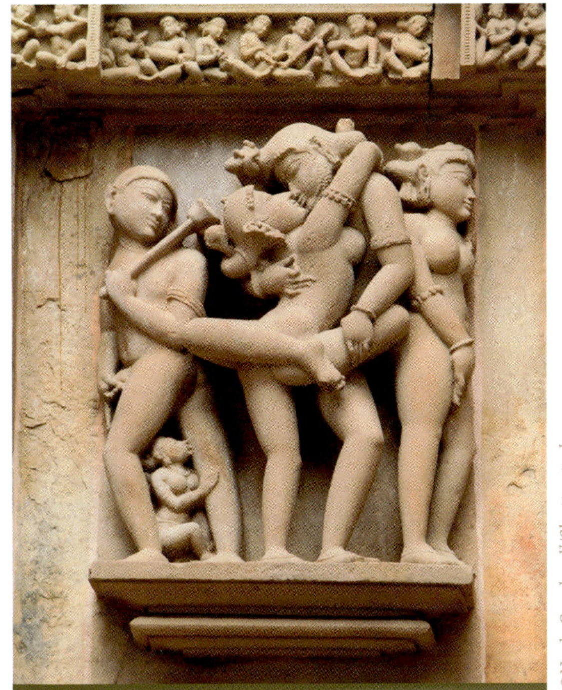

©Neale Cousland/Shutterstock.com

FIGURE 1.37 – Hindu Temple (detail). Khajuraho, India. Stone.

Gustav Klimt's style was influenced by the Art Nouveau and Arts and Crafts movements. This can be seen in part where he incorporated extensive patterning and gold coloration within his paintings. Klimt was also influenced by Japanese art. He incorporated traditional techniques of eighteenth to nineteenth century Japanese woodblock prints, such as flattening of forms and perspective and contrasting areas of decorative patterns with broad planes of color. This influence can clearly be seen in such images as *The Kiss* and *Hope II.*

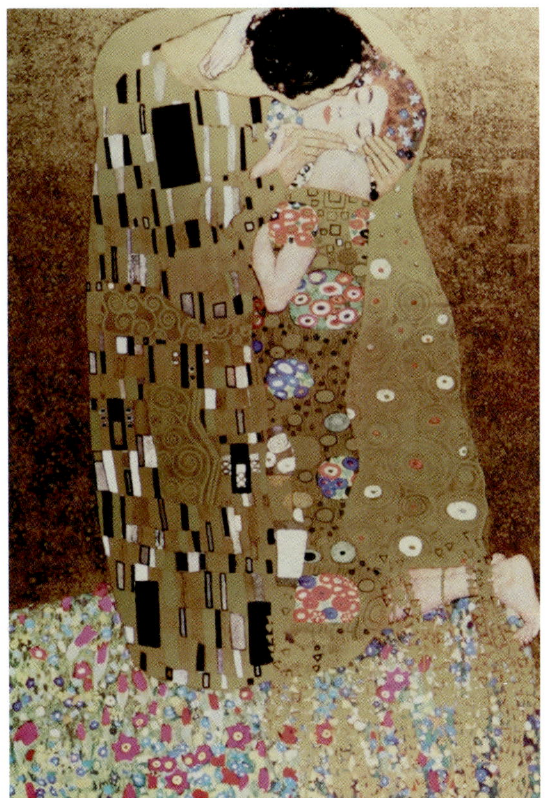

Courtesy of Corel

FIGURE 1.38 – The Kiss, Gustav Klimt. c. 1908. 180 x 180 cm. Oil on canvas.

By nature, Gustav Klimt was a very sexual person and sexuality found its way into his art. *The Kiss* (see Figure 1.38), created in 1908, depicts a woman on her knees with her head tilted upward towards her lover. He passionately embraces her as he leans in for a kiss. Klimt's style explores the use of patterning created through repeated shapes and colors, typical of the Art Nouveau style. This was employed in slightly different ways throughout the painting. The man's garment consists of repeated rectangular forms relating to concepts of masculinity—stability, strength, and structure. While the woman's garment consists of circular forms relating to concepts of femininity—nurture, empathy, and sensitivity. In the way Klimt paints the garments, the three-dimensionality of the figures' bodies was flattened, which helped draw the viewer's attention to the couple's faces. The patterning continues on more subtlety into the background and more vibrantly on the ground upon which the figures are positioned. Both the ground and the woman's dress and hair are filled with flowers, perhaps symbolizing her fertility. Klimt incorporated gold into many of his works, perhaps inspired by his trips to Italy and exposure to Venetian mosaics.

MOSAIC - an image created from combining small pieces of material, such as glass, stone or tile.

American artist, Carrie Pate (1963–) is a painter, sculptor, and owner of her own landscaping company. In her clay sculptures and mixed media paintings, the human figure is predominant. Pate pulls from emotional remnants of her personal experiences, fears, hopes, and dreams for her subject matter. In her mixed media paintings, the imagery is intentionally murky in order to evoke a sense of mystery—for herself and the viewer—and create the illusion of waking from a watery dream.

MIXED MEDIA - a work of art created from two or more materials.

In *Not So Sugary* (see Figure 1.39), Carrie Pate says, "The painting... depicts an almost damsel like heroine contorting her way through a buttery world of colorful demons, suitors, and mystery." She applied dozens of hand drawn/cut out butterflies to the canvas, running through and around the figures. The use of the butterfly is a symbol to Pate of the delicate predicament of a man and woman's relationship with nature, the soul, and self. The title 'Not So Sugary' is meant to imply there is more going on within the image than the viewer first perceives. Upon closer look, the 'sugary' colors used throughout the painting serve as a distraction from the subdued, eerie faces floating in the middle ground and the exact intentions of the 'yellow man' looming over the heroine.

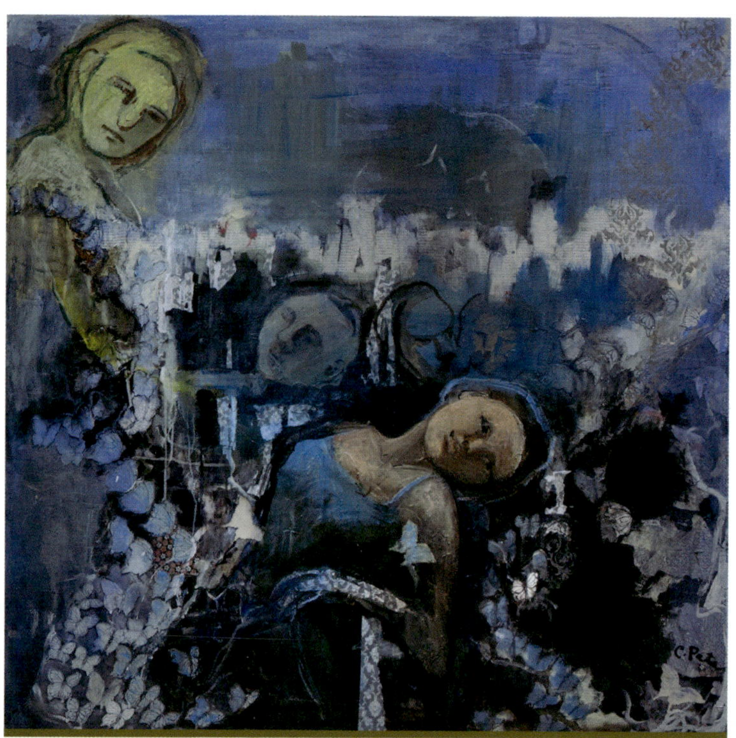

FIGURE 1.39 – Not So Sugary, Carrie Pate. 2016. 42 x 42 in. Acrylic and paper on wood.

Carrie Pate says, "how often have you known something was not quite right but you talked yourself out of that feeling?" In *Not So Sugary*, the uneasy 'gut feeling' is being shown through the bending backward of the woman's body away from the faces and man. Yet, her face remains passive to communicate that she is doubting her feelings and trying not to offend others in her state of uncertainty.

PREGNANCY, MOTHERHOOD, AND FAMILY

Pregnancy, motherhood, and family are frequent subjects' artists use within their work, whether personally or culturally inspired. These images can capture the fears, hopes, desires, and cultural norms of the people involved.

One theme Gustav Klimt focused on during his artistic career was the pregnant form. In *Hope I*, the mother-to-be is shown fully naked in profile, except for her direct gaze at the viewer. She appears to be healthy and unfearful of what lies ahead. While a mass of people occupies the space behind, Death can be seen prominently next to her side, a constant companion—as life and death are intertwined.

In *Hope II* (see Figure 1.40), Klimt has taken a very different approach to this theme. Death is still present, but reduced to a small form protruding from the woman's belly just below her extended arm. The tangle of figures previously in the background are now shown as three women kneeling at her feet and intertwined in her clothing. The woman has closed eyes, no longer looking at the viewer, and appears sickly as shown in her pallor and sunken cheeks.

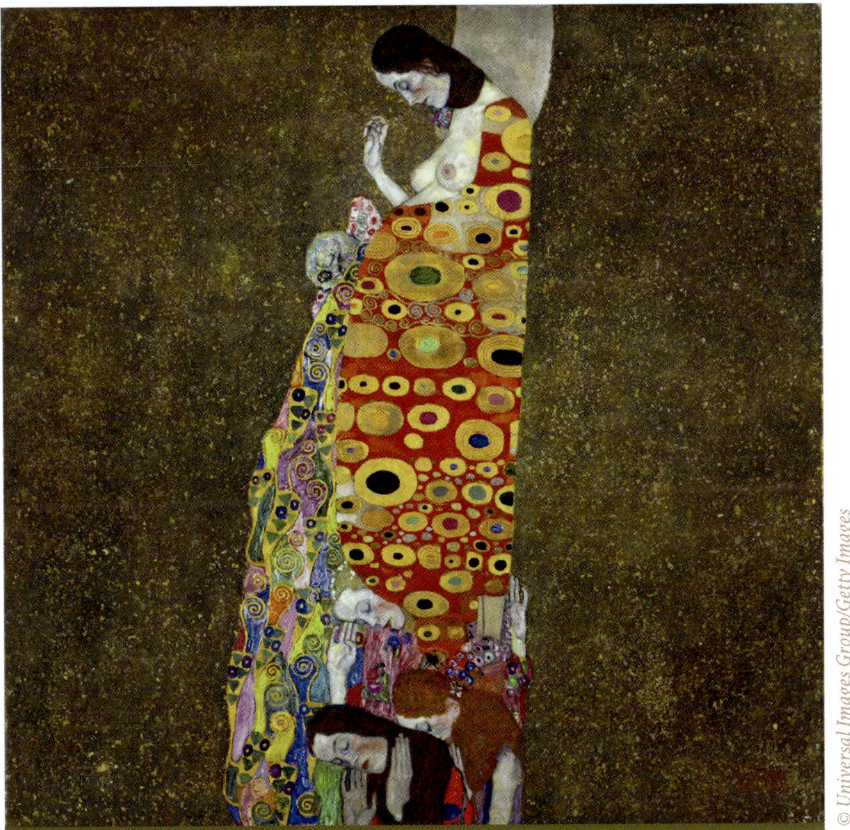

FIGURE 1.40 – Hope II, Gustav Klimt. 1908. 110.5 x 110.5 cm. Oil, gold, and platinum on canvas.

During the first millennium of the Moche culture of Peru, artisans created an enormous amount of functional pottery. The subject matter was widely varied, including people, animals, healing practices, sexual activities, and birthing processes. With the absence of written records, the exact purposes of these various pots is unknown. One theory is that they may have been used as teaching tools.

The *Moche Birthing Pot* (see Figure 1.41) depicts a woman in the process of delivering her child. There is a woman behind the mother providing physical support through this process and another who is helping to deliver the baby, gently holding its head as it emerges from the birth canal. So the purpose of this specific vessel could be twofold. First, it might indicate that midwifery was common in the Moche culture. Used as a teaching tool to those in training, it would show the various roles a midwife was expected to perform. For a first time mother, the image would show that she would deliver the baby in a seated position and assistance and support would be provided during the process.

GENRE PAINTING - a form of painting where the subject matter focuses on aspects of everyday life.

American born, Mary Cassatt (1844–1926) was a well-known genre painter. Her paintings depicted the everyday moments between a mother and child. The etching *In the Omnibus* (see Figure 1.42) depicts a mother and her young daughter while riding on a bus with a companion. This image communicates the nineteenth-century rules of conduct for women, in particular those of the middle- and upper-class. At that time, respectable women were not permitted to be alone in public and must be accompanied by an escort of either sex. Women who could afford to hire nannies, did so to assist in the raising of their children and to provide them with greater freedom to pursue personal interests. To communicate social status, Cassatt focused on the different styles of clothing. Both women are well-dressed, indicating they are not from the working class society. Although both are middle class, the two women are not equal in status, which can be seen in the simple difference between the styles of their hats. The young mother's companion has a more ornate and larger hat. In addition, she is depicted without a child. This may indicate she is unmarried or without a family, but could also suggest that she is of higher standing having the means to hire a nanny to assist her.

PRINTS - an image that is produced through various photography or printmaking techniques.

While in Paris in the spring of 1890, Mary Cassatt visited an exhibition of Japanese ukiyo-e prints. She was so taken with the traditional style of woodblock printing, the use of broad planes of color and flattened figures that it impacted the direction of her work for the next year. While she continued using various printmaking techniques, she translated the feel of the Japanese prints to her images. This can be seen in Cassatt's *In the Omnibus*, where she combined dry point and aquatint techniques. Like Klimt, the influence came out mostly in the simple color washes of the background and the flattened bodies of the figures, while the heads appear more dimensional.

DRY POINT - a printmaking (etching) process where the image or design is scratched onto a surface prior to inking and printing.

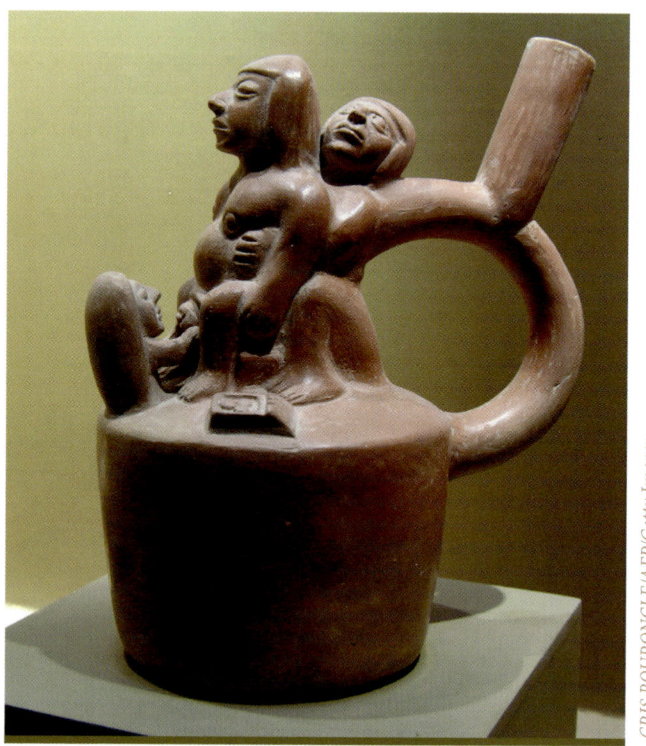

CRIS BOURONCLE/AFP/Getty Images

FIGURE 1.41 – Moche Birthing Pot. Sipan, Peru. c. 1-800. Approximately $5\,^5/_8 \times 6\,^7/_8 \times 6\,^3/_8$ cm. Ceramic.

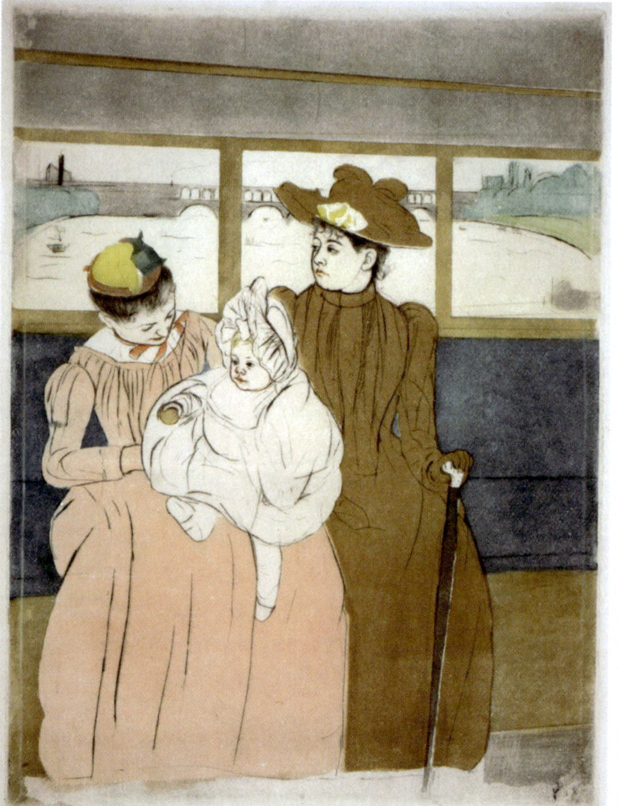

©Everett Historical/Shutterstock.com

FIGURE 1.42 – In the Omnibus, Mary Cassatt. 1891. $14\,^5/_{16} \times 10.5$ in. Drypoint, aquatint and etching.

AQUATINT - a printmaking process where an image is created through a range of tonal values rather than distinct lines on a surface prior to inking and printing.

One of Michelangelo's best known pieces is *Pieta* (see Figure 1.43) created in 1499. Cardinal Jean de Billheres commission the artist to create sculpture for the side chapel in the Old St. Peter's Basilica in Rome.

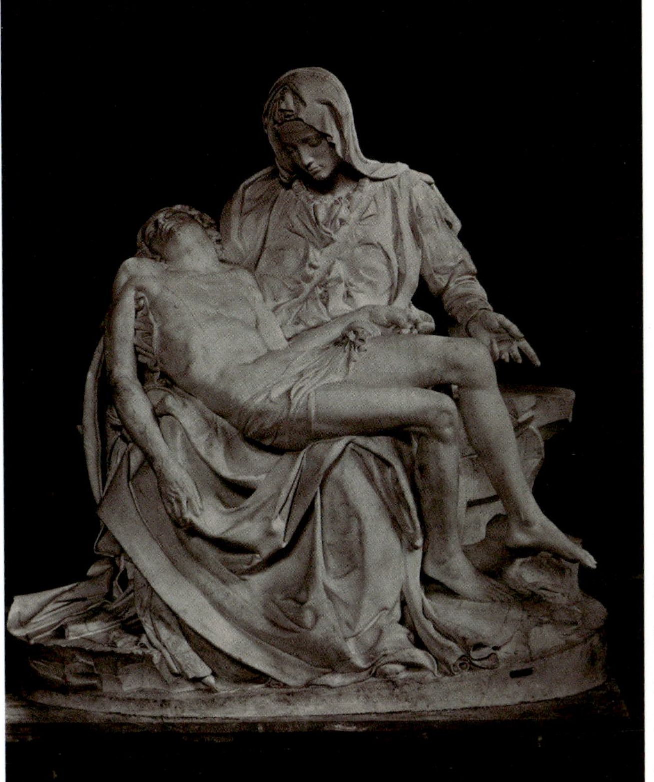

Alinari Archives/Alinari/Getty Images

FIGURE 1.43 – Pieta, Michelangelo. 1499. 68.5 x 76.8 in. Marble.

Michelangelo chose a common subject, that of the Virgin Mary holding her dead son, Christ, after his removal from the cross, prior to entombment. At that point during the Renaissance period, multi-figured sculptures were rarely created. Not only did Michelangelo take this on, but he exaggerated the dimensions of the figures in such a way as to enhance the overall impact of the sculpture. Mary's overall body size is much larger than Christ's. The artist's purpose in doing this was to create the illusion that she could gracefully support her adult son on her lap. Although devastated by her son's death, Mary appears to be resigned to the tragedy. Michelangelo heavily drapes her in clothing to contrast the starkness and vulnerability of her son's nudity. Mary's right hand is covered in cloth rather than directly touching his skin which symbolized the sacredness of Christ's body.

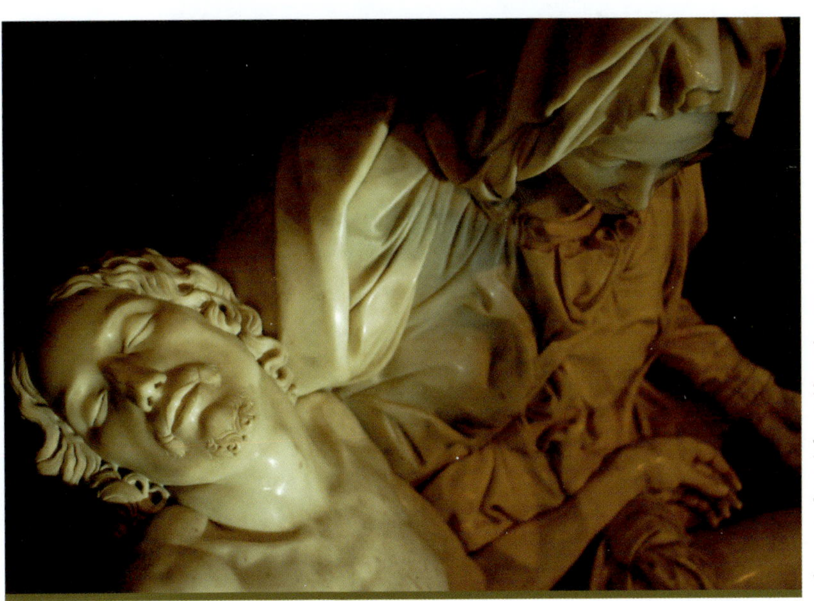

Alinari Archives/Alinari/Getty Images

FIGURE 1.44 – Pieta (Close-up of Christ's Head), Michelangelo. 1499. Marble.

Michelangelo made a unique choice in depicting the face of Mary as more youthful than that of Christ's, who is shown with facial hair (see Figure 1.44) indicating that he is no longer a youth. The artist's choice was said to reflect the idea that chaste women retain their beauty longer; therefore, she has aged very little since Christ's birth. Christ appears in a peaceful slumber, rather than bloodied and bruised from the events that had recently taken place. The bond between mother and child is reflected in the simple yet poignant gesture of Christ's fingers slightly entangled in Mary's robes.

Immediately after its installation, the *Pieta* became famous. The success of this piece would help cement Michelangelo's future success in the art world.

American artist, Andrea Knarr (1945–) was creative from a very early age, pursuing her interests in both dance and the visual arts. After receiving her Master's degree in printmaking, she began a long, distinguished career as an educator. When asked about her work, Knarr says, "There is something about making art that speaks to what it means to be human. A precise moment is captured by the hand and is then recorded, forever unchanged. In making these images, I seek to push the boundaries of time and space and to use the quality of light as an emotional barometer. The suggestion of the horizon as a place of longing and fear is a universal metaphor for the human condition." Knarr's work has been shown extensively in galleries, museums, and universities across the United States.

In *Dismissal* (see Figure 1.45), Andrea Knarr addresses the point in a parent's life when their child leaves home for the first time. She uses chairs to reference the human form, allowing the viewer to connect more personally to the piece by imagining themselves sitting in the chairs. In the foreground, Knarr places two chairs. The one on the left symbolizing the mother; the one on the right the father. The position of the chair reflects the emotions of each parent, as they watch their first born child leaving in the distance. The mother is angled toward the father, communicating her sense of apprehension. Meanwhile, the father is looking more directly at his child, communicating the sense of confidence that he has in him. The child's chair casts a shadow that reaches back toward the parents showing his apprehension. Despite those feelings, the child is moving toward the future, indicated by the position of the chair facing the horizon.

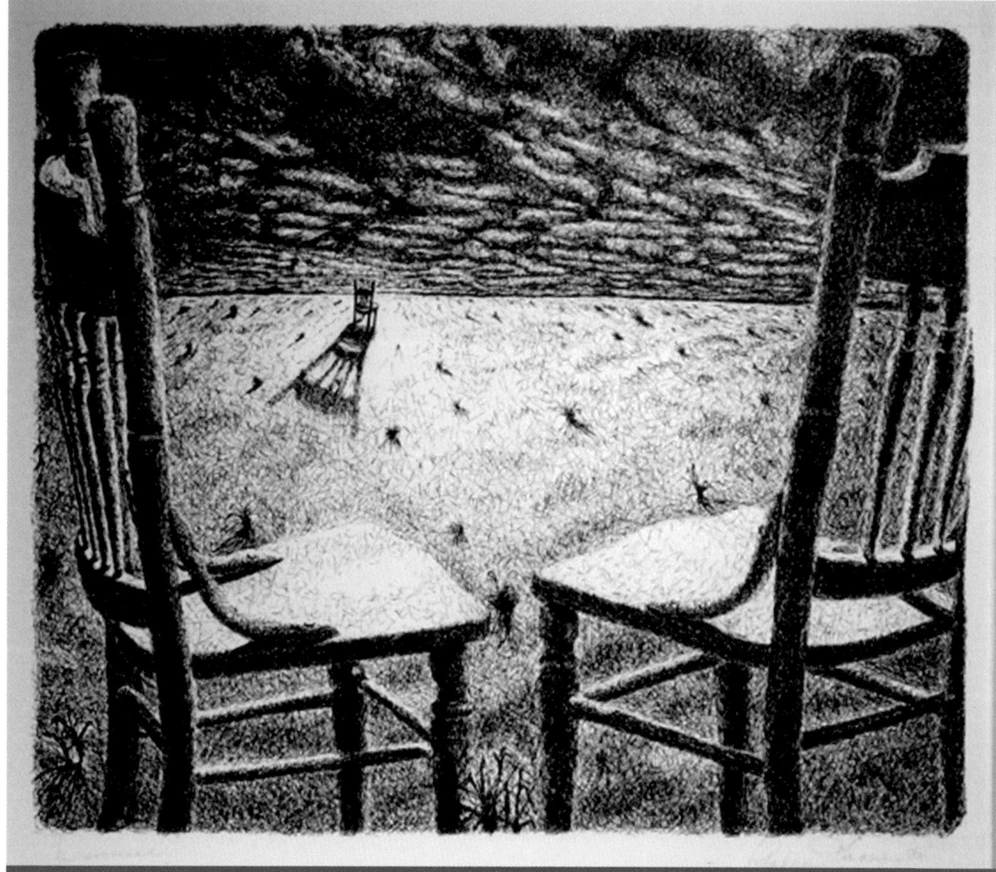

FIGURE 1.45 – Dismissal, Andrea Knarr. 1988. 17 x 14 in. Pen and ink.

part 3

RACE

In every time period, issues of race have plagued mankind. Differences that make us unique individuals can also lead to discrimination, hatred, and prejudice. Cultures around the world use art as a means to express their racial identity and culture. Artists, concentrating on these issues, channel their ideas, feelings, and thoughts about race through their art.

Throughout American history, African-Americans have found themselves at odds with society. Brought to the Americas for slavery, men, women, and children found themselves in an unfamiliar and unfriendly land. Their rights, identity, and cultural heritage were stripped away as a means to control them. They were perceived as savages lacking the same feelings and needs of the 'cultured citizens.' Such misguided perceptions of society continue to be addressed by artists today.

In the early 1900s, the Harlem Renaissance was emerging in New York City. Musicians, writers, and artists were making huge contributions to their fields that would impact those of every race. While new forms of music were emanating from the studios and clubs, artists were equally as exploratory in the visual arts. Some were specifically trying to change the way African-Americans were viewed. Prior to this time, images of African-Americans used in advertising and for entertainment were derogatory in nature, depicting them in positions of servitude, as victims in need of saving, in 'black face' or in other unflattering ways. It was artists like photographer James Vander Zee (1886–1983), and others, that wanted to change societal perceptions of racial identity. As seen in images like *Society Ladies* (1927), Vander Zee captured strong African-American business owners, writers, and intellects, fighting for equal rights in politics and society. Vander Zee not only showed strong people who were anything but victims, but also focused on women who were fighting for these rights. This was not something that would have been typically thought of at that time, for women's rights were almost as restrictive as those of the African-Americans.

In various parts of the United States, as the push for women's rights was taking hold and women were no longer willing to be placed solely in the role of 'caregiver' or 'homemaker', many organizations began to emerge. The Women's League was one such group. Their goal was to address issues of education, health, sanitation, and woman suffrage. While the majority of these organizations were created by white women, African-American organizations (see Figure 1.46) emerged as well. The white organizations held a similar societal prejudice, preventing the admission of African-American women into their groups. This did not prevent African-American women from standing up for themselves, creating their own organizations, and pushing the boundaries on similar issues. In addition, they fought to combat racism and stop lynching.

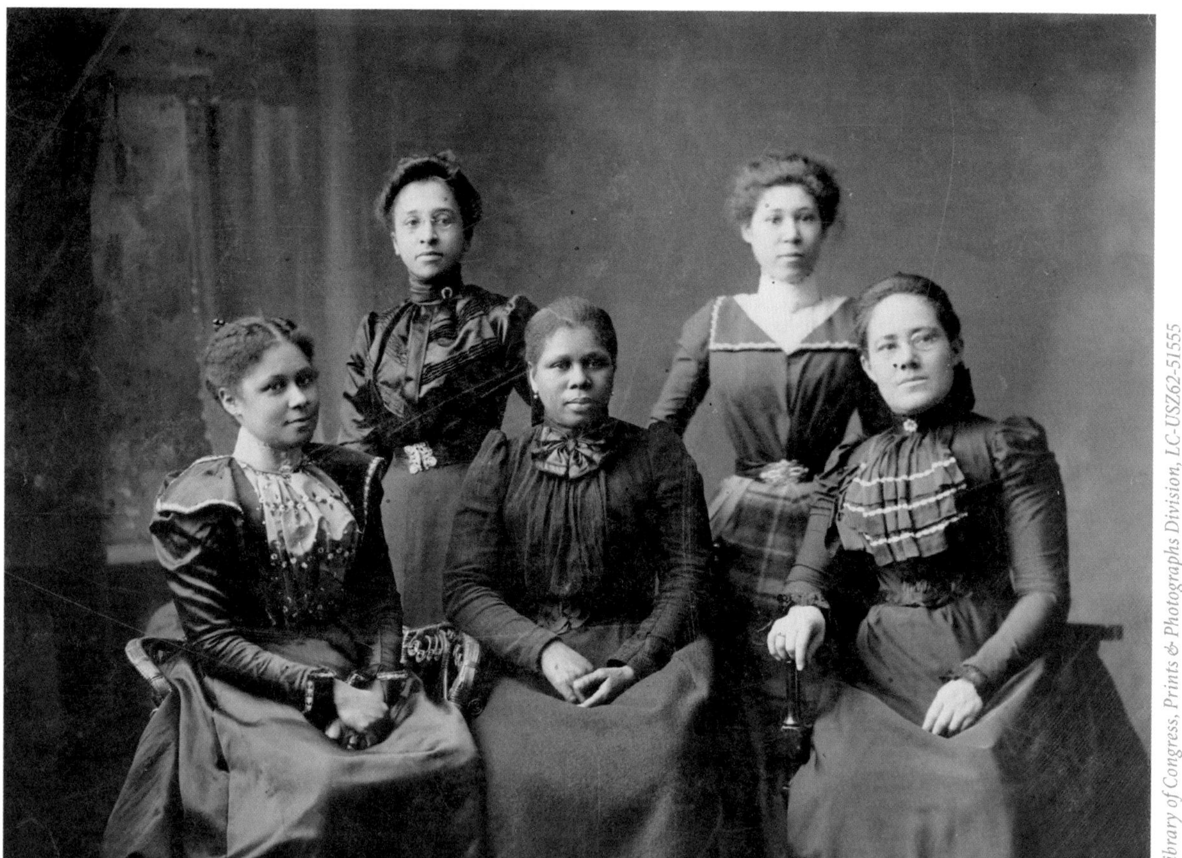

FIGURE 1.46 – 5 Negro Officers of Women's League. Newport, RI. 1899. Photograph.

Contemporary artists continue to deal with issues of racial perception and injustice artistically. While huge strides have been made in some areas of the world, these are still issues that plague people of different races. Artists embrace their racial history and traditions in ways to visually communicate where they came from, what they did to survive, their changing world and to show their continued presence in society.

Michelle Red Elk (1972–) began drawing at the age of five. Her father's artistic pursuits and her frequent visits to museums served as sources of inspiration to her. It was also through her father, and his family in Oklahoma, that Red Elk learned of her Comanche and Kiowa heritage. An integral part of her life, the Indian culture and her father's stories have impacted the way she thinks and sees things as she moves through life. Red Elk finds that aspects of this come through her art, both intentionally and subconsciously. In *Wood Cutter* (see Figure 1.47), the artist depicts Wovoka's vision.

Wovoka, an Indian prophet of peace, claimed that Spirits had provided him knowledge of certain movements and songs that when performed together could bring about the regeneration of the earth. When white peoples' expansion led to the destruction of the land and of the Native people's traditional way of life, the performance of the ghost dance was extended to aid in the restoration of the earth's caretakers to their traditional way of life. Many tribes, even those with a history of conflict, came together to perform this ritual dance. The solidarity it created among the Native people was threatening to the white government and led to the massacre of many ceremonial dancers in 1890 at the Wounded Knee site on the Pine Ridge Indian Reservation in South Dakota.

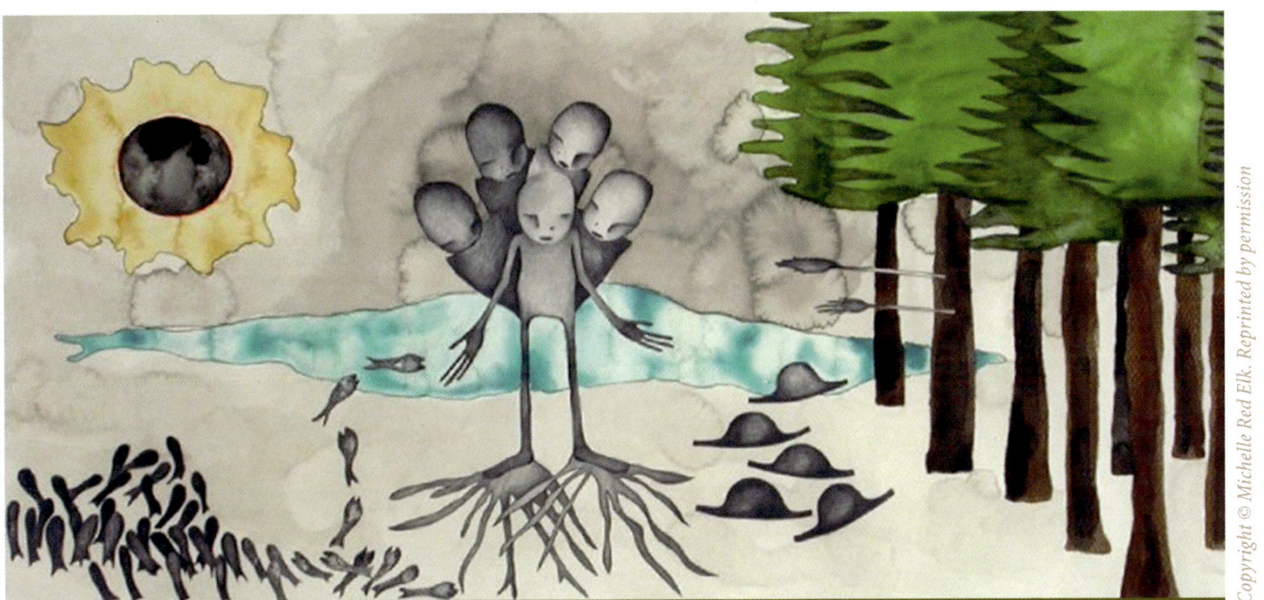

FIGURE 1.47 – Wood Cutter, Michelle Red Elk. 2005. 22.25 in. x 11 in. Watercolor and pencil on paper.

In *Wood Cutter*, Michelle Red Elk shows aspects of the traditional way of life, through the ghost dancers, and the abundance of food and resources, through the fish, bright blue lake, and dense forest. The indication of the encroaching white man is simply communicated through the hats near the trees. Part of the message that is coming from her work on a grander level is one that translates to all races. People are an active part of society, while adapting over the generations to overcome the restrictions and influences outsiders put upon them. They have not faded away; they have not assimilated into another culture to the point of losing their own identity; they continue to live among us and embrace their unique heritage.

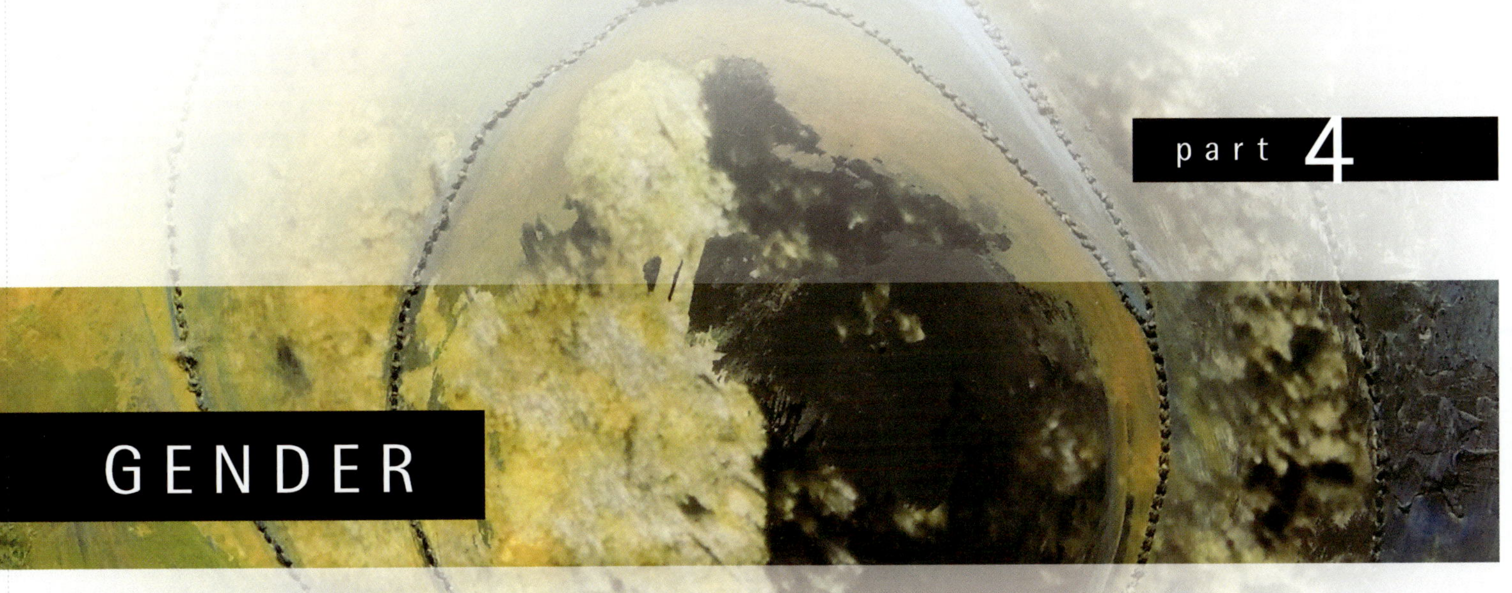

part 4

GENDER

Gender can be expressed artistically through the use of the human form, the natural world, and man-made architecture. Artists can also use their art as a means to address and challenge societal perceptions of gender identity and roles. In various ancient societies, artwork reflected an unusual cultural acceptance of equality between the genders. In an ever-changing world, gender-related issues continue to be addressed through art.

IDENTITY

As early as Paleolithic times in Europe (40,000 BC), humans have not been only making 'art' on cave walls but have also been leaving art in the form of their handprints. Our perceptions of our distant ancestors is one that is changing with each new discovery. Through the information available from the past, Paleolithic humans and their lifestyles seemed to be simple and focused solely on survival. As more caves have been discovered, more theories are being posed that show early man as more similar to modern man. While it was thought that males were responsible for creating the images of animals on cave walls, new studies have opened up the possibility that men, women, and children were responsible for these creations. The work of British biologist, John Manning, suggested that by studying hand size, finger shape, and finger length, it was possible to determine the gender of the 'artist' when no other information is available.

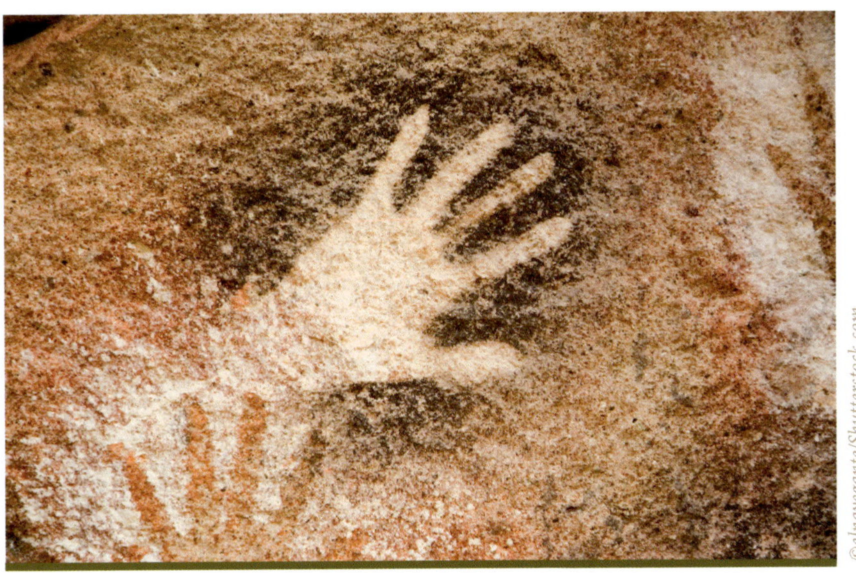

FIGURE 1.48 – Ancient Cave Paintings. Patagonia, Argentina. c. 8000 BC. Pigment on rock.

Using these parameters, archaeologists can look at the outlines of hands left on the cave walls by early humans and make educated guesses as to who might have been responsible. While impossible to prove without a shadow of doubt, it would appear that more often than not, it was the women who were painting the images of animals on the cave walls. Additional analysis of imagery from the Chauvet Cave, discovered in Southern France in the mid-1990s, indicates that the outlines of hands are unique. As seen in *Ancient Cave Paintings* (see Figure 1.48), the brown outlined hand in the center shows the third and fourth fingers to be spaced closer to one another than the other fingers. By making notations of these differences, the archaeologists have discovered that certain hand outlines appear next to certain images throughout the cave. Perhaps, this acted as their signature and they were thereby claiming the image as their own creation.

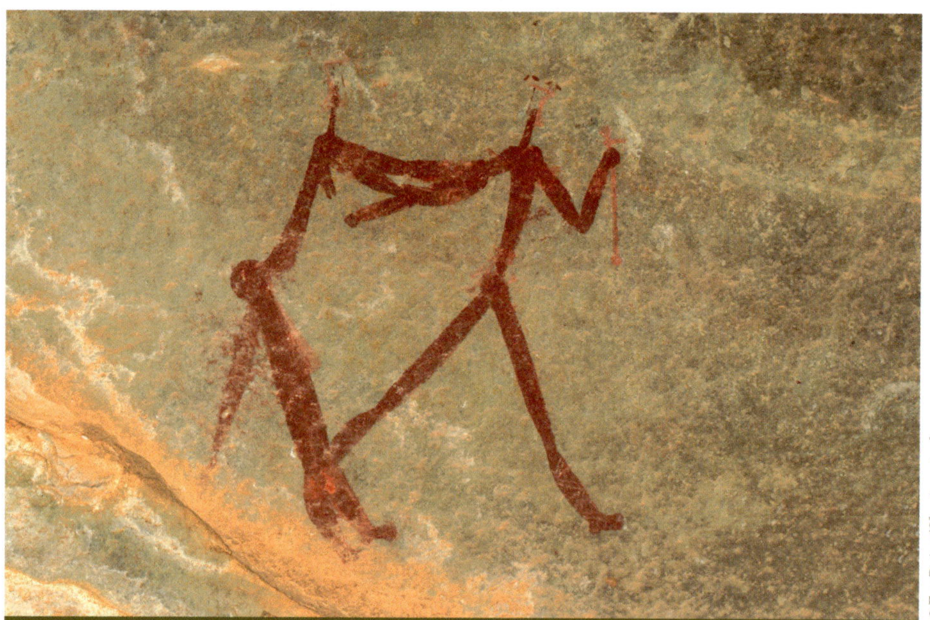

FIGURE 1.49 – Bushmen (San) Rock Painting Depicting Human Figures. Drakensberg, Africa. c. 1200. Pigment on rock.

In the Drakenburg mountains in South Africa, extraordinary images of humans can be seen depicted on rock surfaces. In some cases, imagery shows hunters with spears, or bows and arrows, in hand and running among a herd of animals. Other images show Bushmen with antelope, which is a spiritual animal associated with various rituals tied to rites of passage into adulthood and marriage. In *Bushmen (San) Rock Painting Depicting Human Figures* (see Figure 1.49), the rock art depicts the way the San people visually communicated gender between the sexes. The male and female are similar in the rendering of their upper bodies. A distinct difference however is in the chest where the breasts of the female are clearly depicted. Another distinctive difference to show gender in the figures is through the lower bodies. The male's lower body appears to be lean, athletic, depicting slightly larger calf muscles. The female's body, however, appears to have larger buttocks and thighs. This ties into their cultural ideal of beauty and femininity. Although not seen in this image, another way to indicate gender in male figures is to display an erect phallus. This not only clearly communicates his gender, but also his virility as a hunter and potential mate.

MURALS - images painted on or covering a wall.

In the Minoan culture, bull imagery is found in murals, on musical instruments, and in sculptures. The horns of bulls have been found in altars of homes throughout the region, suggesting that the bull played a significant cultural or religious role. Although its true significance is unknown, the bull appears to symbolize fertility and strength.

In the *Minoan Toreador Fresco* (see Figure 1.50), the image is showing three individuals in the act of 'bull jumping.' The exact purpose of bull jumping to the Minoans is also unknown. There are theories that this was a form of entertainment, taking place in a venue similar to the Roman coliseum where many people could gather for such events. Others suggest that this may be a form of religious ceremony. Whether for entertainment or ritual purposes, the act of bull jumping could be seen as a means of exerting man's dominance over the natural world. The mural shows this ritual was practiced by both sexes. The Minoans, Etruscans, and other cultures used color as a means to distinguish between the genders. Females are painted a whitish tan color; males are painted a reddish brown. The choice of color can reflect common perceptions of gender roles within their society. Males tend to dominate the 'outer world' governing and business, while women the 'inner world' tending to home life and child rearing. The figures are depicted in a similar fashion with similar styles of clothing. Aside from color to differentiate their genders, the only other visual contributor to gender is that the women's upper bodies are more exaggerated to indicate the presence of their breasts.

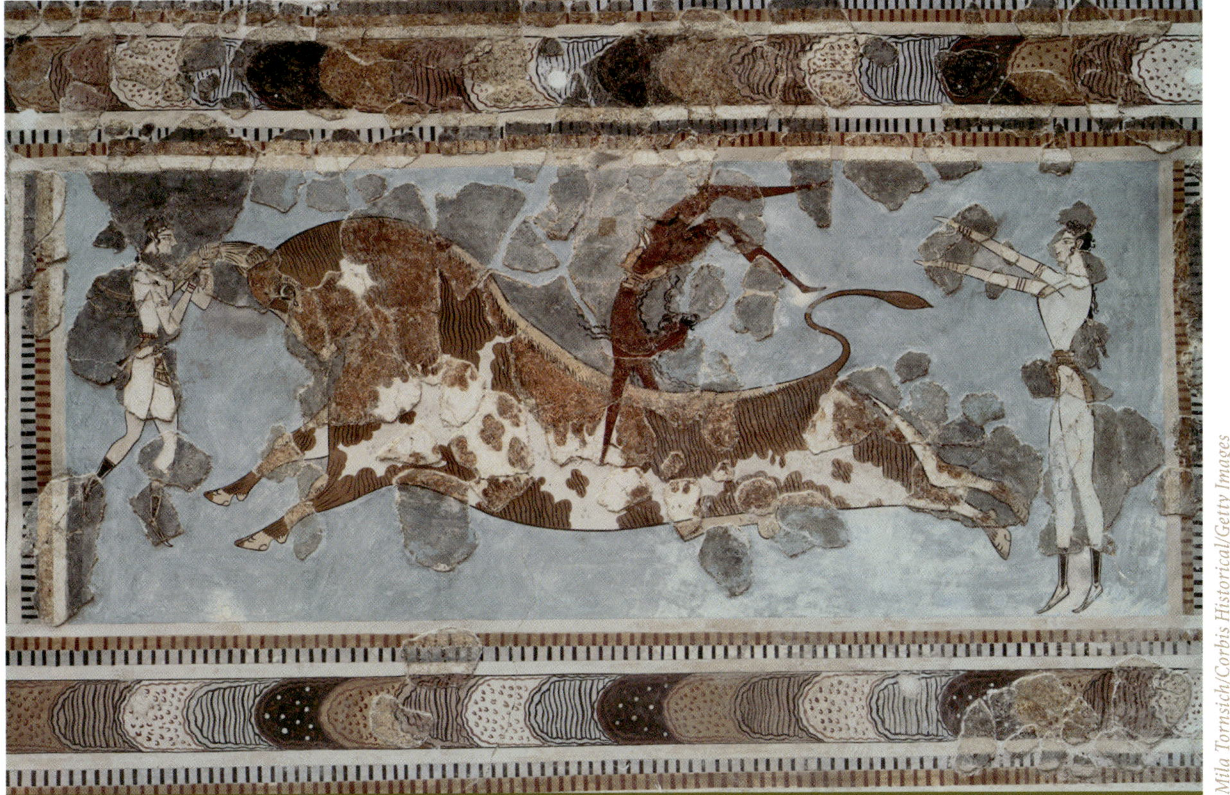

Mila Tornsich/Corbis Historical/Getty Images

FIGURE 1.50 – Minoan Toreador Fresco, Crete, Greece. c. 1550 BC. Approximately 60 x 31.5 in. Fresco mural.

EQUALITY & INEQUALITY

Throughout Egyptian royal art, the queens were often depicted in a similar position as the pharaohs, whether seated or standing. However, they were usually shown without a headdress, a step behind the pharaoh and smaller in height—all to communicate that their role in society was not equal to that of their husband. However, there was one pharaoh that had a significant impact on the depictions of royalty during his reign. Akhenaten (1380–1336) took the throne around 1334 BC upon his father's death. Unlike his father, he was not interested in politics and the expansion of his territory. What did seem important to him was family, how royalty was depicted artistically, and a monotheistic practice of worship.

Egypt, historically a polytheistic culture, was forced to practice monotheism during Akhenaten's rule. Egyptians were to worship Aten, god of the sun. During this time, Akhenaten claimed that he alone was able to communicate to Aten on his people's behalf and by worshipping him, they were worshipping Aten. Some historians suggest this was a political move on his part. Evidence shows that the priests associated with Amun, god of air, had gained increasing power, wealth and influence almost equal to that the pharaoh's.

Another area where Akhenaten impacted Egyptian traditions was through the depiction of royalty and royal life. He demanded the traditional, more stylistic approach give way a more naturalistic representation—showing them as they really were. In addition, royalty was rarely depicted in an intimate way or engaged in family situations. Because the pharaoh believed in the dignity and beauty of family life, Akhenaten had a great deal of artwork created to reflect this. Discoveries have been made of images depicting the royal family in everyday acts, such as eating a meal and relaxing together. Even more atypical within Egyptian royal art were the intimate moments captured between Akhenaten and his primary wife, Nefertiti (1370–1330 BC). Carvings were discovered showing the queen resting her head on the pharaoh's shoulder and of the two engaged in a kiss, openly acknowledging their love for one another.

NATURALISM - rendering an image or object so it closely resembles as it is seen in the natural world.

In *Akhenaten and Nefertiti with Their Children* (see Figure 1.51), the royal family is being depicted in an interesting way. There is an implication that Akhenaten and Nefertiti were perceived as equal by their god, Aten, and were actually co-rulers during his reign. Both are shown seated on thrones and on equal ground. They are facing one another and dressed in royal attire, consisting of similar headdresses and clothing. These visual elements support the idea of co-rulership. In addition, each is holding one or more of their children. While communicating the importance of family, the image also suggests that Akhenaten had more of a hand in home life than was traditional of a man's role in Egyptian society. The final element within the image suggesting a sense of equality in power between the two is Aten, represented by the disk from which the rays are emanating. The rays are almost shining equally down on the royal pair in the ultimate recognition of equality.

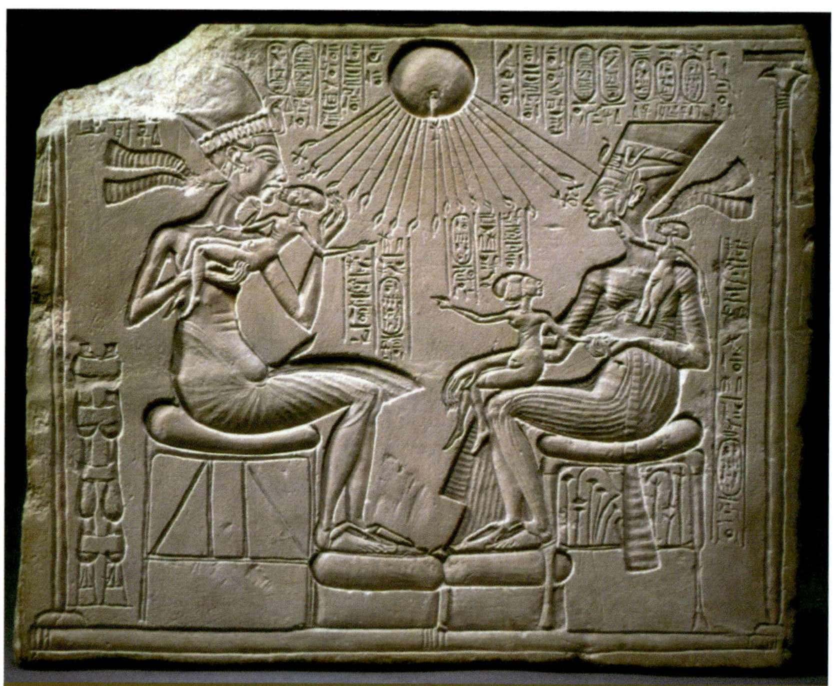

Heritage Images/Hulton Archive/Getty Images

FIGURE 1.51 – Akhenaten, Nefertiti and Their Children (The Royal Family). Egypt. c. 1350 BC. Limestone.

American artist, Carole Winters (1951–) pursued a degree in printmaking in 1973. She turned her attention toward a career in graphic design as an extension of fine art printmaking. After working within various printing and publishing companies in a variety of roles, such as art director and publisher, Winters became a self-employed graphic designer and visual artist. One subject the artist explored was the inequality still seen today between men and women in the workforce. She says, "Unfortunately, our society is still debating equal pay for equal work…choice, assertiveness, and the role of women in the workplace."

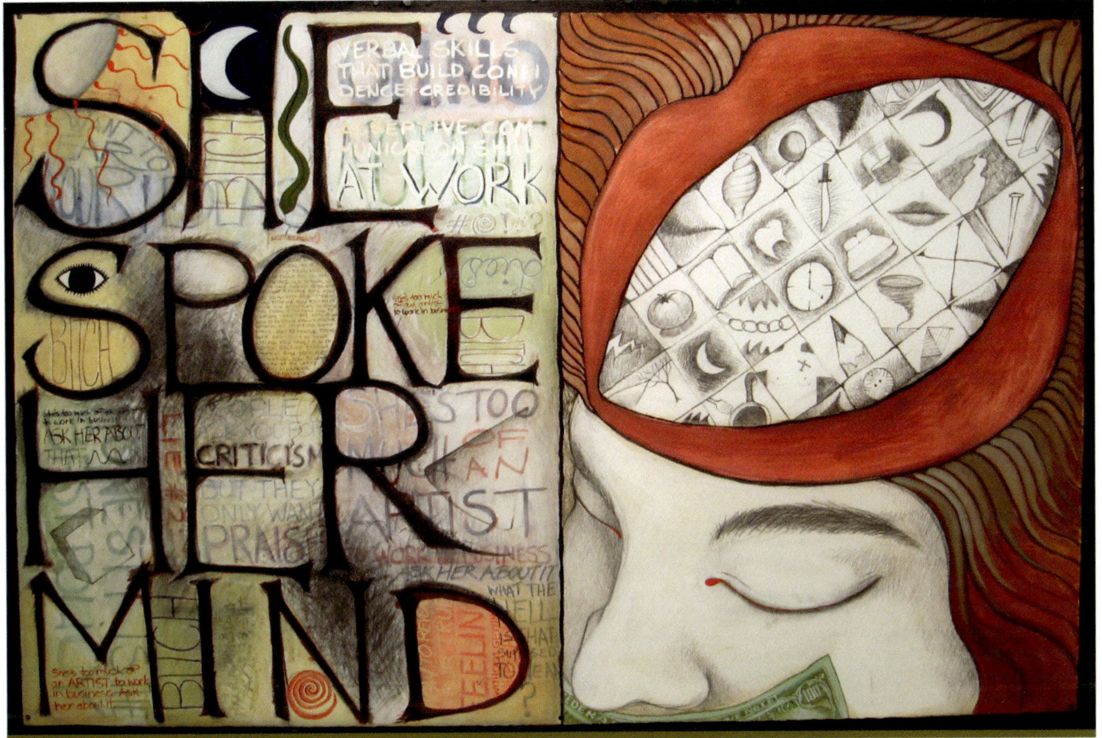

FIGURE 1.52 – She Spoke Her Mind, Carole Winters. 2013. 41 x 28 in. Watercolor, gouache, pencil on paper.

In *She Spoke Her Mind* (see Figure 1.52), Carole Winters addressed her termination from a publishing house where she served as a magazine art director for a decade. The format of the painting resembles that of a magazine spread, where both text and illustrations are essential to the design. Within the left side of the image, the artist includes various euphemisms and actual comments that were said to her around that time. One comment directed at Winter's which struck a chord with her was 'You spoke your mind,' implying that it was inappropriate for a woman to do so in the workplace. The right hand side of the painting is a visual culmination of all that transpired and a final thought that she wanted to communicate to the viewer. Of the depiction of a hundred-dollar bill seemingly taped across the woman's mouth, Winters says, "The need to make money silences one from actually saying what's on one's mind." Although colorful and pleasant to the eye, this painting is a powerful message that gender inequalities are still experienced within the society today.

GENDER IN ARCHITECTURE

While perhaps not an obvious idea, architecture and monumental sculpture can convey a sense of gender. The architect's or artist's choice of material, décor, and scale can all contribute to this. Characteristics traditional of different time periods in art, like Rococo or Arts and Crafts, can also contribute to the impression of gender artistically. The Egyptian obelisk is an example of the masculine in a monumental structure. It is phallic-like in appearance, made of solid stone, gray in color and towers above other structures nearby. These qualities can convey societal attitudes toward masculinity and the traditional roles of males, such as strength, consistency, and dominance. In contrast, a Russian Orthodox church can be seen as more feminine, through the use of multiple bright colors, elaborate patterning, and ornate shapes used throughout its design. These qualities can convey societal attitudes toward femininity and traditional roles of females, such as vivaciousness, playfulness, and life giving.

ROCOCO - an early eighteenth century Western art form distinguished by its ornate style and light colors.

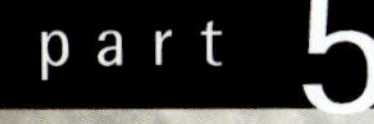

CLAN

Clan is defined as a group of individuals that are associated through blood ties or marriage. This group can consist of two people or up to thousands. Art can be used to communicate the history of a clan or to provide a way for the living to maintain a connection with their clan ancestors.

In ancient Rome, it was a common practice to take a wax casting or impression of the face of a recently deceased family member. This provided an image of the person for the family members to hold onto, serving a similar purpose as a photograph does for many people today. The wax casting could be brought out during family events to not only remind the group of their connection to one another, but as a means to have the presence of their deceased during such times. However, wax is not a permanent material and is susceptible to heat and other elements. The Romans turned to creating stone busts to serve the same function. Traditionally, images of the aristocratic ruling class would depict individuals in a more stylized way, often not showing their age or imperfections. The middle class preferred the more naturalistic portraits for their funerary works. *Ancient Marble Statue of Roman Emperor Julius Caesar* (see Figure 1.53) is a bust of the emperor, created in the traditional style more commonly associated with middle class memorial art. As seen in this piece, the figure is depicted in an aged state, heavily creased lines around his mouth and on his forehead and heavy bags beneath his eyes. Although there is a slight indication of the irises, the eyes appear to be vacant and lifeless to further indicate the individual represented by the sculpture is deceased. Owning an ancestral bust can define a family's status within the larger clan. Wealthier families may only possess such a statue because of the expense involved in its creation and the material used. The invention of photography eventually made owning images of one's ancestors more accessible to the masses.

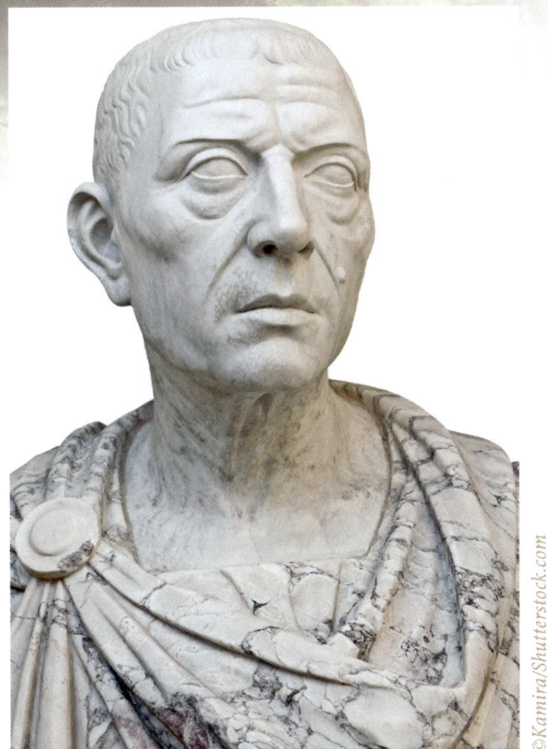

FIGURE 1.53 – Ancient Marble Statue of the Roman Emperor Julius Caesar. Italy. c. 44 BC. Marble.

There is a long history of the samurai and their significance within Japanese culture. During the Tokugawa era (1585–1598), the highest of military officials, known as shoguns, ruled the country in the name of the emperor. Serving under a shogun were regional lords, or *daimyo*, who employed a group of samurai warriors.

Shoguns, daimyo, and samurai warriors were expected to follow the Code of Bushido or the 'way of the warrior.' Part of this code consisted of one's loyalty to one's master and fearlessness in the face of death, which sometimes included ritual suicide.

There were times, however, when a samurai would find himself in the position of being without a master. Reasons for this were the commission of a dishonorable act or the fall or death of his master. If the samurai was unable or unwilling to serve under a new daimyo, the bushido required ritual suicide, or *seppuku*, in such cases to preserve the honor of the samurai and ultimately to prevent revenge killings. However, there were many who chose the dishonorable path and continued to live. They were called *Ronin*, a samurai without a master, and they lived a drastically different lifestyle. These men were not legally allowed to take on respectable positions in society, such as farmers or merchants, and often had to turn to crime for survival.

In Japanese history, there is a true event that is known as *Chushingura* or the *Story of Forty-seven Ronin.* In 1702, Asano Takumi no kami Naganori (1667–1701) was chosen by his shogun to entertain envoys from the Imperial family. Before taking this position, he was to receive training on matters of etiquette from Kira Kozukenosuke Yoshinaka (1641–1702), a high ranking master of protocol. There was a misunderstanding between the two men and animosity developed. Emotions escalated over time, until one day Asano attacked Kira. He was placed under confinement, eventually sentenced to death and his land was confiscated. Asano's Ronin were divided to the direction they should proceed. Some chose to leave and lead the life of a Ronin, while the others chose to defend the castle, help re-establish the Asano family and prepare revenge on Kira. Over the course of a year, these Ronin, led by Ôishi Kuranosuke, created an elaborate façade of falling into ill repute and of being harmless. Once Kira had fallen into a state of complacency, the forty-seven Ronin took their revenge.

In *Chushingura* (see Figure 1.54), the Ronin descended upon Kira's mansion. Battle ensued, as seen throughout the image, on the bridge and land towards the background. In the foreground, three of the Ronin, dressed in similar attire, are seen attacking Kira. Once captured, Kira refused to commit suicide and he was decapitated by Ôishi. The Ronin then turned themselves in and were sentenced to commit ritual suicide. Because many of the Japanese people felt these Ronin followed aspects of the warrior code and were honorable in turning themselves over to the authorities for judgment, there was public outrage over the verdict and fate of the men. In order to calm the situation, the shogun's government returned the title and part of Asano's lands to his eldest son.

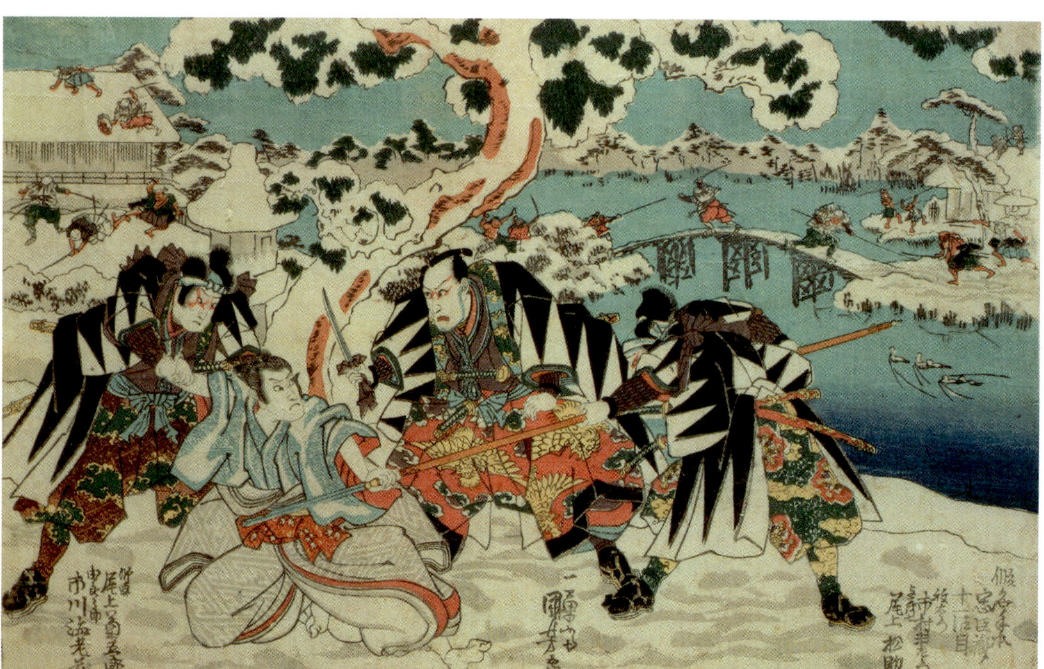

FIGURE 1.54 – The Chushingura (the Story of the 47 Ronin), Utagawa Kuniyoshi. 1854. Color woodcut.

In various Native American tribes in the Pacific Northwest Coast region of the United States and Canada, one way a clan's history is displayed is on totem poles. The creation and erection of a totem pole is steeped in tradition. Once a family decided to have a totem pole carved, they began the process of gathering enough food, creating gifts, and other preparations for all who would attend the Potlatch ceremony for the raising of the pole.

A feller, person who was chosen to find and cut down the right tree, was hired. Once the tree was cut down, a carver could then start the process of depicting important people and events within the clan's history. Every image, including animals, was deliberately chosen to describe this clan's history and mythology. Then they were carefully carved and painted. Once the family was prepared, a potlach ceremony was held. This was when the community and those from surrounding villages would gather for feasting and raising of the pole. Music, dance, games, and gifts were all part of this ceremony. All who attended and participated in the potlatch were acknowledging that family's status in society.

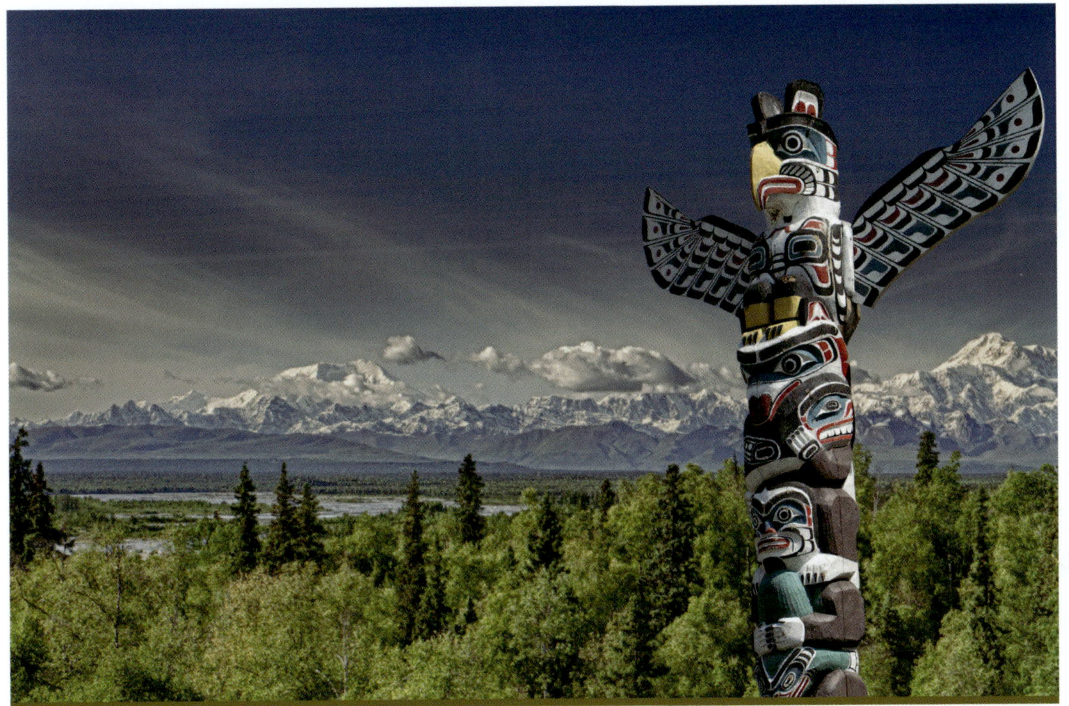

FIGURE 1.55 – Totem Pole. Native American. Carved, painted wood.

Ellen Neel (1916–1966), a master Kwakwaka'wakw carver from Vancouver Island in Canada, was known for carving totem poles. She created a range in size from the large-scale commissioned totem poles to be displayed outside to the small ones purchased by tourists. In 1955, Woodward's department store commissioned Neel to create five totem poles for their mall in Alberta. Thirty years after their installation, three of the totem poles were returned to the coast, one of which still resides in Stanley Park near their site of creation.

In *Totem Pole* (see Figure 1.55), the imagery depicted reflects the Native American animism beliefs and cultural myths. At the top of the pole resides an Eagle, one of the most respected beings in the Pacific Northwest Coast tribes' art and mythology. He was highly regarded for his intelligence, power, and extraordinary vision. Those belonging to the Eagle clan families were viewed as the most prominent and the Eagle Chiefs the most powerful. Located directly beneath the Eagle is the Grizzly Bear (see Figure 1.56), who was respected for its strength and fierceness. Bears were closely associated with humans because of their similar behavior in standing on their hind legs, hunting and gathering food, and nurturing their young. In addition, they were associated with shamans and guardians of the tribe's warriors.

The Bear stands on the shoulders of a woman holding a frog. The Frog was a symbol of knowledge and power to the native people. The woman stands on the head of Bak'was, the Wild Man of the Wilds, representing the forest realm. He was traditionally depicted with a skeletal face, large mouth, and predominately green, brown, and black in coloration. At the bottom of the pole is the Raven. The Raven was known by many names, such as Trickster or Transformer. He was believed to possess the ability to alter his persona into something else. The Kwakwaka'wakw culture attributed the discovery of fire to the Raven. He was typically painted black and depicted with a strong, straight beak that tapered towards its tip. His ears were not prominent and his wings were folded close to his body. While this totem pole was not created for a specific clan, it clearly reflects aspects of their cultural beliefs and myths.

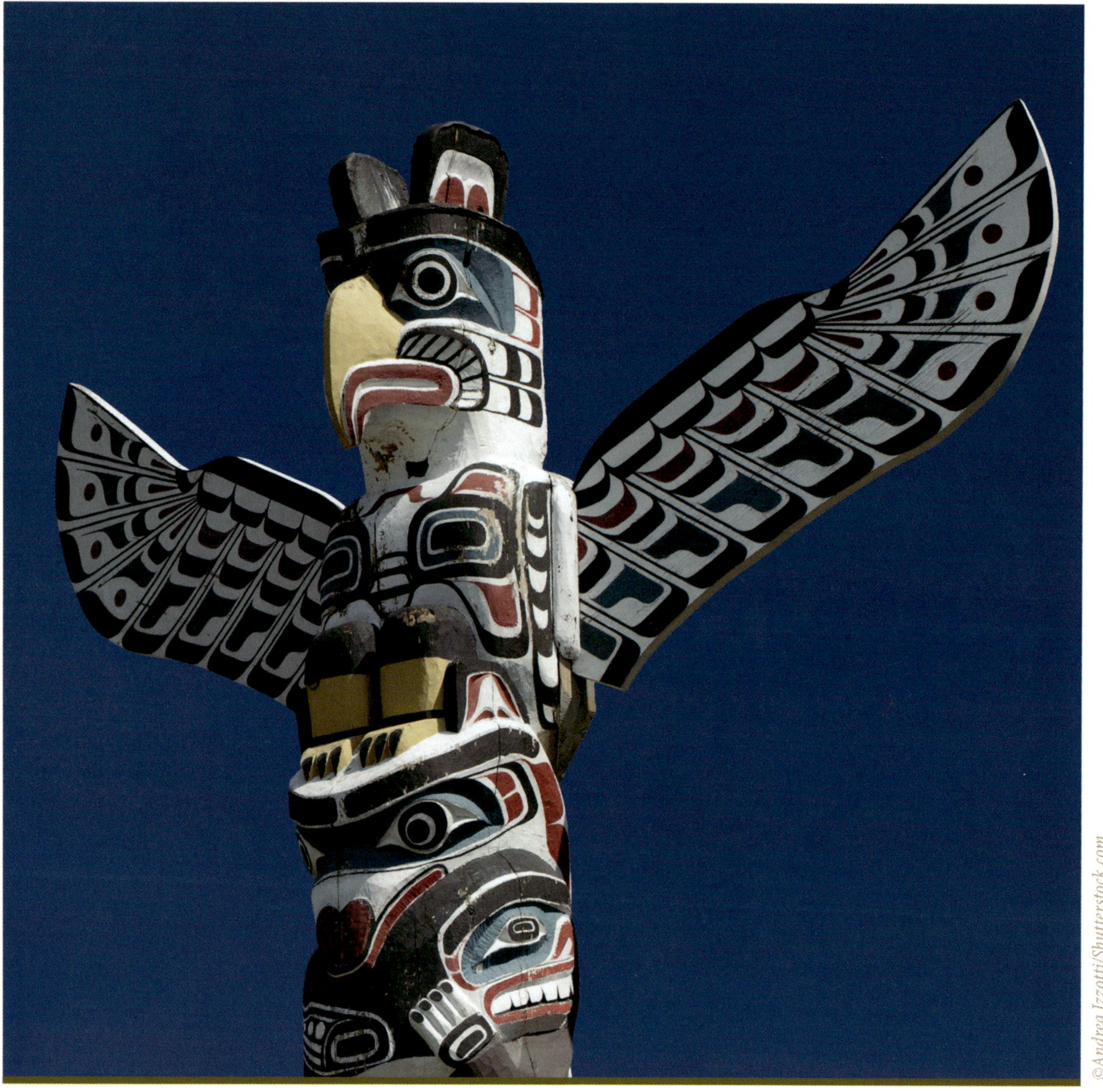

FIGURE 1.56 – Totem Pole (detail). Native American. Carved, painted wood.

part 6

CLASS

Class is defined as a person's social position within a society or culture. In some cultures, a person is born into the same class as their ancestors. In other parts of the world, a person's social class can be easily changed through marriage or the accumulation of wealth. In these situations, a person can just as easily move into a lower social class as they can a higher one. Artwork can be a tool to communicate a person's class, whether through the way they are physically depicted in their environment, through their activities, or by the possessions they own.

In the Etruscan culture, it was an artistic practice to use *hierarchical scale*. This technique showed the person of importance as larger than the others depicted within the image. In *Detail of Standard of Ur (Side B)* (see Figure 1.57), the king is shown seated on his throne facing servants and members of his court. Although seated, he is shown almost a full head higher than the figure directly in front of him. In contrast, the figure seated opposite of the king is eye level with the man standing in front of him. This is an easy way for the artist to show the social standing or importance of a figure within an artwork. As with the Etruscan culture, the Egyptians had a similar practice. Along with the differences in scale of the figures, Egyptian royalty also had a distinct way their physique was depicted to further communicate their status as discussed earlier.

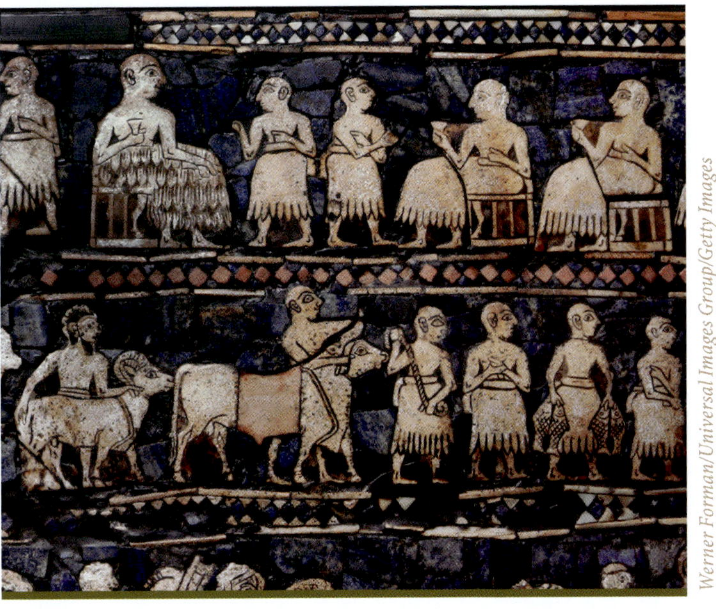

Werner Forman/Universal Images Group/Getty Images

FIGURE 1.57 – Detail of Standard of Ur (Side B). Iran/Iraq c. 2600–2400 BC. 19.5 x 8.5 in. Bitumen inlaid with shell, lapis lazuli and red limestone.

In America, many people were struggling to survive during the Great Depression (1929–1943). President Franklin D. Roosevelt was trying to provide economic relief to citizens, including artists, who were struggling to find work during this difficult time. After several failed attempts in this government effort, artist George Biddle (1885–1973) went to his friend, President Roosevelt, to recommend a unique approach. He suggested that the government hire artists and craftsmen to create large-scale public works of art. United States politicians, intrigued by the idea, envisioned the works expressing patriotic values to rally the dispirited American citizens. From 1935 to 1943, the Works Progress Administration (WPA) was a success that led to many large-scale art projects as well as building efforts that can still be found around the country. Many artists who had a major impact on the art world during or after their careers also worked on the WPA project. Some of these artists include Louise Nevelson, Jackson Pollock, and Mark Rothko.

George Biddle is an American artist who participated in the WPA program. The detail from *Society Freed through Justice* (see Figure 1.58) created in 1936, shows the working class in two specific ways. In the foreground of the painting, a family is planting their own food just outside their home. The artist's choice of not including the front wall of the house allows the viewer a clear view of the possessions and lifestyle of those that live within. While their possessions are nice and the interior is in good shape, the house appears to be too small to accommodate the number of people residing within its confines. In the distance, a more populated town with factories can be seen along the river's edge. On the road coming into view on the right, there are a group of men, some with what appear to be black lunch pails, heading into town to earn their wages.

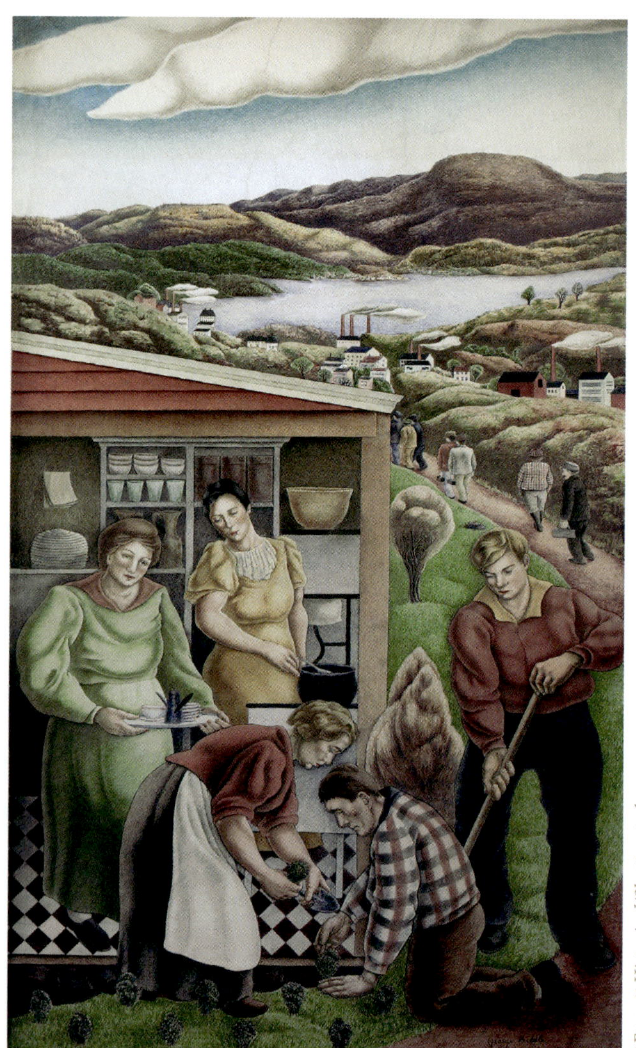

FIGURE 1.58 – Detail from Society Freed Through Justice (WPA Mural), George Biddle. 1936. Fresco mural.

During the eight years of its existence, the Works Progress Administration artists created over 200,000 works. Approximately 5,000 artists were employed and paid an average of $23.50 per week. While some of the WPA art still exists, many smaller works were auctioned off in 1943 by the government. The artwork was sold off by the pound rather than for its artistic value, resulting in individual pieces being sold for a few dollars each.

In 1940s American Midwest, people were experiencing severe droughts that were threatening their crops and ultimately their survival. The extremely dry soil was easily picked up by the strong winds blowing across the flat plains, creating dust storms. These storms would cover their homes, crops, and livestock with layers of dust. Eventually, many people chose to move further west in search of work and a better life. Farmlands and orchards were spread throughout the west coast territory. Due to their scale and the amount of produce grown, the farmers hired migrant workers at low wages to quickly harvest their crops. Migrant working camps popped up to serve as temporary housing for the workers and their families. As the work was completed in one area, they would move on to the next in search of more work to feed their families.

In 1936 in California, farmers experienced something that was very unusual for this warmer part of the country—a sudden temperature drop that led to a crop-killing frost. This not only severely impacted the farmers and consumers, it greatly threatened the workers and their families. Photographer Dorothea Lange (1895–1965) was in California at the time and documented the people and the situation that resulted from the frost. Many parents were left wondering how they would feed their children, when they would be able to work again, and if it would be soon enough to save them. In *Migrant Agricultural Worker's Family* (see Figure 1.59), Lange shows a working class mother, with two of her seven children. The rough fabric of her clothing and its tattered appearance coupled with her weathered skin visually communicates that she is not part of the middle or upper classes. In addition, the photographer captured the make shift shelter of branches and a tarp that she is using to protect her family from the elements. This further indicates that she is not only of the working class but of the poor class, as well. This image was taken shortly after she sold the tires off the family truck to put food on the table for her seven children. The resulting loss of transportation severely limited her ability to find work elsewhere.

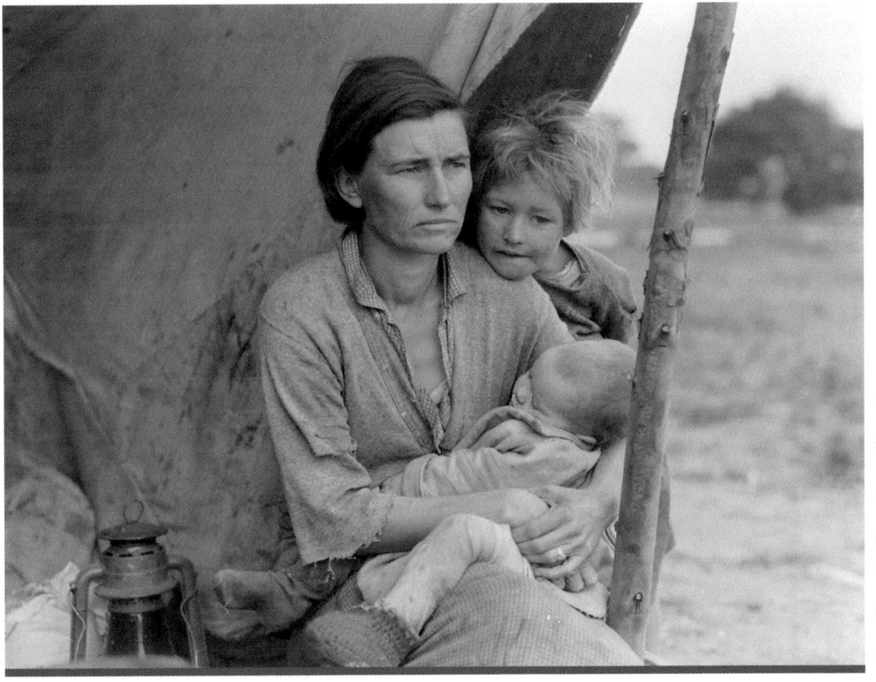

FIGURE 1.59 – Migrant Agricultural Worker's Family, Dorothea Lange. Nipomo, California. 1936. 30 x 20 in. Photograph.

Dorothea Lange's photographs were shown across the United States, bringing national attention to a situation that might otherwise have gone unnoticed. Because of this raised awareness, concerned citizens sent money and other means of support to the aid of the migrant workers.

As with clothing and shelter, one's possessions can communicate one's class. Pottery was a development seen with the emergence of large-scale societies, initially solving the need for storage of liquids and food. Overtime pottery began to change in shape, decoration, and the types of materials used. These all became factors later that were used to determine one's status or class ranking within a culture. The *Decorated Clay Pottery* (see Figure 1.60) is an example of a small, simple pot made from earthenware clay. This type of clay consists of sand and/or minerals and is found near river beds, in earth crevices and in canyons. It is fired at low temperatures, causing it to remain porous and retain an earthy clay color. In contrast, the *Chinese Antique Porcelain Vase with Gold Paint* (see Figure 1.61) is larger in scale and made from porcelain. This type of clay consists mainly of kaolinite, a clay mineral that is whitish in color, and lacks extraneous materials like sand. The pureness of the clay produced a silky smooth texture. Historically, porcelain is used to make small, delicate objects.

Both examples show vessels that are heavily decorated. Yet there is a distinction in how the vessels communicate commonness or refinement. In the earthenware pot, the design is created with two minerals from the earth to create the reddish brown and dark brown coloration. While the design covers the entire vase, it is simple in its pattern and shapes. This type of vessel would be for serving or storage purposes. In comparison, the porcelain vase is too large with too small an opening to serve any real purpose to the owner. It is decorated with gold paint and intricate dragon-like animals out of a deep, rich blue pigment—made from finely ground cobalt oxide mixed with water. The combination of these elements suggests that it was for decorative rather than functional purpose. At the time of its creation, the owner would have been someone of a higher social class who could afford a large vase made from expensive materials that was used for purely decorative purposes.

PIGMENT—color in the form of powder which can be mixed with a binder to create paint.

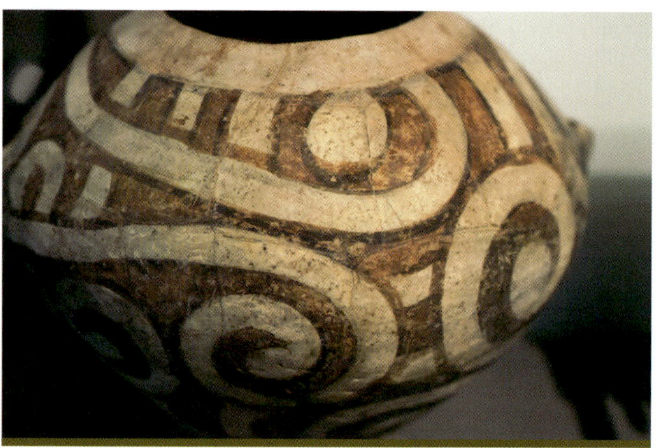

FIGURE 1.60 – Decorated Clay Pottery Ancient.

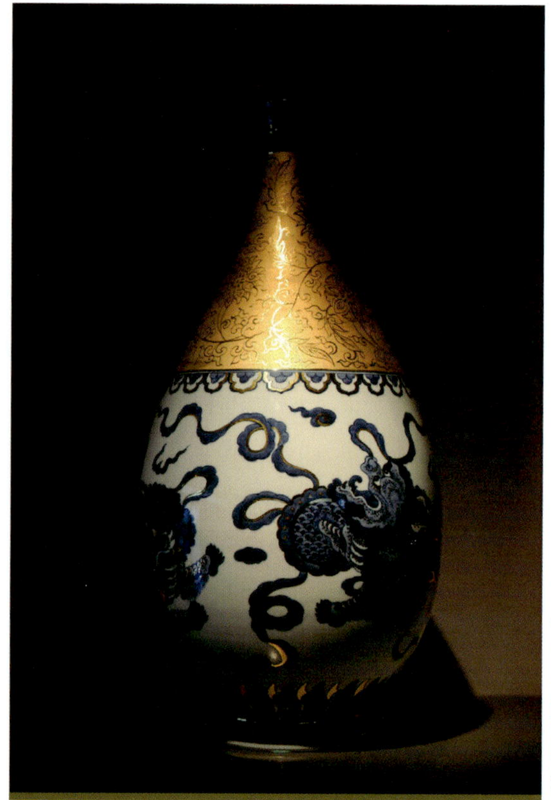

FIGURE 1.61 – Chinese Antique Porcelain Vase with Golden Paint. China.

part 7

CHANGING SOCIETAL PERCEPTIONS

Discrimination is an issue humans face around the world. The characteristics that help to define a person or group of people as something unique are the same factors that can lead to discrimination, hatred, and prejudice. Artists, whether working from personal experience or from a strong sense of right and wrong, use their works to challenge negative societal perceptions and promote positive change.

English-born, artist David N. Martin (1967–) is an educator and photographer. His work addresses social justice and gender identity through self-portraiture, visual systems, cataloging, data collection, and a wry sense of humor. Through his work, Martin says, "I seek to engage the viewer in a discourse that opens the possibility that visual relationships may not always be what they appear."

In *Straight Bed/Queer Bed I* (see Figure 1.62), David Martin asked a group of people to leave their beds exactly as they were in the morning when they woke. He was given permission to then photograph each one. Martin feels the bed is an elemental place, as well as a stage. Regardless of who one is, many things happen in one's bed—birth, death, love, love-making, fighting, arguing, crying, and much more. The artist says, "The bed is also a place that has been used to control and divide based on gender, race, and sexuality. The ultimate premise of this piece is that you cannot tell which beds belong to the straight people and which beds belong to queer people. They are ultimately a neutral visual and performative space."

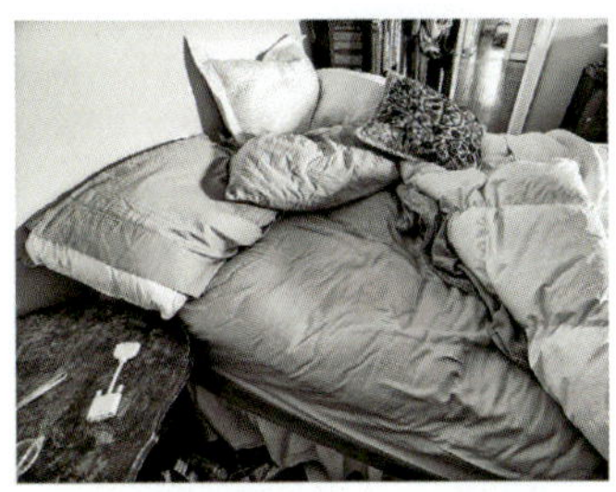
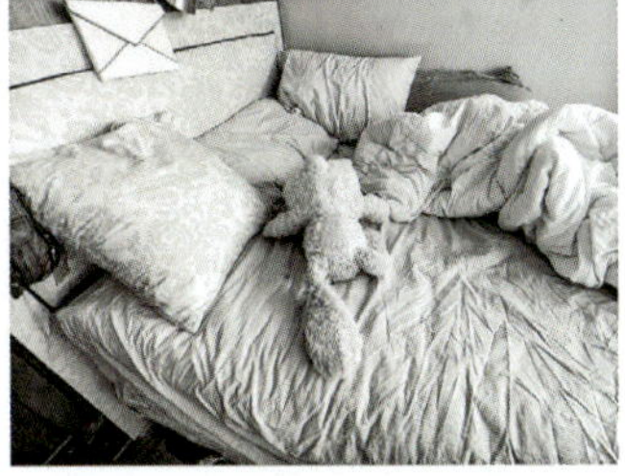
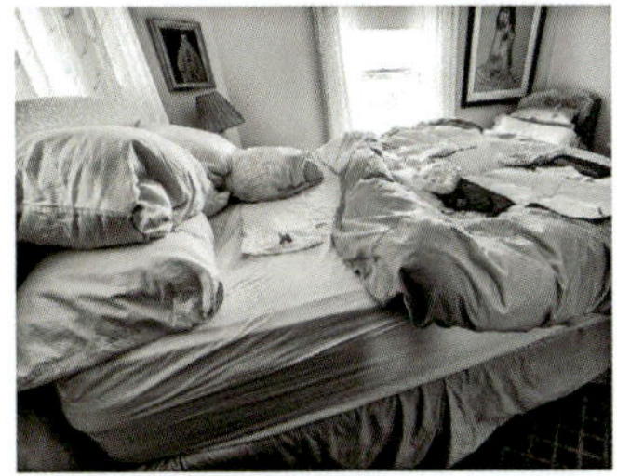
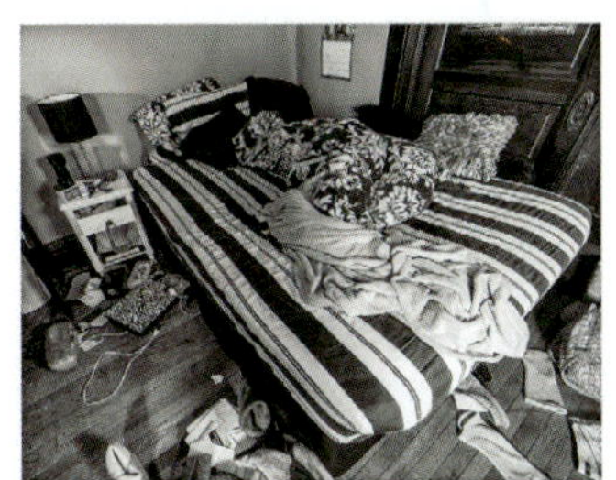
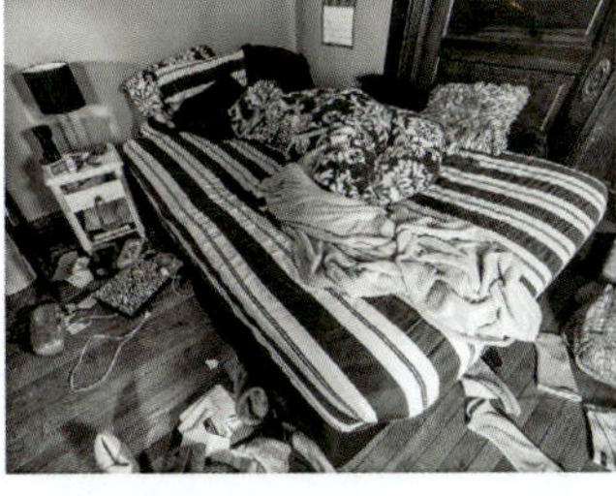
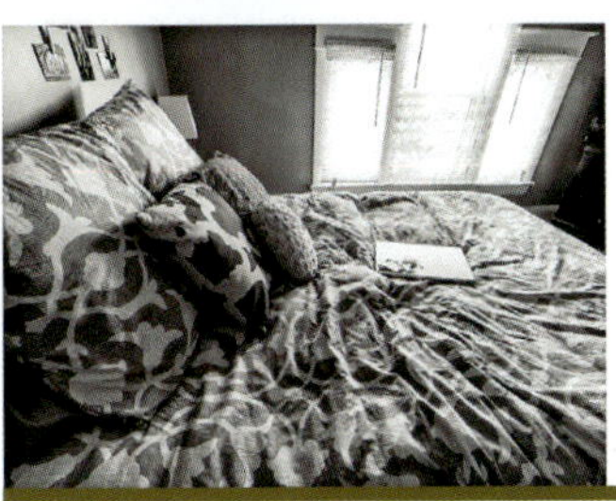
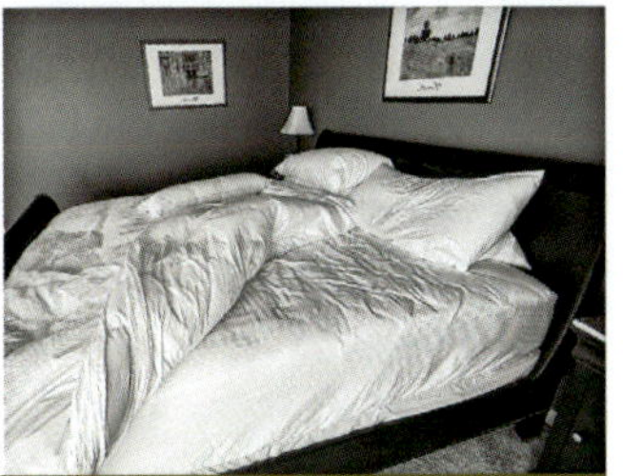

FIGURE 1.62 – Straight Bed/Queer Bed I, David Martin. 2012. 36 x 28 in. Digital photography.

Many of David Martin's series revolve around the idea of data collection and cataloging. If he is photographing a series of beds (see Figure 1.63), hands, fingers, or food, the images are often accompanied by data. The data he collects—age, gender, profession, and sexual orientation—will be consistent from each person and displayed within their photograph. Martin allows each individual to use their own terminology when answering the requested information. This allows the viewer to see how each individual identifies or categorizes themselves.

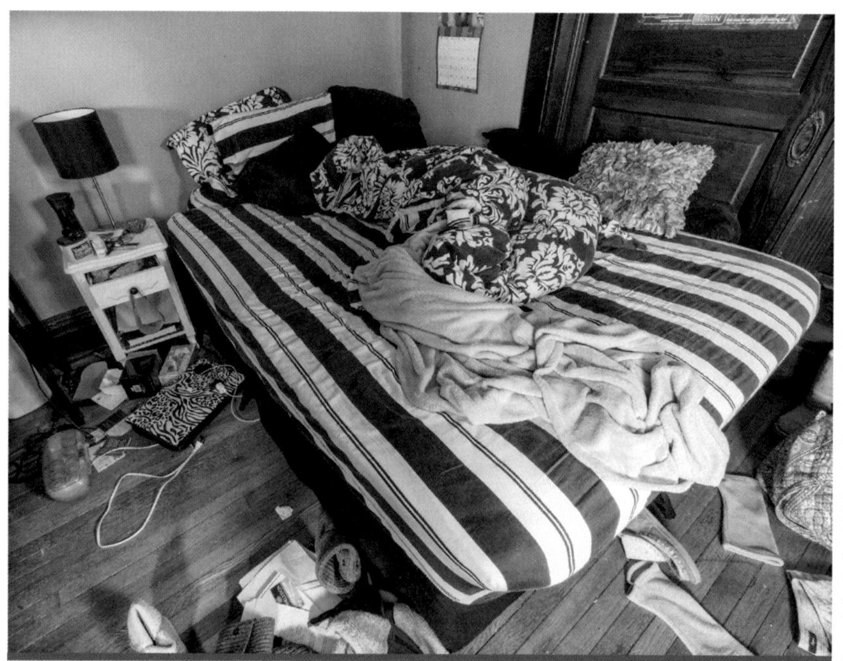

FIGURE 1.63 – Straight Bed/Queer Bed I (detail), David Martin. 2012. Digital photography.

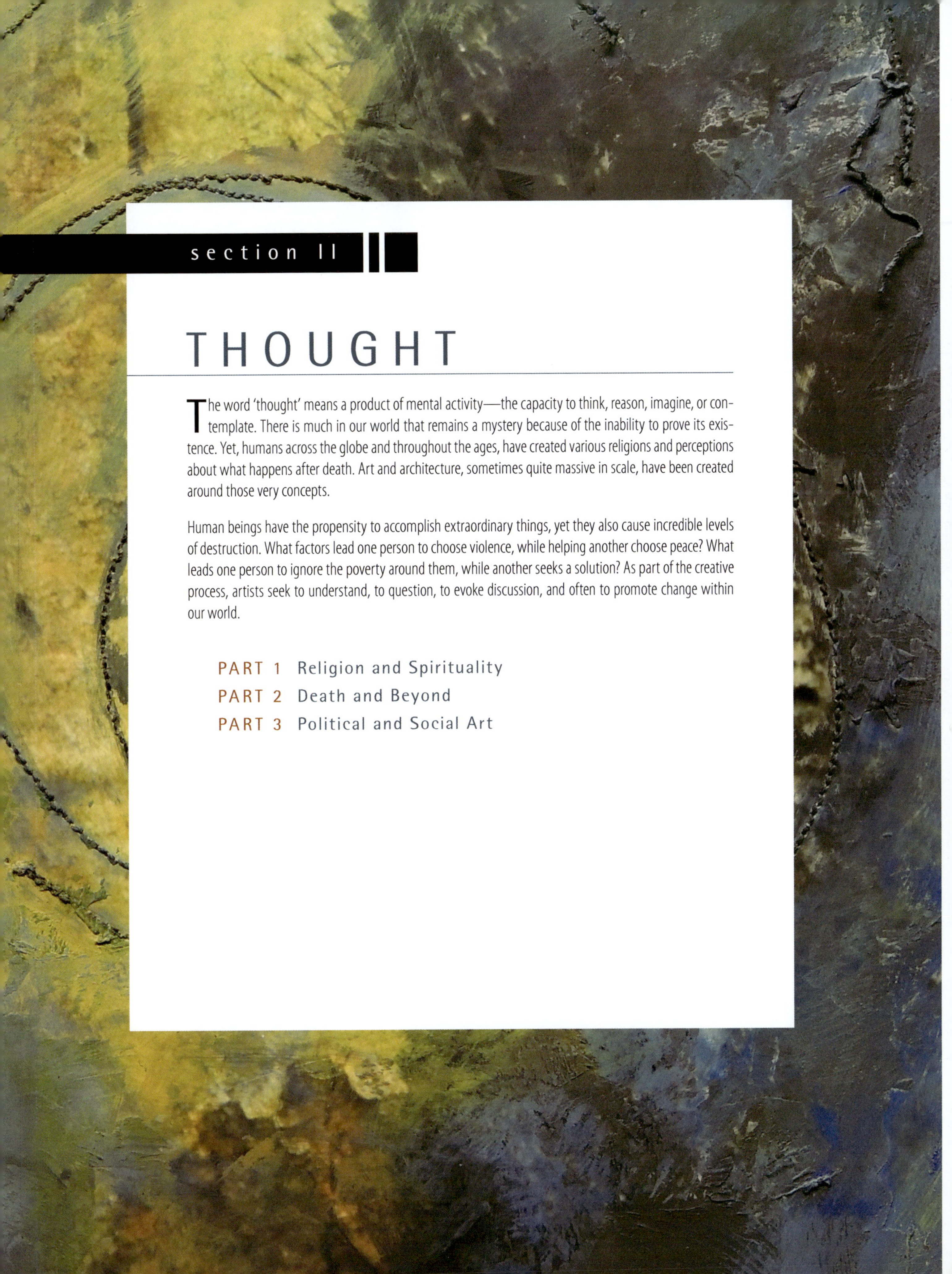

section II

THOUGHT

The word 'thought' means a product of mental activity—the capacity to think, reason, imagine, or contemplate. There is much in our world that remains a mystery because of the inability to prove its existence. Yet, humans across the globe and throughout the ages, have created various religions and perceptions about what happens after death. Art and architecture, sometimes quite massive in scale, have been created around those very concepts.

Human beings have the propensity to accomplish extraordinary things, yet they also cause incredible levels of destruction. What factors lead one person to choose violence, while helping another choose peace? What leads one person to ignore the poverty around them, while another seeks a solution? As part of the creative process, artists seek to understand, to question, to evoke discussion, and often to promote change within our world.

part 1

RELIGION AND SPIRITUALITY

The supernatural is something that lies beyond our senses. Devoid of tangible form, it is beyond our ability to understand or prove it. In almost every age and culture, people have attempted to create diagrams, symbols, and pictures that represent aspects of their beliefs. Images of spiritual beings created by artists, throughout the ages, have been used to assist people in religious ceremonies or rituals, and to provide a tool to deepen their connection to their faith.

REPRESENTATIONS

Examples of geometric representations of deities exist. In indigenous cultures, a circle often represents the masculine god, while a triangle usually represents the feminine goddess (see Figure 2.1). These shapes can take on different symbolism in Eastern and Western religions. For example, the circle in Hinduism represents both the Supreme Being, as well as the totality of the universe. In Christianity, the triangle represents the Trinity (Father, Son, and Holy Ghost), which is masculine in orientation.

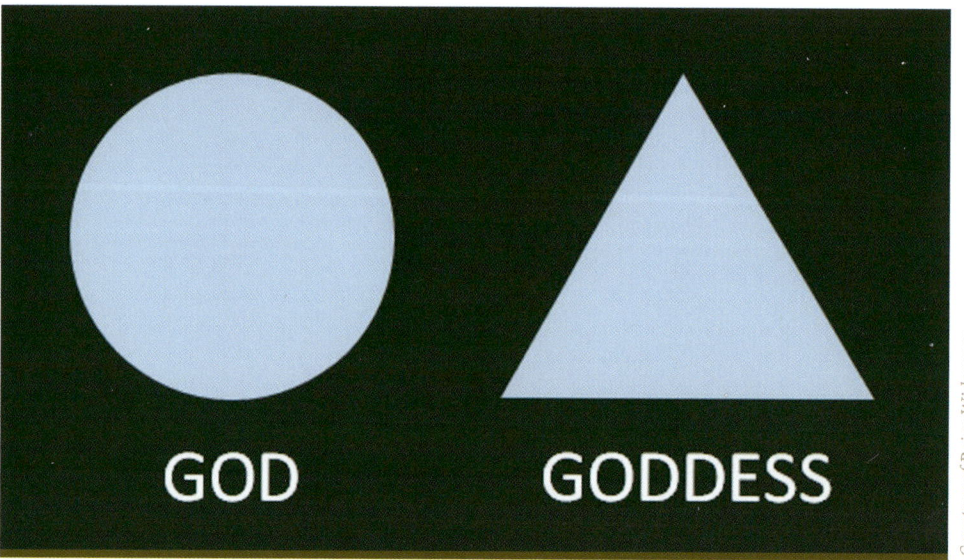

Courtesy of Paige Widemans

FIGURE 2.1 – God/Goddess Geometric Shapes.

GEOMETRIC - description of the simple shapes such as circles, squares, triangles or rectangles in a design.

Many indigenous people find a spiritual connection to the animal kingdom and the natural world that helps bridge the gap to the unknown. Animism is the belief in spiritual beings concerned with human life, who can impact it in helpful or harmful ways. A unifying factor common to animism practiced worldwide is the belief people communicate with these spiritual beings for survival-based issues, like securing food, curing illness, and providing safety.

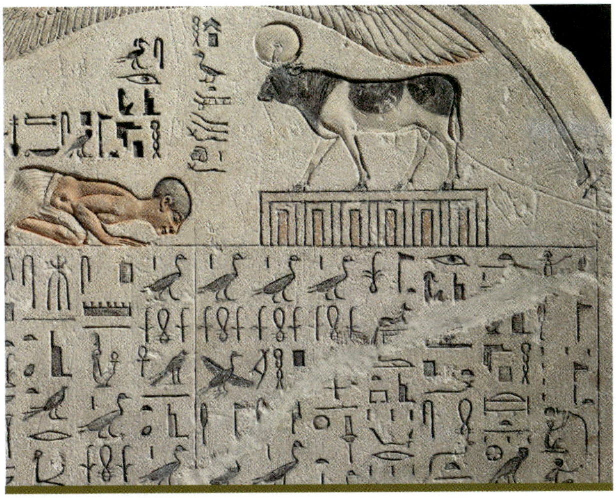

Painted limestone stele of god Apis, detail with the deceased in adoration before the Apis bull / De Agostini Picture Library / G. Dagli Orti / Bridgeman Images

FIGURE 2.2 – Painted Limestone Stele of God Apis (detail). Egypt. c. 1075 BC. Painted and carved limestone.

Animals and nature then become messengers and symbols of things greater than themselves, giving humans a tangible image to connect with, communicate with, or exert control over. Because of a perceived connection between human and animal behavior, animals have been and continue to be perceived as physical manifestations of deities in many cultures. In some, the living animal takes on the same role as an artistic representation of a deity. In ancient Egypt, the Apis bull (see Figure 2.2) was considered to be the physical receptacle for the essence (or Ba) of Ptah, god of wisdom. Ptah was believed to be the creator of the 'Opening of the Mouth' ceremony, typically practiced on the mummified bodies of pharaohs. Only one living bull served this role at any given time. Upon its death, the bull was mummified and then ceremoniously buried before another took its place. The Apis bull, like other animals, was viewed as sacred because of the people's perception of its link to a god. In Christianity, there are examples of using animals as metaphors for religious figures, such as Jesus depicted as a sacrificial lamb and the Holy Ghost (see Figure 2.3) as a dove.

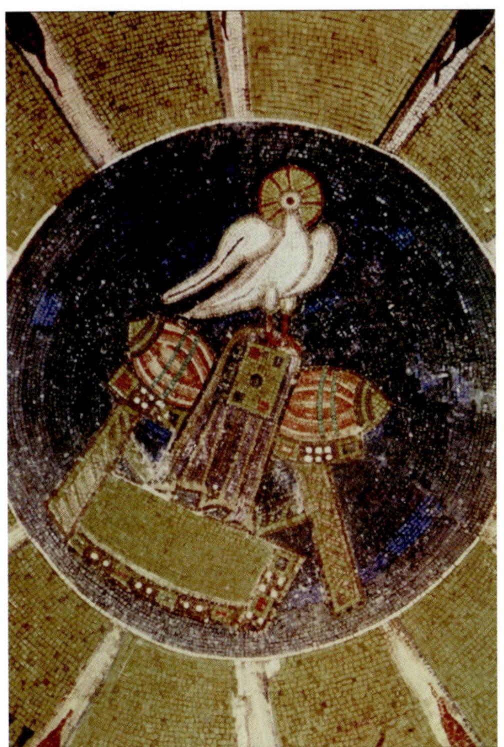

Courtesy of Corel

FIGURE 2.3 – Pentecost, The Holy Ghost. Greece. Mosaic.

Earth Mother has been considered the original deity in almost all areas of the globe throughout history. She controls life and death, and is often associated with fertility and agriculture. There are elements of nature that destroy, and those that generate growth—a kind of a rebirth of the landscape around us. So in many cultures, the earth itself is perceived as a feminine force, while its counterpart, the sky or universe, is perceived as masculine. A well-known example of the Earth Mother in ancient Greece was Gaia. Her descendants were the Greek gods who occupied Mount Olympus, and were responsible for various aspects of the natural world and human life—like the seasons, love, and warfare. Goddesses in many cultures are believed to have stemmed from this original Earth Mother, like the *Minoan Snake Goddess* discussed earlier. In some African sculptures, the extended belly of a male figure is meant as a visual way to show the female's role in fertility and reproduction. In a similar vein, the use of snakes in the Minoan Snake Goddess sculpture could symbolize the presence of male fertility.

RELIGIOUS RITUAL AND PRACTICES

Throughout the ages, humans found ways of making sense of the world around them, and the things they experienced. The unknown and mysteries of the world can, at times, create fear and uncertainty. A loud crack of thunder becomes the wrath of an unhappy god, whereas a torrential downpour becomes proof that our actions are pleasing to the gods. Perhaps deriving from a need to make sense of the world, and feel the ability to exert control over it, humans have created deities and rituals to assist in the process. We will take a closer look at a few examples to better understand their role in the lives of people who participate in these customs.

Having existed for over 30,000 years, shamanism is a practice of accessing alternate realms for spiritual guidance and healing. In many cultures, shamanism permeates all aspects of life, making their role important in influencing and protecting society. It also creates deep appreciation and respect for all life. Although there are cultural variations to their roles, historically the shaman is believed to help cure, perform miracles, communicate with and control spirits, effect divination, be clairvoyant, and even control the weather. Although mainly perceived to be a positive force, in some cultures, shamans can also possess the ability to cause suffering and destruction.

Shamans believe a magical dimension is present around us at all times and an *axis mundi* (or vertical pole) connects the earth to it. Through their intuition and the use of various tools, they tap into this dimension to communicate with the spirits or ancestors of their culture, and in some cases, they do this to gain control over them. Rhythmic sounds created through drumming and chanting and rhythmic movements created through free-form dancing assist shamans in entering into a trance-like state to communicate with their spirit helpers who appear to them in animal or human form.

Shamans follow different practices and traditions, which dictate the costumes and tools used in their rituals. There is no standard 'attire' among shamans worldwide. Some utilize elaborate costumes, while others practice ritual nudity. In any case, the essential aspect is that the shaman is not wearing ordinary, pedestrian clothing. Their specialized clothing is perceived to transform the shaman into a super human being before the people's eyes. Whether or not a costume is worn, other objects can be perceived as a part of the shaman's sacred wardrobe. A belt, cap (headdress) or mask can, therefore, be used to assist in contacting the spiritual realm. A headdress can be an important part of shamanic dress and can vary in overall design and materials in which they are made. In some cultures, shamans incorporate parts of animals or birds into their headdress. The shaman (see Figure 2.4) is wearing a headdress in the shape of an eagle's head. To some shamans, animals serve as totems and spirit guides, assisting them in their various duties. Referred to as power animals, they represent a shaman's personal strength and qualities of character.

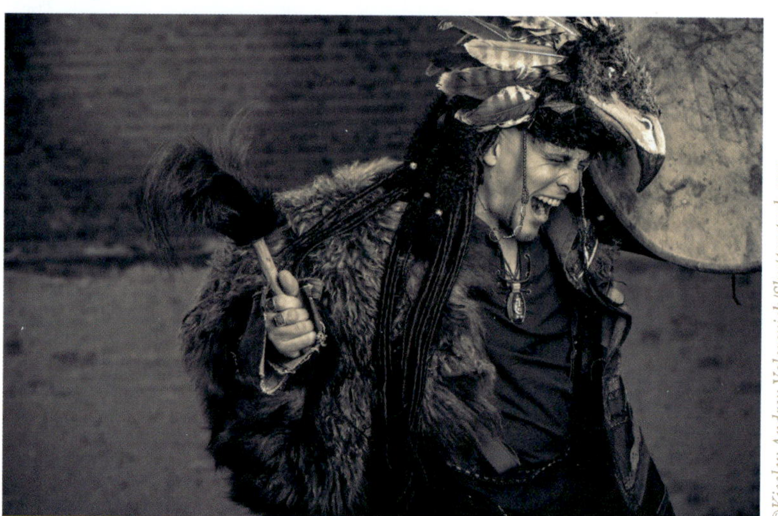

FIGURE 2.4 – Portrait of a Shaman Dancing with a Drum Outdoor. Native American. 25 x 14 in. Photography.

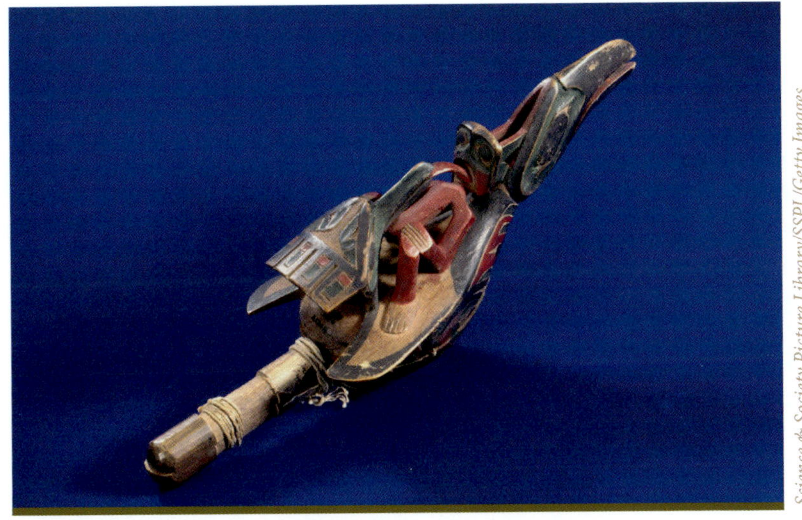

Science & Society Picture Library/SSPL/Getty Images

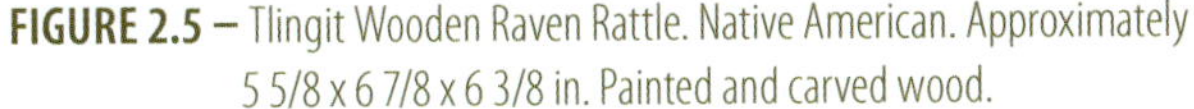

FIGURE 2.5 – Tlingit Wooden Raven Rattle. Native American. Approximately 5 5/8 x 6 7/8 x 6 3/8 in. Painted and carved wood.

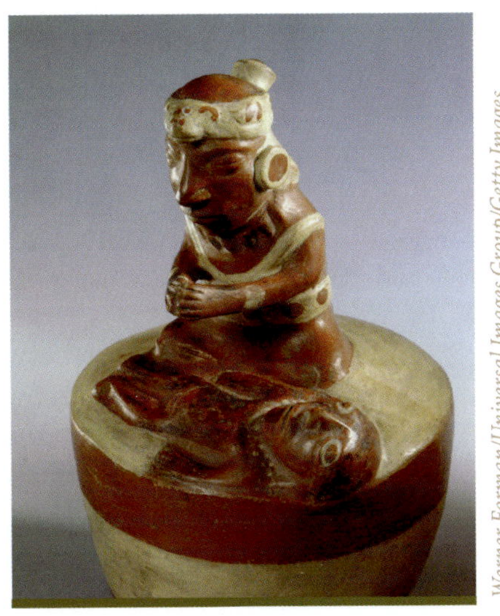

Werner Forman/Universal Images Group/Getty Images

FIGURE 2.6 – Moche Shaman Pot. Peru. c. 1–800. 78 x 109 x 6 cm. Ceramic.

Like a headdress, masks can take on animal or human forms, sometimes representing ancestors. When these are worn by a shaman, the animal or ancestor is considered to be present during a ritual to aid in its purpose. Masks are kept in special locations or containers when not in use, because they are believed to contain a spirit or special powers. They can be created out of wood, animal skins, feathers or cloth and can be painted or adorned with feathers, horns, fur, and more.

Other tools of a shaman include bells, rattles, and drums. These play a significant role in their rituals and practices. Ceremonial rattles come in many forms, depending on the cultural or spiritual influences of the shaman and his/her needs. They can be made from dry gourds, turtle shells or carved wood, and filled with pebbles. Rattles are used to accompany songs in sacred ceremonies, and to invoke spirits. The *Tlingit Wooden Raven Rattle* (see Figure 2.5) is used in their healing rituals. The rattle is carved in the shape of a raven, with the shaman lying on its back. The raven is perceived as the creator of the world, populating it with people and animals. The shaman's mouth is open and tongue extended towards the mouth of a frog, which represents good luck and fortune to the Tlingit people.

Another important tool used by shamans is a drum. The beat of a drum serves multiple purposes. The repetitious sound created by the beating of a drum helps to focus the mind of the shaman in preparation for his/her journey. As the shaman enters into an altered state, his soul is free to leave its human vessel to travel. The beat of the drum then carries the soul of the shaman to the spiritual realm. It can also be used to summon the spirits to the earthly realm.

Songs are believed to imbue the shaman's voice with power, and for that reason, used to call upon the spirits for assistance in the healing process. While songs can be important, the shaman also uses his hands as a tool. Laying on of hands can be through a rubbing, brushing, or a push-pull motion, which allows a shaman to heal or repair injury to a person's body. In this process, ritual herbs and ointments can be used. The *Moche Shaman Pot* (see Figure 2.6) from Peru shows shamans played a role in the Moche society. While one cannot completely be sure of the function of such a vessel, it clearly depicts a shaman leaning over a person and preparing to use his hands in the act of a healing.

Human sacrifice was practiced by many pre-Columbian cultures, such as the Maya. Often in cultures that practice sacrifice, there exists the belief that their gods gave up their flesh and blood to create the universe in which the people live. To show respect for this perceived sacrifice of their deities, the people give back in kind. Extreme forms of sacrifice involve cutting out the hearts of captured warriors or sacrificial victims as an offering. Through this ritual, they hope for the continuation of mankind and the universe. These cultures also performed self-sacrifice through the ritualistic practice of bloodletting. The rulers or priests shed their own blood as a way to communicate with their deities, whether assisting their safe travel to the spiritual world or calling the deities to them on earth. In the *Bloodletting Ritual of Lady Xoc* (see Figure 2.7), the Queen is seen piercing her tongue and threading a thorny, braided rope through it during a bloodletting ritual. The blood travels down the rope into a bowl filled with fibers resting at her feet. The fibers are then set on fire and its smoke rises towards the heavens. As the smoke coiled upwards, it could visually be interpreted as a serpent escorting them or delivering their message to the spiritual realm. Rituals like this were performed at pivotal times to assist a ruler in preparation for battle, or in his accession to the throne.

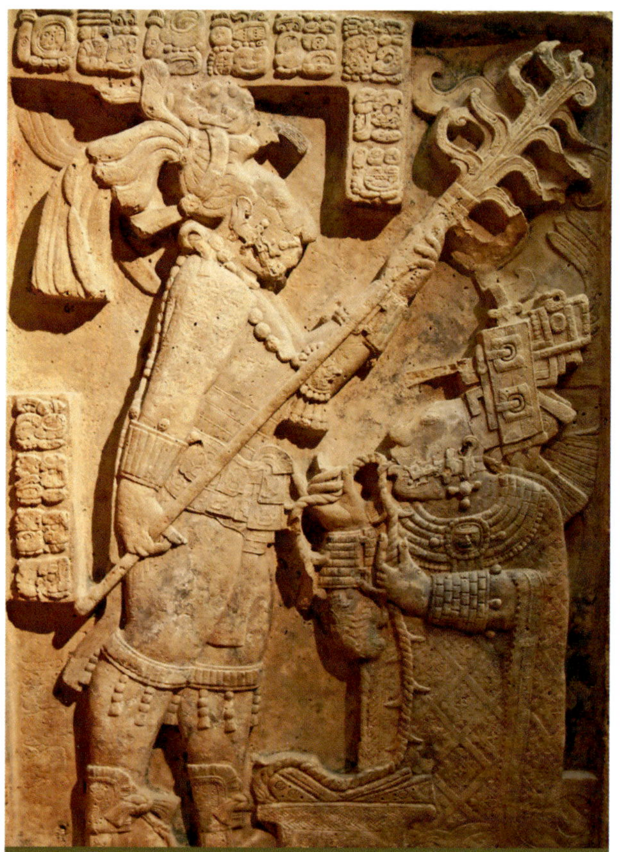

FIGURE 2.7 – Bloodletting Ritual of Lady Xoc. Maya. c. 725. Carved limestone.

In ancient Egyptian culture, mummification was a common practice, especially among royalty. Their belief in the afterlife required the preservation of the human body. This intricate process included cleansing the body, removing its organs, wrapping it with linens, and burying it with the luxuries of their earthly life. Upon successfully entering the afterlife, an individual would live in eternity as they did on earth. Early Egyptians frequently saw jackals scavenging for food in graveyards. Perhaps because of this, and their concern for protecting their dead, more elaborate tombs and burial rituals were created. It seems a natural leap for Egyptians to have perceived the god of mummification as a jackal-headed man, known as Anubis. Anubis had three main roles associated with death and the afterlife. His first role was to oversee the embalming process of the body. Preserving the body through mummification required great care, so that it could be resurrected for the afterlife. In *Anubis Concluding Mummification of Dead Man* (see Figure 2.8), this message is communicated clearly. His second role was to oversee the 'Opening of the Mouth' ceremony, which was required to re-animate the deceased's soul so that it could eat, drink, breathe, and enjoy aspects of the previous life, throughout the afterlife. This ceremony was also performed on animals, like the Apis Bull. But most importantly, Anubis' third and most essential role is in the second part of their judgment day, where he watches over the Scale of Truth in order to protect the dead from deception and eternal death. Egyptians believe that by worshipping him, Anubis will protect the deceased from the jackals that roam the gravesites, and provide a safe journey for them into the afterlife.

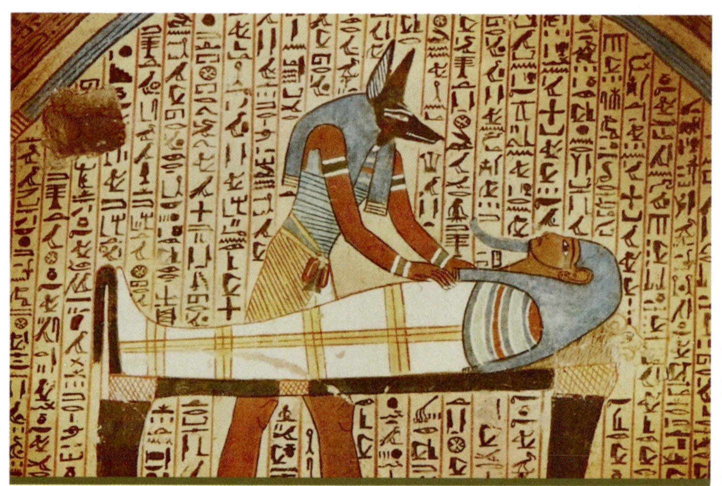

FIGURE 2.8 – Anubis Concluding Mummification of Dead Man. Egypt. Ramessid Period. Mural.

MANDALA - often a circular design which includes other geometric elements and other shapes representing deities and the cosmos in Hindu and Buddhist traditions.

Tibetan Buddhist monks have an ancient artistic form known as the *mandala* (or sand painting). Its circular shape, visually brings together that which is visible and hidden, and that which is sacred and secular. A mandala represents the following:

- birth and death
- a two-dimensional blueprint of the world in a state of balance and harmony
- a bird's eye view of Buddha's multi-level celestial realm, filled with enlightened beings
- re-consecrating of the earth and its inhabitants
- dispelling negative energy and replacing it with peace

Tibetan monks are trained for years to learn ancient symbols, representations of their deities, and geometric shapes used to create these mandalas. The mandala is believed to consist of three levels of meaning—the world in divine form, a map of transformation from an ordinary state to one of enlightenment, and balance between mind and body. Purification and healing occurs on these levels through the creation of a mandala.

OUTLINE - a line that defines the outer boundaries of an object or figure.

Tibetan monks consecrate the area where the *mandala* is to be created through a ceremony involving chants, mantras, and music. Afterwards, a monk carefully draws the detailed outline of the mandala to be created on a board using white chalk. The monks then begin laying down the different colors of sand, using a tool called a chak-pur (see Figure 2.9). This tool consists of two parts—a funnel-like piece where the sand is placed and a rod to rasp against its ridged surface. The speed at which they move the rod over the funnel, controls the amount of sand being dispensed. This tecÚique allows for large areas of a single color of sand to be laid down more efficiently, and makes fine detailing and outlining of small shapes possible (see Figure 2.10). A completed mandala is approximately four feet in diameter and can take several days to complete. Almost immediately upon its completion, the monks deconstruct it. Why destroy something that took so long to create and contains sacred symbols and representations of their deities? The deconstruction represents their belief in the impermanence of life. It is a reminder that everything has a beginning, middle, and end.

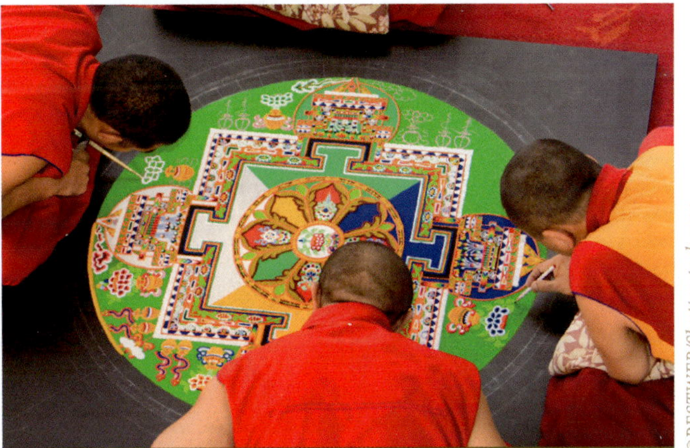

FIGURE 2.9 – Tibetan Mandala (monks creating sand mandala).

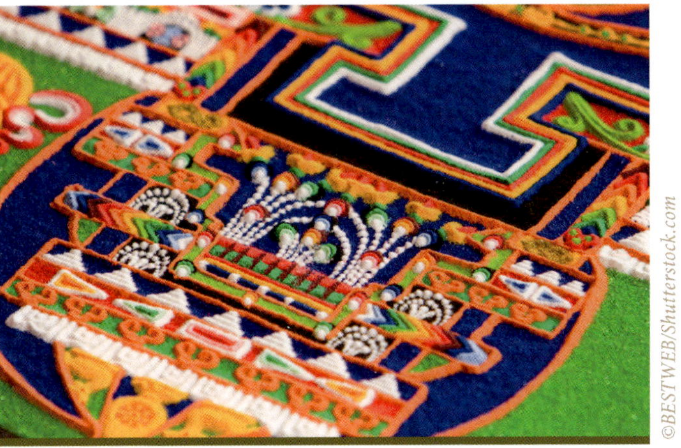

FIGURE 2.10 – Tibetan Mandala (detail).

Prior to the dismantling of a mandala, the monks offer prayers of apology for any mistakes made during its creation, as well as releasing any claim to rewards gained through making it. Then, a monk begins to cut the power of the mandala (see Figure 2.11) by pushing the end of a bell through the sand from the outer edge into the center from its four cardinal points. Eventually, all the sand is swept into the center and put into an urn. The act of sweeping the sand into a single pile and placing it into a vessel fulfills the function of healing. The monks then carry the sand-filled urn to a body of water. All water on the planet is believed to be interconnected. Therefore, by pouring the sand into one water source, the blessing on the mandala will spread worldwide. This process also communicates the idea of a mandala not only benefiting human beings, but the environment as well.

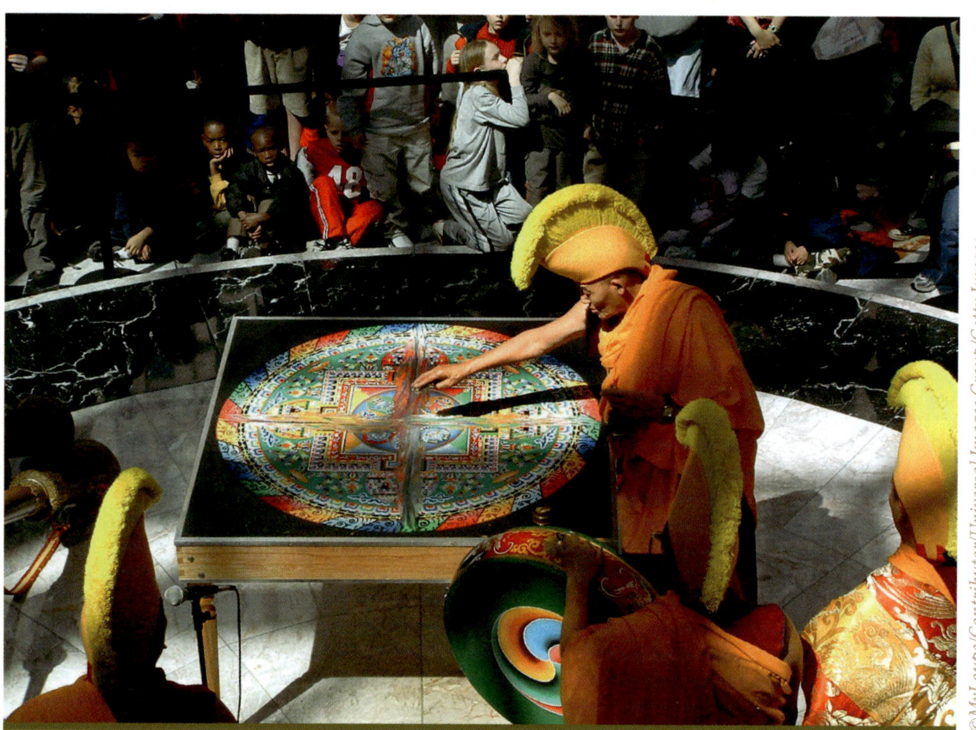

FIGURE 2.11 – Buddhist Ceremony—Dismantling of Sand Mandala.

RELIGIOUS IMAGERY AND ARCHITECTURE

Religion is an organized collection of beliefs, cultural systems, and worldviews that provide an understanding of the intangible. In this section, we will take a closer look at Eastern philosophies and Western religions. In addition to understanding the core concepts of each, we will look at the artwork and architecture associated with them and what they communicate.

THE EASTERN WORLD

In the Eastern world, Hinduism and Buddhism are two philosophies that share common core concepts from which they developed uniquely. In these philosophies, there is a shared belief in reincarnation. The theory of reincarnation is based on the idea that upon one's death, a part of the living being survives and is reborn into a new body. This consists of multiple manifestations, as it is an endless cycle of birth, life, death, and rebirth. In both, one's journey in life is about breaking free of this endless earth-bound cycle. Each philosophy believes in a different path to achieve this. Once the cycle is broken, Hindus are able to join Brahman and Buddhists, the universal life force.

Hinduism is a collection of beliefs and traditions. One aspect of Hindu thought is a symbolic way of understanding our cosmos through geometric forms. The circle is used visually in art and architecture to represent the totality of the universe. The square is used to represent the divine force made physical on earth. And the vertical pole (axis mundi) is used to represent the link between heaven and earth. Another branch of Hindu thought includes the belief in reincarnation, ethics and right action. It is a way of life, known as Dharma, which governs all actions. By following a path of righteousness, followers of Hinduism strive to break free of the endless cycle of reincarnation.

In Hinduism, there are many gods and goddesses who are responsible for all life forms. Even within this context, there is something greater, referred to as a 'supreme universal force.' This force is known as Brahman.

Brahman is never pictured in human form, but is believed to exist in all aspects of the cosmos, including nature, humans, and the various deities. Like we will see in Christianity, Hinduism has a Trinity consisting of the gods Brahma, VisÚu and Shiva. Each of these gods represents different aspects of the Brahman – as the creator, the protector, and the destroyer of the universe and all that resides in it. There are four central principles in Hinduism: *Dharma* (ethics and duties), *Samsara* (rebirth), *Karma* (right action), and *Moksha* (liberation from the cycles of Samsara).

One of the physical manifestations of Brahman is VisÚu, who is responsible for protecting the world and restoring moral order or *Dharma*. Multiple arms on a Hindu deity symbolize the unlimited powers of a god. VisÚu (see Figure 2.12) is visually depicted with four arms, each holding a symbol of his divinity—a conch, discus, lotus, and mace (club). The sound of the conch represents the primordial creative voice (or breath) of VisÚu. Its spiral design denotes eternity. The discus, also known as a *chakra*, represents the mind and a waterwheel, which both empties and fills its vessel in a continuous motion. The lotus symbolizes creation and fertility. It was believed that when VisÚu contemplated creating mankind, a lotus sprang from his naval. His image is sometimes depicted with a lotus on his torso to reference that moment. The lotus held in VisÚu's hand represents his companion, Lakshmi—the goddess of prosperity. Similar to the Minoan Snake Goddess holding snakes in her hands, the lotus becomes a visual representation of feminine force on a male image. This feminine force helps activate VisÚu's creative power. The mace symbolizes mental and physical strength, and the power of time. As time is unconquerable, the mace becomes a powerful weapon that can conquer or destroy all who oppose it. This image of VisÚu depicts his body straight as a rod referencing the axis mundi, where he becomes the pillar that joins the earth to the heavens, visually providing comfort to his followers.

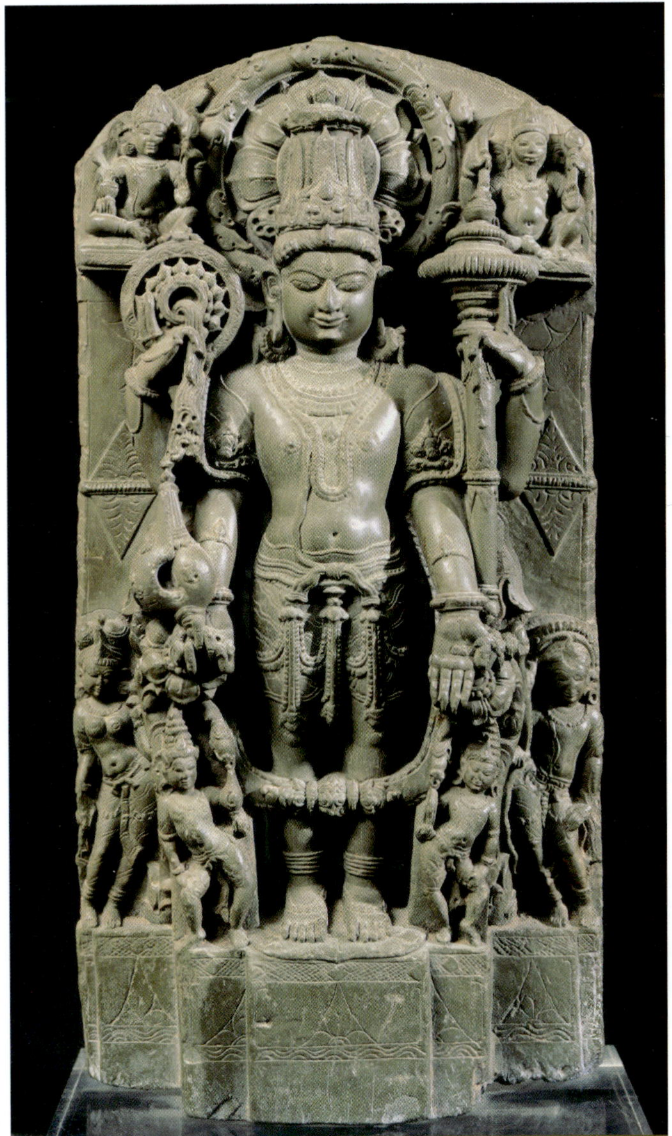

FIGURE 2.12 – VisÚu. Northern India. 14th century. Stone.

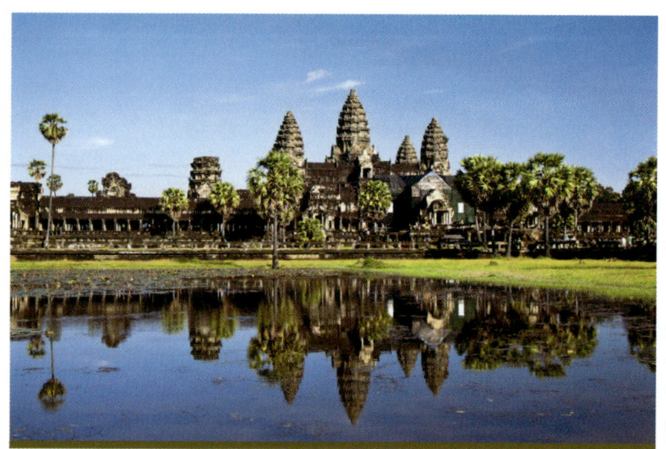

FIGURE 2.13 – Angkor Wat Seen Across the Lake. Cambodia. c. 1113–1150. 500 acres complex.

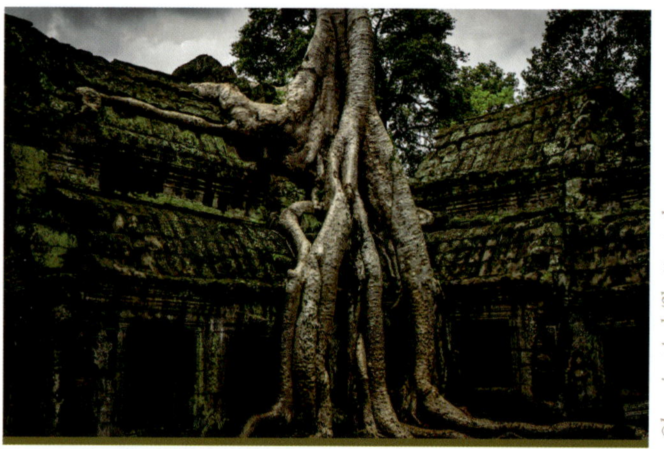

FIGURE 2.14 – Trees Growing Out the Ruin of Ta Prohm (Angkor Wat). Cambodia. c. 1113–1150.

The architecture associated with Hinduism is a temple. Each temple was built to honor one of their deities, and was carved with elaborate imagery communicating aspects of the deity's life, and aspects of Hindu beliefs. Followers will visit a temple to leave offerings to the deity and to reflect upon their spiritual path, making temples a place of pilgrimage. Priests tend to the temples and the offerings people leave behind.

Over a span of 400 years, the Khmer civilization constructed Angkor Wat, a complex of stone temples, in honor of the Hindu god, VisÚu. Like many man-made temples and structures around the world, Angkor Wat appears to align with star constellations in the sky. While the reason behind such alignments is often unknown, one speculation is that man is trying to mirror the heavens on earth. The spectacular construction of Angkor Wat (see Figure 2.13) became a significant place of pilgrimage for those throughout southeastern Asia.

In Arusha National Park in northern Tanzania, there is a mountain range called Mt. Meru, which to Hindus and Buddhists also represents the center of the cosmos. The overall structure of Angkor Wat represents the Hindu cosmology. The largest temple represents the mythical Mt. Meru. Multiple intersecting rectangular walls are symbolic of mountain ranges, while the moats are symbolic of the cosmic ocean. A little over 200 years after its construction, Angkor Wat was conquered by the Thai people, an indigenous group from Thailand, and abandoned. Nature began to overtake its structures and it remained lost for centuries, until rediscovered in 1860 by Henri Mouhot, a French naturalist. (see Figure 2.14).

Buddhism is a non-theistic philosophy, based on the teachings of a Sakya prince from today's Nepal, named Siddhartha Gautama, who lived around 563 BC. He was overwhelmed by the idea of people suffering and experiencing illness. So he left the comforts of his position as a prince in search of understanding as to why humans must experience such things. Siddhartha became known as Buddha—the awakened one—after taking a profound journey that led to a realization of the nature of life, death, and existence. Rather than teaching people what he came to realize, Buddha taught people how to come into enlightenment through their own path. Through this, Buddhism is seen as a practice rather than a religion. At the foundation of Buddhism lies the Four Noble Truths: *Dukkha* (truth of suffering), *Samudaya* (truth of the cause of suffering), *Nirhodha* (truth of the end of suffering), and *Magga* (truth of the path that frees us from suffering). Buddhism, like Hinduism, holds that humans are perpetually reincarnated. The lives they are born into in the present are based on the deeds of their past lives. By following the teachings of Buddha, one can overcome desire and break free of the cycle of reincarnation to transform and become part of that universal consciousness or energy.

In early Buddhist art, there is a clear absence of Buddha in human form. Artists conveyed his presence through footprints, an empty throne, or other imagery as a way to communicate his mortality. In the example of an empty throne, its image represents the Buddha's belief in impermanence—as does the destruction of the sand mandala. As seen throughout history, man's need for human connection to their teachers or gods takes hold of, and supersedes traditional practices. Eventually depictions of Buddha in human form become part of reality. In many faiths, images at some point no longer simply visualize their god or teacher, but are believed to possess its presence. So at various points in Buddhism, images like *Resurrection of the Buddha* (see Figure 2.15) were thought to be a physical incarnation of Buddha and used to invoke his blessing, protection, and more.

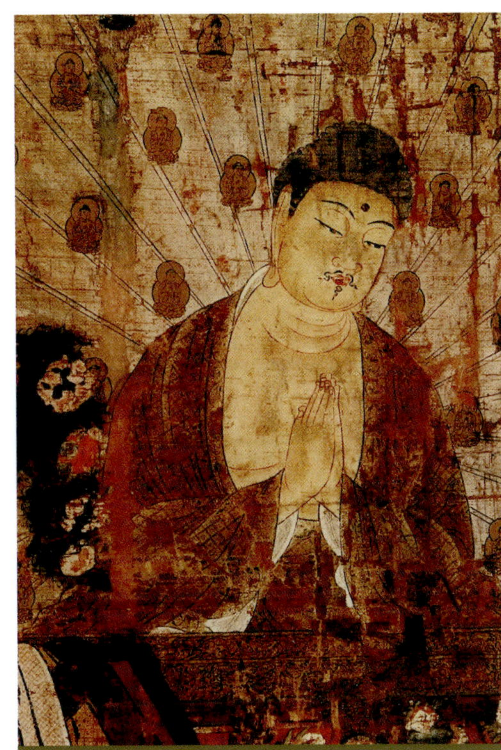

Courtesy of Corel

FIGURE 2.15 – Resurrection of the Buddha. India. Painting.

Buddhism is practiced in many cultures, each having a unique way of representing Buddha in physical form. However, they all share some common characteristics. Taking a closer look at the *Resurrection of the Buddha*, the visual similarities include the topknot of hair and a circle between the eyebrows (both indicators of wisdom), extended earlobes (an indicator of his previous status as a prince), and eyes half-closed in a serene state (an indicator of the practice of meditation). Buddha is commonly depicted seated in a lotus position (legs crossed) on a throne. Cultural differences in depictions of Buddha can be seen in the position of his hands, in his physical stature, and in his clothing.

The architectural structure associated with Buddhism is a stupa. A stupa was first created as a mound tomb, symbolizing the Buddha's presence. Eventually, the stupa transformed into a monument containing ashes or relics of the Buddha. Buddhists visit stupas, walking around them in a clockwise direction, to meditate and reflect upon the special meaning of the carvings created on its surface. Many of the carvings depict various scenes from Buddha's life. So, like a Hindu temple, the stupa becomes a place of pilgrimage. In the past, wealthy patrons determined the imagery that was depicted on some stupas. By making donations, they were able to choose the particular aspect of Buddha's life or teachings most significant to them to have it carved onto the structure. This allowed them to share with others what they felt was important.

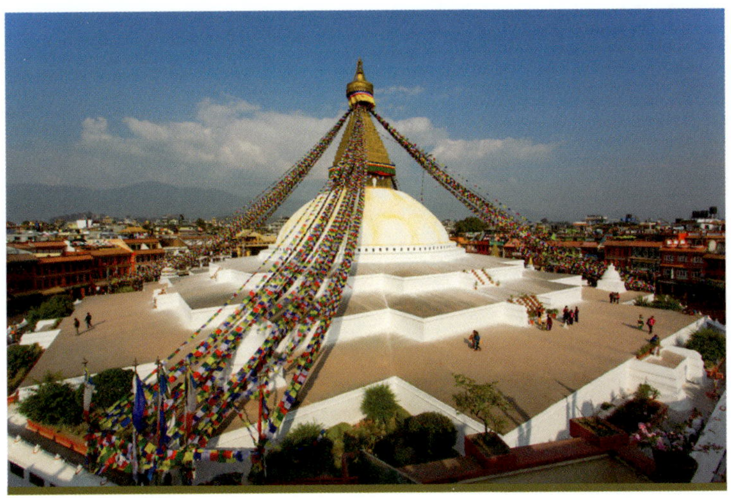

©danm12/Shutterstock.com

FIGURE 2.16 – Buddhist Boudhanath Stupa (overview). Kathmandu, Nepal. c. 483 BC. 118 ft. high.

PLINTH - a base or stone slab on which an object or structure is placed.

Around the fourteenth century CE, the *Buddhist Boudhanath Stupa* (see Figure 2.16) was built in Nepal. It is considered one of the holiest Buddhist structures built outside of Tibet. Like the sand mandala discussed earlier, the overall design of the stupa represents the Buddhist idea of the cosmos. From a bird's eye view, the layout resembles an intricate mandala with thirteen rings radiating out around it. These rings represent the path to enlightenment. Other architectural components of a stupa bringing the cosmos to life include: nine levels to the structure symbolize the mythical Mt. Meru, three platforms creating its base symbolize the earth, and two circular plinths supporting the domed structure symbolize water. A square tower bearing the eyes of Buddha (see Figure 2.17) on all four sides captures our attention. On top of the tower, a 13-level pyramid represents the path to enlightenment in three-dimensional form. This triangular form also symbolizes the element of fire, while the canopy at the top of the tower symbolizes air. Prayer flags secured to the top of the stupa carry mantras and prayers to the heavens on behalf of the people. Over the centuries, this continues to be an important place of pilgrimage for Buddhists.

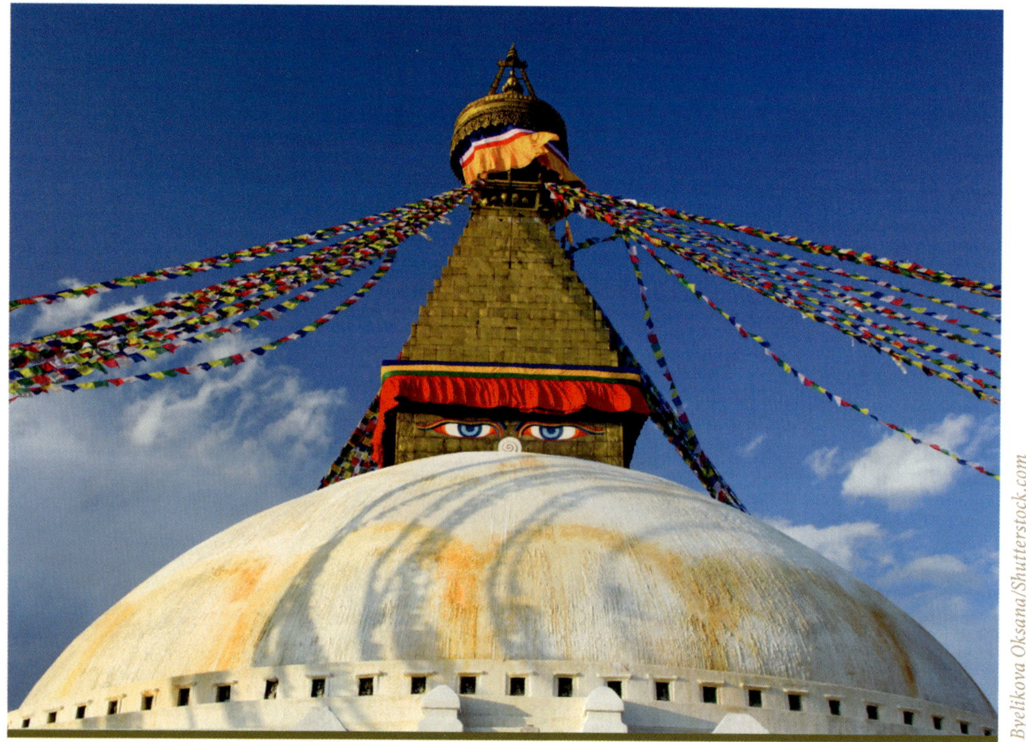

Byelikova Oksana/Shutterstock.com

FIGURE 2.17 – Buddhist Boudhanath Stupa (detail). Kathmandu, Nepal. c. 483 BC.

THE WESTERN WORLD

The followers of Western Abrahamic religions are known as 'People of the Book'. Three such religions that share common concepts are Judaism, Christianity, and Islam. Being the oldest of the three, Judaism was the foundation upon which Christianity and Islam were built. God, humanity, and the universe are all shared ideas of these religions. Each has a belief in a powerful Supreme Being, although sometimes known by different names. Each has a religious book containing the word of God and a group of prophets that spread that word. While believing in similar prophets, each differs in whom they recognize as the central prophet (Moses, Jesus, and Muhammed). Each has a practice of prayer, a belief in judgment day and in life after death in some form. The architecture associated with these religions is primarily used for congregational purposes, and can be varied in overall design.

Judaism has roots as early as the eighth century BC. At the core of Jewish beliefs is that while man is created in the image of the Supreme Being, he has free will to make choices throughout life. Those choices, whether good or bad, will have consequences of which he is responsible for in the end. The Torah is Judaism's sacred text containing stories and commandments, teaching about life and death, and guiding one throughout life. Man's individual path to salvation is not through his own salvation, but that of all Jewish people.

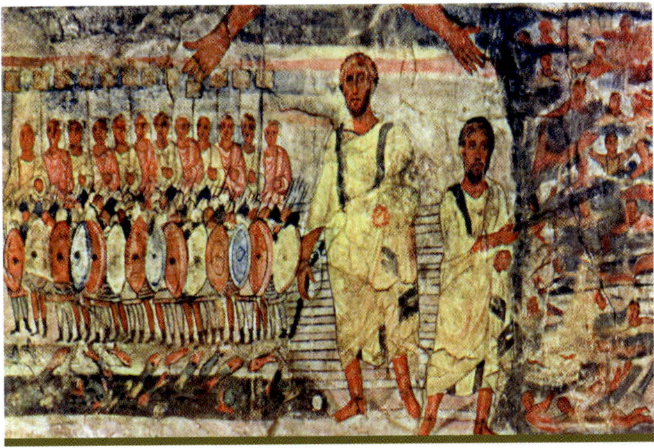

Syria: Moses and the Exodus. The Jews cross the Red Sea pursued by the forces of Pharaoh. Fresco from Dura Europos synagogue, c.250 CE / Pictures from History / Bridgeman Images

FIGURE 2.18 – Syria: Moses and the Exodus; The Jews cross the Red Sea pursued by the forces of Pharaoh. Dura Europos Synagogue, Egypt. c. 245. Mural.

In this religion God is never depicted in human form because the Hebrew Bible forbids praying to idols. On a rare occasion, God's presence will be referenced artistically as a hand emerging from the sky (see Figure 2.18). Little to no representational sculptures exist, because Jewish law forbids praying to images or idols.

CATACOMB - a multi-level subterranean cemetery with recessed areas in the walls for graves.

Historically based on their faith, Jews found themselves facing restrictions controlling various aspects of their life in relation to education and profession. They also faced persecution for those differences. During times of persecution, religious art and architecture was the target of destruction. As a result of such actions, very little ancient Jewish art has survived. A few remnants of early Jewish art are found in catacombs, and are often fragments of larger mosaics and murals that visually tell the stories from their sacred text.

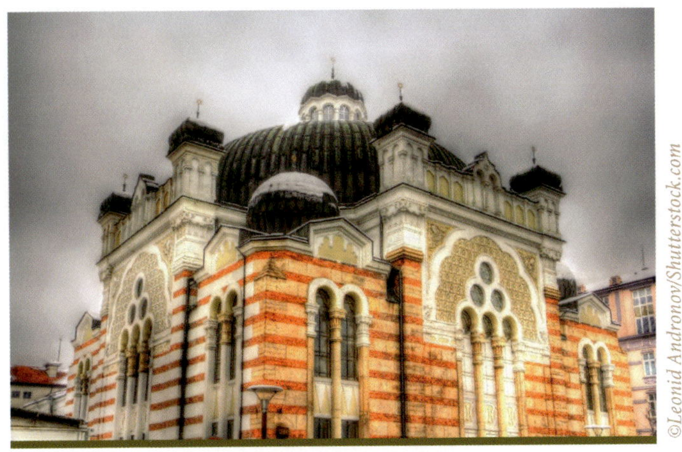

©Leonid Andronov/Shutterstock.com

FIGURE 2.19 – Sofia Synagogue, architect Friedrich Grunager. Bulgaria. 1909. 102 ft. high.

The architectural structure associated with Judaism is a synagogue, a place of congregational worship and education. These buildings range in their construction from simple to ornate. An extraordinary example is the *Sophia Synagogue* (see Figure 2.19) in Bulgaria. Built on the site where another synagogue once stood, it was completed in 1909 and became a symbol of Bulgarian Judaism almost immediately. Over time it was eventually recognized as the second largest Sephardic synagogue in Europe. The Sophia synagogue has a central dome structure, where the congregation gathers underneath for worship. It also has a narthex (or entryway) leading into the congregational space, where people gather prior to, and after a service. The octagonal-shaped prayer hall has niches positioned at the four corners of its construction. There is a separate prayer room for women above these niches. The floor of the interior is covered with Venetian mosaics, while the walls are ornately decorated with rich colors and designs. The outside of the building is decorated with stone carvings, and a variety of different materials are used to create its unique look. During its history, the Sofia synagogue has only been closed for a year spanning 1943–1944 due to the deportation of the Jews from Sofia to the countryside. In 1944, the Synagogue was bombed several times, destroying various parts of its structure. Recently, an extensive fund-raising campaign has led to its restoration. Under the supervision of a Jewish architect, Bulgarian craftsmen began restorative work using the original plans.

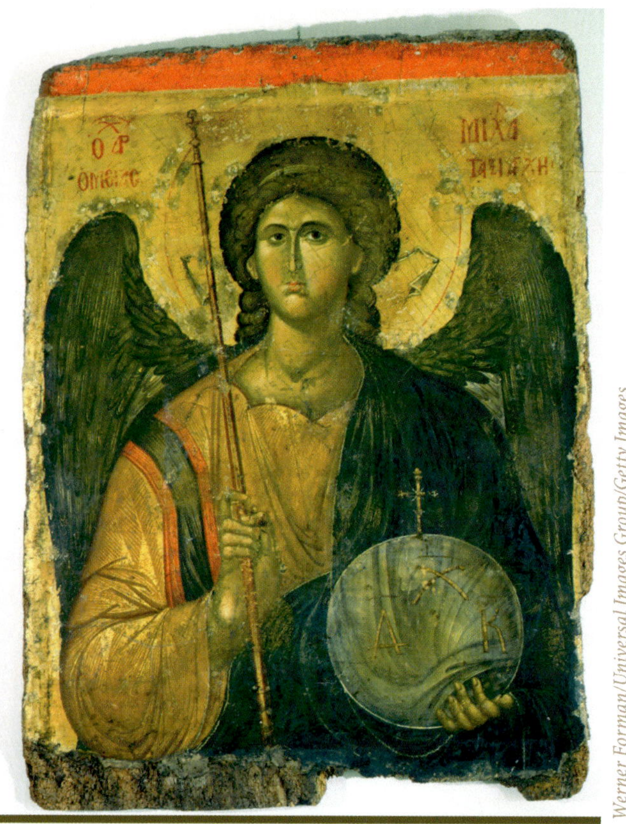

FIGURE 2.20 – Archangel St. Michael. Byzantine, Greece. 14th century. Mural.

Starting as a small movement within Judaism, Christianity began to shape into its own unique religion during the first century CE. Therefore, this religion stems from Judaism on basic principles such as monotheism, man created in the likeness of God, and a central prophet among many others. Christianity has differing views from Judaism. Their tenets, belief in who Jesus was, prayer to and belief in saints, are just a few of these differences. One central difference is the belief that man's salvation is through Christ's passion, death, and resurrection.

Throughout the ages, art is used as a visual tool of communication. Images depicting scenes, like those of Adam and Eve, and the resurrection of Christ are used to visually communicate the teachings of the Bible to the masses. This was extremely important in times where the general population was illiterate. Originally, there were no human representations of God because he was not considered of this earth. Eventually, through the need of its practitioners, artists began creating depictions of him, usually as an aged patriarch who is wise and powerful. Other religious imagery includes images of saints, angels, the Virgin Mary, Jesus, and the Holy Spirit.

Within a religious context, an icon is a visual depiction of a spiritual being—like the Virgin Mary or Archangel Michael. Icon paintings of an individual were called portrait icons. These are different than those that visually illustrate stories from the Bible, like that of Adam and Eve.

Archangel Michael is one of the most frequently depicted spiritual beings in Christian art. Known for fighting for good to prevail over evil, his characteristics are courage and strength. Artistically because of this role, he is often depicted wearing armor and wielding a sword. Dating back to the fourteenth century, *Icon of Archangel St. Michael* (see Figure 2.20) is shown differently. He is wearing a chiton (a basic, simply designed garment) and draped with a himation (a cloak). Rather than wielding a sword, he is holding a sceptre (or staff) in one hand and a globe of the world in another. The globe has the initials X Δ K standing for 'Christ Just Judge'. The cross on top of the globe was a Roman tradition, in this case communicating Christ's dominion over the world.

During the middle ages, these icons were directly tied to Christianity and served as models of the ideal Christian lifestyle. As seen with images of Buddha, icon paintings were believed to be more than a simple representation of a spiritual being. At times, the images of saints or other religious personages were viewed as possessing the presence of that individual, allowing the people to directly communicate with, or pray to them. Rather than relying on a priest to be the intermediary, the religious personage depict could intercede on the individual's behalf with God. This allows the person to maintain a strong connection to his/her faith in times when they were unable to be part of a congregational experience.

RELIQUARY - a receptacle designed to store or display a holy relic, such as ashes or bones of a spiritual figure.

In addition, the creation of reliquaries were used to store bones and other artifacts of saints (see Figure 2.21). These, like icon paintings, were placed in various churches and monasteries around the world, popularizing them as places of pilgrimage.

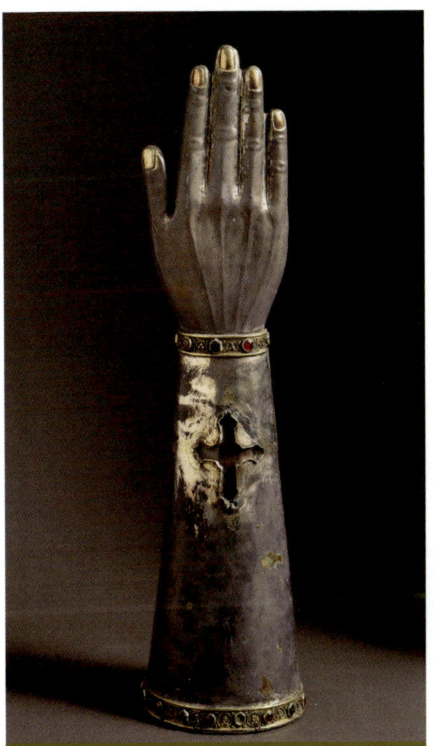
DEA PICTURE LIBRARY/De Agostini/Getty Images

FIGURE 2.21 – Silver Reliquary of the Arm of Abbot Giovanni Bove. Cathedral of Veroli, Italy. 13th century. Approximately 18 5/8 x 5 7/8 x 3 7/8 in. Silver, semi precious stones on wood form.

In 313 CE, the two Emperors who controlled the Roman Empire were Constantine (272–337) and Licinius (263–325). Seeing the following Christianity had among the people, the Emperors put an end to the persecution of Christians in Europe with the creation of the Edict of Milan. The Edict provided Christians the same religious freedoms as followers of other religions. Shortly thereafter, Constantine made Christianity an official religion. In time, it led to an increase in the building of churches and cathedrals, which are places for congregational worship. These large-scale buildings towered over others and varied in their construction.

During the twelfth century Zagwe dynasty in Ethiopia, King Lalibela (1162-1221) commissioned a series of spectacular churches to be fashioned out of the subterranean volcanic tuff rock (see Figure 2.22). Some of the churches were carved as free-standing monolithic structures, while others were carved directly into the wall of the rock. One of the most iconic of these is the cross-shaped structure of St. George (see Figure 2.23). The architects of these churches created a complex system of subterranean passageways that connected these underground structures. In an effort to preserve them, a drainage system was created. While these churches are located in a remote mountain town in northern Ethiopia, people will walk the rugged terrain for days and even weeks to get to them, thus turning the site into an important place of pilgrimage for worshippers of Orthodox Christianity. In 1978, UNESCO made this area a World Heritage Site and has taken measures to preserve the churches from environmental forces that have been eroding them over time.

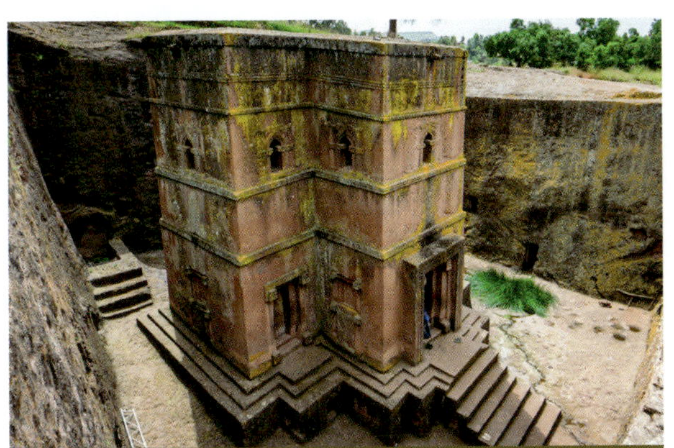
©Anton_Ivanov/Shutterstock.com

FIGURE 2.22 – The Church of St. George. Lalibela, Ethiopia. c. 1220. Approximately 40 ft. high. Tuff (rose colored limestone).

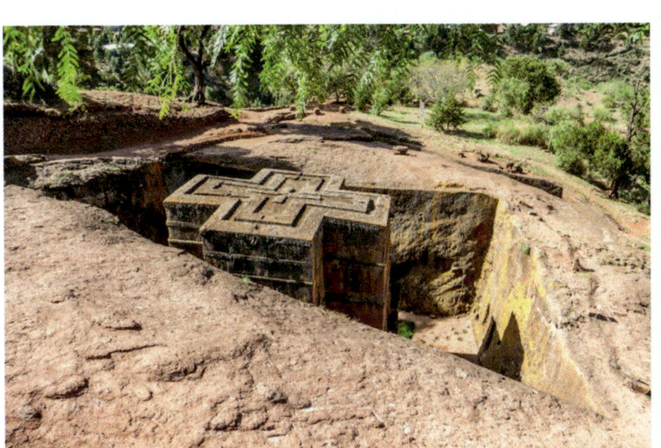
©milosk50/Shutterstock.com

FIGURE 2.23 – The Church of St. George (Bete Giyorgis). Lalibela, Ethiopia. c. 1220. Approximately 40 ft. high. Tuff (rose colored limestone).

UNESCO - (United Nations Educational, Scientific, and Cultural Organization) A United Nations agency established to promote education, communication and the arts.

Often churches were decorated with imagery communicating teachings of their faith to help them reflect upon, and strengthen those beliefs. Churches serve multiple functions from a congregational space, to a burial place, to a pilgrimage shrine containing relics of a holy person.

Before Islam came into being, the Arabs were polytheistic. Among the many deities they worshipped, the most powerful of them was Allah. As with the two religions that came before, Islam shares the core concepts of monotheism, a supreme being (Allah), and prophets. Common concepts shared solely with Christianity include the virgin birth, the idea of heaven and hell, and the second coming of Jesus. Like Christianity, it also developed into its own unique religion. Islam came into being in the seventh century CE, based on the revelations of Muhammed (their greatest prophet). Muhammed (570–632), like Jesus, is meant to confirm and renew beliefs in Allah to the people. Man's path to salvation is based on correct belief, good deeds, and the Five Pillars of Islam, which include faith, prayer, fasting, pilgrimage to Mecca and alms.

Islam's holy book, the Qur'an, prohibits the representation of human and animal forms in a religious context. Therefore, there are no images of Allah depicted in human form throughout the history of Islam. In addition, religious architecture is often decorated with calligraphy and complex geometric designs and patterns (see Figure 2.24).

CALLIGRAPHY - a form of decorative handwriting.

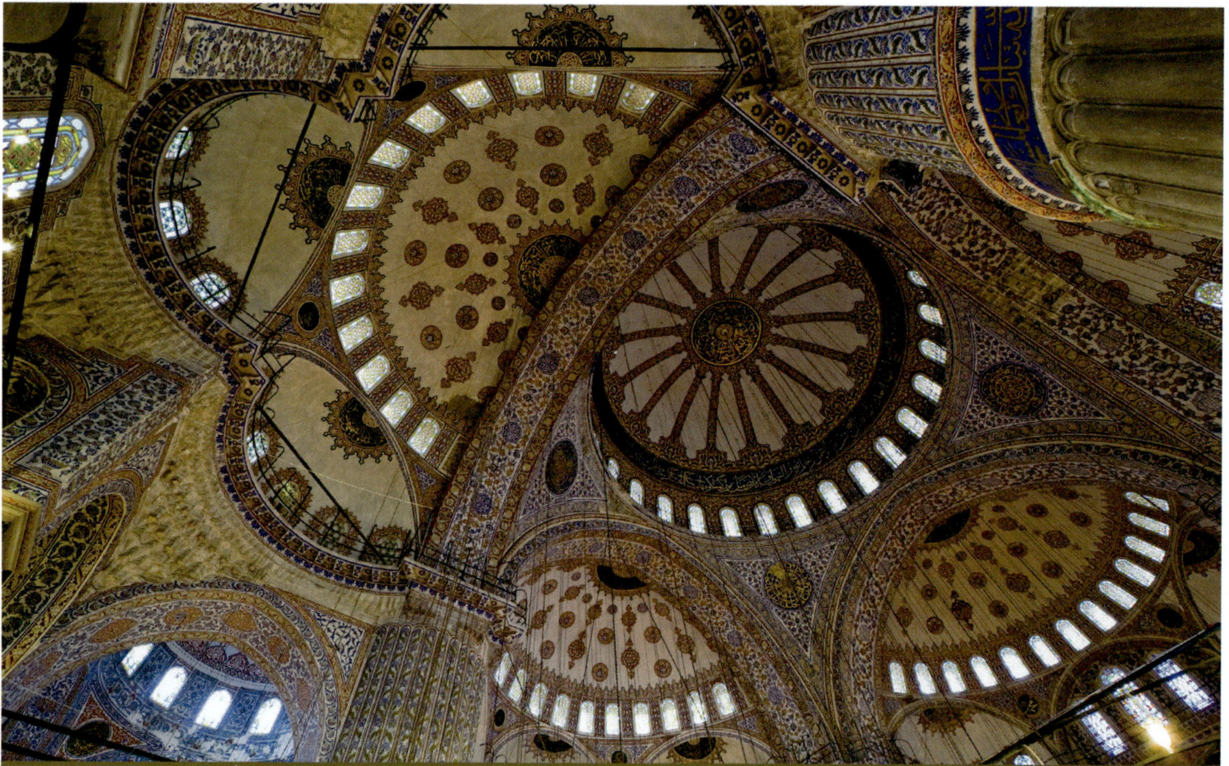

FIGURE 2.24 – The Blue Mosque (ceiling detail). Istanbul, Turkey. c. 1616. Ceramic mosaic.

The mosque is the Islamic place for congregational worship. Also known as the Sultan Ahmed Mosque, the *Blue Mosque* (see Figure 2.25) was built in Istanbul, Turkey between 1609 and 1616. It was built on the same location where a Byzantine palace once stood. It gets its name of the Blue Mosque from the many blue tiles used to decorate its interior walls. The interior space is heavily decorated with verses of the Qur'an done in calligraphy and over 20,000 handmade tiles with images of flowers, fruit and cypresses.

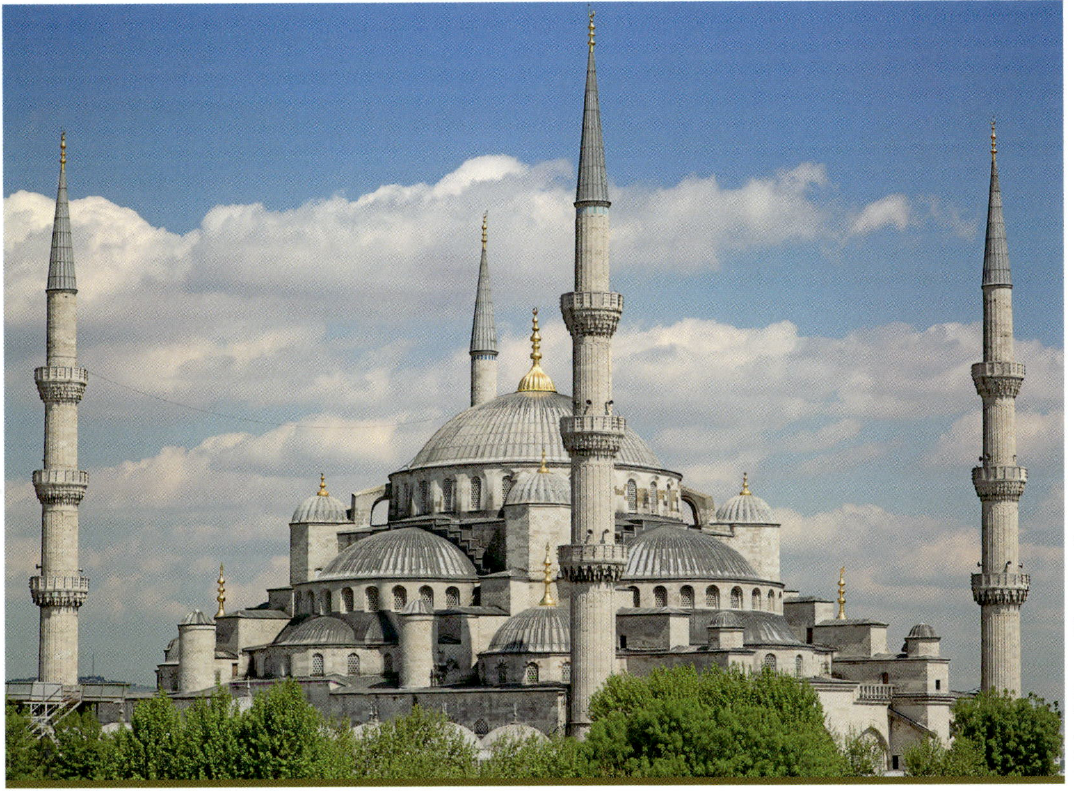

FIGURE 2.25 – Blue Mosque, architect Sedefkar Mehmed Agha. Istanbul, Turkey. c. 1616. 141 ft. high.

DESTINATIONS OF PILGRIMAGE

Throughout history, places of worship have come to serve many purposes for humans. As seen in westernized religions, they are used as a shelter for congregational worship. In some cases, they house sacred objects (whether text, imagery or artifacts) as seen in both Buddhism and Christianity. Places of worship can incorporate elements of nature. This can be seen in their overall design, like a Buddhist stupa representing an earthen mound. But in cultures where permanent architecture is not something normally created, elements of nature, like a tree or body of water, can serve as a sacred gathering site for a congregation, rituals or ceremonies. Places of worship, in any of the above contexts, can also provide sites for ritual celebrations or as the final destinations of pilgrimage. Often, people travel to these destinations in hopes of receiving special blessings or as a way to deepen their faith, linking the physical journey to that of their spiritual one.

SHRINE - a holy place, a receptacle for sacred objects, and/or a place devoted to a holy person or deity.

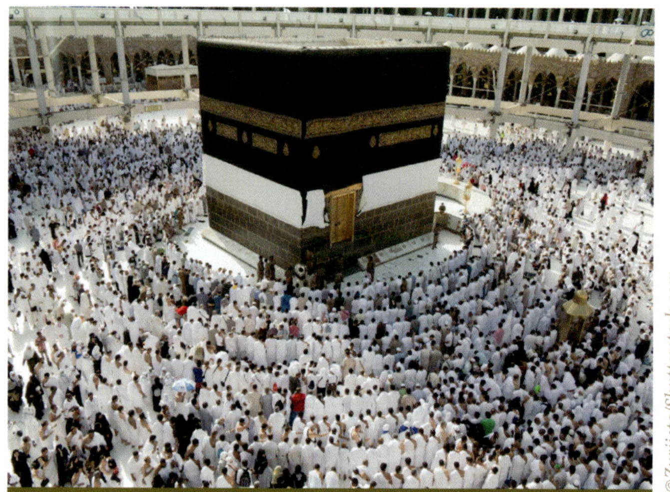

©Zurijeta/Shutterstock.com

FIGURE 2.26 – Ka'aba the Holy Mosque. Mecca, Saudi Arabia. c. 5th century. 36.2 x 43 x 42.2 ft. Granite, marble and limestone.

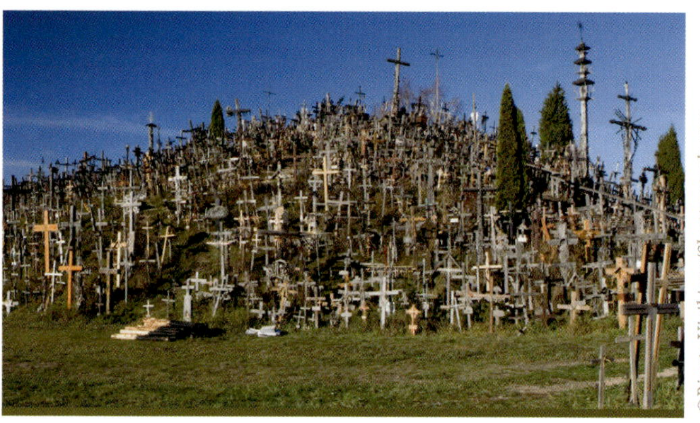

©Birute Vjeikiene/Shutterstock.com

FIGURE 2.27 – Hill of Crosses. Siauliai, Lithuania. c. 1830.

Places of pilgrimage exist all around the world, ranging from natural sites to man-made structures. Hindus and Buddhists turn to shrines, Jews to Jerusalem, Christians to places with holy relics, and Muslims to Mecca.

In the fifth century CE, people began to settle in Saudi Arabia, many choosing Mecca located near the West Coast. Mecca is the location of a large shrine, known as the *Ka'aba* (see Figure 2.26). It was once dedicated to various pagan deities in pre-Islamic times. Eventually, Muhammed removed all idols and established it as the structure to a monotheistic shrine. This granite structure stands approximately forty-nine feet high and is covered in black silk, emblazoned with gold-and-silver calligraphy. Embedded in its eastern corner and revered by Muslims, the Black Stone is believed to have been a gift from the angel Gabriel to Ibrahim. The stone is believed by some to be an angel who will protect all that kiss it prior to the Day of Judgment. Whether due to the changing needs of the community, or damage sustained over time, the Ka'aba has undergone many renovations throughout its history.

Mecca was eventually recognized as one of Islam's holiest cities and a place of pilgrimage. People travel to Mecca, if possible, at least once in their lifetime. When they arrive, people enter the courtyard and begin walking around the Ka'aba seven times in a counter-clockwise direction. Muslims attempt to kiss the stone each time they circle the Ka'aba to emulate the actions of Muhammed centuries earlier. The sheer number of pilgrims prevents many from actually touching or kissing the stone. So the act of pointing in its direction is now accepted as having the same result.

Since the fifteenth century CE and perhaps even earlier, there has been a long-standing tradition of creating wayside shrines in Lithuania. These started as grave markers to mark burial places of loved ones. They eventually evolved into a variety of objects from shrines to totems created to memorialize key events in both individual lives, and those of the community at large. Sometimes the wayside shrines were used to commemorate those who participated in political uprisings. One such example is the *Hill of Crosses* (see Figure 2.27).

TOTEM - an emblem or symbol, such as an animal, plant or natural form, representing a group of people with family ties or a clan.

The Hill of Crosses consists of an oblong mound approximately thirty feet high by eighty feet long. The earliest reference to this location described a castle destroyed by fire in 1348 that once stood on this spot. It was not referenced again in writing until the early 1830s, when it described this location as a site where crosses were erected by relatives to honor victims of the 1831 rebellion against the czarist rule. At this time, the Soviet government forbade its people from creating such shrines, seeing the action as a destabilizing force. Despite the government's efforts, the Hill of Crosses became a symbol of community and hope that was perceived to support rebellious activities. The Lithuanian people continued to leave roadway shrines and crosses throughout the 1800s for other rebellions.

For a twenty-year period starting in 1961, the government went to great lengths to suppress their people by occasionally using bulldozers to destroy the Hill of Crosses. Wooden crosses were burnt; metal ones were turned into scrap metal; and stone or concrete ones were broken and buried in the earth. This occurred four times over that twenty-year period that eventually became known as "bulldozer atheism." While often guarded to prevent people from putting crosses back, they somehow reappeared immediately and grew in number. At one point, the government tried to flood the area around the hill to prevent access.

However, no matter what extremes they took to guard the hill, the next day crosses (see Figure 2.28) would reappear. By 1988, the Hill of Crosses gained a new status as both a Lithuanian and world phenomenon. Today, there are over 50,000 crosses, statues, and pictures of Saints and rosaries marking this location. Because of the people's determination to honor their loved ones, and protest the political oppression of their government, the Hill of Crosses has become a worldwide symbol of people's persistence of faith. To this day, it continues to be an important pilgrimage destination for people of all faiths and nationalities.

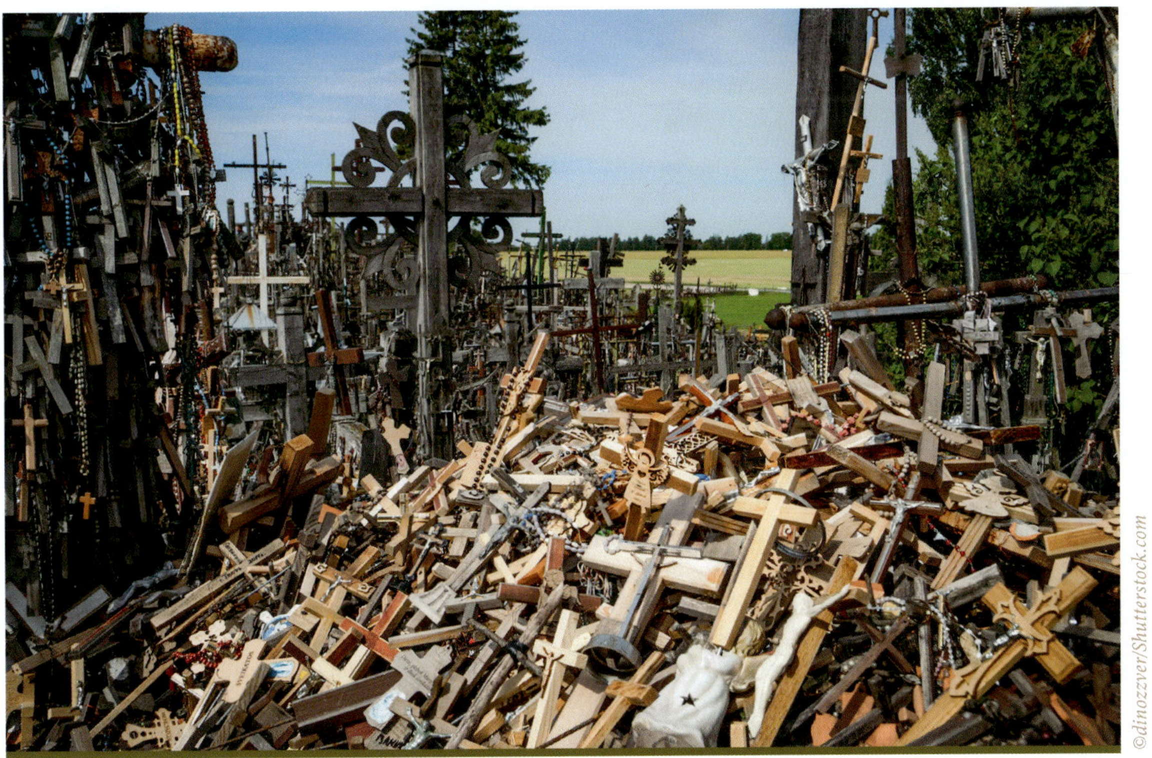

FIGURE 2.28 – Crosses on Hill of Crosses. Siauliai, Lithuania.

Take a closer look at the way that Christ (see Figure 2.29) is depicted. How would you describe him compared to imagery that you normally see? Upon closer observation, Christ appears to be tired and beaten-down. The environment and way of life for many Lithuanians over the centuries has been one that challenged their ability to thrive. Having the image of Christ depicted similarly to how they feel, gives them the strength to persevere and to follow the teachings of their faith, no matter what the circumstances are before them.

Another example of a place of pilgrimage is the *Yungang Grottoes* (see Figure 2.30) in China. The site is a huge complex of shrines and caves, housing thousands of inscriptions dedicated to and sacred statues of the Buddha (see Figure 2.31). Although it has become a destination for people from all over the world who practice Buddhism, sites like these exude a sense of spirituality and sacredness that appeal to those of other faiths, as well.

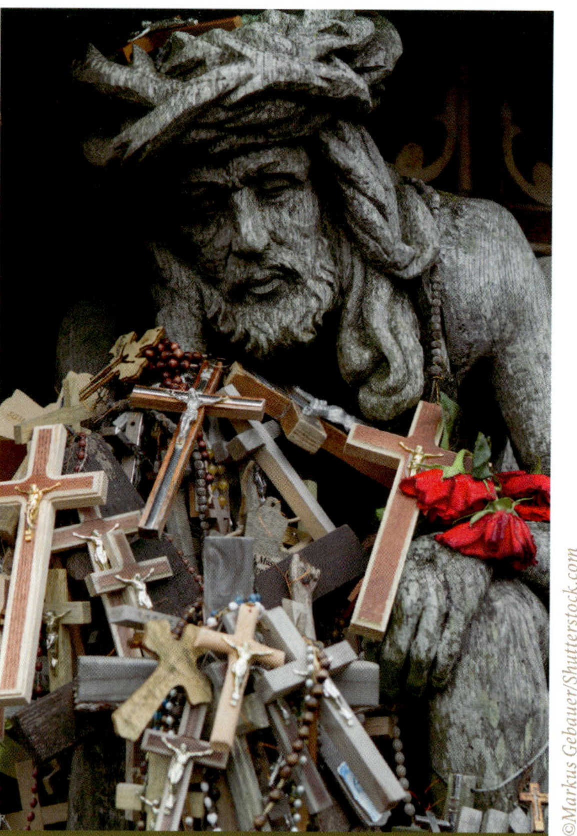

FIGURE 2.29 – Hill of Crosses (detail of Christ). Siauliai, Lithuania.

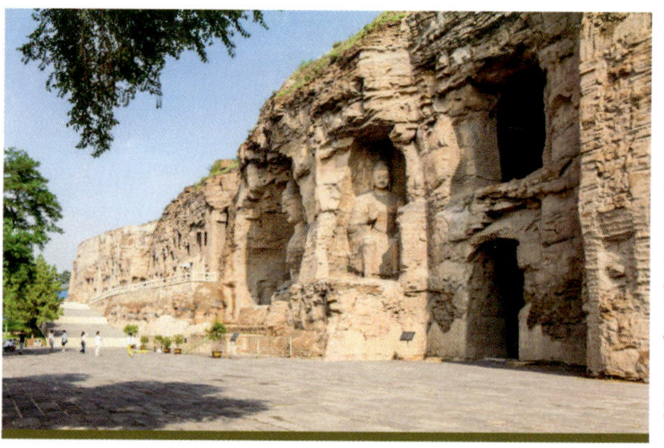

FIGURE 2.30 – Yungang Grottoes. Province of Shanxi, China. c. 460. 18,000 m^2.

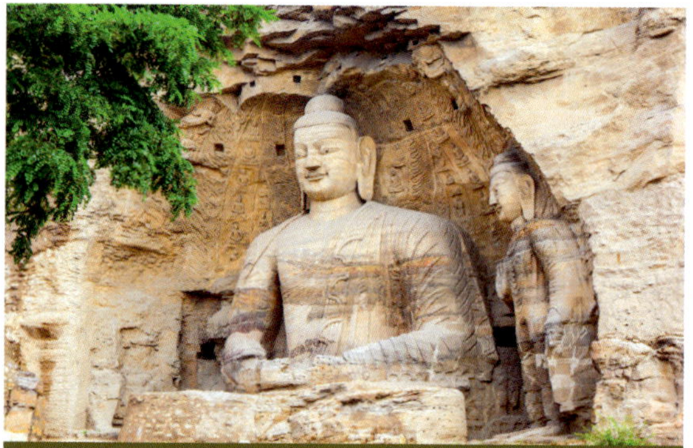

FIGURE 2.31 – Yungang Grottoes. Province of Shanxi, China. c. 460. 13.7 m. high.

DESTRUCTION OF RELIGIOUS ART AND SITES OF PILGRIMAGE

The practice of iconoclasm has occurred in many cultures throughout history. When an outside culture overtakes an area, there is a need to exert control over its people. One effective way is through the destruction of cultural identity by destroying religious architecture and imagery. Such actions, that visually eradicate what came before, strike at the core of a person mentally and emotionally. The destruction of culturally significant art typically includes mutilating of parts—the face and eyes (see Figure 2.32), rather than the entire piece—hence the term 'defacing.'

RELIEF - form of sculpture, with a partially raised image projected from a flat surface and meant to be viewed from the front.

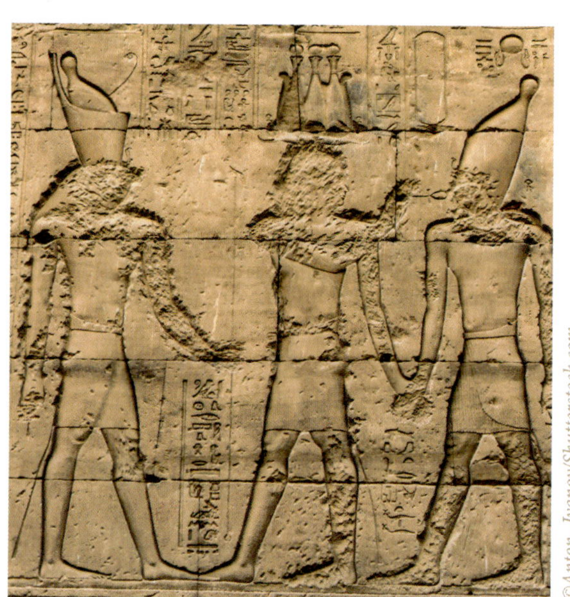

FIGURE 2.32– Hieroglyphic Illustration of the Egyptian God Horus on the Wall in a Temple. Temple of Horus, Egypt. c. 237–57 BC. Relief carving.

In Afghanistan, large-scale relief sculptures of the Buddha (see Figure 2.33) were carved into the side of a mountain in Bamiyan Valley. They range in size from 124 feet to 180 feet in height. This became a site of pilgrimage over the centuries. In March 2001, the Taliban committed a modern-day act of iconoclasm. They were ordered to use these large sculptures of Buddha as target practice. Using rockets, explosives, and tank shells, the Taliban reduced these majestic images of Buddha to rubble. Afterwards they released images and videos of the act to the world. Actions like these serve multiple purposes for the perpetrators, such as spreading their message and ideals to the masses, humiliating and harassing the people they are intruding upon, and leaving in their wake massive cultural destruction. In Afghanistan, the Taliban did this to rid the nation of reminders of its pre-Islamic past. Soon after their destruction, there were various efforts made to reconstruct some of these reliefs from the pieces discovered in the debris at the base where they once stood.

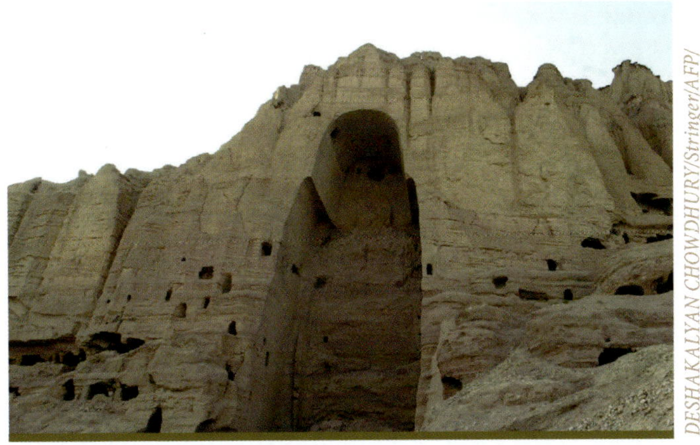

DESHAKALYAN CHOWDHURY/Stringer/AFP/ Getty Images

FIGURE 2.33 – 53 m. High Buddha. Bamyan Valley, Afghanistan. c. 14th century. Destruction occurred on August 31, 2002.

SALVAGING RELIGIOUS ART AND SITES OF PILGRIMAGE

Over the centuries, some military and political leaders have ordered the destruction of important cultural and religious sites and artifacts. However, there are now a growing number of individuals and organizations that are willing to risk a great deal to protect or salvage these important artifacts and sites.

ARTIFACT - an object crafted by a human being, often having cultural or historical significance.

During the sixteenth century CE in Italy, there were several reasons for the destruction of religious art that were not always tied to political strategies. Frescos were often painted over or destroyed, when a new artistic style or patronage led to renovations of churches and homes. At times, stiff penalties were put into place to prevent the removal, defacing or destruction of religious Christian art. In 1519, an Italian homeowner, Bernardo del Beccuto, was going to lease his property to a Jewish family. He felt they would not appreciate having sacred Christian images in their living space. Del Beccuto went to Florentine authorities to seek assistance in preserving the frescos. He went to great lengths, covering them in a way to prevent damage so they could be preserved until uncovered again.

In 1812, Napoleonic troops occupied Granada, Spain. While there, the army excavated Alhambra, a hilltop palace originally built in 889 CE, which they used as a fort. The military's effort to reform the locals had failed and before they left the area, the commander ordered his troops to demolish the palace. A low-ranking Spanish officer, willing to risk his life to prevent the destruction of a cultural heritage, located and cut the already lit fuse without being detected.

As discussed earlier, the large-scale relief sculptures of Buddha in Afghanistan that had been destroyed by the Taliban brought international attention to the continuing practice of iconoclasm. It is also an example of the global acknowledgement and support of the sacredness of such art and sites of pilgrimage. In 2002, the Afghanistan Minister of Information and Culture at the time, Raheen Makhdoom, supported efforts to reconstruct the statues of Buddha. Doing so, not only held religious significance, but also helped restore Afghanistan's once-thriving tourist industry. Since Makhdoom's support, there have been three main issues preventing anyone from moving forward on the reconstructions. The first is that the bombing has weakened the cliffs where the sculptures once stood, and they must be stabilized before any reconstruction can start.

The second is that UNESCO, which has put this area on its World Heritage List, requires that any reconstruction of the statues must be done with original materials. The third is the discovery that most of the debris at the base of the destroyed Buddhas was hauled away and sold by local residents. Therefore, to meet UNESCO's requirements and to remain on the list of protected sites once restored, someone has to trace and reacquire all of the rubble—a hopeless task.

There are two schools of thought regarding the reconstruction of the statues. The first argues for leaving them in their current state as a reminder to future generations of the ignorance and/or lack of acceptance by others. The second argues for reconstruction to give back the Afghan people their spectacular site of pilgrimage. When asked, the local residents are in favor of such efforts in a way that supports both schools of thought. The rebuilding of the smaller Buddha statue would allow them to regain part of their history, while sending a message to the world in support of religious understanding. In contrast, by leaving the larger Buddha niche empty, it serves as a universal reminder of the damage done, and history lost at the hands of the intolerant.

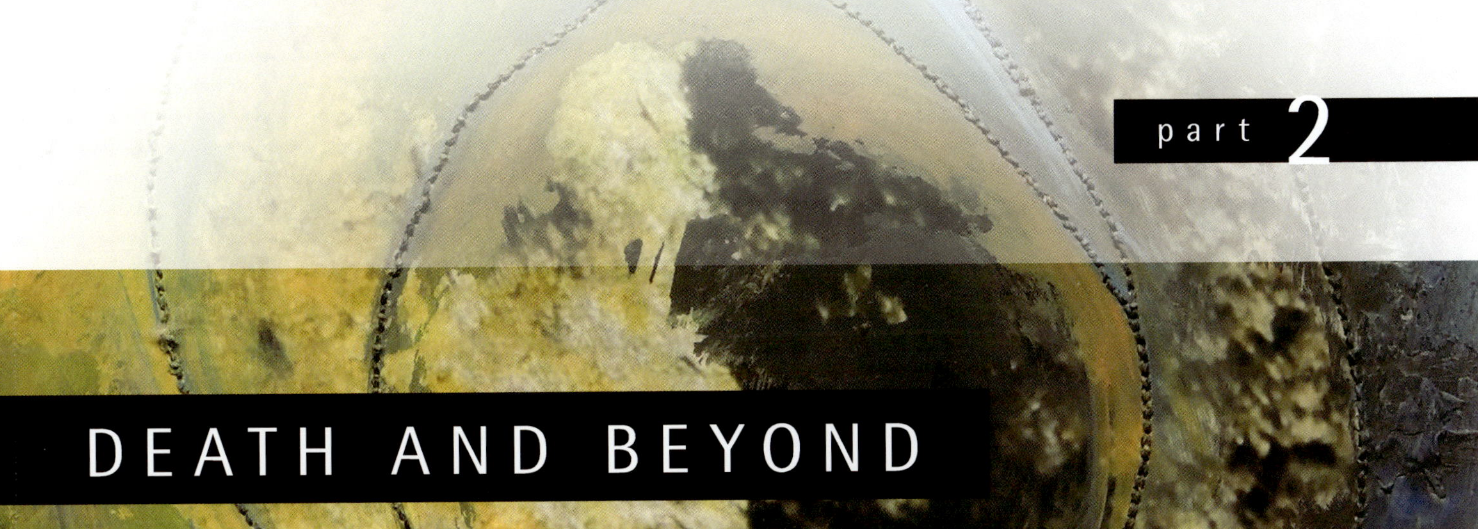

In cultures around the world, humans have created rituals and practices surrounding their concept of death and what lies beyond. In addition, humans have created funerary art as a way to honor or memorialize their ancestors, political leaders, and fallen heroes. These can take on many appearances from a single, small stone marker placed at the head of a grave to large-scale monuments placed within a city.

CULTURAL PRACTICES

In Sulawesi, Indonesia, the Tana Toraja society had ancient traditions associated with death that are still practiced today. The traditions include a celebration of life with the recounting of stories of the deceased, ritual sacrifice and feasting on buffalo and pigs, and placement of the deceased in their final resting spot. To this culture, life revolves around death in that they work hard to accumulate wealth to be able to provide a good send off in death, rather than to acquire possessions during life. It is in death that a person's status (or that of their family) is established. When Torajans die, they are placed into the home of their surviving family members where they 'live' until enough money can be raised to perform the funerary ceremony and festivities. Until the ceremonies are completed, the deceased is not truly considered to be dead, but is viewed as sick or sleeping during this time. This can take several months to years to acquire enough money to be able to purchase the required number of buffalo and pigs to be sacrificed. The sacrifices hold three distinct purposes. The first is to be able to feed all of the attendees who have traveled great distances for the celebration. The second is the belief that through the slaughtering of the animals the deceased will live peacefully in the 'land of the souls' once the animals have joined them. The third is directly tied to the buffalo, which is a status symbol among the Torajan. The horns of the sacrificed buffaloes are placed outside the family home. The number of horns for the individual is significant in determining his/her status. The number of horns accumulated over the generations outside the family home indicates their status as a family among the community at large.

EFFIGY - a sculpture of a human being created for a variety of purposes, like political, cultural, or personal.

On the eleventh day of the festivities of the celebration of life, the body is placed in a coffin within a cave on the side of mountain at Lemo (see Figure 2.34). This location overlooks the rice fields and homes of the Torajan. A life-size wooden effigy of the dead (see Figure 2.35), called a *tau tau*, is perched high in the cliffs on a balcony near the burial caves. The figure is usually adorned with the favorite jewelry or outfit of the deceased, and is believed to ward off evil and to protect the Torajans living below. A common color seen in the clothing of the effigies is red, which is the color of death in Sulawesi.

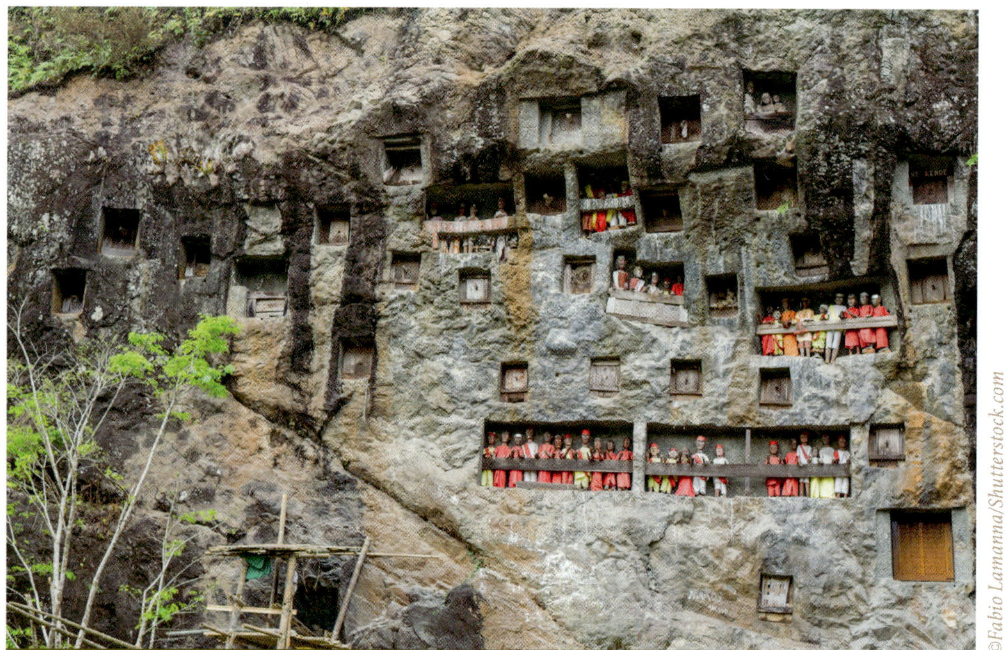

©Fabio Lamanna/Shutterstock.com

FIGURE 2.34 – Lemo (Tana Toraja, South Sulawesi, Indonesia), famous burial. South Sulawesi, Indonesia.

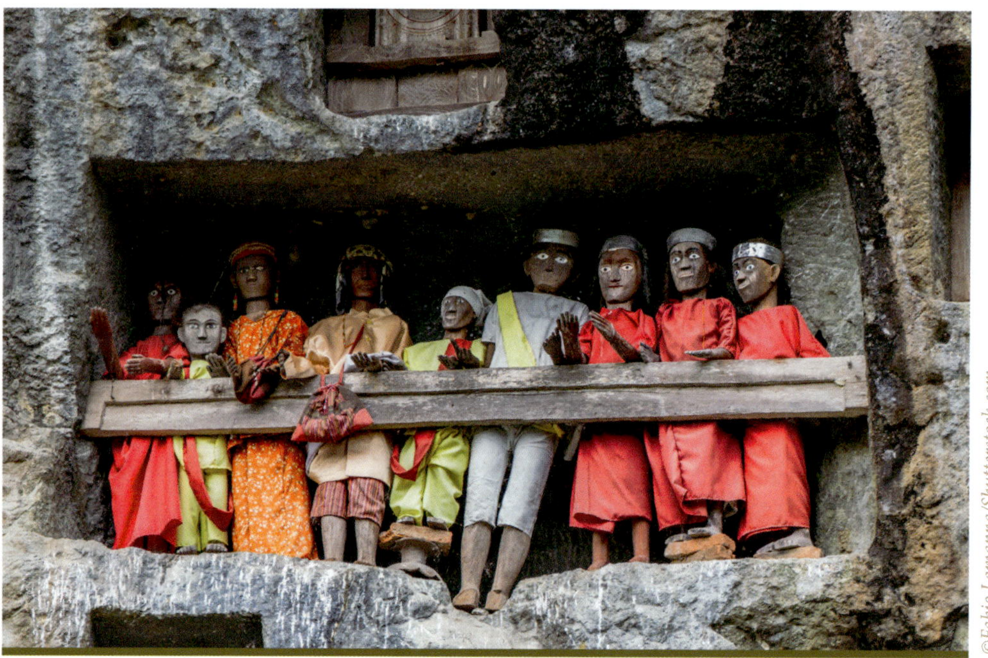

©Fabio Lamanna/Shutterstock.com

FIGURE 2.35 – Lemo (Tana Toraja, South Sulawesi, Indonesia), famous burial site (detail). South Sulawesi, Indonesia.

In August of every year, the Ceremony of Cleaning Corpses or *Ma'Nene* occurs. The bodies of the deceased are exhumed at this time to be washed, groomed and dressed in new clothing. If there is any decay or damage to their coffins, repairs are made at this time, as well. Before returning a deceased to their cave, the family walks the mummy around the village in a ceremonial way. While not clearly understood by outsiders, this seems to be linked to the belief that when a person dies they must be accompanied by family members back to their village of origin.

Various ancient cultures throughout Peru buried their dead in bundles. Folding the body into a fetal position, the deceased (see Figure 2.36) was carefully wrapped in several layers of hand woven textiles and leaves. A braided rope made from the fibers of local plants was tied around the bundled body to hold it together. The prepared body would then be buried in a variety of ways, depending on the cultural traditions of the deceased. This could range from being placed on cliff edges, to simple pit graves, to sturdily constructed tombs. In the pit graves or tombs, the mummy bundles were buried along with earthly items that were perceived to be needed for the comfort of the individual throughout their afterlife. In some cases, perhaps that of an important individual, additional bundles were found buried in a tomb. It is believed that these could be young children who were sacrificed at the time of the deceased's burial as a sacrificial offering to one or more of their gods.

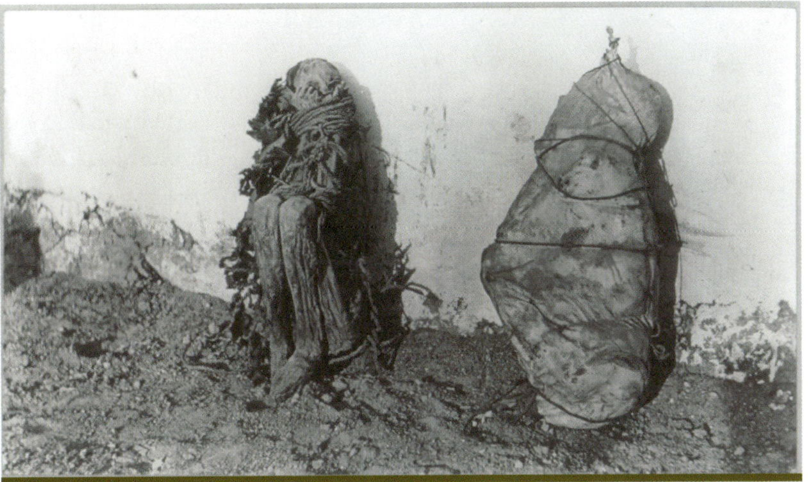

FIGURE 2.36 – 2 Mummies. Cerro de Pasco, Peru. c. 1890.

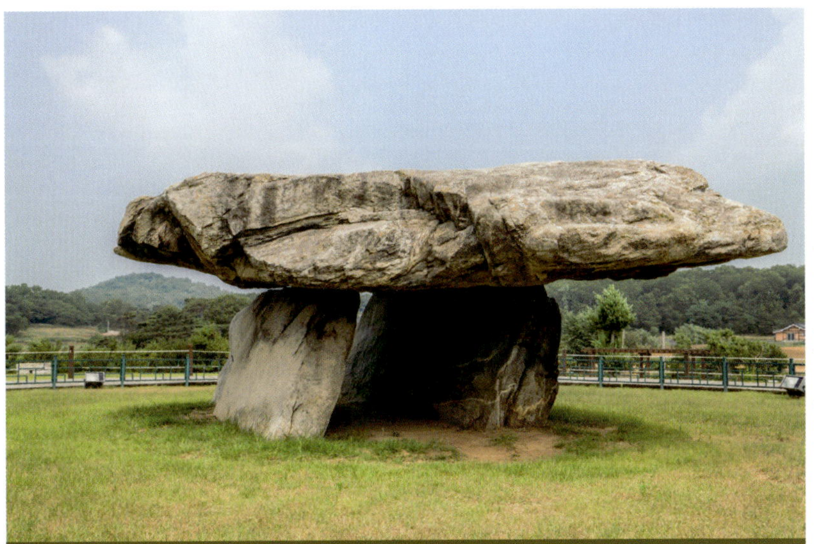

FIGURE 2.37 – Ganghwa Dolmen, a stone grave or tomb. South Korea. c. 7th century BC. 2.6 x 7.1 x 5.5 cm. Stone.

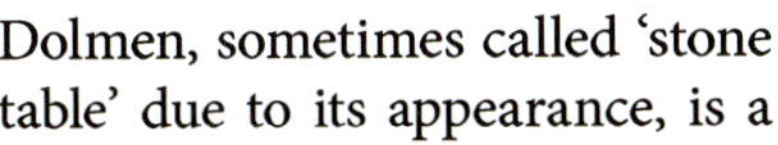

Dolmen, sometimes called 'stone table' due to its appearance, is a type of construction that consists of using two or more upright stones that support a *capstone* (a large flat horizontal stone). Historically, dolmen construction was used for ceremonial sites, like *Stonehenge* in England, or to create passageways into burial chambers, like *Newgrange* in Ireland. Dating back over 4,000 years ago in various parts of Korea, the practice of using dolmens for funerary purposes or ancestral rituals was common. There are approximately 30,000 dolmens still remaining throughout the country. Excavations have revealed bodies and grave goods under some dolmens, indicating that they served as grave markers for the elite or ruling class. Others, as seen in *Ganghwa Dolmen* (see Figure 2.37), due to their size, most likely served as ceremonial locations where various rituals would be performed. While the purpose of such ceremonies remains a mystery, the large number of these sites indicates that at one time the use of dolmens were very significant to their culture. UNESCO designated the Korean dolmens collectively as a World Heritage Site in 2000.

Vikings were maritime raiders from Scandinavia who traveled to remote destinations like Iceland, England, and North America during the eighth, ninth and tenth centuries. They practiced polytheism, worshipping many gods and goddesses, who exerted control over various aspects of Viking life. They were considered a pagan culture to the more 'civilized' people of the Western world at the time. Their way of life revolved heavily around farming, family, and warfare. In the end, a Viking wished admittance into *Valhalla*, their concept of the Christian heaven.

Because of the significance of their seafaring ways, Viking burials, from the commoner to the wealthy, included a boat in some fashion. In a Necropolis (graveyard), over the burial site stones would be laid out in the outline of a boat (see Figure 2.38). In more common burials in this case, the deceased (see Figure 2.39) was buried in traditional attire, with a weapon across his waist. The weapon could be seen to represent one's ability to protect oneself in the afterlife.

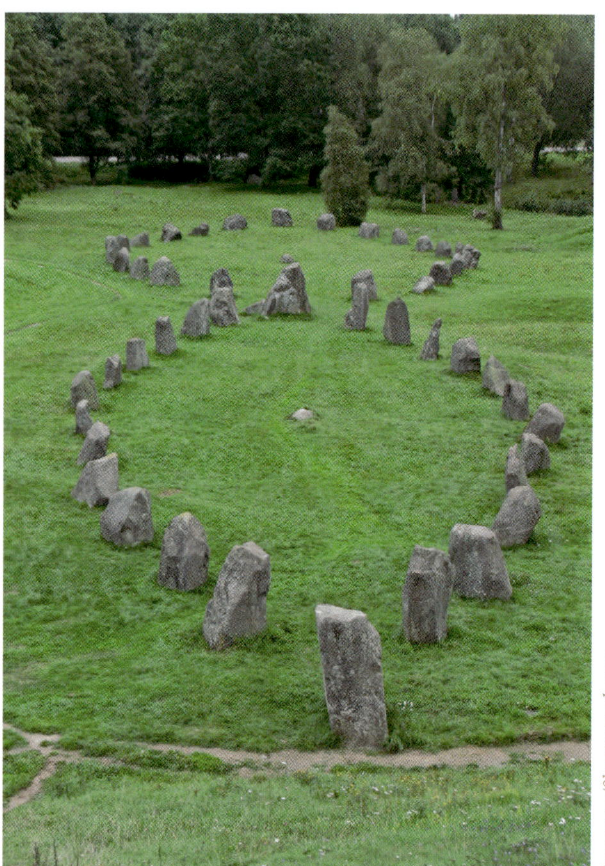

FIGURE 2.38 – Anundshog Cemetery, rune stone. Sweden. c. 500 BC–1050 CE.

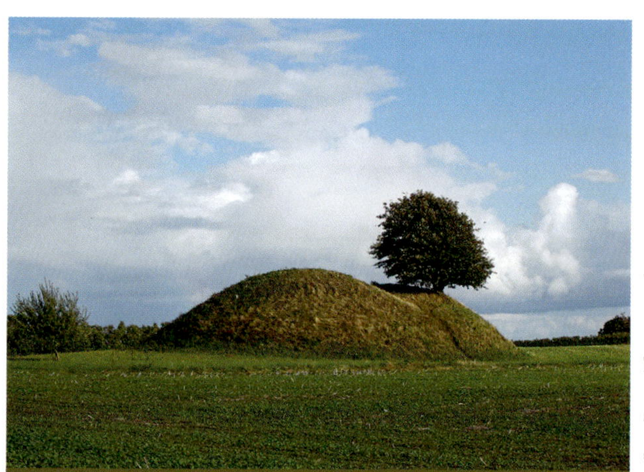

FIGURE 2.40 – Traditional Viking Age Grave Burial Site. Funen, Denmark. c. 925.

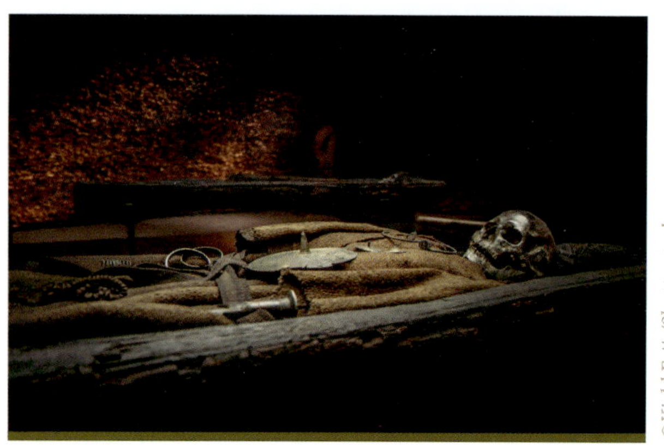

FIGURE 2.39 – Skeleton of a Bronze Age Man in a Burial Mound.

The Vikings who were wealthier, or had higher standing, often had earthen mounds (see Figure 2.40) constructed on their farmsteads. The deceased would be placed inside a life-size boat (up to 60 feet in length), typically one that would have been used along the coastline or inland waterways. Tools of their trade—weapons, jewelry, food, and drink—would be placed along with the deceased in the boat. Servants and animals, like horses, would be killed and placed with the body, as well. This provided the individual with all of the necessities and comforts of their earthly life for the afterlife.

In many African cultures, reliquaries reflect their views on the link between the living and the dead. These figures take on many different forms and incorporate many different materials specific to the cultures creating them. They contain ashes or bone fragments of important ancestors and other perceived powerful materials. The Tsogho people in Gabon create reliquary figures to commemorate specific ancestors and assist in initiation rituals. In addition, the reliquaries are used to consult with their ancestors on important matters, regarding illness, infertility, and warfare. Although each family within the tribe creates a reliquary of their own, they are all stored within the hut of the village's chief.

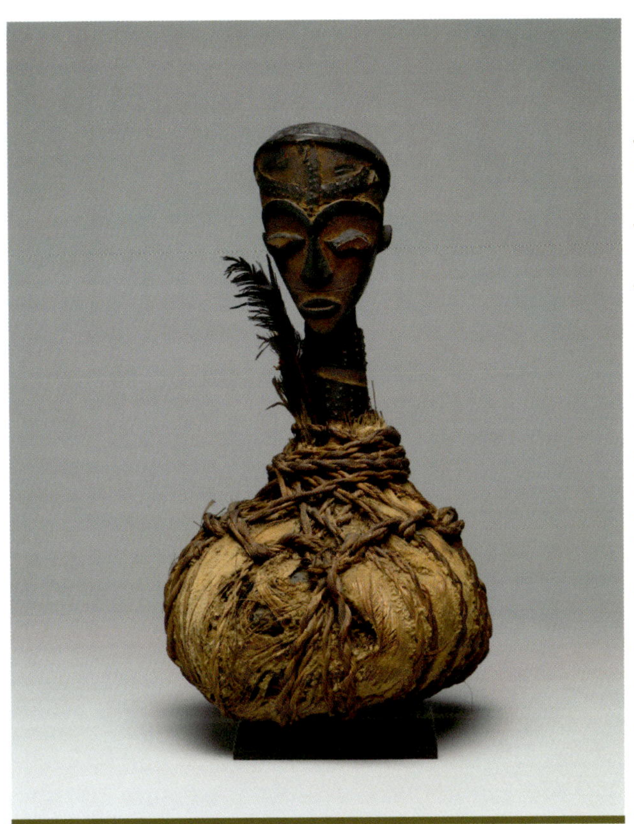

Reliquary Guardian Figure (Boumba Bwiti), Tsogho, late nineteenth or early twentieth century (wood, raffia, metal, bark cloth, glass, feathers), African School / Brooklyn Museum of Art, New York, USA / Gift of Mr. and Mrs. John A. Friede / Bridgeman Images

FIGURE 2.41 – Reliquary Guardian Figure (Mbuma Bwete). Tsogho, Africa. c. Late 19th century. 30.5 x 18.4 cm. Wood, raffia, metal, bark, cloth, glass, feathers.

Mbuma Bwete (see Figure 2.41) is an example of a Tsogho reliquary guardian figure. The statue's purpose was to evoke *Bwete* or the spirit that mediates between the divine and the Tsogho people. These reliquary figures were viewed as the personification of their ancestors, because they contain partial remains of venerated forebears of their community. These figures could be called upon by healers to assist in their healing practices.

The construction of the reliquary guardian consisted of a wooden head atop a truncated body carved from a reddish colored wood called *tukula*. The color red is associated with blood or life force, therefore increasing the figure's power. Small arms are shown resting on the figure's chest in a ritual gesture. Its oval-shaped eyes are made from a reddish-brown stained glass, providing a dramatic quality to the figure during ritual use, as the material reflects light. The shiny quality of the eyes also conveys the spiritual power the figure possesses. On the forehead and neck of the figure, embossed metal strips are attached. The reflective nature of the once untarnished metal symbolizes daylight and offers the figure protection against the evil forces, often at their strongest during the night. In addition, the use of copper signifies the wealth of a family, honoring both the dead and the living. The carved part is attached to a bundle containing the remains or relics of the ancestor within. It is perceived as the rest of the body (or the stomach) of the ancestral figure.

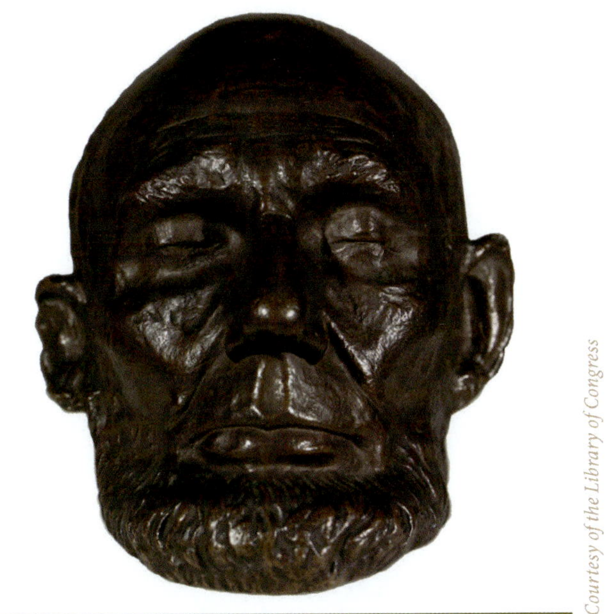

Courtesy of the Library of Congress

FIGURE 2.42 – Life Mask of Abraham Lincoln, Clark Mills. United States. 1865. Bronze casting.

The ritual of taking a mask of a recently deceased person was a common practice historically, as discussed earlier in Roman times. Eventually life masks became of equal importance because they captured a person of importance during various aspects of their life. A common practice in American culture was to take life masks of the presidents. Over the years, life mask creations were then practiced by people of all ages, professions, and social status.

During Abraham Lincoln's political career, two artists had the privilege of taking life mask castings of his face. In 1858, the first artist, Leonard Volk (1828–1895), met Lincoln while he was campaigning for the U.S. Senate. Volk invited him to sit for a bust. Although Lincoln agreed, it took two years of Volk's urging to get him to finally come to his studio. At this point, Lincoln was the Republican nominee for presidency. Volk started by taking a plaster casting of Lincoln's face. The mold took over an hour to set and due to Lincoln's prominent ears and high cheekbones was very difficult to remove. Lincoln himself took over the process and was able to gradually remove it in one piece, remarking that the process was 'anything but agreeable.' The casting from this mold has continued to be used as a reference by artists when creating images of Abraham Lincoln.

CASTING - the process of making a 'positive' or image from a mold out of a range of materials, such as bronze, clay, or plaster.

The second artist, Clark Mills (1810–1883), took a casting of Lincoln's face two months prior to his assassination in 1865. The difference between the two masks is very revealing. The earlier casting, although taken when he was fifty-one, shows a youthfulness and lack of burden when compared to the one done in his later years. *Life Mask of Abraham Lincoln* (see Figure 2.42) by Mills shows that the stress of the presidency and Civil War had taken a toll and aged Lincoln considerably. The change was so dramatic in its effect that a fellow American sculptor, Gustus Saint-Gaudens (1848–1907), thought it was a death mask when he first saw it.

ARCHITECTURE AND ART

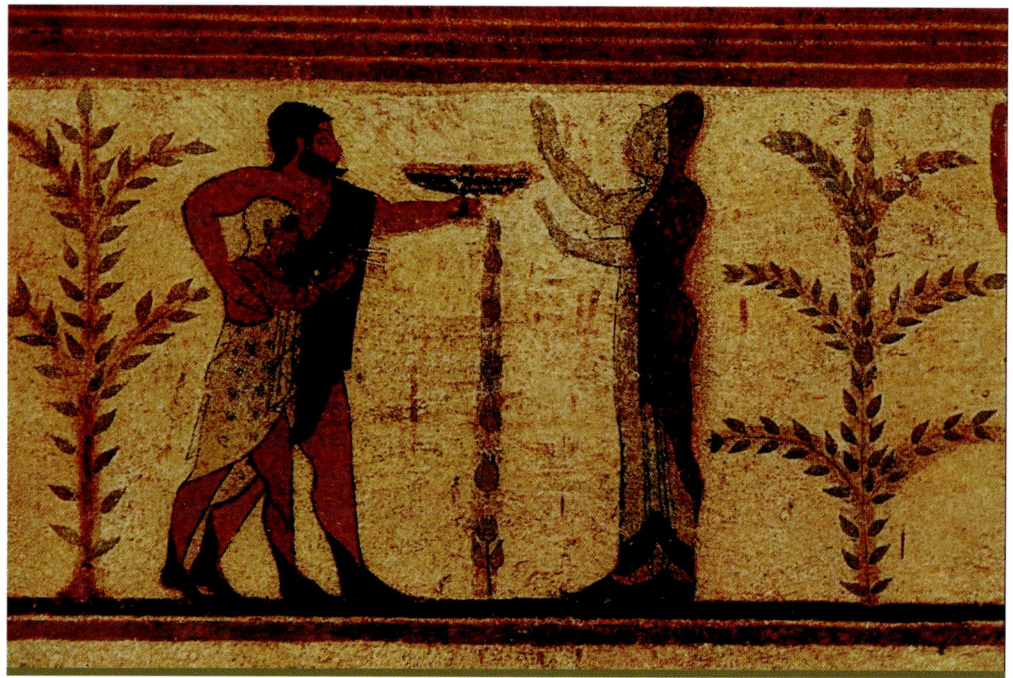

Courtesy of Corel

FIGURE 2.43 – Offering Fresco Etruscan Tomb of the Barons Tarquinia. Ionian School, Italy. c. 510–500 BC. Fresco.

In Etruscan culture, people were originally cremated and buried in urns in the ground. Eventually, when the notion of needing one's body to exist within the afterlife took hold, they created house-like tombs for their dead. They were a people who celebrated the enjoyment of life more than the importance or position they held within it. The murals decorating the inside of the tombs focused on such pleasures as banquets, feasts, music, and dancing. In addition, some murals showed the process of one entering into the afterlife. In the full image of the *Offering Fresco*, there are two horses that represent life and death. They engage in a race to see who will win. Ultimately, the final winner is always death. The deceased woman is then escorted by death into the afterlife. In the detail of the *Offering Fresco* (see Figure 2.43), the image shows the husband and son of a recently deceased woman coming to say their farewell to her, before she moves onto the afterlife. Here, as in other cultures, the artist uses a difference in coloration of skin for the genders.

In Egyptian culture, there was an evolutionary development of funerary architecture. The first stage was the *mastaba*, a single-level rectangular structure that was built over the top of a burial chamber. Pharaoh Djoser decided that for his burial he wanted something that towered above what came before. Around 2667 BC, the construction of the 203-foot-high stepped pyramid began. It consisted of six mastaba structures stacked on top of one another, gradually getting smaller in size towards the top. The next major evolution in funerary architecture came under Sneferu's reign. Eventually around 2600 BC, the architects failed at their first attempt of a four-sided slopped pyramid. This initial attempt is known as the *Bent Pyramid*. The architects discovered their miscalculations and refined their process to achieve structures like the *Great Pyramid* (see Figure 2.44) located in the Giza Plateau in Egypt. This structure towers over the stepped pyramid, standing at 481 feet high. These structures, like the mastaba, were built on top of the burial chamber that went below the surface of the ground.

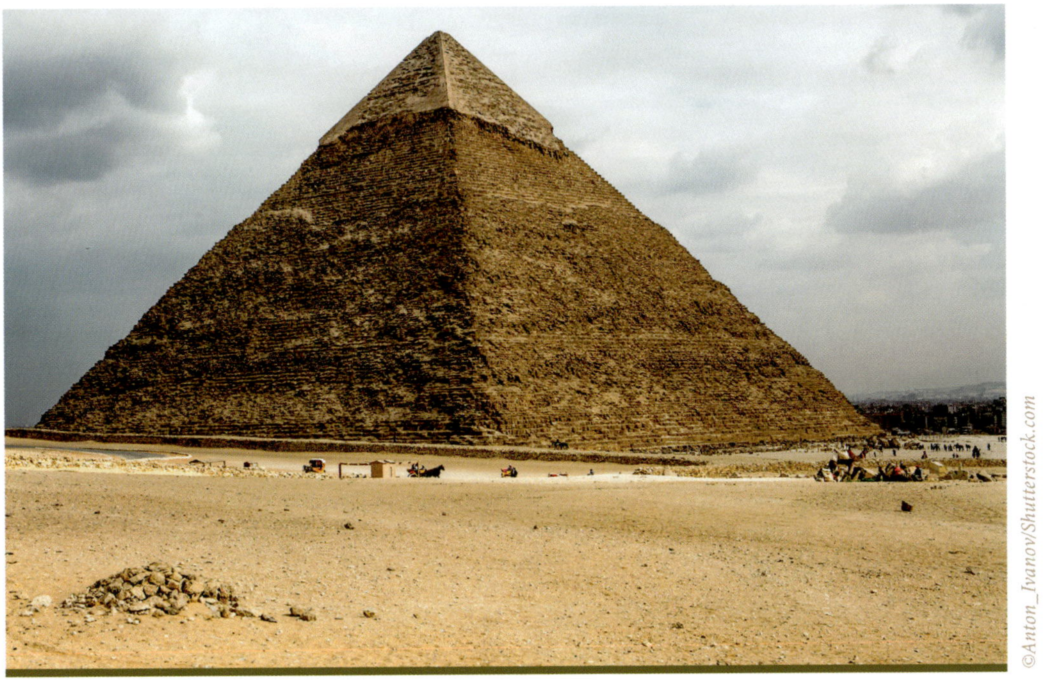

FIGURE 2.44 – Ruins of the Great Pyramids at the Giza Necropolis. Giza Plateau, Egypt. 2560 BC. 455 ft. high. Limestone.

HIEROGLYPHIC – an ancient form of writing utilizing pictures or symbols rather than letters. Most commonly associated with the Egyptian culture.

Inside the burial chamber, the walls were decorated with imagery associated with the life and achievements of the pharaoh buried inside. In addition, it was common to have imagery associated with their Judgment Day and entrance into the afterlife depicted. Judgment day consisted of two parts. The first was for the deceased to stand before a panel of deities who asked about the individual's life and deeds. If the deities believed the person, he/she was then led into the next phase of judgment. In the *Antique Egyptian Papyrus and Hieroglyph—Scale of Truth* (see Figure 2.45), this image details the second phase where the deceased is brought into in the Scale of Truth room. Here the heart of the deceased was placed on a scale against an ostrich feather, symbolic of Maat, the goddess of truth. If the scale remained balanced, the deceased was then escorted by Anubis into the afterlife to live as he/she did on earth.

However, if someone outwitted the deities during the initial phase, their heart would weigh heavily upon the scale tipping it downward. Nearby, Ahemait, a creature that was part lion, crocodile and hippopotamus, lay in wait to devour the heart of the deceitful. This was a devastating prospect to the Egyptians, who could not enter into the afterlife unless they had all aspects of their soul intact. In that case, they would simply cease to exist.

In Egyptian culture, the boat was the vehicle that took the deceased into the afterlife. In 1954, buried along the outer edge of the Great Pyramid, archaeologist Kamal eh-Mallakh (1918–1987) discovered a full-size boat. The boat was believed to have been made to transport Pharaoh Khufu (2620–2566 BC) into the afterlife. The 143-foot-long boat is made of wood and perfectly preserved due to the dry climate of the desert. In *Barge of the Sun on its Night Course* (see Figure 2.46), the deceased is being escorted to the afterlife by the gods Isis, Thoth, Ra and Hu. These gods are associated with creation, death and the afterlife.

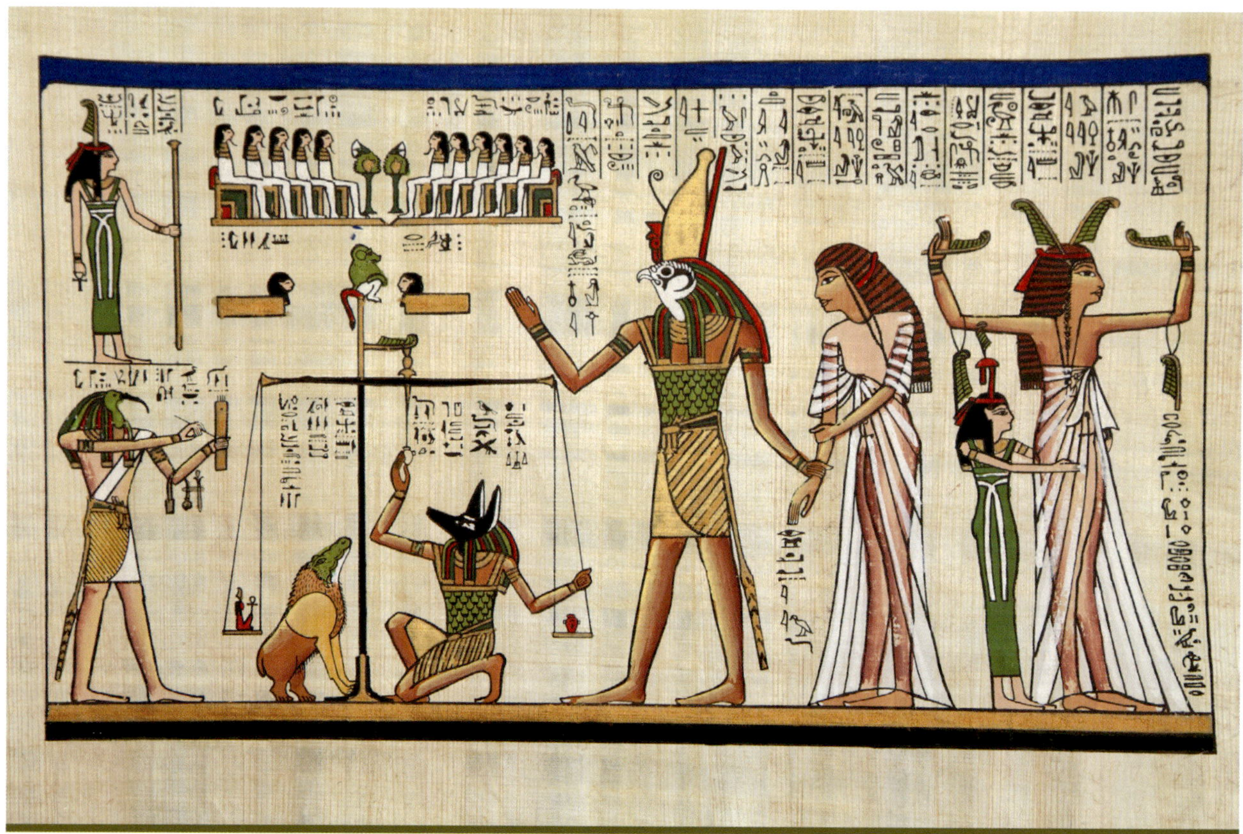

FIGURE 2.45 – Antique Egyptian Papyrus and Hieroglyph—Scale of Truth. A page from the Book of the Dead. Egypt. c. 1550 BC. Papyrus.

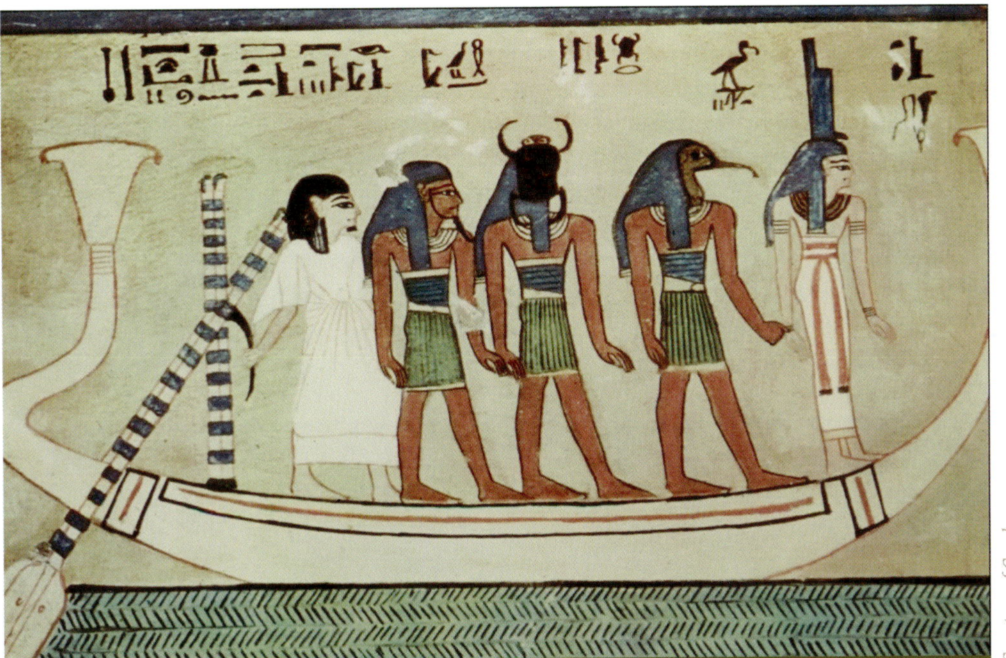
Courtesy of Corel

FIGURE 2.46 – Barge of the Sun on its Night Course Tomb of Anhurkhawi. Egypt. Mural.

Inside the burial chamber, as in a Viking burial, all of the amenities of one's life on earth, along with food and drink are buried with the deceased. However, the Egyptians placed tableaus of servants preparing food, washing clothing and more, rather than sacrificing real people. As seen in *Bread Preparation* (see Figure 2.47), there are several individuals performing various tasks of making bread.

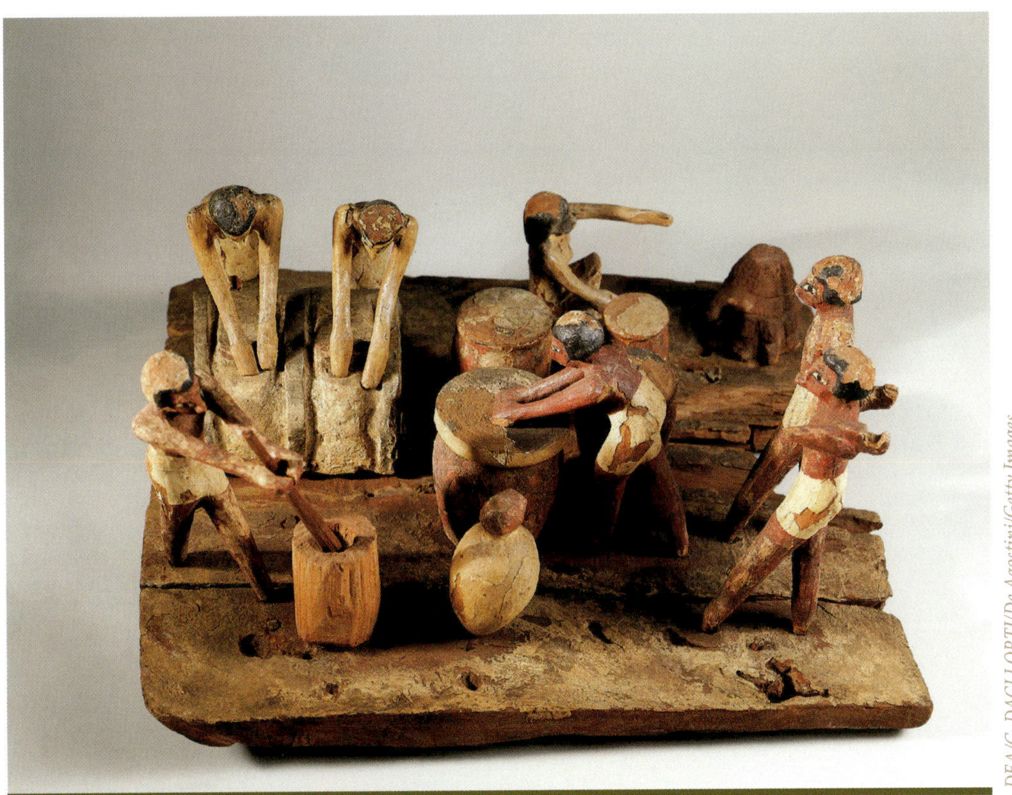
DEA/G. DAGLI ORTI/De Agostini/Getty Images

FIGURE 2.47 – Asyut, Bread Preparation. Egypt. Wooden model.

In Egyptian history, Hatshepsut (1507–1458 BC) is recognized as the first female pharaoh during the fifteenth century BC. Her father, Pharaoh Thutmose I who reigned until 1493 BC, married her to her step-brother at the age of fifteen. Upon her father's death, Hatshepsut's husband, Thutmose II succeeded him in 1493 BC. When her husband passed away fifteen years later, her stepson was the next in line to power, with her serving as his regent until he was old enough to take control. However, she thought twice about this situation and found an opportunity to change her fate. She had artwork created to show that her father had intended for her to succeed him in power. This visually communicated the message to the masses and secured her place of authority as pharaoh. Artistically she depicted herself with the traditional stylized male body of a ruler, along with the headdress, false beard, and kilt traditional of that rank. All of these moves artistically were to reinforce her abilities to rule as competently and successfully as any male counterpart before her. She had a very successful and peaceful reign for twenty years.

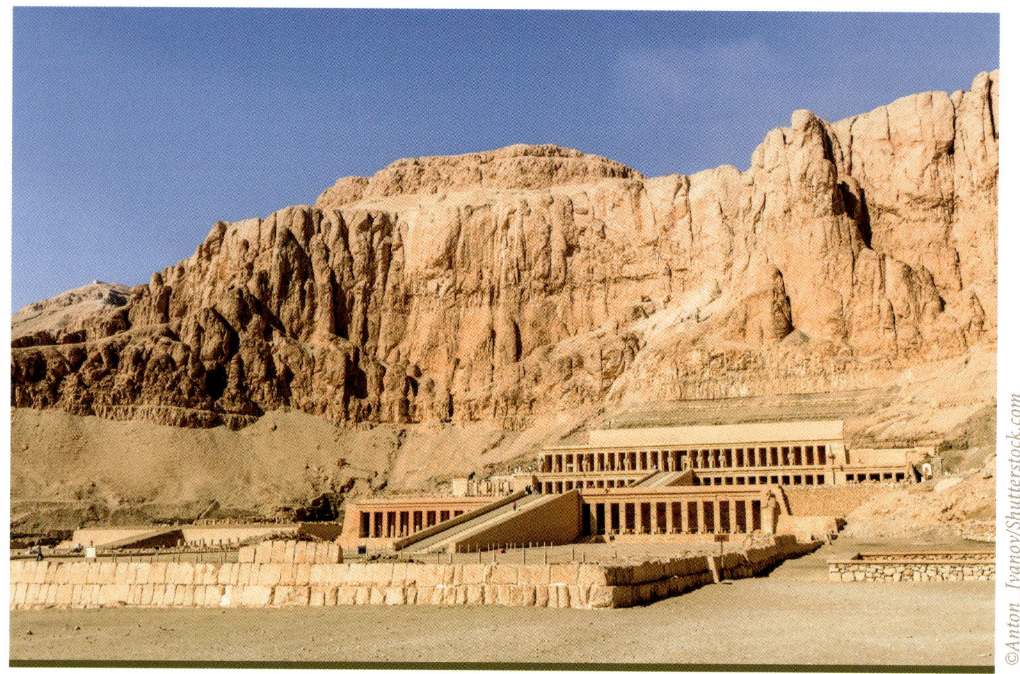

FIGURE 2.48 – The Mortuary Temple of Hatshepsut (Dayr el-Bahari). Egypt. c. 1470 BC.

During her lifetime, Hatshepsut saw the looting of the pyramids. In an attempt to protect her burial from such a fate, she altered the architecture and burial practices of the pharaohs from her reign onwards. Large-scale mortuary temples were created, like Hatshepsut's (see Figure 2.48), to provide a place for people to leave the deceased pharaoh offerings and to be used by the pharaoh's cult after death. While some distance away, she had her funerary complex and burial chamber constructed underground out of the sight of looters in what was named 'Valley of the Kings.' Over the centuries, this has become a massive underground complex of funerary architecture.

MAUSOLEUM – an above ground-tomb which is majestic or grand in manner

In India, the Taj Mahal is an exquisite mausoleum built to honor Mumtaz Mahal (1593–1631). She was the favorite wife of Shah Jahan (1592–1666), a Mughal ruler who reigned in India from 1628–1658 CE. The mausoleum took thirty-two years to build and was completed a few years after she died giving birth to her fourteenth child. This structure was built to show the Shah's love for her.

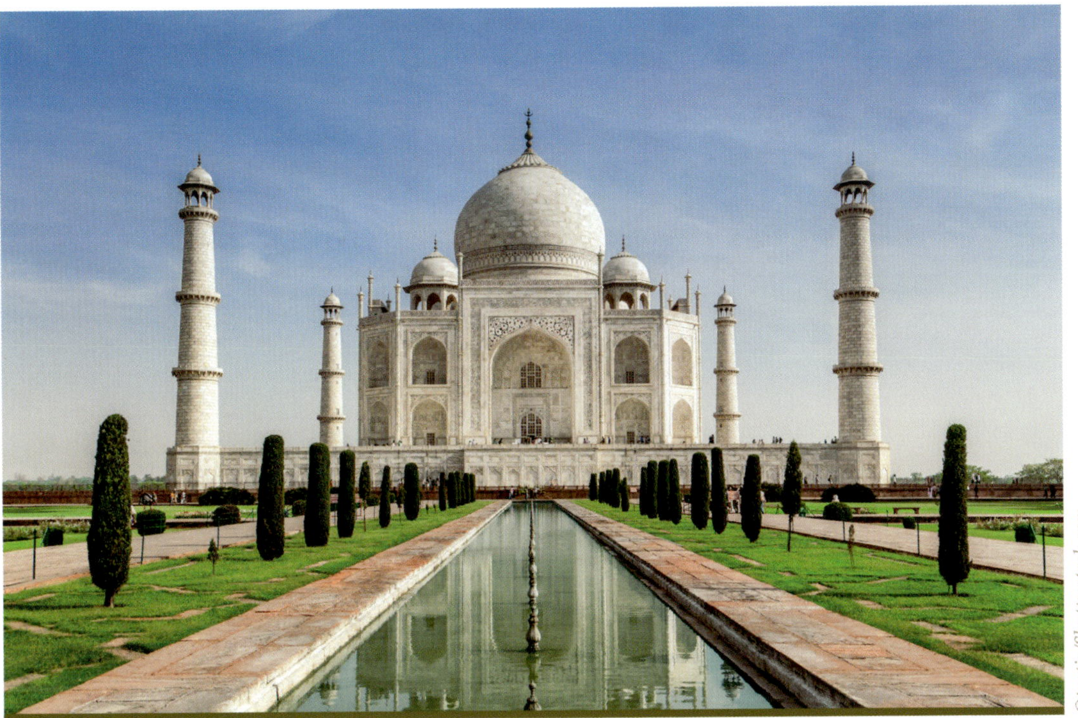

©turtix/Shutterstock.com

FIGURE 2.49 – Taj Mahal. Commissioned by Mughal emperor Shah Jahan. Agra, India. 1648. 240 ft. high. White marble inlaid with semi-precious stones.

SYMMETRICAL – creating visual balance through equal distribution of color, shape, line, and other formal elements throughout a composition.

The Taj Mahal is made out of white marble and sits in the center of thirty-five acres of gardens in Agra, India. It is completely symmetrical with a reflecting pool on each side that dissects the gardens into four equal quadrants. Everything about the Taj Mahal and its location is symbolic. The building represents the throne of Allah, the Islamic name for God, therefore not of this earth. The canals represent the four rivers in Paradise; the gardens the four gardens in Paradise.

Take a closer look at the Taj Mahal and the canal (see Figure 2.49) in front. The reflection of the structure, and the way that the canal seems to end just before it, creates a visual line and the illusion that the building is hovering just above the ground. While physically impossible, it reinforces that this is not just a man-made structure but something much more—like the throne of Allah. In addition, the white of the marble is highly reflective and changes in appearance with the varying colors of the sky from the bright yellows and oranges of the rising sun to the deeper oranges and pinks of the setting sun. This, too, creates the illusion that the building is not of this earth.

SARCOPHAGUS – a coffin made of stone, typically decorated with images or inscribed with words.

The Shah had begun to build his mausoleum on the opposite shore in black marble. He was exiled before his death and the structure was never completed. Once he died, he was placed inside the Taj Mahal alongside Mumtaz's sarcophagus, becoming the only asymmetrical component within the thirty-five acres and the Taj Mahal itself.

ASYMMETRICAL – creating visual imbalance by positioning more color, line, and other formal elements on one area of the composition.

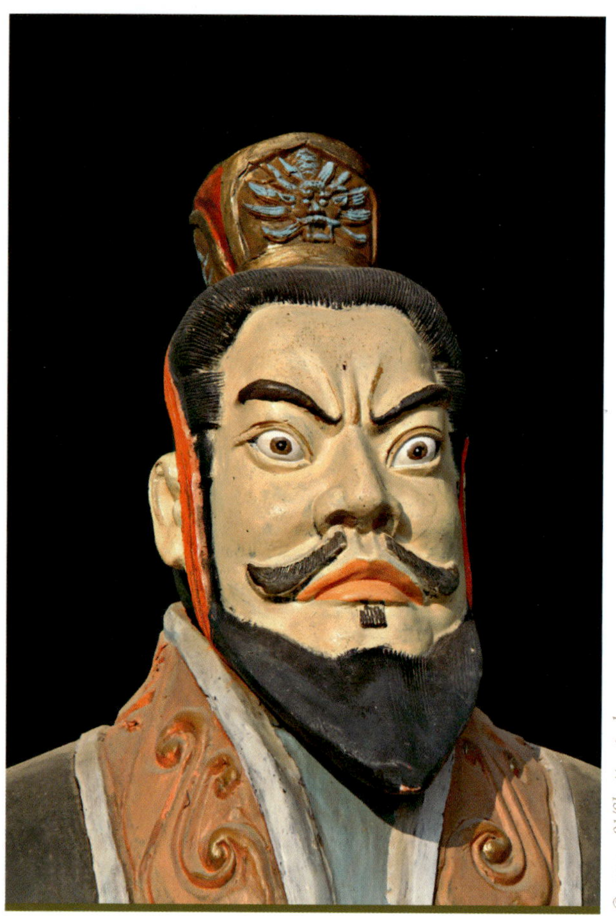

FIGURE 2.50 – Shi Huangdi, China's First Emperor (Qin Dynasty). China. Painted sculpture.

In contrast to the Etruscan and Egyptian funerary architecture, and even that of the Taj Mahal, the man who named himself China's First Emperor or *Shi Huangdi* (see Figure 2.50) went to far greater lengths to honor himself in death. Ying Zheng (260 – 210 BC) acceded the throne at the young age of thirteen, having a regent help govern until he began to exercise his sovereign authority at the age of twenty-two. By 221 BC, Zheng had ruthlessly conquered and unified all the states of China under his rule, establishing the Qin dynasty. Wanting to eradicate any history of what existed before his reign, Shi Huangdi had all historical records and books confiscated. After preserving a single copy of each book in the central Qin archives, all others were destroyed. Any historian who did not agree with him, or the changes that he made, was murdered to prevent any rebellion or return to the old ways.

While his destruction was great, Shi Huangdi had a positive impact upon China, as well. Roadways were built throughout China. While most likely to assist the military in their movements and control of the country, these roadways made it possible for not only the people of China, but traders, to move more freely throughout the lands. Measuring weights, currency, and script styles that were once unique to each state were now unified throughout all of China. This, in addition to unified laws and regulations, led to the substantial growth of society and its economy. The emperor is also responsible for the building of the Great Wall.

Upon taking the throne, Shi Huangdi immediately ordered the construction of his underground mausoleum to begin. He believed that his soul would rule the underground kingdom for an eternity and wanted everything from this life with him in death. Therefore, the funerary palace was to be as grand as that in which he currently resided. It took nearly thirty-seven years and over 700,000 people to complete its construction. This incredible mausoleum and its guards remained relatively untouched from the time of his burial in 210 BC. It wasn't until 1974 when two peasants digging a well came across some broken pottery that they assumed were from an ancient kiln. After deciding to continue to dig in that spot, they found pieces of ceramics in the shape of arms, legs, and heads another ten feet down. Realizing this was something of importance, they stopped their efforts and archaeologists were called in to begin excavating the site. To the present day, over 8,000 terracotta soldiers have been unearthed.

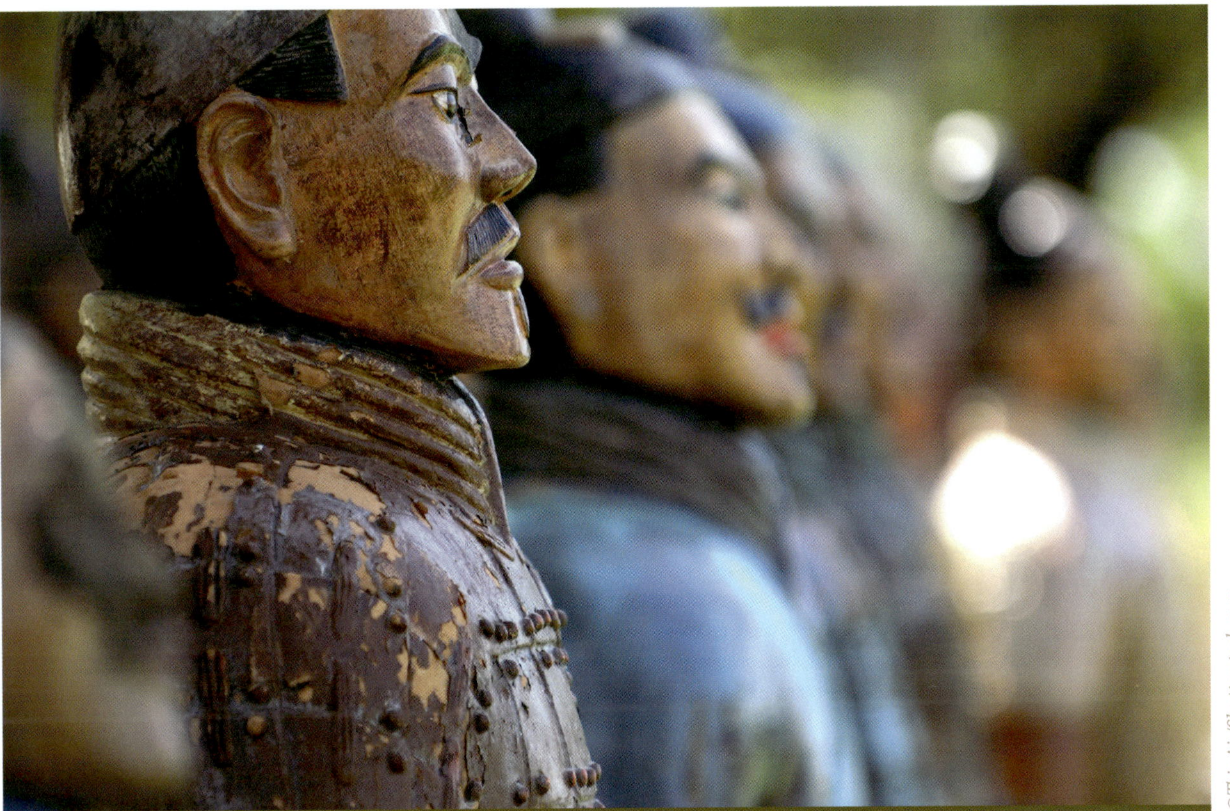

©ThinAir/Shutterstock.com

FIGURE 2.51 – Army of Terracotta Warriors. China. c. 246–208 BC. Approximately 6 ft. high. Ceramic.

KILN – a type of furnace or oven used to bake, dry, or harden various materials, such as clay and brick.

Extensive study, documentation, and analysis have led to the discovery that a complete army was created to guard the emperor throughout eternity. Speaking to Shi Huangdi's ego, this army was not a simple representation of an army, but rather contained thousands of individuals who were to guard him. While the mass production of the body parts was essential in completing the quantity of soldiers needed, after they were pieced together and before they were put into a kiln, each face was carved to represent a unique individual. No two faces are identical. Further development of technology has also led to the discovery that even body parts like the earlobe or nose that might be easy to reproduce in a similar way to quicken the process or out of habit, were also individualized. The rank of each soldier was clearly communicated through the design of their uniform, the weapon(s) they bore, and even the style of their hair. In addition, traces of mineral pigments survived on some pieces of the soldiers suggesting that they were once brightly colored (see Figure 2.51). Real weapons, like crossbows, spears and swords were placed with them and found to still be functioning and effective after centuries of being buried under the earth. Life-size chariots and horses (see Figure 2.52) made of clay were also buried along with the army, since they were an important part of military tactics. The emperor's fondness of hunting in life led to rare birds and animals being buried in a separate pit that was part of the massive underground construction.

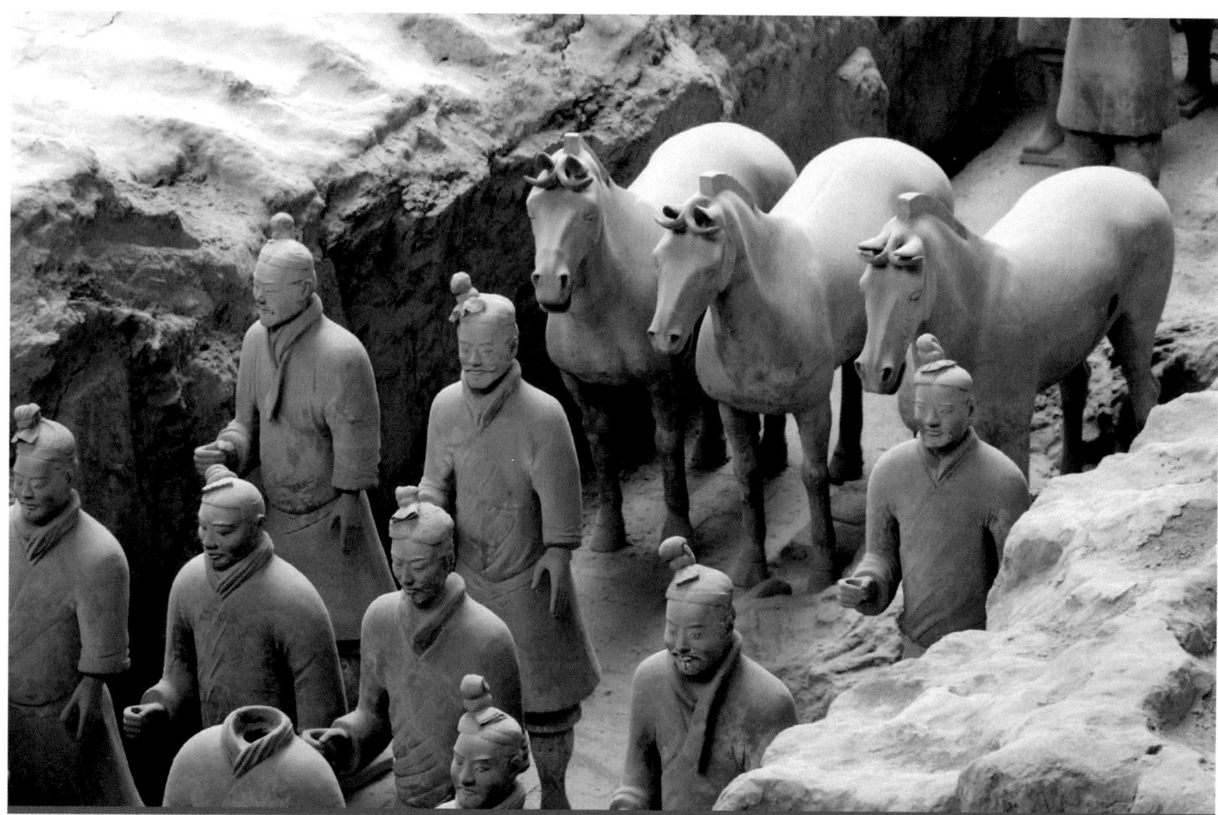

©Ke Wang/Shutterstock.com

FIGURE 2.52 – Terracotta Warriors and Horses. China. c. 246–208 BC. Ceramic.

TERRACOTTA – a type of low-fired clay that is brownish-orange in color.

To this day, the funerary palace has not been completely excavated. Written records describing its layout, suggest that there are rivers of mercury throughout to mimic the bodies of water on earth. Recent testing has indicated high levels of mercury near the location of the palace. Due to its toxic nature, the excavation of the tomb will have to be painstakingly slow and carefully monitored to prevent any contamination to the environment.

CONTEMPORARY MEMORIALS

While large-scale memorials for individual people are being created even today, another tradition is for memorials to be created for the demise of large numbers of individuals from wars and other significant events. These memorials can vary in form and scale from a single monument, to a museum, to a small installation or temporary exhibition displayed for a short period of time.

INSTALLATION ART – a form of art created for a specific location, sometimes incorporating materials or physical aspects of the site. or site.

Christian Boltanski (1944–) is a French artist, painter, sculptor, and filmmaker. Through his art, he explores aspects of life, death, and memory. Though not a religious person, Boltanski is interested in its aspects, and feels that art should be about some kind of moral. Through this exploration, his artwork has often addressed universal subjects such as life and death, guilt or innocence, and various moral problems humans face.

EXHIBITION – a public showing of a body of artwork within a space, such as a gallery or museum.

Although Boltanski tries to leave his work open-ended so the viewer can take something more individual or personal away from it, he feels his work has increasingly become more about the Holocaust. While it is a serious part of history and important to him, it also remains an example of something all humans face—death.

Christian Boltanski came across a 1931 class photograph from a Jewish school in Vienna, Austria. While he is unsure if those in the photograph are still alive or even victims, he finds it emotionally easier to use this image than the ones specifically from the Holocaust. For *Autel Chases* (see Figure 2.53), he re-photographed the small image and enlarged certain faces from it. In doing so, they appear grainy and the identity of the individual is hard to distinguish. This can be seen as a means for the viewer to project their own ancestors or the memories of them into the piece for a more personal connection to the work. Beneath the photographs are a series of tins, filled with a variety of objects. The viewer is left to ponder what the objects and the significance of them might be—to the people depicted in *Autel Chases* or to the artist himself.

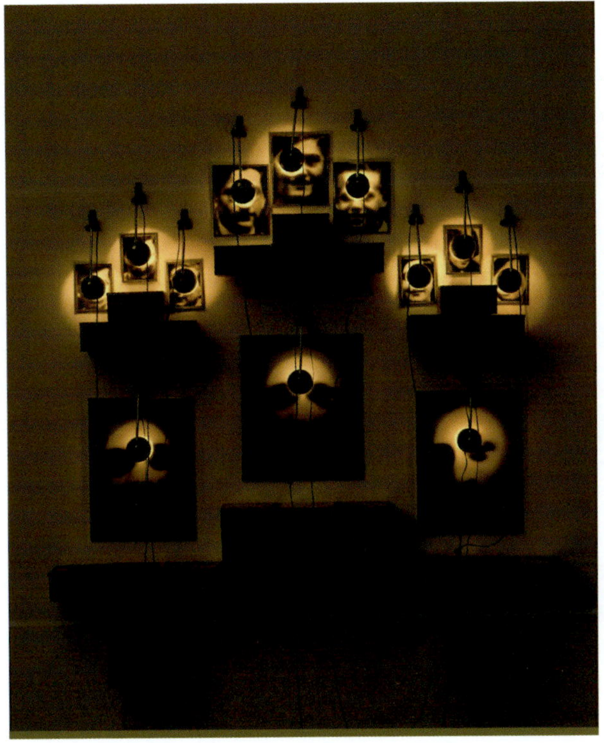

Autel Chases, 1987 (biscuit tins, 12 black & white photos, 12 lamps, cable), Boltanski, Christian (b.1944) / Hamburger Kunsthalle, Hamburg, Germany / Bridgeman Images

FIGURE 2.53 – Autel Chases (Altar to Chases High School), Christian Boltanski. 1987. 250 x 207 x 22 cm. Biscuit tins, 12 black & white photos, 12 lamps, cable.

Another piece more directly tied to the victims of the Holocaust is *Stumbling Stones* by German artist, Gunter Demnig (1947–). He feels that memorials in the form of large monuments and museums remain in the abstract. A person must decide to visit these locations. And may never get there as intended, due to daily life and the distractions it creates. In *Stumbling Stones*, a person literally stumbles upon these small memorials.

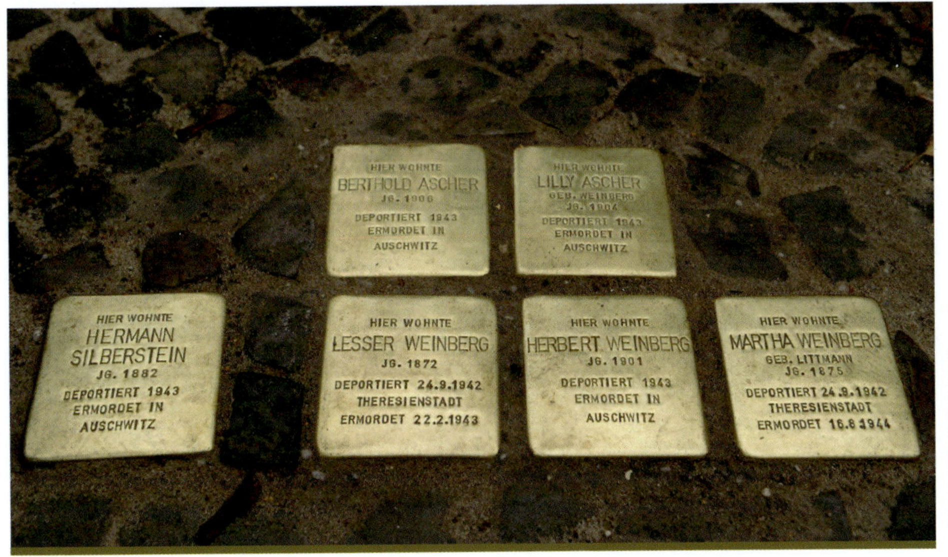

AXEL SCHMIDT/DDP/Getty Images

FIGURE 2.54 – A Cluster of Six 'Stolpersteine' or Stumbling Stones, Gunter Demnig. Berlin, Germany. 1992–present. 3.9 x 3.9 in (each). Inscribed brass plates.

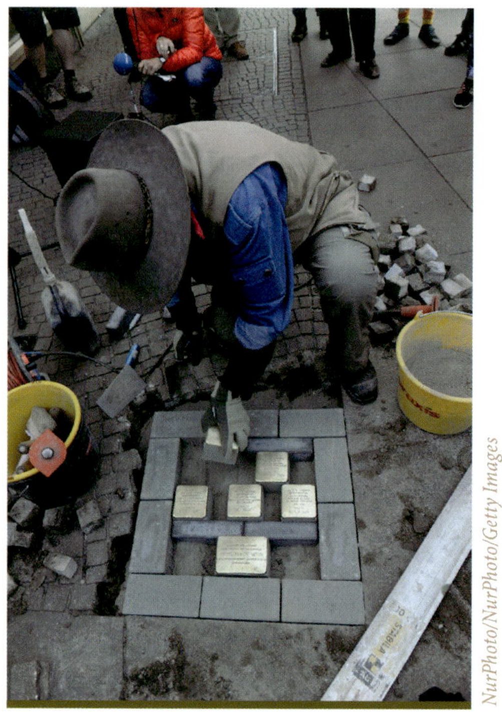

NurPhoto/NurPhoto/Getty Images

FIGURE 2.55 – Stumbling Stones in Berlin, Gunter Demnig. Berlin, Germany.

The idea behind the piece is to create a small brass cobblestone (see Figure 2.54) with the victim's name, date, and details of their death engraved in its surface. The artist is provided this information by the victim's family. Demnig digs up the sidewalk in front of the deceased's former home and secures the stone into the ground with concrete (see Figure 2.55). There are over 30,000 of these throughout Germany and other European countries. As one is walking around, the glint of light bouncing off the brass might catch their eye, causing them to stop and investigate. They are 'stumbling' upon the memorial first in a physical way and then hopefully in an emotional way, as they bring the memory or voice of the Holocaust victim to life by reading the information on the stone. The viewer is standing where the victim once lived, remembering them in this more intimate way. The artist feels a large-scale memorial cannot do this.

Gunter Demnig typically installs these stones without fanfare. However, based on the location of some sites being in areas where sympathizers of the Nazi Germans still live today, police insist on escorting him into those sites during installation. The artist says he will continue the memorial for as long as he physically can. The project continues on today through private funding and depends heavily upon locals and school children who want to assist by doing the research for him.

As with many works of art and memorials throughout the ages, there is controversy surrounding *Stumbling Stones*. Some feel that the dead are being victimized again as people, animals, and bikes are trampling over the stones each day. While others, who suddenly find the stones in front of their homes or businesses (see Figure 2.56), argue that the negative associations of the Holocaust lead these small monuments to devalue their property.

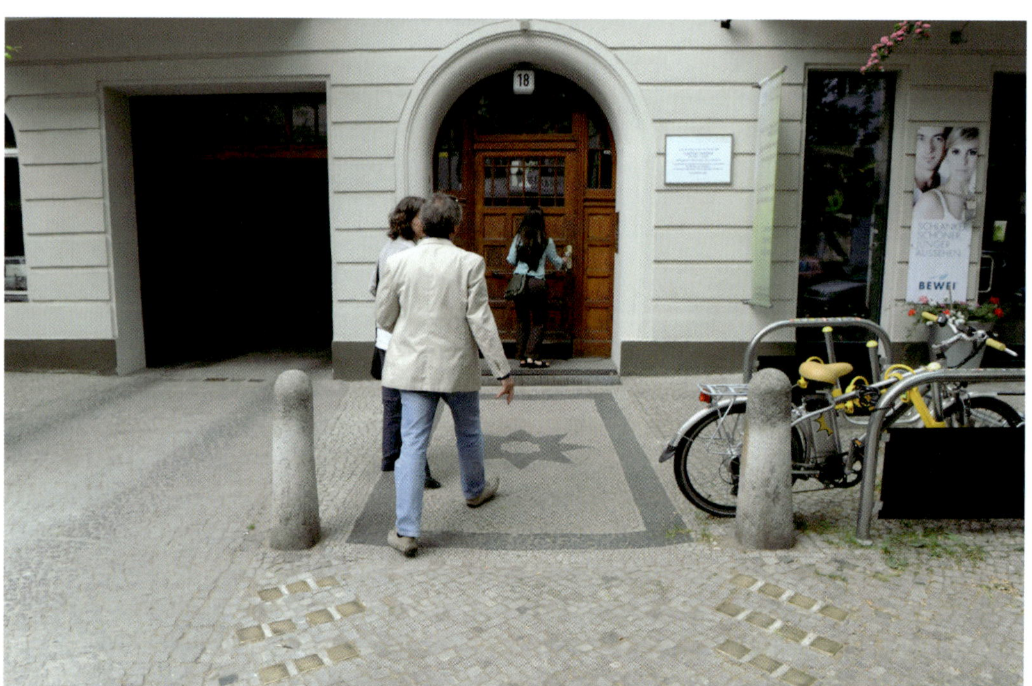

ullstein bild/Getty Images

FIGURE 2.56 – Brass Stolpersteine (Stumbling Stones), Gunter Demnig. Berlin, Germany.

Maya Lin (1959–), a 21-year-old architecture student at Yale University in 1980, completed an assignment for a funeral architecture seminar. She had designed a wall monument for the Vietnam veterans who lost their lives during the war. Inspired by the university's Memorial Rotunda, where the names of alumni who died in service of their country were engraved in its marble walls, she incorporated this element into her design. "I think it left a lasting impression on me," Lin wrote, "the sense of the power of a name."

At the encouragement of her professor, Maya Lin entered the design into the national design competition for the Vietnam Veterans Memorial, which was to be built on the National Mall in Washington, D.C. There were a total of 1400 designs submitted. Following the rules of the competition for the memorial to be apolitical and contain the names of the confirmed dead and missing in action, she listed 58,000 American servicemen's names in chronological order of their loss. The overall design was a black granite wall (see Figure 2.57), laid out in a V-shape, partially sunken into the ground. It stands eight inches at either end, and rises to ten feet at its center.

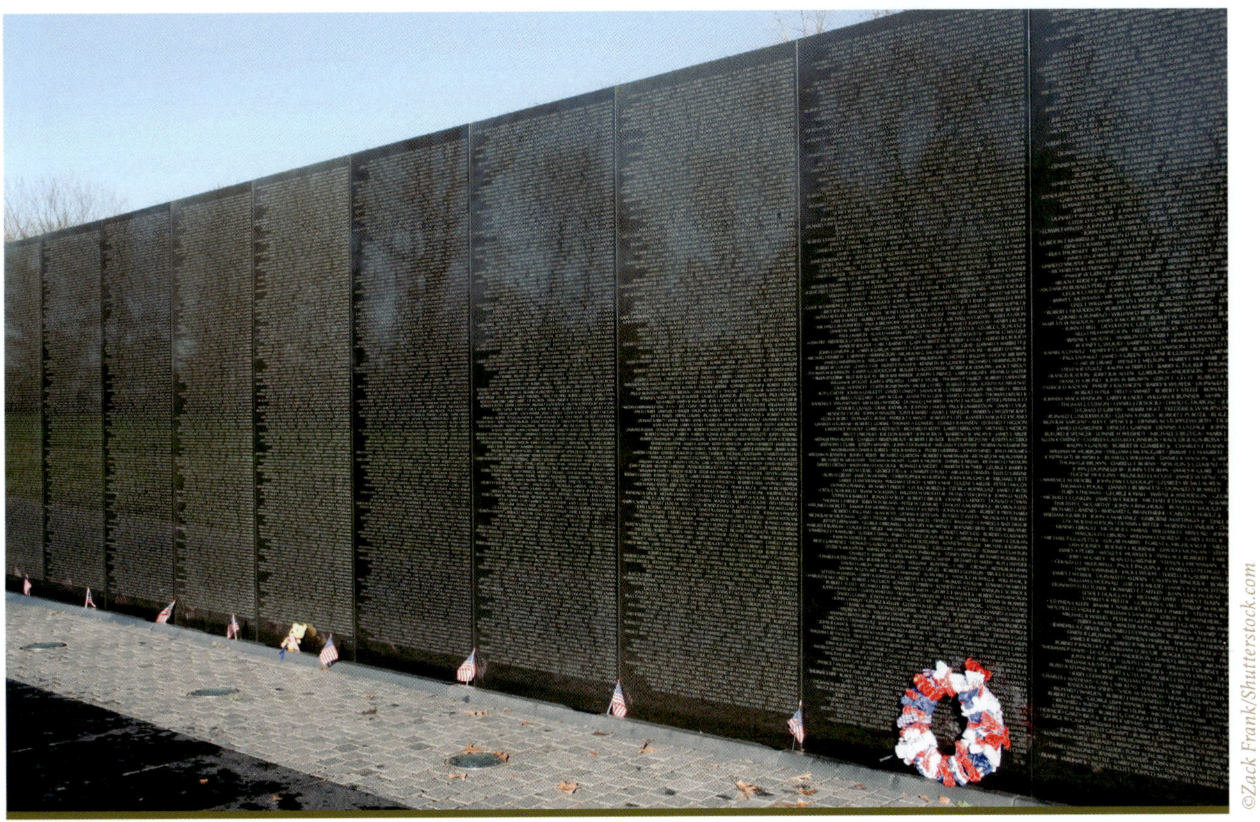

FIGURE 2.57 – Vietnam Veterans Memorial and reflection, Maya Lin. Washington, DC. 1982. 493 x 10 ft. Black granite.

Although Maya Lin adhered to the competition rules, the design outraged many American veterans who felt it lacked patriotic symbols and did not honor the living soldiers along with the dead. Many thought the use of black conveyed the idea of shame and sorrow associated with the war. The overall V-shape of its design was thought to represent the two-fingered peace sign often used by protestors against the war, turning the monument into a subliminal anti-war symbol. Bowing to the pressures of the critics of Lin's design, the Secretary of the Interior at the time, James Watt, approved the addition of a 50-foot-high flagpole on which to place the American flag and a large-scale sculpture depicting three soldiers, created by American sculptor, Frederick Hart (1943–1999), to be added nearby.

Upon its unveiling to the public in November of 1982, the controversy surrounding the monument quickly subsided. It has since become a pilgrimage site for all connected to the Vietnam War, providing a place for healing and remembrance. The reflective quality of the granite brings together the past and the present—the ancestor and the living—through the reflection of the person standing before it (see Figure 2.58).

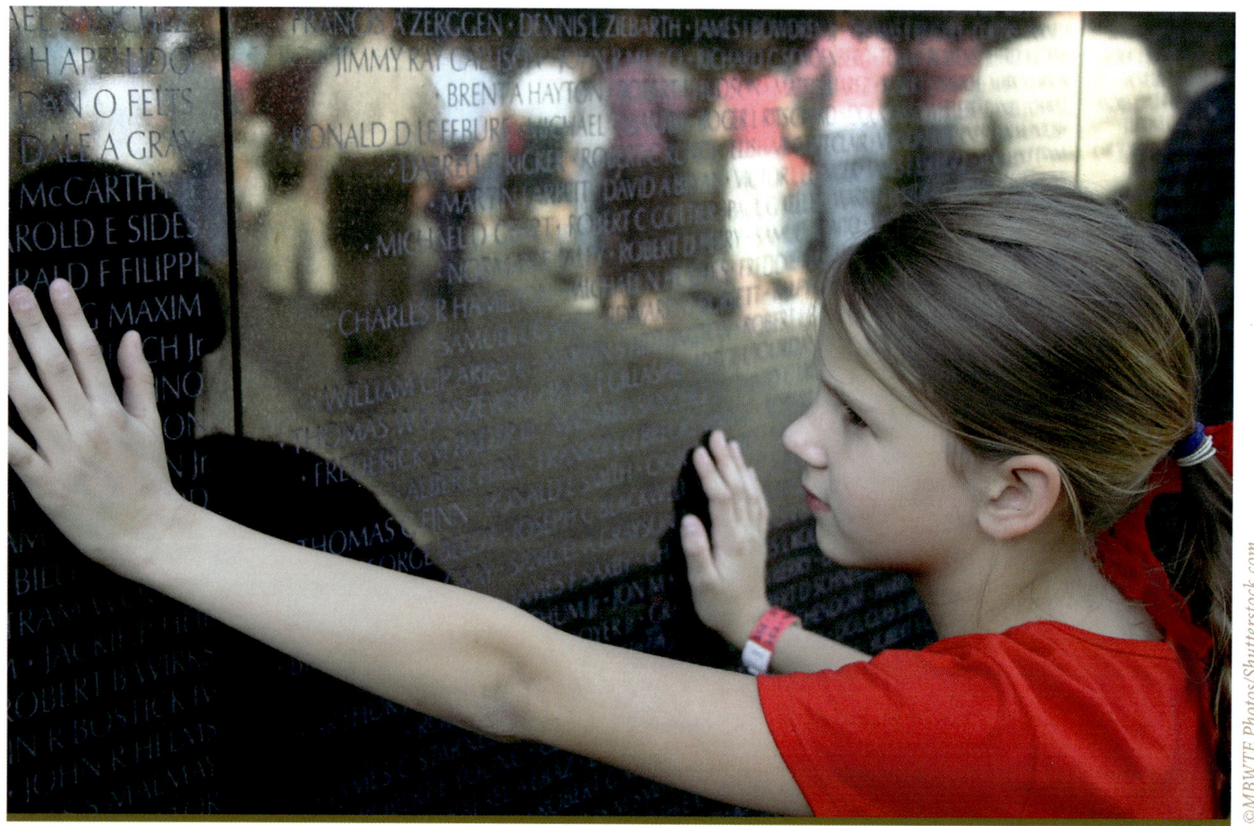

FIGURE 2.58 – Child Viewing the Vietnam Memorial Wall. Washington, DC.

part 3

POLITICAL AND SOCIAL ART

Political and social concerns have plagued humans since the development of large-scale societies. Artists find themselves compelled to create works addressing such issues to educate or incite the masses.

POLITICAL ART

Élisabeth Vigée-Lebrun (1755–1842) was a French painter who became very well-known for her portraits of royalty. Her ability to capture a flattering and elegant depiction of those that she painted caught the eye of many important people, including Marie Antoinette (1755–1793).

Antoinette's husband, King Louis XVI of France, seemed to be heavily influenced by her. She had a penchant for the luxuries of royalty, often at the expense of the French people. She was often blamed for the fall of the economy and other events that led to the start of the French Revolution (1789–1799). In 1779, Marie Antoinette commissioned the first of thirty portraits to be painted by Vigée-Lebrun. Soon after, the artist became her official painter for approximately a decade. In *Portrait of Marie Antoinette* (see Figure 2.59), Vigée-Lebrun depicts the Queen in extravagant clothing befitting royalty. Because of the public's negative view of Antoinette, she had the artist paint a family portrait of her with her children. *Marie Antoinette with Her Children* (1786) shows a loving mother, with her children surrounding and clinging to her. On the right, her son, Louis Joseph, is seen with his hand on a bassinette that represents the loss of Antoinette's youngest child. This image was to elicit sympathy towards the Queen and hopefully a change in attitude towards her, as well.

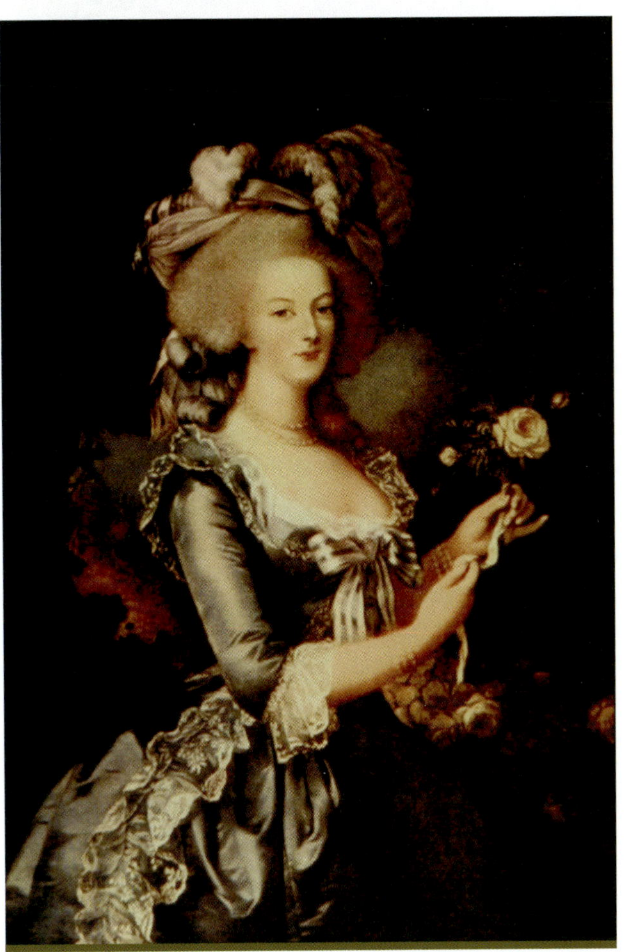

Courtesy of Corel

FIGURE 2.59 – Portrait of Marie Antonietta. Élisabeth Vigée-LeBrun. c. 1783. Oil paint.

Diego Rivera (1886–1957) was a twentieth century Mexican muralist. During several points between 1907 and 1920, Rivera studied the various European artistic traditions. He came into contact with artists like Picasso, who had some influence on his style. While in Italy, Rivera studied fresco painting techniques more intently before starting mural works in Mexico in the 1920s. The culmination of his studies led to a unique approach and choice of subject matter. The artist used this unique approach to communicate to the Mexican people various aspects of their history and the socio-political issues of the present day. While many of the people were illiterate at the time, Rivera saw the power of murals as a communication tool to educate. One of the many focuses of his work was the history of his country and the people who had impacted Mexican culture and way of life, whether positively or negatively.

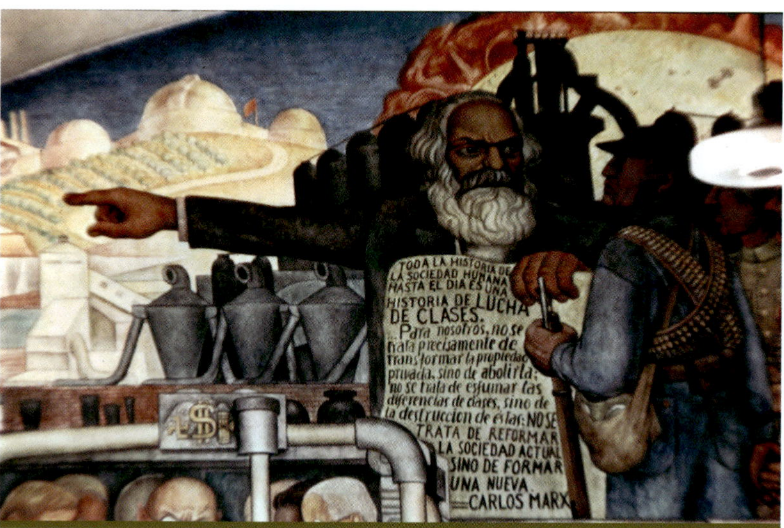

FIGURE 2.60 – Marx Talking to Latin American Peoples, Diego Rivera, Mural at Palacio Nacional de Mexico, 1935. Fresco mural.

Marx Talking to Latin American Peoples (see Figure 2.60) is part of a large-scale mural called *Class Struggles* painted in Palaciao Nacional de Mexico in 1935. While the entire mural addresses the lack of reform in spite of the 1910–1920 Mexican Revolution, this section depicts Karl Marx (1818–1883), a philosopher and socialist responsible for publishing anti-capitalist literature, such as the *Communist Manifesto*. He is holding a copy of the manifesto in his left hand. To Marx's right, Rivera painted workers who have gathered to listen to Marx. Painted just below him are the perceived villains—corrupt military, clergy, and capitalists—attempting to prevent free speech from occurring.

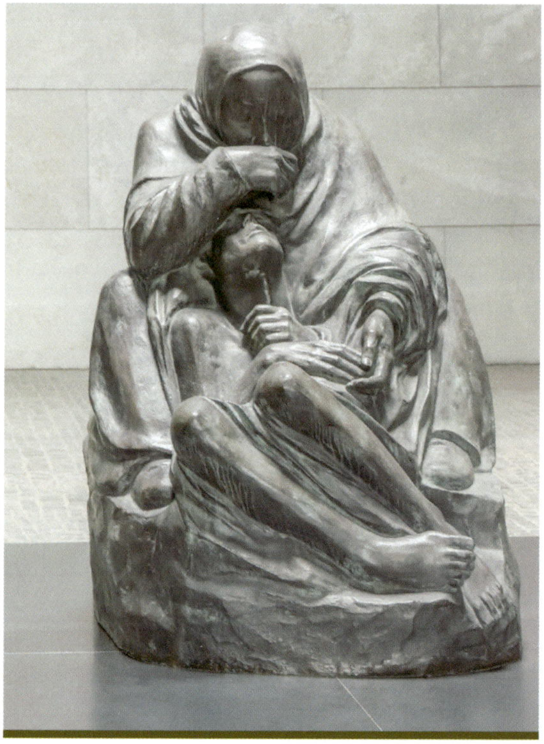

FIGURE 2.61 – Mother and Her Dead Son (Pieta), Käthe Kollwitz, c. 1914, Cast bronze.

Käthe Schmidt Kollwitz (1867–1945) was a German artist who became very well known for addressing important social and political issues of her time, many of which continue to plague the world. She was born into a middle-class family that was politically progressive. At the time, women were barred from government-run art schools and had to attend academies established just for them in order to pursue their artistic ambitions. With the support of her family, Kollwitz studied at the Women's Art School in Munich. During her time there, she was heavily influenced by a fellow German artist and printmaker named Max Klinger (1857–1920). By the 1890s, her focus on painting would switch primarily to printmaking as her main form of expression. Upon graduating in 1891 from the Women's Art School, she returned to Berlin to marry fiancé, Karl Kollowitz. Karl Kollowitz was a physician who opened a clinic for the working-class of Berlin. His patients became the artist's first real introduction to the miserable conditions and suffering of the urban poor, ultimately leading to her lifelong artistic focus on social and political issues.

In 1928, Käthe Kollwitz was the first woman elected a member of the Prussian Academy of the Arts, where she was head of the Master of Studio Arts for Graphic Arts. Her time at the Academy was cut short with the Nazis' rise to power in 1933. Kollwitz's work was deemed 'degenerate' by the Nazis. She lost her position and standing at the academy and in society as a result. Within a decade, most of her work was destroyed when her home and studio were bombed during an allied invasion.

Käthe Kollwitz was witness to the Russian Revolution (1917), the German Revolution (1918) and both the World Wars. The loss and suffering of human life was great, leaving an indelible mark upon her. *Mother and Her Dead Son* (see Figure 2.61) was cast in bronze c. 1914. She created this as a memorial for the many victims of war and tyranny. While this piece is universal, it speaks about her personal pain and loss of her own son, Hans, during World War I (1914–1918) and of her grandson, Peter, during World War II (1939–1945). The pain ran deeply throughout the remainder of her life. This piece is also reflective of Michelangelo's *Pieta* (1489). There are distinct similarities in the sculptures between the mothers holding their dead sons. Both mothers are cloaked in heavy garments, while their sons lay lifeless and exposed in their laps. Each son is depicted as a mature adult, appearing too large for his mother to hold. Yet they bear the weight of their dead sons, who each appear to be holding onto their mothers in some way.

Saad Ghosn (1951–), a native from Lebanon, has resided in the United States since 1976. He has spent many years working as a medical professional and educator. Recently retired, Ghosn has now had the opportunity to focus more attention on his various artistic pursuits. He believes that 'activism is at the heart of art expression' and uses his art to express his social and political views. Ghosn supports and provides multiple venues for other artists to voice their views through art and writing.

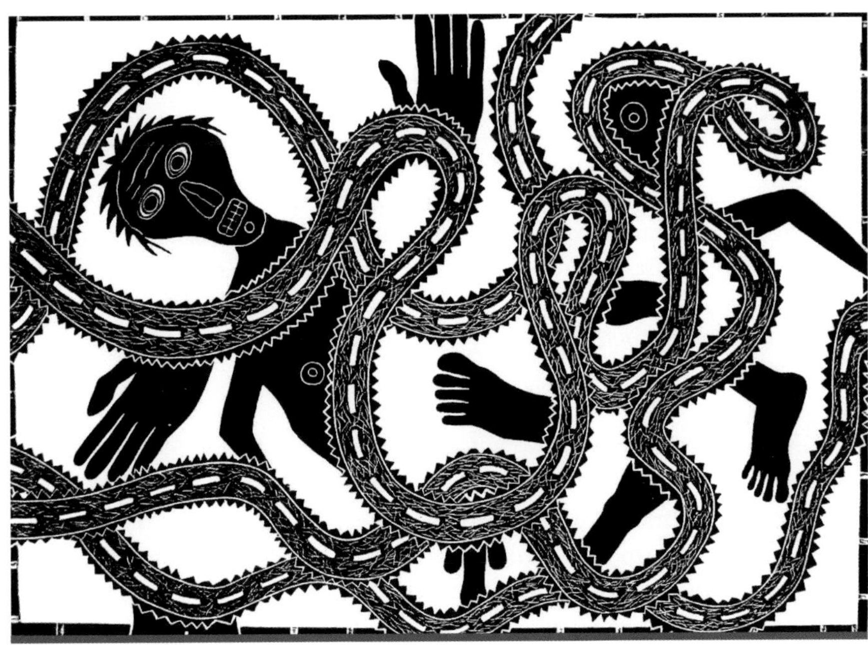

FIGURE 2.62 – The Road to Peace, Saad Ghosn. 2008. 30 x 22 in. Woodcut on Rives BFK paper.

In *The Road to Peace* (see Figure 2.62), Ghosn expresses his concerns that when peace is unjustly imposed there will be severe human consequences. He says, "To impose 'peace' not founded on justice cannot but perpetuate a convoluted situation conflicting with the essence of human beings, denigrating their rights, contributing to their suffering, and basically to their violent 'dismembering.' A just and transparent peace, on the contrary, can be straightforward, stable, and conducive to harmony; it is, however, often opposed by the powerful and strong, unwilling to give up some of their privileges."

Saad Ghosn is visually communicating this idea by filling the page with a spikey, convoluted road seeming to have no sense of direction. To convey the seriousness of the suffering and damage that can be caused by this path to peace, he uses a dismembered body, scattered about and trapped by the road. When looking more closely at the figure's face, its skull-like appearance can be seen to address the ultimate impact—death—of misguided actions.

Matt Reed (1975–) is an American artist and educator. His illustrations have appeared in various magazines, comic books and music album covers. Reed has strong political views that are sometimes addressed within his work.

Election Day (see Figure 2.63) addresses Reed's frustrations with the democratic process. In particular, he feels the two-party system does not provide candidates that represent all members of the public or their views, leaving many voters to choose between the 'lesser of two evils.' The image depicts a man standing in a voting booth, while the world around him seems to be falling into a state of chaos and destruction. The large, venomous snakes towering over the man on either side represent the two political parties in America—Democratic and Republican.

About this piece, Reed says, "...as the world falls apart around him, the voter has to choose between two equally poor candidates represented by the two snakes. (Snakes being a frequent symbol of evil in Western culture due to the Biblical allusion.) The work is meant to call to mind the cliché phrase, 'choosing between the lesser of two evils,' which comes up during every election cycle."

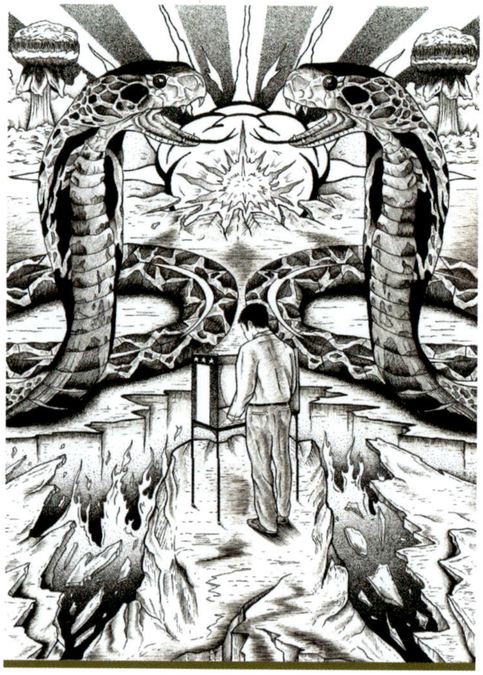

FIGURE 2.63 – Election Day, Matt Reed. 2008. 22 x 18 in. Pen and ink.

SOCIAL ART

In the mid-1800s in Germany, industrialization led to the creation of new jobs that impacted the cottage industries, like linen weavers. These weavers worked on looms in their homes, but quickly discovered they could not keep up with the output of the new mechanical devices. Many families now found themselves poverty-stricken and unable to take care of themselves or their families. Some families packed up and left their homes, while others stayed to rebel against their former employers. The weavers were defeated in the end, violently oppressed, and victimized.

WEAVING – interlocking of threads or fibers to create cloth or an artwork, often using a loom.

Käthe Kollwitz's time with fellow artist Max Klinger showed her that printmaking could be a powerful vehicle for social commentary. In addition, printing allowed for multiples of a single image to be reproduced inexpensively, allowing the artist to reach more people. In 1893, she began to work on a series of six images called *A Weaver's Revolt*, bringing national attention to their situation. These works were created by using the etching and lithography processes.

Misery (see Figure 2.64) is the first image in the series where Käthe Kollwitz addresses the severity of the situation. The mother is clad in black and seen hunched over, clutching her head in despair as she sits before her starving child. The severe malnutrition of the child is communicated through the skin stretched so tightly against the skull. Its body is so small that it is swallowed up by the bed and its coverings. In the background, the father and another sibling sit helplessly looking upon the dying child. The family's loom consumes most of the interior space, perhaps suggesting how reliant on weaving they were for survival.

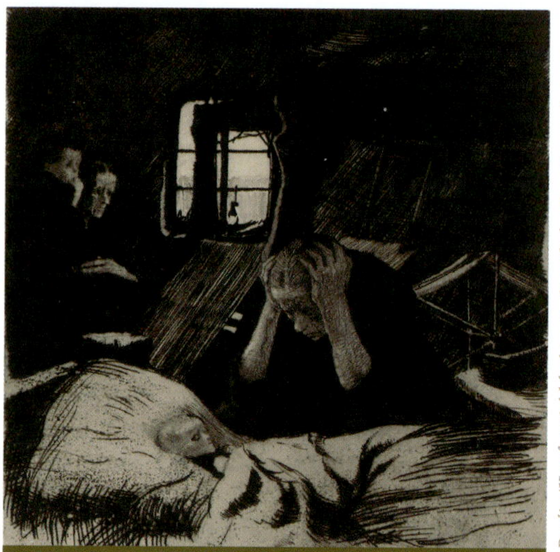

FIGURE 2.64 – Misery (Need), Käthe Kollwitz. 1895–1896. 28 x 22 cm. Aquatint.

Swedish artist, Carl Fredrik Reuterswärd (1934–2016) began his artistic career at the age of fourteen. He studied art in Paris under a well-known painter named Fernand Léger, and later at the Art Academy of Stockholm. During his education, he experimented with new ways and modes of creative expression. This served him well after a stroke left his dominant hand impaired and he had to rely upon his other hand to draw and write. From 1965–1969, Reuterswärd was a professor of painting at the Art Academy of Stockholm.

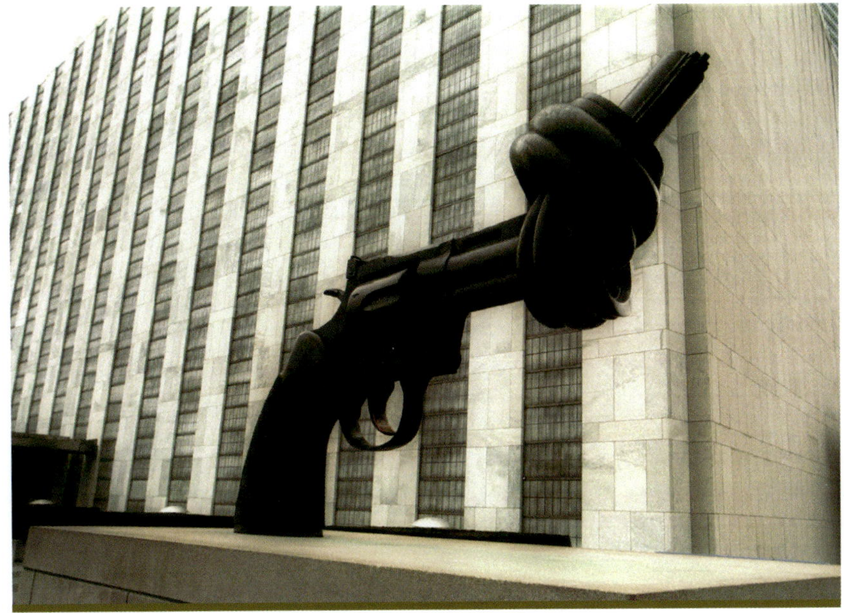
Ulrich Baumgarten/Getty Images

FIGURE 2.65 – Non-Violence, Carl Fredrik Reuterswärd. New York, USA. 1985. Bronze.

In 1980, former Beatles singer/songwriter and political activist, John Lennon, was shot to death by a fan. At the time, Lennon had been a very vocal and public advocate for non-violence and peace. When Carl Reuterswärd learned of his friend's senseless death, he was so overtaken by it and all of the unnecessary violence that plagued society that he immediately channeled those emotions into art. The image of a knotted barrel of a gun was the first to enter his mind. The end result is *Non-Violence* (see Figure 2.65). It shows a revolver cocked and ready to fire. Yet, the barrel is twisted and facing upward rather than in a straight trajectory. Because a bullet cannot leave the barrel, the piece perhaps implies that violence has been narrowly averted.

The sculpture was first installed in Central Park across from where Lennon and his wife, Yoko Ono, lived. Later in 1988, it was donated by the Luxembourg Government to the United Nations. It now resides outside the UN Headquarters in New York City. Over thirty replicas can now be found in various countries around the world. *Non-Violence* has grown to become a powerful symbol for peace.

STENCIL – a sheet of plastic, wood, or other material in which a design and/or lettering has been cut out. Ink or paint can be applied to the surface of the sheet or through the open areas to transfer an image onto another surface, like cloth or a building's wall.

Banksy is an English graffiti artist who primarily uses stencils and spray paint to create his works of art. At the age of eighteen, he was freehand spray painting a train car with some friends, when the British Transport Police showed up to run them off. His friends made it back to the car, while he hid under a dump truck for over an hour before he was in the clear. During this time, he realized he needed to shorten his painting time dramatically or give it up altogether. His eye eventually caught sight of a stenciled plate on the bottom of the truck, sparking the idea for a new technique. He once explained to a friend, "As soon as I cut my first stencil I could feel the power there. I also like the political edge. All graffiti is low-level dissent, but stencils have an extra history. They've been used to start revolutions and to stop wars." The stencils are created in his studio and then can be easily transported to a location that he wants to put the image.

Outside an English pub called Prince Albert, Banksy tagged one of its walls with the image of two London policemen kissing in a passionate embrace. Because society often labels and portrays gay men as being less masculine then straight men, the artist specifically chose to use policemen as the figures within the image.

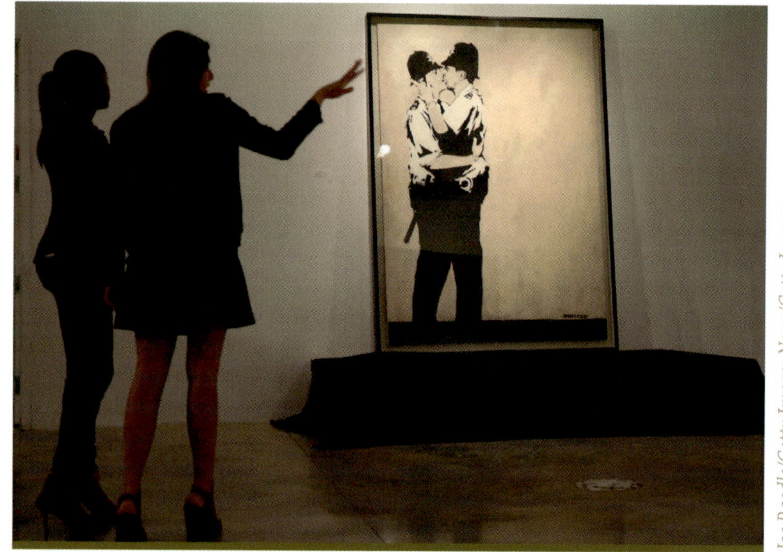

Joe Raedle/Getty Images News/Getty Images

FIGURE 2.66 – Banksy Wall Painted in New York (Gay Cops Kissing), Banksy. 2004. Life-size. Stencil and spray paint.

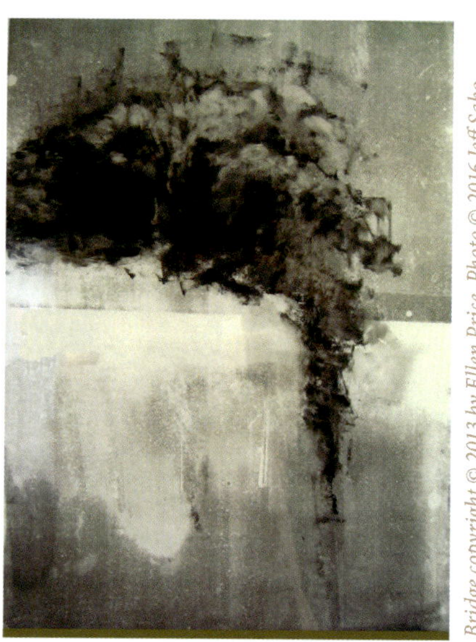

Bridge copyright © 2013 by Ellen Price. Photo © 2016 Jeff Sabo.

FIGURE 2.67 – Bridge, Ellen Price. 2013. 18 x 18 in. Monotype.

Gay Cops Kissing (see Figure 2.66) challenges that stereotype since police officers are perceived as strong, authoritative types who hold an important position within society.

American artist, Ellen Price (1955–) was born in New York and eventually pursued her artistic education in printmaking at schools in the Midwest. She is an educator and an artist, who continues to show her work regionally. While her subject matter does not typically focus on current events, the scope of the Deepwater Horizon incident in the Gulf of Mexico in 2010 captured her attention. There was an explosion on the Deepwater Horizon oil rig caused by a gas leak. Nearly two-dozen people were either killed or injured in the incident. Before the well could be properly sealed and shut off, it was estimated that approximately five million barrels of oil had leaked into the gulf. The amount of damage done to the environment and livelihood of people living in that area was outstanding.

In *Bridge* (see Figure 2.67), Ellen Price uses the monotype process to create a simple, but striking image of a rising plume of smoke to remind the viewer of one of the worst oil spills ever recorded. The ultimate devastation an event like this can have on the environment can take decades to fully understand. In this monotype, the gulf waters appear to be calm and lacking of any evidence of life. The sky and air are filled with the heavy black smoke.

MONOTYPE – a form of printmaking by which an image is created with ink or paint on a flat surface before printing, producing a single, unique print.

Mary Barr Rhodes (1954–) is an American artist living in the Midwest. While she pursued degrees in Art Education, Barr Rhodes has pursued a career that focuses on living sustainability forging a movement that addresses income inadequacies. Artistically, she focuses more on the abstract, mindfully exploring colors, shapes, and textures through the painted surface. Painting is part of Barr Rhodes personal journey and spiritual practice, which help to express her reverence of the natural world and her place within it.

Art can be part of the healing process for many artists. In 2011, Mary Barr Rhodes processed her emotions relating to physical abuse and emotional suppression in the piece *Worn Down* (see Figure 2.68). The central figure, a woman, is naked and exposed to anything that happens to her. The drooped shoulders speak to how worn down she has become from the abuse and the need to suppress her true feelings. The hand resting heavily on her shoulder references the physical pain she suffers. Barr Rhodes created the image loosely and lacking definition in order to visually communicate that she is a mere semblance of the person she once was and truly is. The subdued colors communicate the idea of suppression. The texture in the background was created through writing down angry thoughts and feelings and then erasing them, leaving simple marks behind.

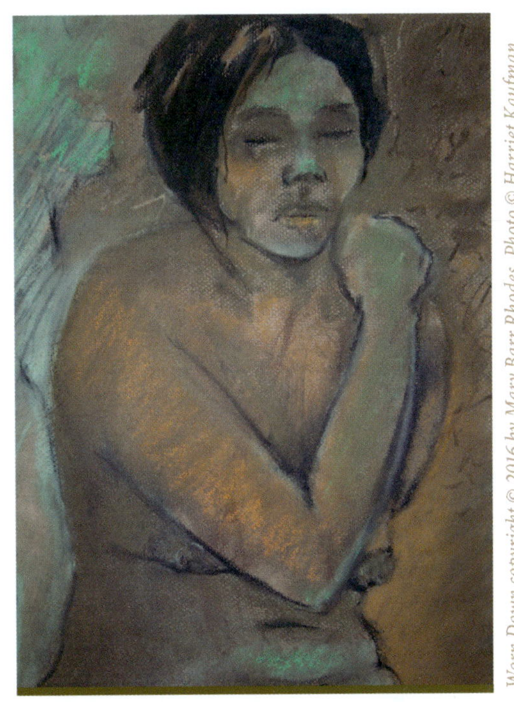

FIGURE 2.68 – Worn Down, Mary Barr Rhodes. 2011. 18 x 24 in. Pastel drawing.

Not only addressing political concerns in his work, Saad Ghosn often addresses social issues such as societal injustice, violence, discrimination, and abuse of the vulnerable and weak. In *We See Nothing, We Hear Nothing* (see Figure 2.69), the artist is bringing attention to the deliberate ignorance or dismissal of what occurs around the world. In order to protect or prevent one's privileges and comforts from being disrupted, people often choose to look the other way when a wrong is being committed to another. On the right side of the image, an affluent couple is enjoying each other's company while at a restaurant. Separated by just a brick wall, outside a policeman is seen beating a young, defenseless boy.

While religion (represented by the cross) is meant to positively guide our actions towards others, a well-decorated policeman meant to serve and protect the community seems to be driven by other forces. He is stepping on the boy who lies unprotected and exposed (shown through lack of clothing) on the ground below. The image is shown on a white background to show such incidents occur openly around us. The couple is depicted on a black background to show they are choosing to ignore what is happening just a few feet from them, while the brick wall can reference the imagery one person creates in their mind to justify not taking action against the injustice.

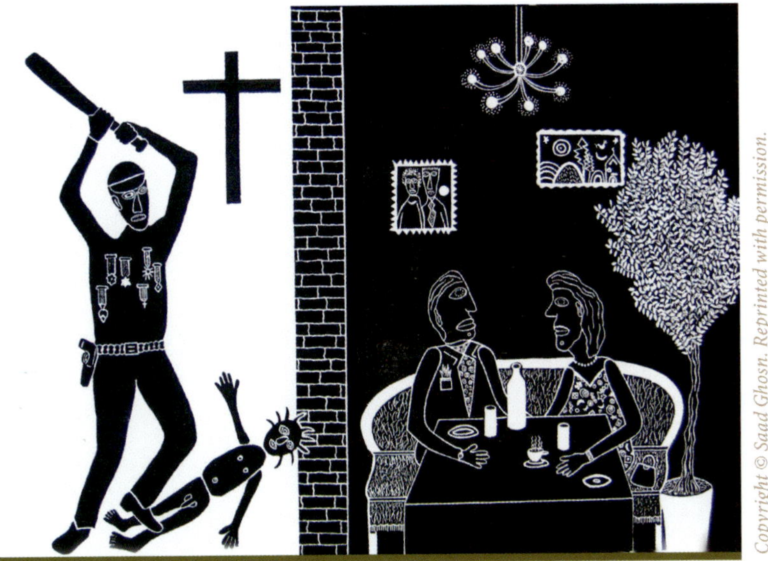

FIGURE 2.69 – We See Nothing, We Hear Nothing, Saad Ghosn. 2013. 30 x 22 in. Woodcut on Rives BFK paper.

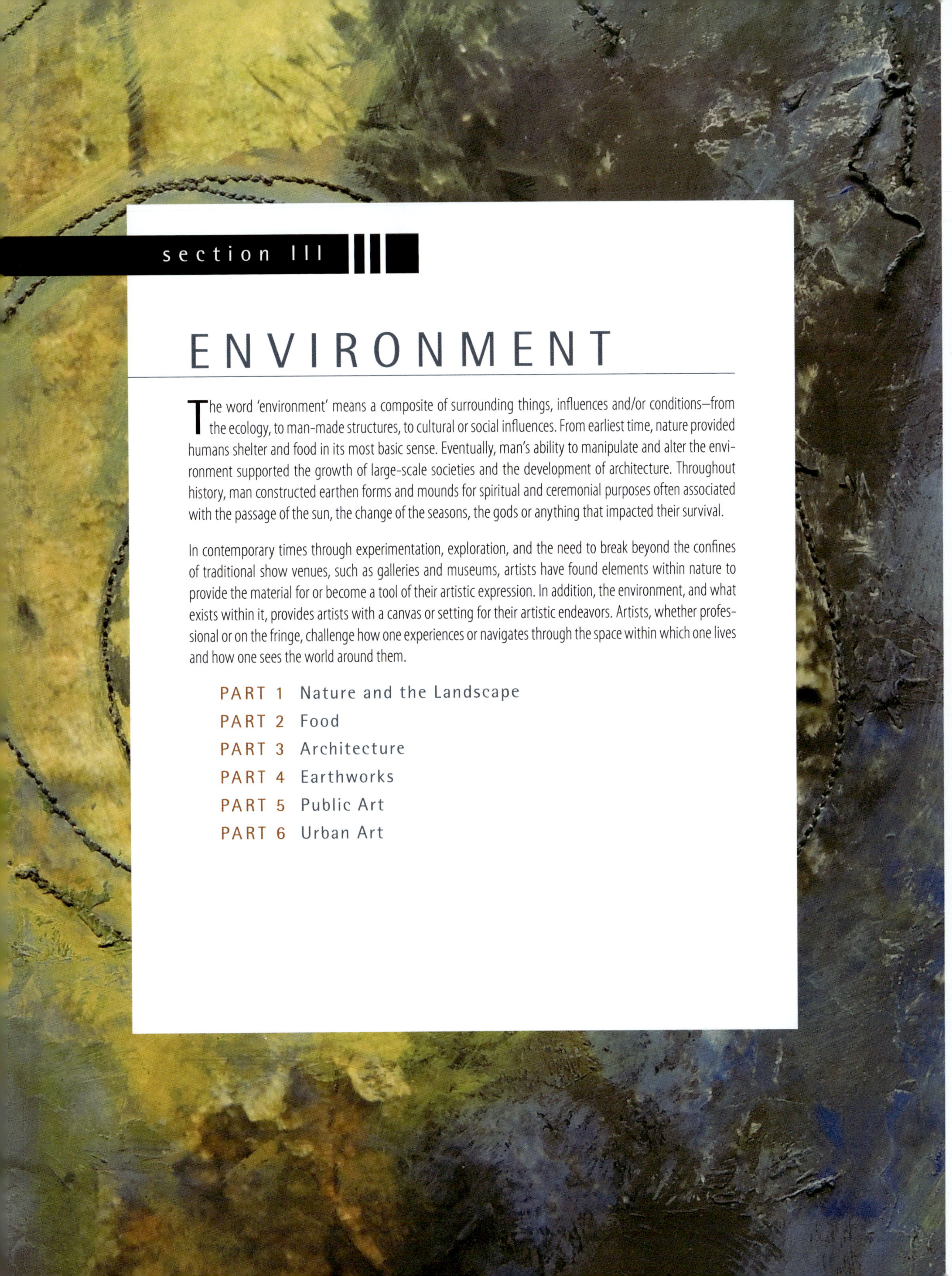

section III

ENVIRONMENT

The word 'environment' means a composite of surrounding things, influences and/or conditions—from the ecology, to man-made structures, to cultural or social influences. From earliest time, nature provided humans shelter and food in its most basic sense. Eventually, man's ability to manipulate and alter the environment supported the growth of large-scale societies and the development of architecture. Throughout history, man constructed earthen forms and mounds for spiritual and ceremonial purposes often associated with the passage of the sun, the change of the seasons, the gods or anything that impacted their survival.

In contemporary times through experimentation, exploration, and the need to break beyond the confines of traditional show venues, such as galleries and museums, artists have found elements within nature to provide the material for or become a tool of their artistic expression. In addition, the environment, and what exists within it, provides artists with a canvas or setting for their artistic endeavors. Artists, whether professional or on the fringe, challenge how one experiences or navigates through the space within which one lives and how one sees the world around them.

part 1

NATURE AND THE LANDSCAPE

THE NATURAL WORLD

A subject frequently explored by artists throughout the ages is nature. The varying types of landscapes, from the mundane to the majestic, have been explored through art. In addition, other aspects of the natural world, from insects to flowers to animals, have captured the imagination of artists. These elements from the natural world are then used to further explore one's relationship with nature and all that resides within it.

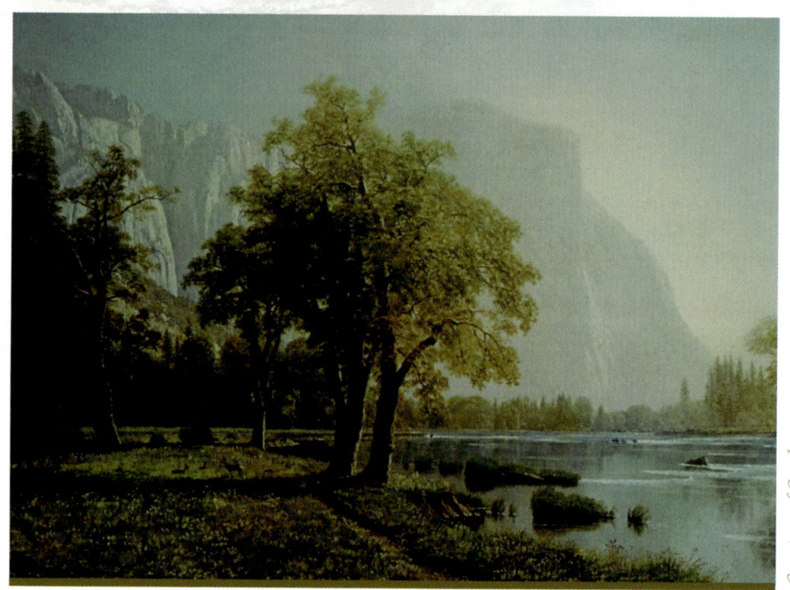

Courtesy of Corel

FIGURE 3.1 – El Capitan, Yosemite Valley, California, Albert Bierstadt. 1875. 48.03 x 32.28 in. Oil on canvas.

German-born, Albert Bierstadt (1830–1902) lived in America from the age of two. At the age of twenty-three, he returned to Germany to study painting. His focus during this time was on the Alpine landscapes. Bierstadt returned to America after four years and joined a survey expedition that took him to the underdeveloped west. On his journey, he photographed and sketched the mountain ranges and dramatic rock formations, which inspired a great deal of his work. Bierstadt was fortunate to have witnessed and enjoyed his artistic success during his lifetime.

Albert Bierstadt's paintings romanticized the rugged landscapes of the American West, through dramatic lighting and an abundance of detail. Often artworks like his were the only means for those living in the east to have a glimpse at the untamed beauty of the American West. In *El Capitan, Yosemite Valley, California* (see Figure 3.1), the artist draws the viewer first into the landscape through the soft, inviting light and then through rich colors and the realism of the landscape in the foreground. In the background, El Capitan's monumental cliff face emerges from a haze. Although it lacks detail like the rest of the image, Bierstadt's depiction of El Capitan made it the most recognized site in Yosemite Valley.

Paul Cezanne (1839–1906) was born in Aix-en-Provence in Southeastern France. He developed a close relationship with nature from his childhood explorations of the countryside around Aix. Cezanne went on to study painting and drawing. His father, however, discouraged his artistic pursuits and persuaded him to enroll in law school. After trying to follow his father's wishes, Cezanne dropped out. He convinced his father to support his move to Paris, where he met several painters who were exploring a new direction artistically, eventually to be known as Impressionism. One of the artists he met and worked alongside was Camille Pissarro (1830–1903). Pissarro encouraged Cezanne to observe nature more closely, to paint outdoors, to lighten his color palette, and to use smaller brushstrokes to capture the effects of sunlight on his subject matter. Cezanne created and exhibited his impressionistic paintings from 1874–1877.

IMPRESSIONISM – a late nineteenth-century Western painting style characterized by capturing subtle light through small brush strokes and strong color.

In 1878, Paul Cezanne returned home and pursued his own artistic path. He found that he was more interested in understanding the underlying structure or inner geometry of landscapes he painted. In *Mont Sainte-Victoire* (see Figure 3.2), the artist was painting the mountain range that he grew up seeing in his hometown. Rather than trying to capture exactly what he saw or its impressionistic counterpart, Cezanne used patches of color gently overlapping and butting up to one another to create a mosaicked landscape. By capturing architectural structures and elements of nature in this manner, he was laying the groundwork that would inspire the cubist work of Pablo Picasso (1881–1973) and George Braque (1882–1963).

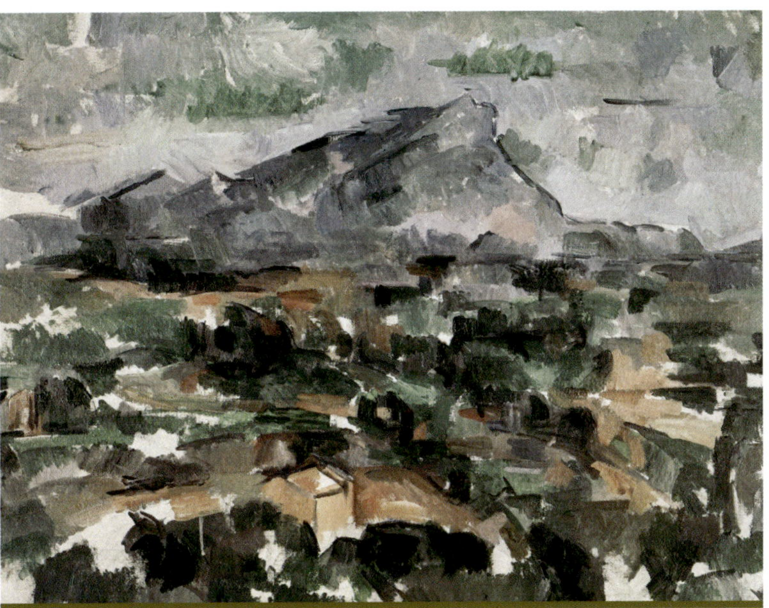

FIGURE 3.2 – Mont Sainte-Victoire, Paul Cezanne. c. 1904–1906. 73 x 9.19 cm. Oil on canvas.

He painted more than sixty versions of this mountain during his career; no two are exactly the same. In a 1906 letter to his son, Cezanne wrote, "The same subject seen from a different angle offers subject for study of the most powerful interest and so varied that I think I could occupy myself for months without changing my place, by turning now more to the right, now more to the left."

CUBISM – an early twentieth-century art movement where by multiple viewpoints of a single object, space, or landscape is captured simultaneously in a single image. Often breaking forms from the natural world down to simple geometric representations.

American artist, Kevin Muente (1971–) has developed a deep appreciation and relationship with nature. After his formal training in painting, he became an educator and continued to pursue his exploration of nature through his travels and work. He continues to exhibit his work in galleries nationwide. Muente says, "My role as an artist is to experience places in a more in depth manner and communicate those experiences to the viewer. I believe in being swept up in the moment, consciously paying attention to the noises, smells, and changes in light and temperature of a place."

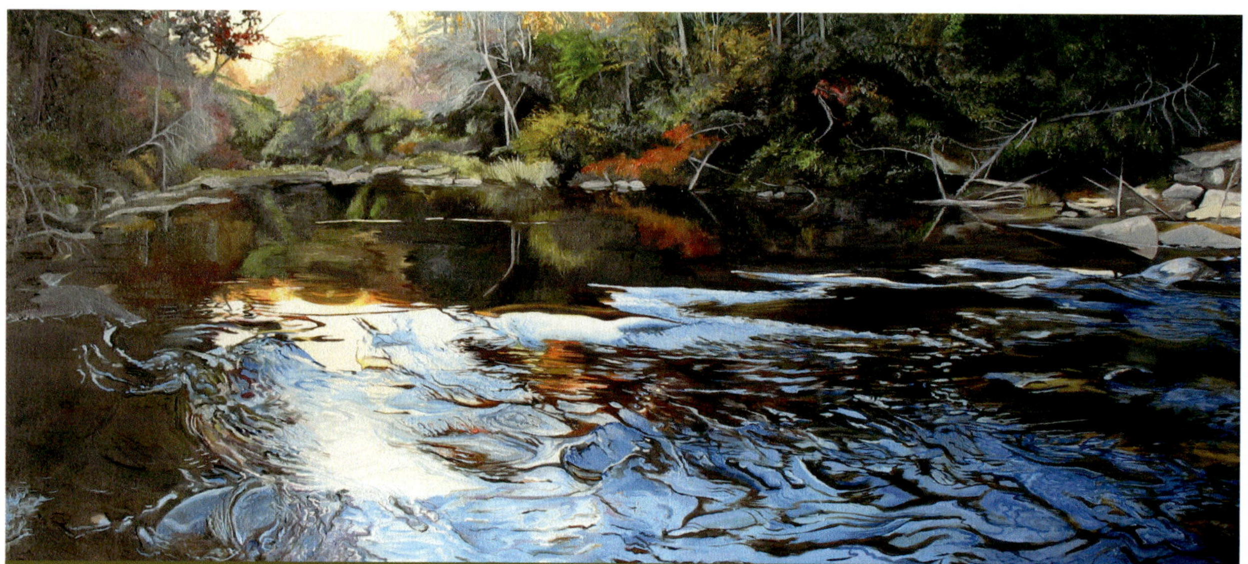

FIGURE 3.3 – Linville River, Kevin Muente. 2007. 24 x 48 in. Oil on canvas.

Kevin Muente works from life, as well as photographs he's taken, to capture the unique moments within nature that help to express the spirit of a place. He feels that a landscape is too complex to be dealt with in a simple manner. Muente pays particular attention to elements within the landscapes he paints, such as branches, leaves, stones, and ripples in water. In *Linville River* (see Figure 3.3), the artist captures a moment in time where the viewer feels isolated within this magical setting. Muente's attention to detail brings the landscape to life before the viewer's eyes. While the ripples and waves created by the current conjure up the sound of moving water, the viewer can meditate on the calm reflection of the trees on the water's surface in the middle ground of the image. In the distance, the soft light of the setting sun signals the end of another day.

Randall Sackerson (1952–) is an American artist, photographer, musician, and writer. He began his artistic pursuit in photography early in life, experimenting with the black and white photography of landscapes. After receiving a formal education and while continuing his photographic pursuits, Sackerson went on to explore abstract painting. He feels the art of abstraction complements his photographic imagery. As he travels around the world, Sackerson captures all aspects of the cultures and landscapes he encounters. His sharp

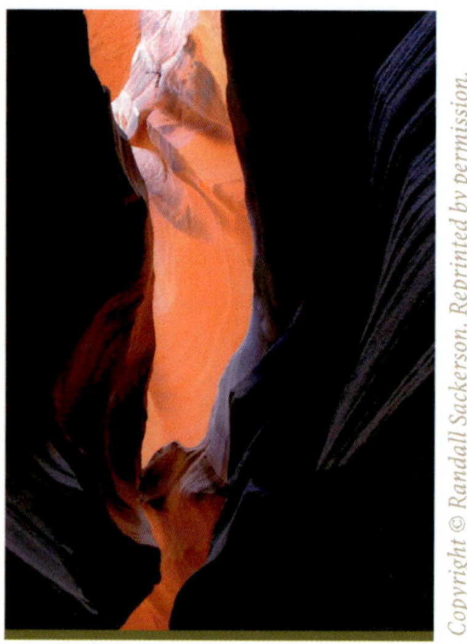

FIGURE 3.4 – Antelope 4, Randall Sackerson. 2005. 24 x 36 in. Digital photography.

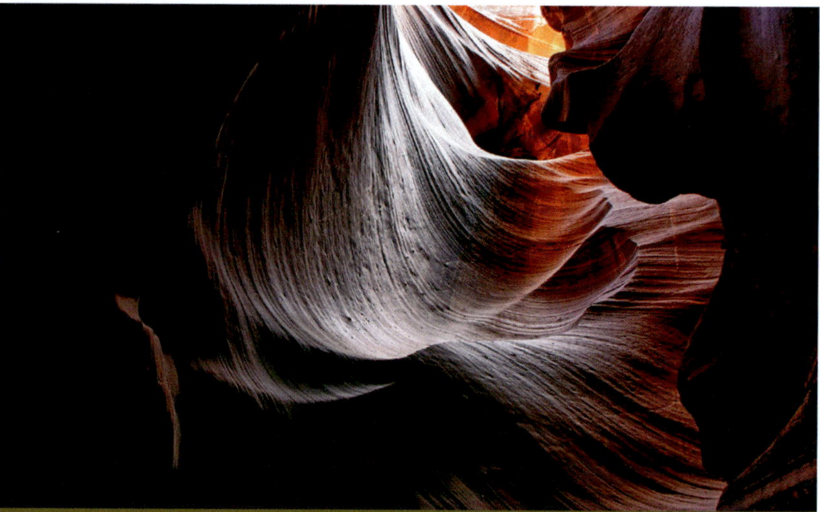

FIGURE 3.5 – Antelope 5, Randall Sackerson. 2005. 24 x 36 in. Digital photography.

attention to detail, composition, and color draw the viewer into a world they can't imagine exists in nature on its own. Yet in his traditional photographic pursuits, he brings nature alive in this dynamic way.

The Antelope Canyon, located in the American Southwest, is a slot canyon. Through the ages, flash floods have caused the soft Navajo sandstone to erode, leaving behind large corridors (or slots) in the rock formations. In *Antelope 4* (see Figure 3.4), the artist captures the light and dark created by the magnificent rock formations. The way the light streams down into the crevice creates the illusion of the rock in the background becoming molten from the heat, while the rock walls closest to the viewer take on the glass-like appearance of obsidian. In *Antelope 5* (see Figure 3.5), Sackerson captures the light softly cascading down the rock formation, accentuating the ridges and colors within. Each photograph focuses on smaller details of a large landscape, turning it into an abstract work of art.

NATURE IN ART

Through the ages, artists and even scientists, have explored the natural world—from the micro to macro—through art. Elements of nature, from microscopic organisms to flora and fauna, to insects and animals, continue to be used by artists within and/or the focus of their art. Whether rendered realistically or abstractly, these individual elements have been used to remind the viewer of the beauty and the dangers that lie within nature and the destruction caused by mankind and societal advancements.

REALISM – a nineteenth-century art style depicting the natural world as it appears, not through distortion or exaggeration.

American artist, Renee Harris (1956–) creates textile and mixed media work. After receiving a formal education in painting, printmaking, and illustration, she worked in galleries and freelance jobs while searching for a direction to pursue her visual narrative. Harris discovered a real passion for textiles and began incorporating them into her work. In addition, her illustration background led to the realization that visual imagery could provide a dialogue where environmental issues could be addressed. Harris says, "The continuous stimulation of everyday life observations inspires the visual dialogues between remembered color, light, texture, form, and the intuitive design in my work...Each stitch through fabric or paper becomes a drawing tool that transforms my ideas into tactile illustrations."

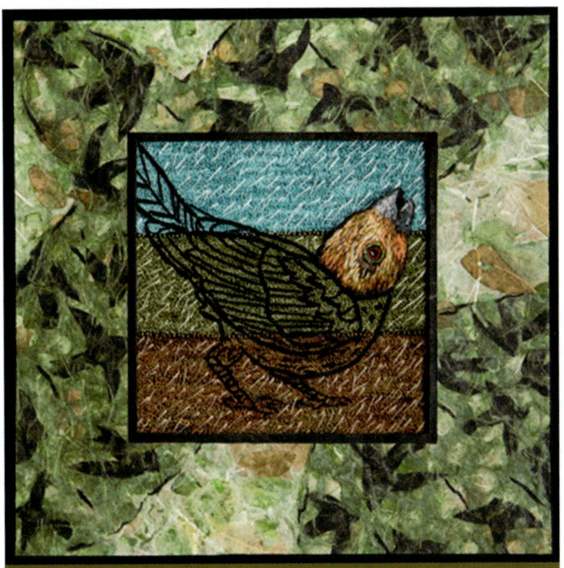

FIGURE 3.6 – Does it See Me?, Renee Harris. 2013. 10 x 10 x 25 in. Fiber.

FORM – the defined shape of an object or natural element.

Renee Harris' recent work has focused on the plight of endangered species. *Does it See Me?* (see Figure 3.6) depicts a small bird looking up towards an unseen danger. The daily life of a bird revolves around finding food and avoiding predators. The border of the image is created by collaging earth colored papers to reference a tree canopy. Subtly within that border, the outline of a hawk, which the small bird looks up towards, was created through selectively placed pieces of dark green paper. Layered within the hawk's body are dark shapes referencing its already consumed prey. Harris chose to embroider the outline of the body to communicate the bird's instinct to remain invisible to its prey. In contrast, the bird's head was created more dimensionally to communicate its awareness of the danger lurking above. The beauty of the overall image draws the viewer in, while the subtlety of its serious message allows it to be more easily contemplated.

DIMENSIONAL – a measurement of an object or work of art in length, depth, and thickness. May also be the appearance of depth within an artwork created through various techniques, such as carving, modeling, or perspective.

Kathleen Piercefield (1949–) is an American artist who formally pursued an education in printmaking and studio arts. While growing up in a large city, she had limited exposure to nature on a grand scale. As a result, Piercefield hungered for nature—treasuring even its smallest manifestations—and incorporated it as an integral part of her work. She does not want to merely replicate what she sees or remembers, but to convey the awe she feels at the amazing things around her.

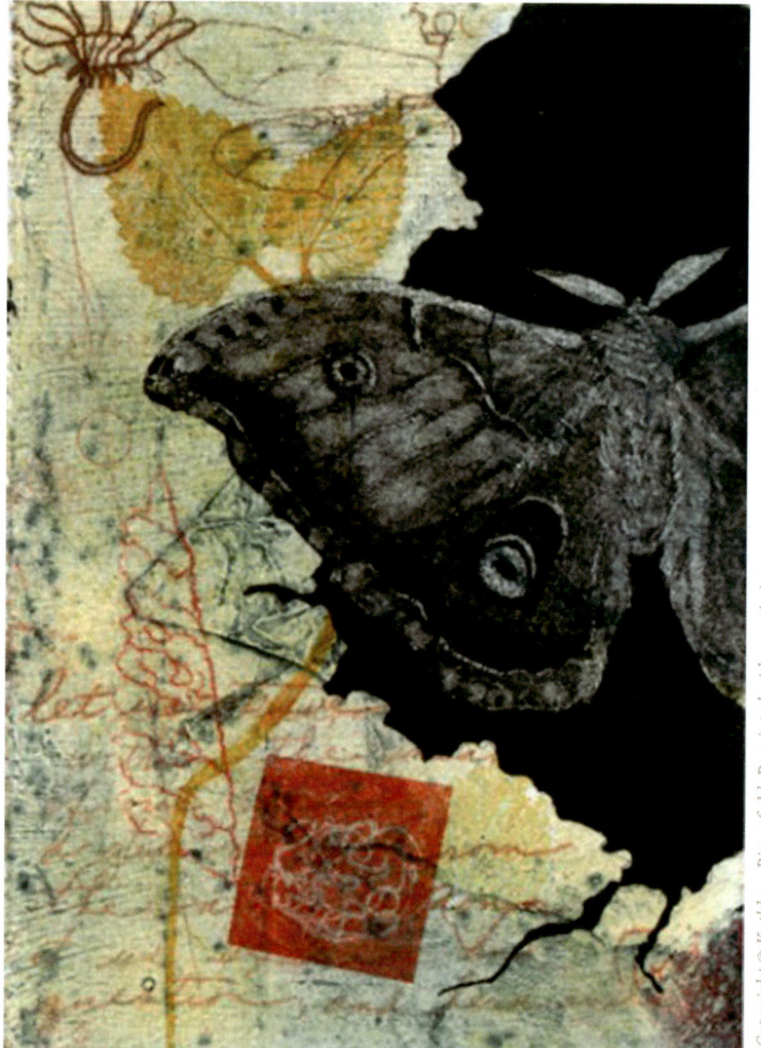

FIGURE 3.7 – Memory Map, Kathleen Piercefield. 2009. 7 x 5 in. Etching, collograph, monotype.

COLLOGRAPH – a form of printmaking where materials and objects are applied to a rigid surface, such as wood or artist board, to create an image before inking and printing.

In *Memory Map* (see Figure 3.7), Kathleen Piercefield depicts a moth as the central image. To the artist, the moth is a symbol of all things mysterious, hidden, strange, and unexpected. The visual impression of the overall image is that of an old map. This is created through the layering of imagery, texture, and color using various printmaking techniques, such as collagraph, monotype, and etching. The dark shape behind the moth could be a hollow in a tree or evoke the shape of a body of water depicted on a map. Piercefield explains, "...the latter interpretation is what suggested the direction I went as I developed the image. The other marks, writing, unreadable script, and fragments of natural shapes are the meandering lines on a map, only partly legible, but suggesting a route, a path that one might follow to find some lost and wonderful place." While the artist continues to utilize various aspects of nature artistically, the sense of mystery and awe she feels is prevalent throughout.

California-based artist, Liliana Duque Piñeiro (1973–) was born in Colombia, South America. She came to the United States in 2001 to further her education, where she earned degrees in sculpture and theater design/

production. Piñeiro has since established a career in set design, both nationally and in South America. While preparing for a recent solo exhibition, the artist's mother was diagnosed with Alzheimer's. This altered the direction of her work and became about 'her childhood hero fading away.' It was a deeply personal experience she shared with the viewer, but felt it was one to which many people could relate.

Liliana Duque Piñeiro, has a unique approach to her set designs, as they also tend to be highly sculptural. Set designs typically need not be as 'finished' or 'polished' in appearance as a work of art because of the distance between the audience and a stage. This distance can create the illusion of something highly detailed or constructed. For her 2015 university exhibition, *Limonar: Stories of Alzheimer's*, Piñeiro had an unique opportunity not only to create sets for an opera of her own choosing, but to have the school's faculty and students perform in them for two nights during the opening week. The performances were videotaped and shown on a monitor in the gallery through the remainder of the exhibition. Because the sets would not be used for more than the first week of a month long exhibition, the artist felt she needed to take the sets a step further, turning them into sculptural forms that could stand on their own merits as works of art.

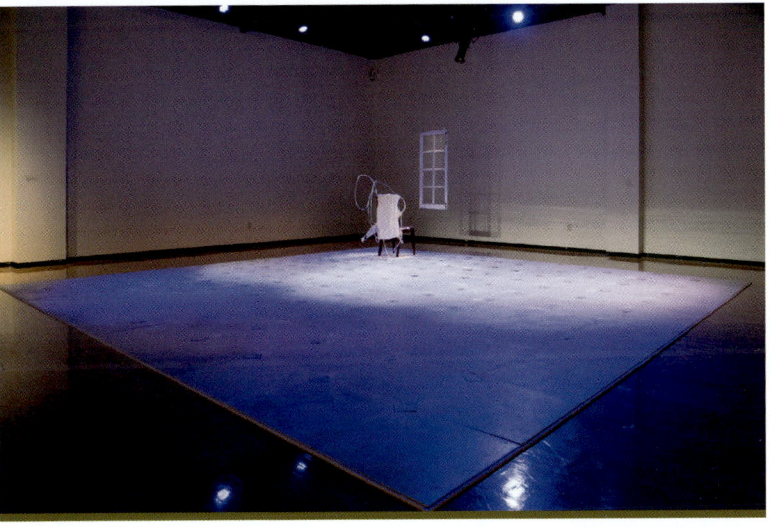

FIGURE 3.8 – From Limonar Exhibition, Liliana Duque Piñeiro, 2015, Performance/Stage Design.

Limonar (see Figure 3.8) was the set Piñeiro created for the performance of excerpts from *Alzheimer's Stories* by composer Robert Cohen (1945–), which loosely mimics the progression of the disease. This set was also used for a single performance at the start of the evening. In the image *Limonar detail* (see Figure 3.9), a woman sits on a chair at the far end of a room, staring out a window. The woman represents Piñeiro's mother, who is slowly entering into a state of isolation through the progression of the disease. In her hand, she holds a music box that she is slowly playing. Piñeiro, with the aid of her friend and composer, Chía Patiño (1967–), created music from something her mother used to sing. However, pieces of the music were removed (see Figure 3.10), creating gaps in the song to reflect the gaps in her mother's memory. On the back of her mother's chair, is a torn shirt in the shape of butterfly wings. Placed across the floor are repeated butterfly images and die cut butterflies. Piñeiro uses the butterfly throughout this piece as a metaphor of the transformation her mother is going through and of her fading memories.

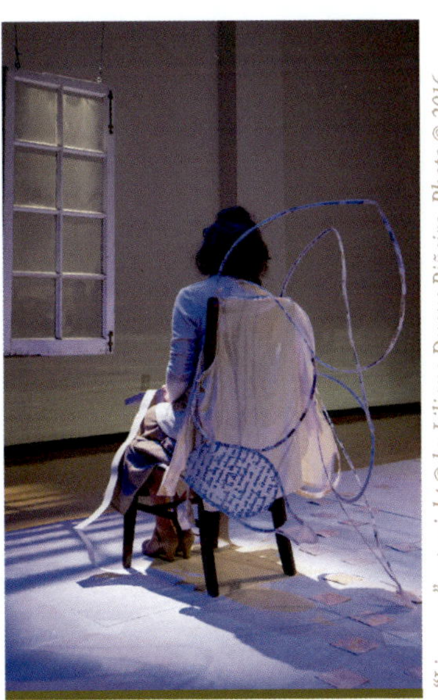

FIGURE 3.9 – Limonar Detail

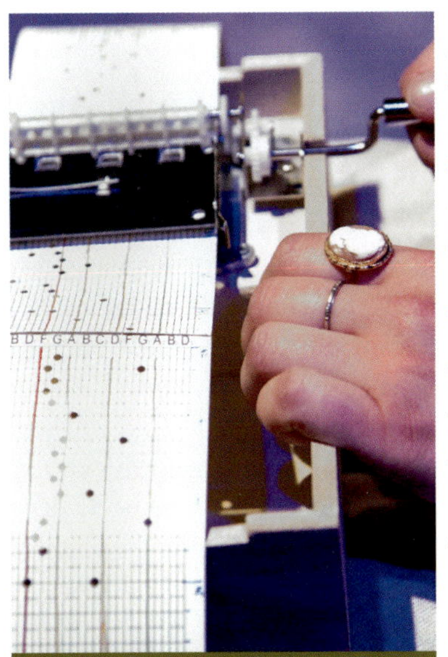

FIGURE 3.10 – Limonar Detail

American artist, Michelle Blades (1972–) was fascinated, at a young age with constructing play spaces for her dolls and toys. She pursued her artistic education in sculpture before entering into the corporate world. In 2009, as a result of the economic recession, Blades found herself in search of a new profession. She became a freelance artist and social media marketer. This allowed her to pursue her own artistic endeavors. Blades says, "I create diminutive imagined realms with which a viewer will interact...By making my works figurative, and thus relatable...I can tell stories that might otherwise seem too fantastical to convey."

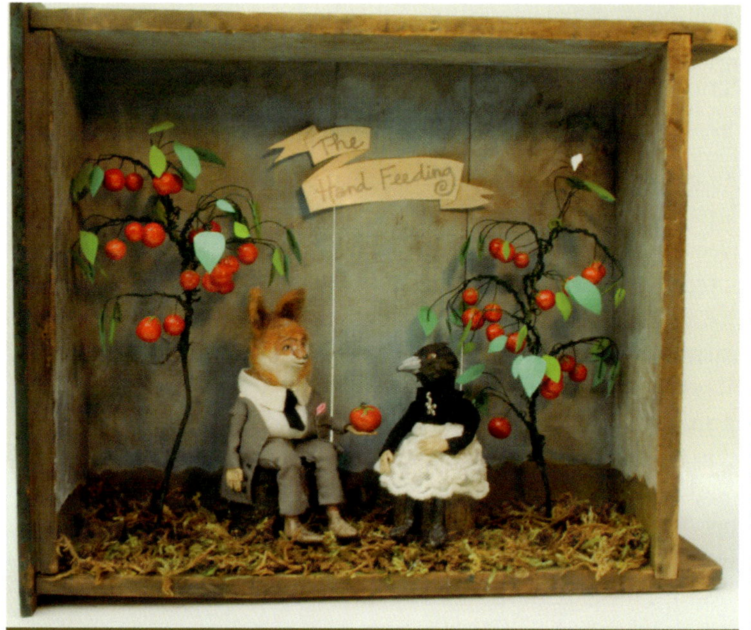

FIGURE 3.11 – The Hand Feeding, Michelle Blades, 2014, 8 x 14 x 5 in. 3D mixed media.

The Hand Feeding (see Figure 3.11) depicts a fox sharing a tomato from his garden with a magpie, he seems to have befriended. Michelle Blades finds humor in the unlikely friendships that can develop between two species. She says, "This piece is an ode to that idea—building an enduring relationship across (and despite) seemingly inherent boundaries." The two figures sit slightly turned toward one another, appear at ease in each other's company, and are placed in an intimate setting, creating the feeling that the viewer has intruded upon a private moment between the two. By humanizing the animals in her work, whether through their clothing, their hands or their actions, the artist creates whimsical scenes to which the viewer can easily relate. Although Blades does not directly say she is addressing social issues or concerns through her art, these delightful works seem to have a message behind them.

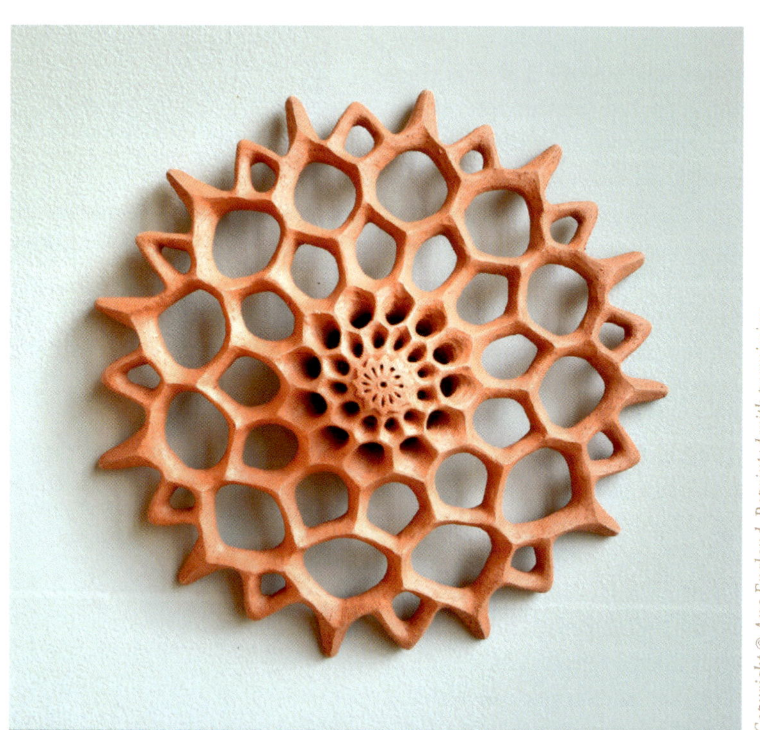

FIGURE 3.12 – Cellular Mind, Ana England, 2016, 13 x 13 x 13 in. Ceramic.

Ana England (1953–) is an American artist residing in Southern Ohio. Her educational pursuits turned towards art in the early 1980s, when she focused on ceramics and sculpture. Recently retired, England has had an illustrious career as a professor of ceramics and continues to exhibit her work nationally. Although, professing no real scientific knowledge, she educated herself through extensive reading on aspects of biology, botany, and physics for both pleasure and artistic inspiration. In one body of work, England explores the forms of radiolarian—microscopic single celled organisms found in water—which create complex structures that protect themselves.

Ana England began working on *Cellular Mind* (see Figure 3.12) in 2016. This large wall installation consists of ceramic forms inspired by the natural designs of single celled organisms (radiolarian), found in the *Art Forms from the Ocean* by Ernst Haeckel (1834–1919). Haeckel was a German zoologist who drew the intricate and complex structures created by the radiolarian. England says, "*Cellular Mind*, loosely based on these forms, is my attempt to understand the difference between brain, which radiolarian do not have, and mind, which it seems that they do have." The artist starts with wheel thrown clay forms, then continues to shape the clay pieces through hand building and carving techniques. The pieces of this series are shown in process, lacking the finishing surface the artist has yet to determine.

WHEEL THROWING – a technique of creating pottery and other ceramic forms using a spinning wheel.

HANDBUILDING – an ancient technique to create pottery and other ceramic objects using various methods, such as coiling or slab construction.

CARVING – a sculptural method for creating a work of art by removing material from a source, like a block of clay, wood, or stone.

In addition to capturing the magnificence of nature through landscape photography, Randall Sackerson explores the imaginary 'worlds' of his own creation. *Biogenesis 2* (see Figure 3.13) is an example of the artist combining two of his photographs—one of foliage and one of a butterfly—in Photoshop, an image editing software. Sackerson worked with selective color ranges and applied various lighting techniques to the layered image. He continued to repeat this process many times to create the resulting visual effect. The textures, rich colors, and lines within the image give the digital creation the look of an abstract painting. Although the foliage and butterfly may not be clear to the viewer, Sackerson created an imaginary world that seems to have things living and growing within.

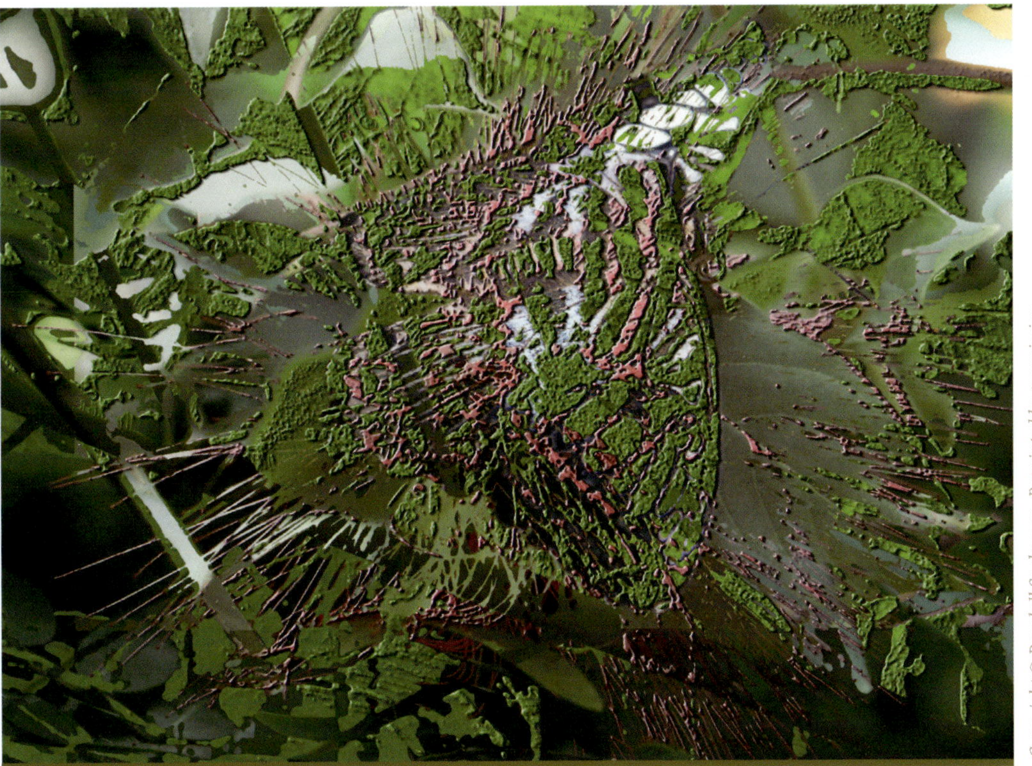

FIGURE 3.13 – Biogenesis 2, Randall Sackerson, 2011, 36 x 24 in. Digital art.

DIGITAL ART – works of art created with the aid of electronic devices and technology.

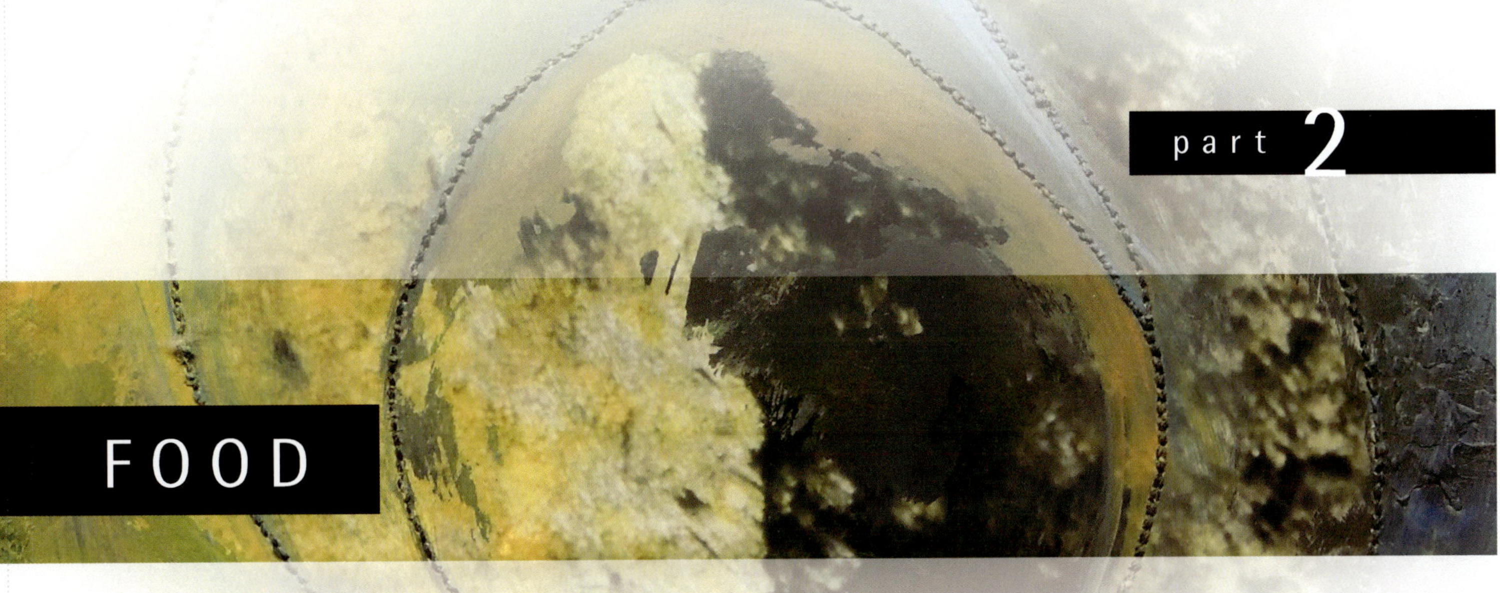

part 2

FOOD

The acquisition, preparation, and storage of food are longstanding needs of human beings. While the process may vary or change throughout history or within a culture, these are essential to our survival as humans. Artists have created art to aid in all the processes, from drawing images on cave walls to performing rituals to creating pottery.

ACQUISITION (HUNTING AND HARVESTING)

Early man painted and engraved a variety of animal images on cave walls. In European Paleolithic (c. 45,000 BC) times, humans sought out caves for temporary shelter and for ritual purposes throughout France and Spain. Images were discovered in the Altamira cave which is located in Southern France and was initially discovered in 1868 by a local shepherd, Modesto Cubillas (1820–1881). A decade later in 1878, the images were brought to the public's attention at the World's Fair in Paris by Marcelino Sanz de Sautuola (1831–1888), the land owner where the cave was found. The theories surrounding the creation of this work and its meaning were not widely accepted until a French prehistorian, Emile Cartaihlac (1845–1921), brought the work to the public's eye again in 1902. From this point forward, cave and other Paleolithic art and tools were part of a larger puzzle from which to try to understand the origins of man.

The various animals depicted on cave walls appear to be indigenous to the location of the caves and include a wide range of animals including bear, deer, lions, bison, and horses. Pigments used to create the images came from the environment—charcoal from fires to create black, minerals like red iron oxide, and ochre from the land to create reddish-brown and yellow respectively. These materials could be ground into a powder and combined with a binder, such as saliva or animal fat, to create the consistency of paint before applying it to the cave wall's surface.

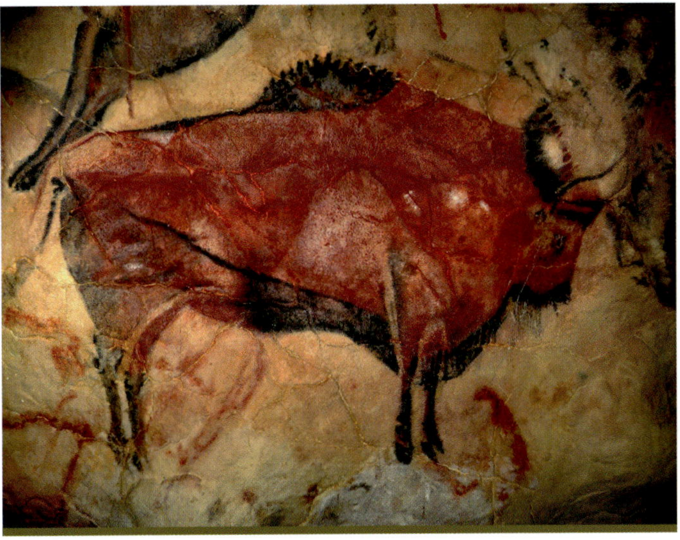

Heritage Images/Hulton Fine Art Collection/Getty Images

FIGURE 3.14 – Neolithic Bison (Painting in the Cave of Altamira). Cantabria, Spain. 35,000–11,000 BC. Pigment on rock.

Images like *Neolithic Bison* (see Figure 3.14) accurately depict the animal and its unique features. The purpose of two colors is to capture the details of the bison's hair, eyes, horns, and hooves. Perhaps images like this were painted to assist the hunter in the successful acquisition of food or as a way to show respect to the animal for giving itself to feed the people. Since there was no written language at this time, one must look to other cultural practices to find similarities that might provide a clue as to what one is seeing. For example, a traditional hunting ritual among the Native American cultures in the United States was to perform a tobacco offering to the animal they just killed. By thanking the animal for giving its life to sustain theirs through an offering and prayer, the hope was that the animal would continue to be a viable food resource for them in the future. Perhaps by drawing animals some early man believed their food sources would continue to be there for them.

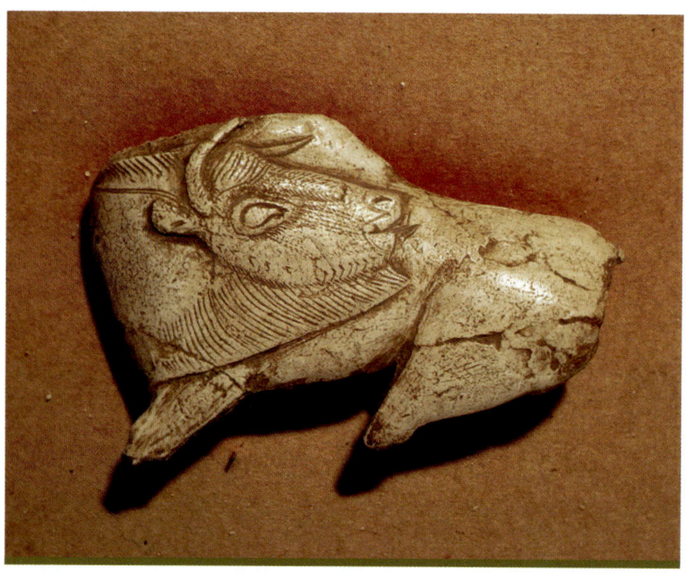

FIGURE 3.15 – Bison Carving. France. c. 12000 BC. 4.5 x 3.5 x 1.5 in. Ivory.

Besides cave art, handheld portable art was created in the form of humans and animals. Discovered in Madeleine, France, the *Bison Carving* (see Figure 3.15) is a realistic rendering of a bison carved from a piece of horn. This piece is approximately four inches long dating back to c. 12,000 BC. The details of the animal are expertly carved. Due to the shape of the material being used, the neck and head of the animal is turned back towards its body. While a creative way to fully capture the size and shape of the bison, upon closer look one can see the bison's tongue is extended and repeated to create a licking motion. This would have been an observation that early man could have made and been intentionally trying to reproduce.

Speculation as to the purpose behind creations such as the *Bison Carving* is varied. One possibility is that it could provide luck to the person who carried it on their hunt.

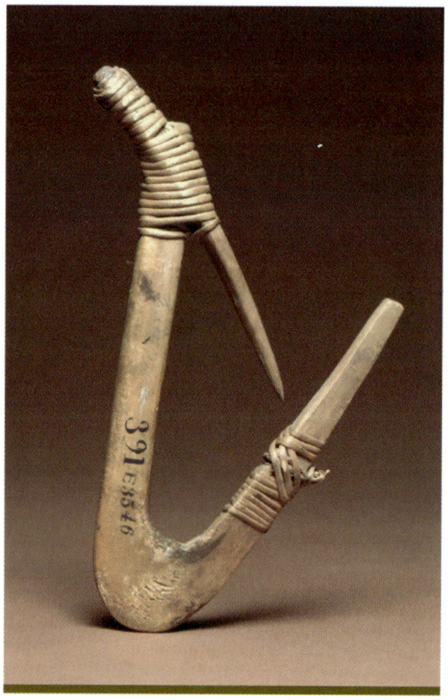

FIGURE 3.16– Halibut Hook. c. 1800. 26.6 cm. high. Wood and spruce root.

In regions of Alaska and Canada, Native American Indians, known as the Inuit, live in extremely cold, harsh climates where snow and ice impacts all aspects of daily life. During warmer conditions, dugout canoes were used for fishing and whaling. However, under colder conditions, when protein resources were more limited, they supplemented their diets by breaking through thick layers of ice in order to fish.

Before the introduction of metal, the Inuit used wood from trees to construct fishing hooks. Fishing line was made from kelp or the inner bark of cedar trees. They would observe their prey and shape the hook specific to what they were hunting. A common food source was the halibut, which inhales its food as opposed to salmon which nibbles at theirs. The hooks used to fish halibut were designed in a V-shape with a barb at the end (see Figure 3.16). This specific design would cause the barb to get lodged into the cheek of the fish when it was sucked in.

Whales were an important resource for Native Americans living in these regions. All parts of the whale would be used, including the blubber, bones, and skin. Important men within the Inuit communities would own a boat or kayak for whaling. Male members from this clan and the community would assist in the hunt. The meat and other resources from the whale would then be divided up among the community at large. A small community could be well fed for up to a year from a single large whale.

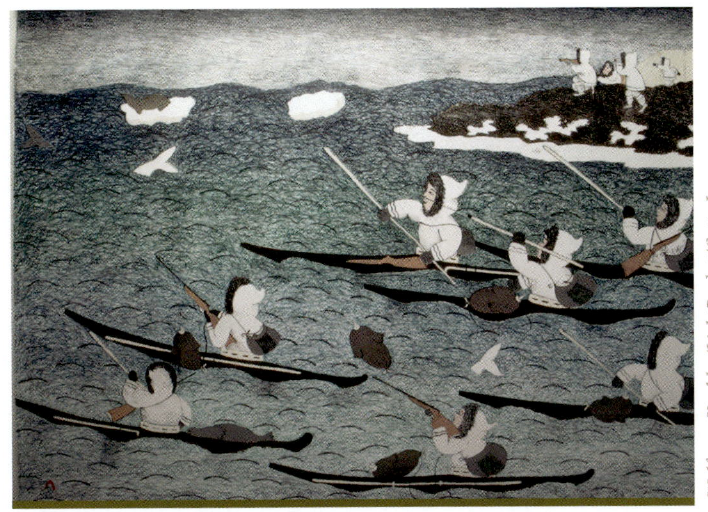
Wolfgang Kaehler/LightRocket/Getty Images

FIGURE 3.17 – The Whale Hunt, Mary Pudlat. Cape Dorset, Canada. 1990. Lithograph.

During harsh winters and the whaling season, in particular, it was essential to keep the fisherman alert and responsive during the long hours of waiting for their prey. The use of 'magical' songs was an important aid in hunting. Children were taught these songs early in life to be sung during hunting expeditions when they were adults. It helped to divert the hunter's attention from the cold, while keeping them alert to see when prey was nearby. *The Whale Hunt* (see Figure 3.17) was created in 1990 by printmaker, Mary Pudlat (1923-2001). Her image shows hunters working together to secure a whale. Some are armed with traditional harpoons, while others are holding rifles. In the upper right hand corner of the print, there are scouts looking to the ocean for signs of a surfacing whale. Once spotted, the hunters would rush forward and attempt to secure the whale. Once the whale has been killed, the hunters would tow it back to shore where it could then be processed. While the image is showing a way of life that is dying out, it also captures how a culture adapts to the changing world around them to survive.

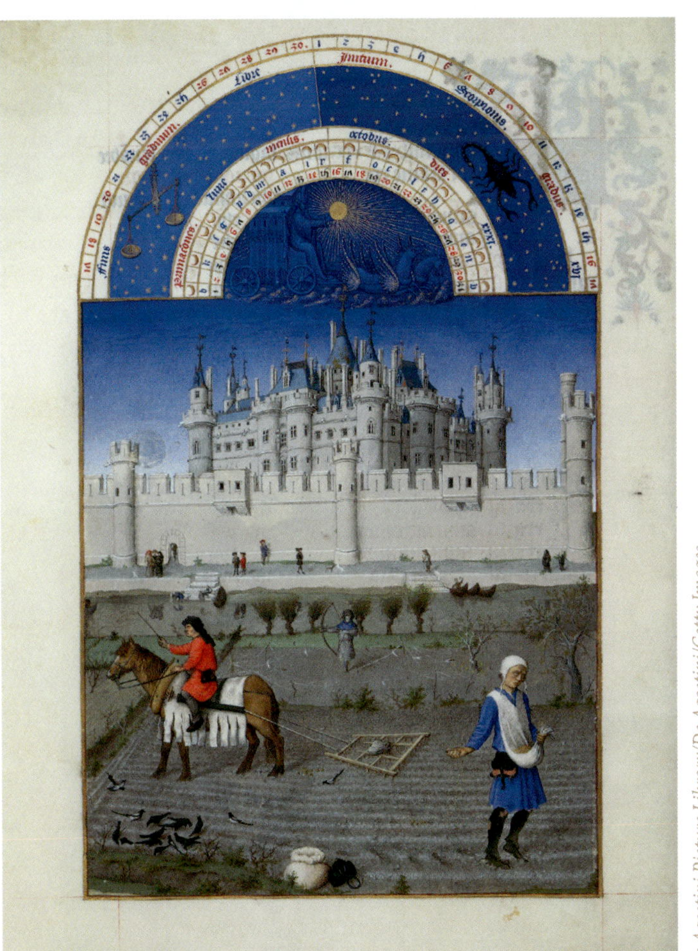
De Agostini Picture Library/De Agostini/Getty Images

FIGURE 3.18 – October, Limbourg Brothers. c. 1412–1486. 21.5 x 30 cm. Illuminated manuscript page from Très Riches Heures.

The Limbourg Brothers (Herman, Paul, and Johan) were well-known Dutch manuscript illuminators from the fifteenth century. Born into a creative family, they were exposed early in life to the materials and techniques of both painting and woodcarving. Their maternal uncle, Jean Malouel (1365–1415), was a court painter and eventually secured the brothers a court position of their own with the Duke of Burgundy. Upon his death, they continued on under the duke's brother, Jean de France (1340–1416), the Duke of Berry.

The Limbourg Brothers quickly established a reputation, initially through their accurate renderings of specific landscape scenes and were often commissioned to capture a patron's castle and surrounding environment. They blended their styles into a singular one characterized by sensitivity to detail and subtlety of line. For the Duke of Berry, the Limbourg brothers created two lavishly illustrated books of hours, known as the *Belles Heures* and the *Très Riches Heures*. Illustrated books like these were private prayer books of the period.

Très Riches Heures was started in 1413, but was left unfinished when the Limbourg Brothers all died in 1416 from the plague or some other epidemic. It was later completed in 1485 by Jean Colombe (1430–1493), a French illuminator, for another owner. This elaborate manuscript had full-page illustrations, containing twelve elaborate scenes of landscapes. Each illustration showed the distinction between the wealthy nobles and the poor working class through the activities depicted. In *October* (see Figure 3.18), the brothers show the Duke's castle towering in the background, with the Seine River just outside its walls. In the foreground, the peasants are seen tilling the fields and planting seeds. Each image within the *Très Riches Heures* is positioned below an arch, decorated with the image of Phoebus, Greek god of the sun (aka Apollo) carrying a sun surrounded by the appropriate zodiac sign of the month.

PREPARATION AND SERVING

Seen in Medieval Europe (fifth to fifteenth century), feasting and enjoyment of food was an important part of life. This led from wars where food was scarce, putting the burden of paying for food and wages of the household upon the nobles. Common dietary staples for all people at that time included chicken, fish, pork, porridge, and bread. Once food was more accessible to the masses, nobles paid for expensive, and therefore more prestigious, game meats upon which to feast. The type of food and how refined it was defined the social norms which dictated what the different classes consumed. Therefore, those performing manual labor should eat cheaper, coarser food than the nobles. During the late medieval period as the wealth of the middle class increased, they began emulating the aristocracy's lavish way of eating. This threatened the symbolic barrier previously created to divide the nobility and lower classes. As a result, laws were passed to prevent non-aristocrats from having lavish banquets.

A medieval handbook, known as *Tacuinum Sanitatis*, was created prior to the 1400s. Its pages were filled with illustrations revolving around various aspects of health, including food preparation and consumption. In *Preparing Tripe* (see Figure 3.19), the scene depicts three women in a kitchen. Two of the women are preparing tripe (stomach lining of a cow, pig, or sheep). The woman on the left is thoroughly cleaning the stomach's content, before placing it in the wooden bin at her feet. Because of the toughness of tripe, it required soaking in water for several hours before cooking it. The woman on the right is cooking the tripe in a kettle filled with water, wine, or milk. This process could take several hours before the tripe was considered edible. The woman at the table in the background appears to be sampling the prepared food.

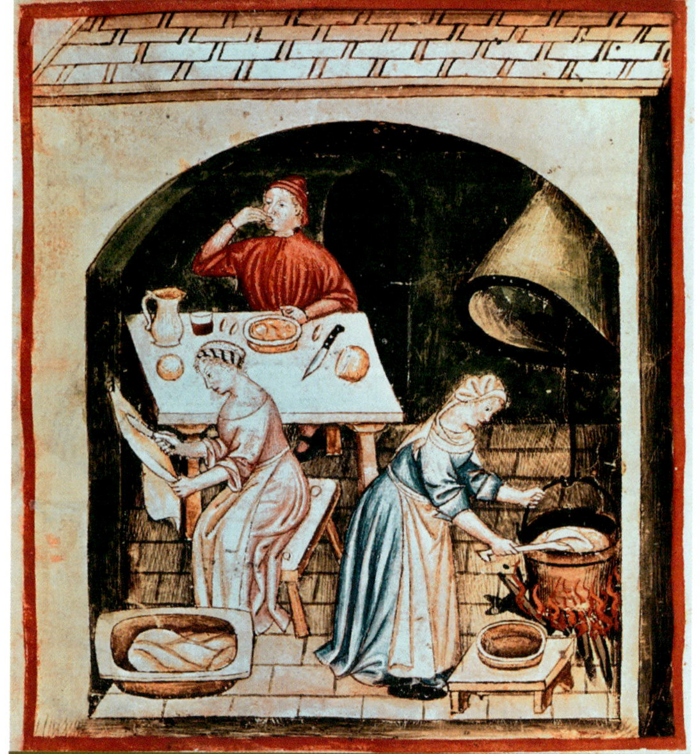

FIGURE 3.19 – Preparing Tripe, Tacuinum Sanitatis. Italy. c. 14th century. Page from The Medieval Health Handbook.

The *Wedding Feast at Cana* (see Figure 3.20) depicts the sumptuous setting of a sixteenth century Venetian wedding. Paolo Veronese (1528–1588) painted this feast in a room filled with exquisite furniture, crystal glassware, ornate plates, and an abundance of food and drink. The scene shows at least 130 people in attendance, from various noblemen to Christ and his disciples. Christ is seated at the head of the table, while the wedding couple is off to his left. It is at this event where Christ performs his first miracle of turning water into wine.

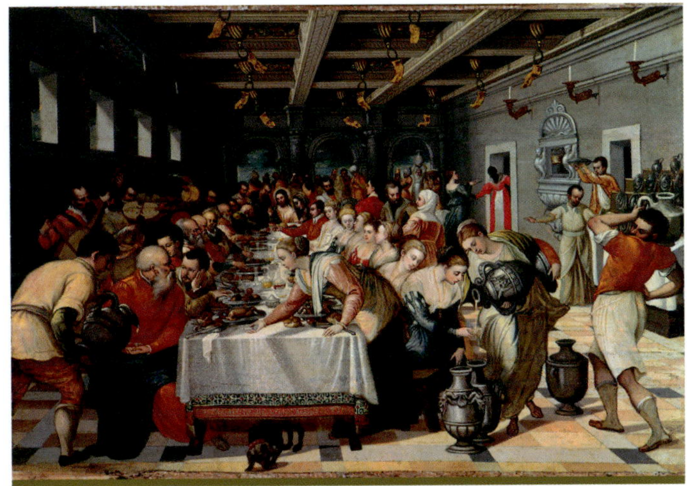

Leemage/Hulton Fine Art Collection/Getty Images

FIGURE 3.20 – The Wedding Feast at Cana, Michael Damaskenos. 1563. 267 x 391 in. Oil on canvas.

The detail view from the *Wedding Feast at Cana* (see Figure 3.21) shows the wealthy absorbed in conversation or distracted by other events to where they are seemingly unaware of those there to serve them. To the right, a servant reaches out to offer a guest dessert—a quince, a small fruit symbolic of marriage.

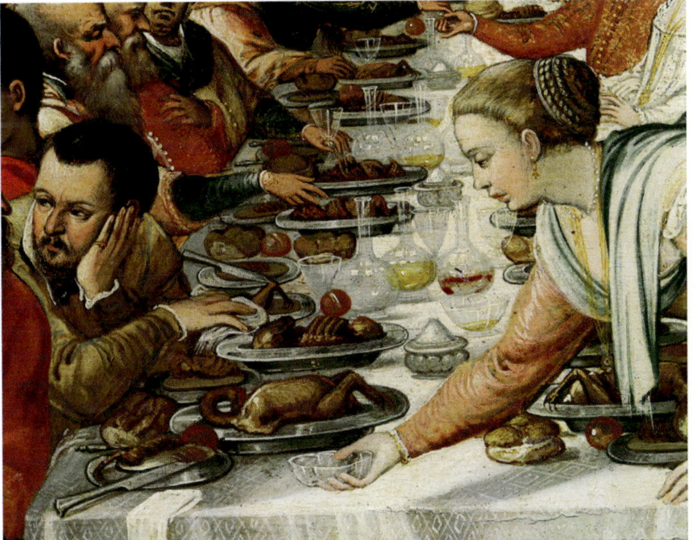

DEA/A. DAGLI ORTI/De Agostini/Getty Images

FIGURE 3.21 – The Wedding Feast of Cana (detail), Michael Damaskenos.

Three-legged bronze wine vessels were created in the Chinese culture for various purposes, which dictated their overall design. The *Jue* (see Figure 3.22) is an example of one of the oldest wine mugs. The overall shape is typically defined by its long beak or spout, with small handles on either side. During the Shang Dynasty (1600–1050 BC), the addition of one or two 'buttons' (posts with knobs on top) was added near the beak. This type of bronze wine vessel was very popular until artists began creating bowls and cups during the Song Dynasty (960–1279 CE).

Many cultures create elaborate serving utensils for special occasions. The Tlingit culture, in the Pacific Northwest Coast region of the United States, is divided into two major clans: raven and eagle. In northwest coast art and mythology, the raven is a highly regarded being. His role may vary slightly from one culture to another, but is often viewed as the trickster, teacher, and chief spirit. The raven has the power to transform himself and others into something else, even into inanimate matter. To the Tlingit people, the Raven is the central figure in their creation myth, for he was responsible for bringing light and other things into the world.

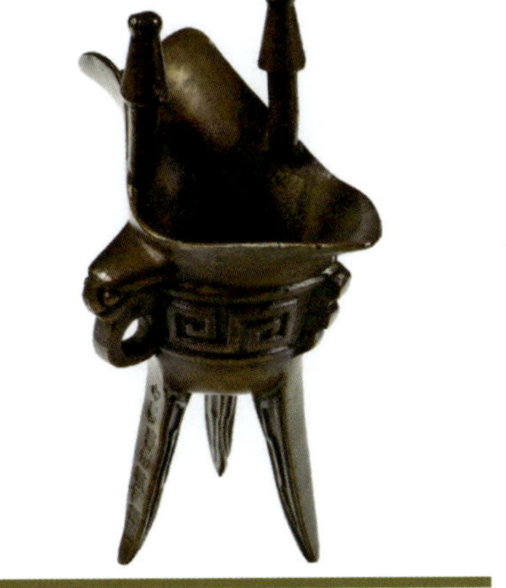

©Nikodem Nijaki/Shutterstock.com

FIGURE 3.22 – Jue—Chinese Bronze Ritual Tripod Wine Vessel on White. China. 12th century BC. 3 15/16 x 7 3/4 x 6 1/2 in. Bronze.

One version of this story tells of a chief who kept the stars, moon, and daylight within his clan house. The Raven learned the chief had a beautiful daughter who drank from the stream outside their home each morning. Raven transforms himself into a speck of dirt to float into the girl's cup as a way to sneak inside the house. The dirt was detected and the water thrown out. So he transformed himself into a hemlock needle, the color of the wood from which the ladle is created, and goes undetected. The daughter drinks the water and becomes pregnant with Raven in the form of a human baby. Eventually, the child is born. As the story unfolds, the boy, raven's mother, and his grandfather find it hard to refuse him any of his wishes out of the deep love they felt for him. The boy eventually finds the treasure boxes that possess the stars, moon, and sun. Although told not to open any of them, he eventually does one by one, which gives the world what was protected within.

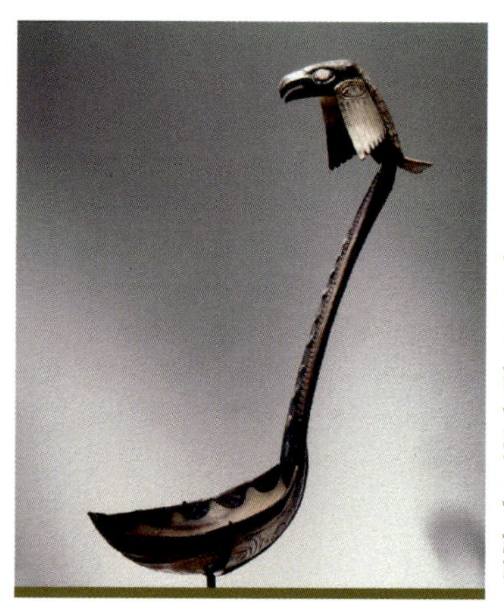

©Nikodem Nijaki/Shutterstock.com

FIGURE 3.23 – Ladle with a Raven Perched on the Handle. Tlingit Culture, Native American. United States. Late 19th century. Horn, bone, copper and abalone shell inlay.

When cultures like the Tlingit create objects for ceremonial purposes, the artists will decorate them with images associated with their specific clan. On this Tlingit ladle (see Figure 3.23), a raven is sitting perched on its handle. It is identifiable as a raven through its straight, tapering beak, slightly curved at the tip. Its ears are not prominent and the long wings are often shown close to the body. The ladle is made of horn and decorated with copper and abalone shell inlay. This type of ladle was most likely reserved for ceremonial purposes.

STORAGE OF FOOD

As cultures settled into a more sedentary lifestyle, the need for food and drink storage became more of a priority. Pottery was developed for such purposes, providing a variety of sizes and shapes to accommodate what was being stored within.

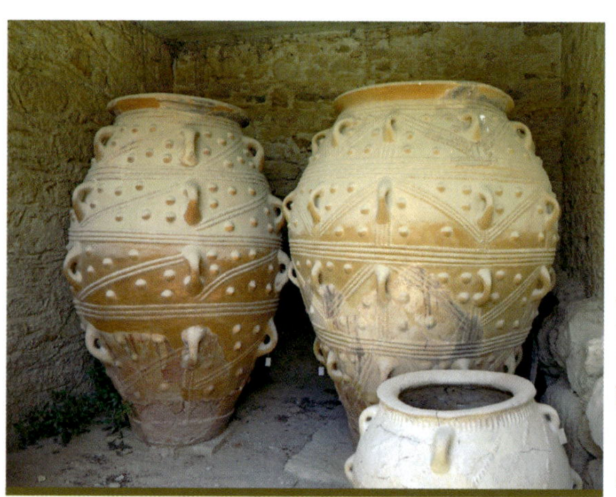

©arogant/Shutterstock.com

FIGURE 3.24 – Ancient Clay Minoan Amphora. Crete, Greece. c. 1900 BC. Ceramic.

In Minoan culture, large amphorae (see Figure 3.24), sometimes taller than a man, were commonly used for bulk storage of commodities, such as oil, wine, and grains. They were unpainted, but often decorated with circular elements, like raised knobs, loops, and lines, perhaps mimicking the ropes that were used to move them.

Throughout the ages, different cultures created food storage that best suited their needs and environmental conditions. The Inuit cultures of Alaska and Canada were able to store food outside on raised platforms for short periods of time due to the severely cold conditions in which they lived. The food was elevated above ground level (see Figure 3.25) to provide protection from animals. The extreme cold was enough to prevent the meat from spoiling in such an open structure.

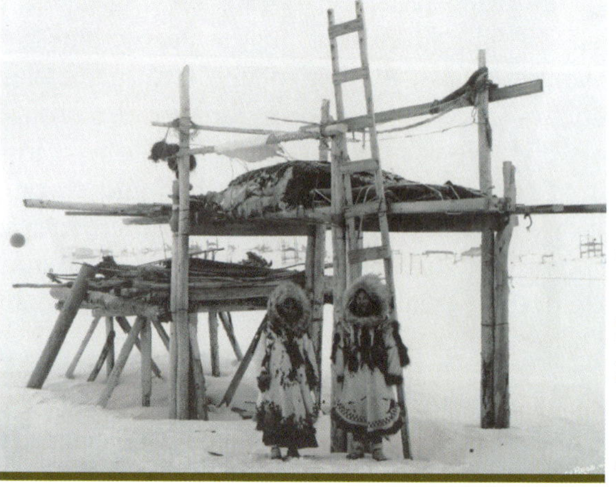

Courtesy of the Library of Congress

FIGURE 3.25 – Eskimo (Inuit) Women and Storage Place, Lomen Brothers. Cape Prince of Wales, Alaska. 1916. Photograph.

In the Maori culture of New Zealand, a *pataka* (or storage house) resembled a house raised up on stilts. The entrance to the pataka was off of a balcony located on the front of the structure. To access the balcony a ladder would be placed through a small hatch in the balcony's floor. The design of the pataka provided the people a tactical advantage of funneling their enemy through a small opening and making it easier to defend the food, ritual objects, and other possessions stored inside. Red in the Maori culture represents something that is sacred. An object or structure that is painted red, like the pataka (see Figure 3.26), and what it stores is therefore perceived to be under spiritual protection.

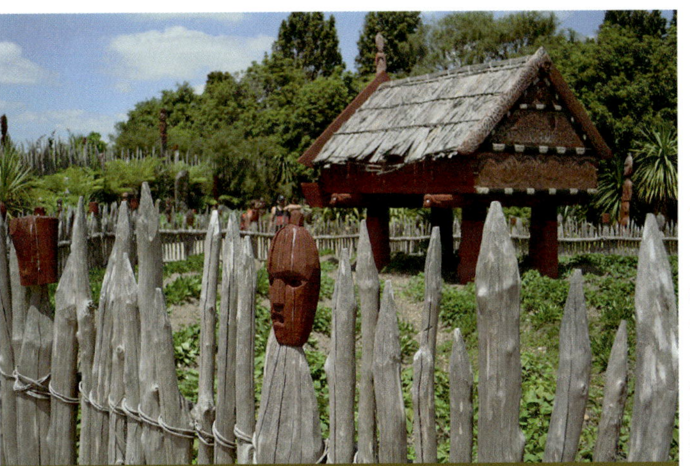

©Vadim Boussenko/Shutterstock.com

FIGURE 3.26 – Pataka (The Parapara Maori Garden). Hamilton Gardens, New Zealand. 1960.

The elaborate carvings on the outside represent various animals and mythical beings. Whales are commonly seen depicted on structures or objects related to food because they are a symbol of plenty to the Maori people. They not only were an important food source, but also provided bone for tools and fishing implements and oil for light and heat. The mythical being called Manaia is considered to be a guardian spirit and can be found on these same items.

RITUALS

Many cultural rituals revolve around food. The living or the dead from a culture could be called upon to aid in them. Artists have created imagery, as well as objects, relevant to these purposes.

In the Minoan culture, the crocus is a flower that holds great significance. The stigma from the center of the flower is dried to make saffron, a subtle, but distinctive spice used for cooking. Its fragrance led to its use in the perfume industry, and eventually its rich color to its use in the clothing industry. When picking the crocus' stigma, a person's fingertips are stained a deep yellow color. This was discovered to be water-soluble and resistant to light, leading it to be used in the dying of fabric. Over the years, saffron was also discovered to have medicinal properties. It eased menstrual cramping and was used to treat various ailments and diseases, ranging from stomach aches to inflammation and infection. It appears in imagery associated with religious rituals, typically shown as an offering.

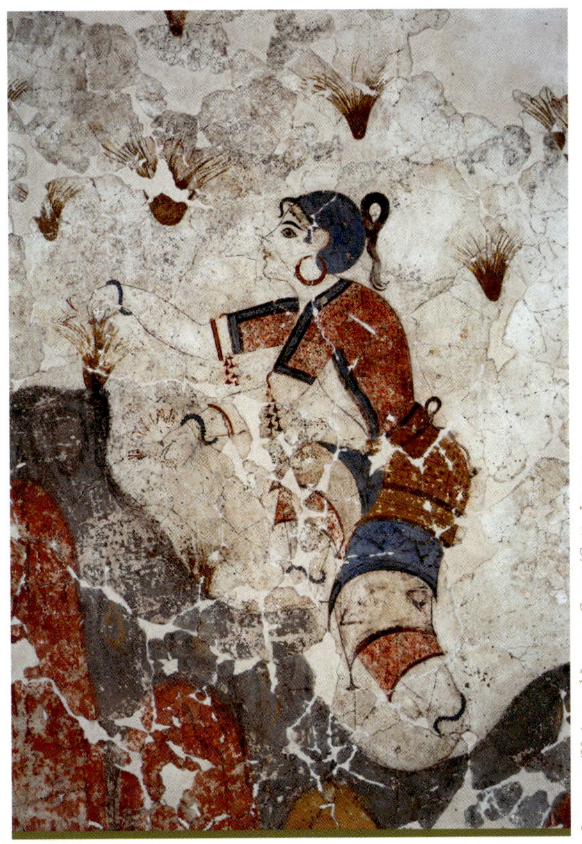

Leemage/Universal Images Group/Getty Images

FIGURE 3.27 – The Saffron Gatherers (detail). Crete, Greece. c. 1600 BC. Fresco.

Women's roles in Minoan society included cooking and the making of clothing. Because of this saffron quickly became associated with female social identity. In *The Saffron Gatherers* (see Figure 3.27), a young woman is depicted harvesting the saffron from the crocus flower. Some art historians believe this was part of an initiation ritual that familiarized a young woman with the significance of saffron to their culture as a whole and to her individually. Further support of the significance of saffron and the crocus flower to women, in particular, may be supported through the visual use of yellow in women's clothing in murals, and the noticeable lack of it in male attire.

In ancient Thailand, there was a custom of providing water for travelers, as they would take a break on their journey. Large clay pots filled with rainwater would be placed outside a person's home (see Figure 3.28). A ladle made from coconut shell would allow the traveler to drink from the pot. Over the years, people used the custom as a way to welcome people into their home, reflecting the cultural paradigm of hospitality and generosity. Earthenware pots were porous allowing the water within to evaporate slowly. This evaporation process reduces the water's temperature, keeping it naturally cool throughout the day.

EARTHENWARE – a type of low-fired clay that remains slightly porous after being fired in a kiln.

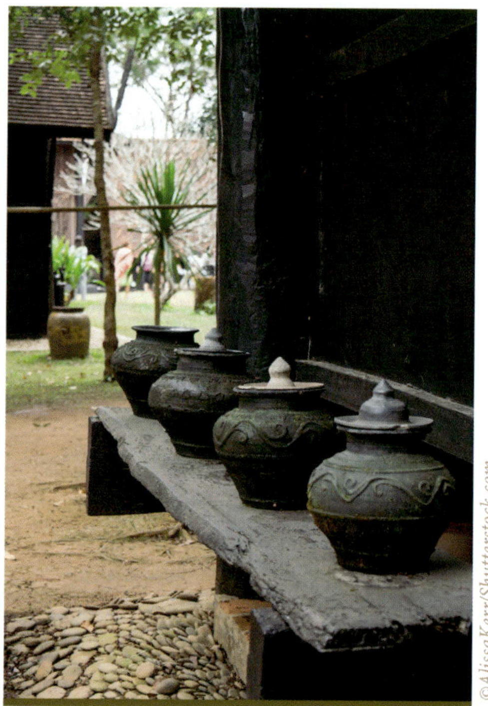

©AlissaKerr/Shutterstock.com

FIGURE 3.28 – An Old Traditional Welcome Water Drink in Clay Pots for Visitors, Alissala Kerr. Thailand.

In more modern times, this custom eventually faded out due to environmental and social concerns. Travelers were now weary of the rainwater because it was tainted by pollution and possibly the germs of others. In addition, the increased theft of these beautifully made pots led to a distrust of strangers near homes, leading to the complete disappearance of this social custom.

Over 3000 years ago, the ancient Aztecs from central Mexico practiced an annual month long ritual to honor their dead. The ritual involved the displaying of skulls, usually trophies collected from battle. To Mesoamerican cultures, like the Aztecs, skulls were a symbol of death and rebirth. They believed life on earth was a dream and that one was truly awake in death. When the Spanish Conquistadors landed in Aztec territory over 500 years ago, they found the indigenous people to be primitive and barbaric. They saw their ritual to honor the dead as something that instead mocked death. The Spaniards attempted to convert the Aztecs to Catholicism thereby eliminating many of the religious practices they deemed sacrilegious. Finding it impossible to completely change the indigenous people and their traditions, the Spaniards compromised by blending the two religions together. While the month long ritual historically took place during what would be August on today's calendar, it was moved to November 1st and 2nd of each year to coincide with the Catholic holiday known as 'All Soul's Day & All Saint's Day.'

The Day of the Dead celebration that takes place now throughout Mexico is varied depending on the region. There are similarities between the practices and a continued use of skull imagery throughout. On the first day, altars (see Figure 3.29) were created in family homes for the deceased, upon which food, drink, and other items were placed. In lieu of using the real skulls of their ancestors, families have wooden skulls made for these altars. In addition, family members would visit the graveyards to pull weeds, pick up debris, and decorate the graves of their loved ones.

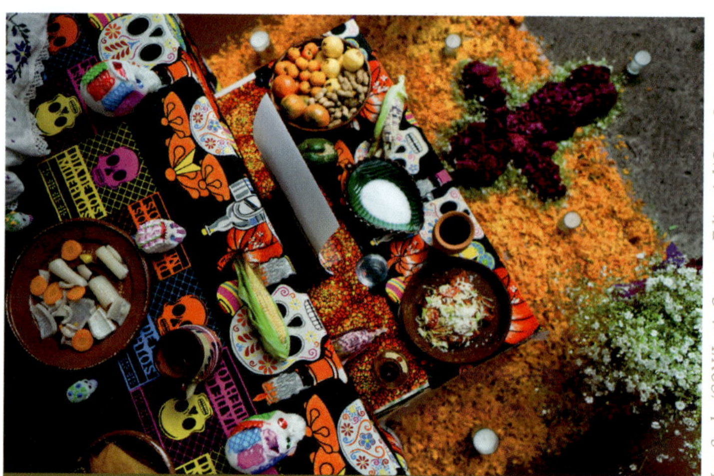

Jan Socho/CON/LatinContent Editorial/Getty Images

FIGURE 3.29 – Day of the Dead Celebration (offering). Michoacán, Mexico. 2014.

On the second day of the Day of the Dead celebration, the families would move the festivities to their ancestors' gravesites. They play games, drink, listen to music, and feast, for this time is perceived truly as a celebration of life. It is believed that happy ancestral spirits will provide wisdom, good luck, and protection to the living as a result.

FOOD AS ART

Like all things relative to humans, food becomes of interest in artistic pursuits throughout the ages. Food has been used as the subject matter of artwork, as the material with which an artwork is made, and as the means to elevate the mundane to something extraordinary in the mind of the viewer.

STILL-LIFE – a group of mostly inanimate objects assembled to create a composition used as subject matter in an artwork.

Dutch painter, Pieter Claesz (1597–1661) was best known for his still-life paintings. He was one of the early pioneers in depicting tabletop still lifes, possessing a sensitivity to how he rendered light and texture. Throughout his career he had three distinct styles. The earliest work possessed a strong use of light and bright colors, with many objects within his compositions. His style evolved over time into one that embraced the subtleties of light and color, and a paring down of objects compositionally. In *Still Life with a Stoneware Jug, Berkemeyer and Smoking Utensils* (see Figure. 3.30), Claesz's more subdued, monochromatic palette is used. He pared the number of objects in the still life down considerably to where there is not much overlap seen between them. In addition, Claesz incorporated the table's edge into his compositions to create a sense of depth not earlier seen in his works. In his later paintings, he returned to the complex compositions with a more vivid use of color.

Giuseppe Arcimboldo (1527–1593) was born in Milan, Italy. Throughout his artistic career, he received major commissions to design stain glass windows for Duomo (an Italian cathedral church) and other locations. Eventually in 1562, he became a court portraitist to Ferdinand I (1503–1564), King of Germany, and later to Maximillian II (1527–1576) and his son, Rudolf II (1552–1612), of Prague.

Throughout his career, Arcimboldo created many conventional works of art based on religious subjects, but he is best remembered for his unusual portraits of human heads made up of vegetables, fruit, and tree roots. They were greatly admired by his contemporaries and centuries later became a source of inspiration to artists, like Salvador Dali.

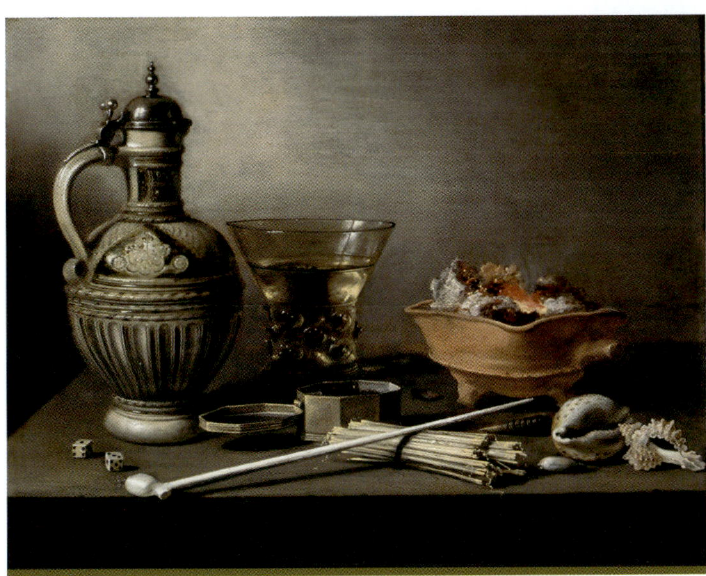

Indianapolis Museum of Art/Archive Photos/Getty Images

FIGURE 3.30 – Still Life with a Stoneware Jug, Berkemeyer and Smoking Utensils, Pieter Claesz. 1640. 17.5 x 23.5 in. Oil on panel.

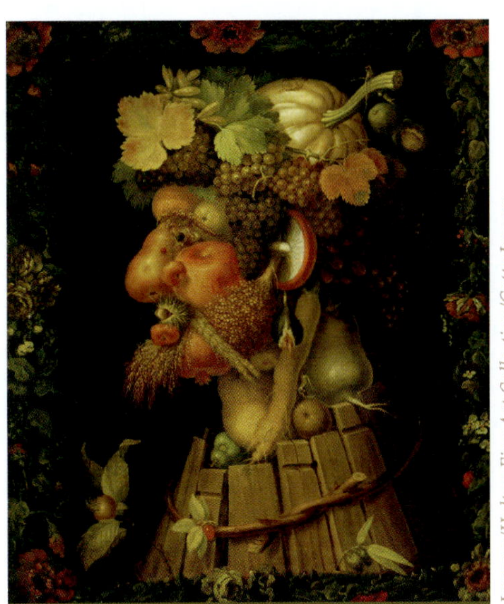

Imagno/Hulton Fine Art Collection/Getty Images

FIGURE 3.31 – Autumn, Giuseppe Arcimboldo. 1573. 24.8 x 29.92 in. Oil on canvas.

What led Arcimboldo to create these unusual portraits has caused great debate among scholars and art critics. Perhaps they were simply whimsical images that came to him or a product of madness, as some claim. However, during the Renaissance period (1300–1700) when he was creating them, people were fascinated with puzzles, riddles, and anything that fell into the realm of the bizarre. One can look to other artists of the time, including Leonardo da Vinci (1452–1519) – a fellow Italian who was drawing grotesque images of heads. Arcimboldo may simply have been exploring and pushing the boundaries of the norm like his contemporaries.

Whatever the case may be, *Autumn* (see Figure 3.31) is an example of Arcimboldo's work in this area. Upon initial glance the face appears to be painted normally and then adorned with a hat of fruit and gourds. However, closer inspection reveals that every aspect of the head from the eyes to the nose, mouth and neck are created from individual pieces of food.

Through the invention of photography, a whole new world opened up to people. Artists were capturing landscapes, portraits, and moments in time with the push of a button where before it would take them hours or months to reproduce through drawing, painting or sculpting.

American photographer, Edward Weston (1886–1958) developed into a strong portrait artist with an inherent understanding of light and composition. Over the decades of his career, he explored many subjects including landscapes, nudes, natural forms, and close-ups. The major impact on Weston's career personally—and on the world of photography—came with his exploration of the abstract. He explored objects, not as a whole, but close-up. In addition to Weston's understanding of light and ability to capture sharp detail, he was able to turn ordinary food into abstract works of art. By photographing food in this way, sometimes revealing the inside of a piece of fruit or a vegetable, one began to realize the beauty of something once simply perceived as a source of nourishment. In *Cabbage Leaf* (see Figure 3.32), Weston captures the unique lines and the visual movement they create through lighting and black and white photography. Stripping away the color of the lettuce and framing it in closely, the focus becomes more about it as an object of art and less about it as food.

Cheryl Pannabecker is an American artist who became a ceramic sculptor. She facilitates art workshops among the senior centers, nursing homes, and assisted living centers in Ohio, while continuing to exhibit her work regionally. Pannabecker's artistic influences are from art history and mythology. In one body of work, she focused on food in ceramic still lifes. Of these, the artist says, "These still lifes commemorate food items—something common to us put into a new context—which helps to elevate or add another layer to the everyday."

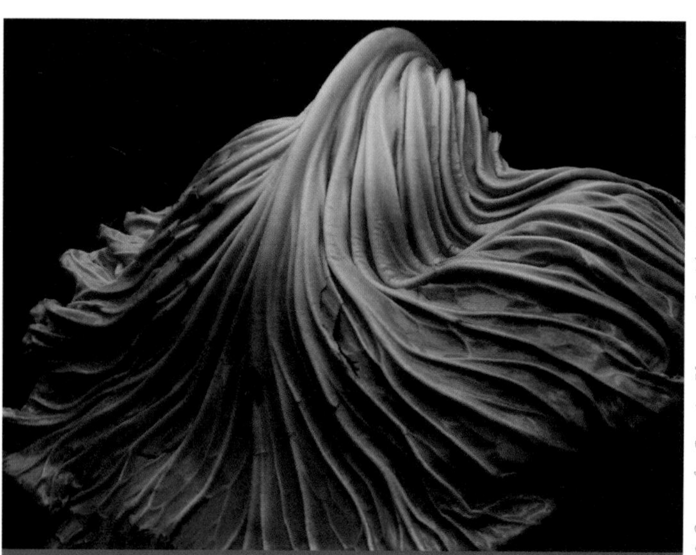

FIGURE 3.32 – Cabbage Leaf, Edward Weston. 1931. 19.1 x 24.1 cm. Gelatin silver print.

In *Blood Oranges* (see Figure 3.33), Cheryl Pannabecker depicts cut pieces of blood oranges on a shelf, surrounded by a dark red swirling frame. In the background, the painted image pulls from the biblical story of the beheading of Holofernes by Judith. The image shows her cradling his head in her arms, more traditional of the early Renaissance interpretations of the 1400s. Behind Judith are army tents with circus stripes and barren trees. The blood oranges are cut open to intensify the bloody scene behind them–the red juice dripping on the piece to the right mimics the Holofernes' blood dripping down Judith's dress. The sharp edges, swirls, and color of the border were chosen to suggest power, energy, and danger.

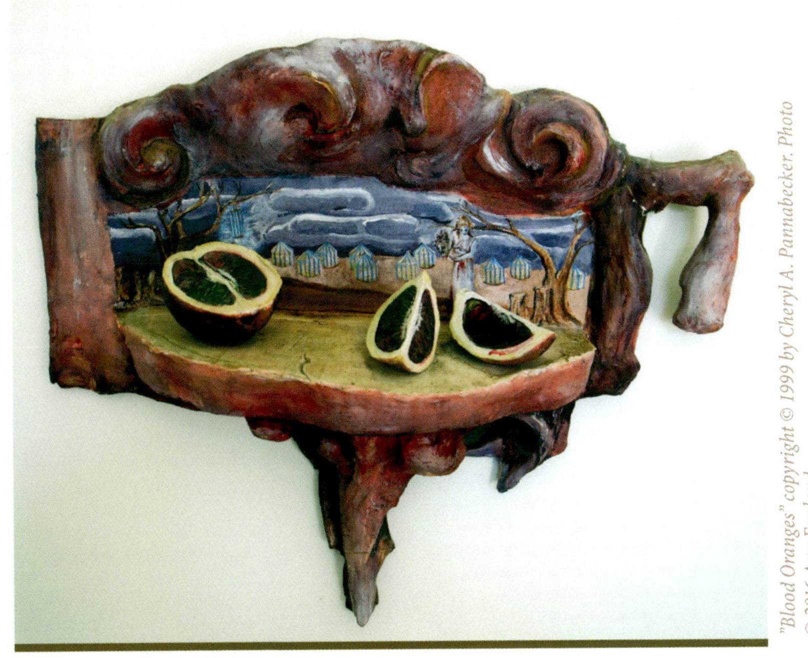

FIGURE 3.33 – Blood Oranges, Cheryl Pannabecker. 1999. 14 x 13 x 5 in. Ceramic, oil paint, canvas.

Photographer David Martin uses food, in addition to the human form, to challenge societal perceptions of race, gender, and sexuality. One day while enjoying a bag of M&M's, the artist realized that not all of the candy was identically shaped. Further exploration of the candy revealed that some were not clearly marked with the company's signature 'm'. Yet, the manufacturing process is intended to produce a consistent product. Martin saw a connection to his other body of work and began collecting these odd pieces from several bags of M&M's over a period of a few months. He then documented the anomalies through photography.

Sexuality I (see Figure 3.34), displays thirty-five pieces of candy that were naturally deformed or misshapen during the manufacturing process. Of this piece, Martin says, "The comparisons to human sexuality were very clear to me. M&M's are just as varied as the sexual continuum in many ways...and we just don't really notice it until we stop to really look." Martin's photographic series may not be self-explanatory, until the viewer takes the title into account while looking more closely at the imagery.

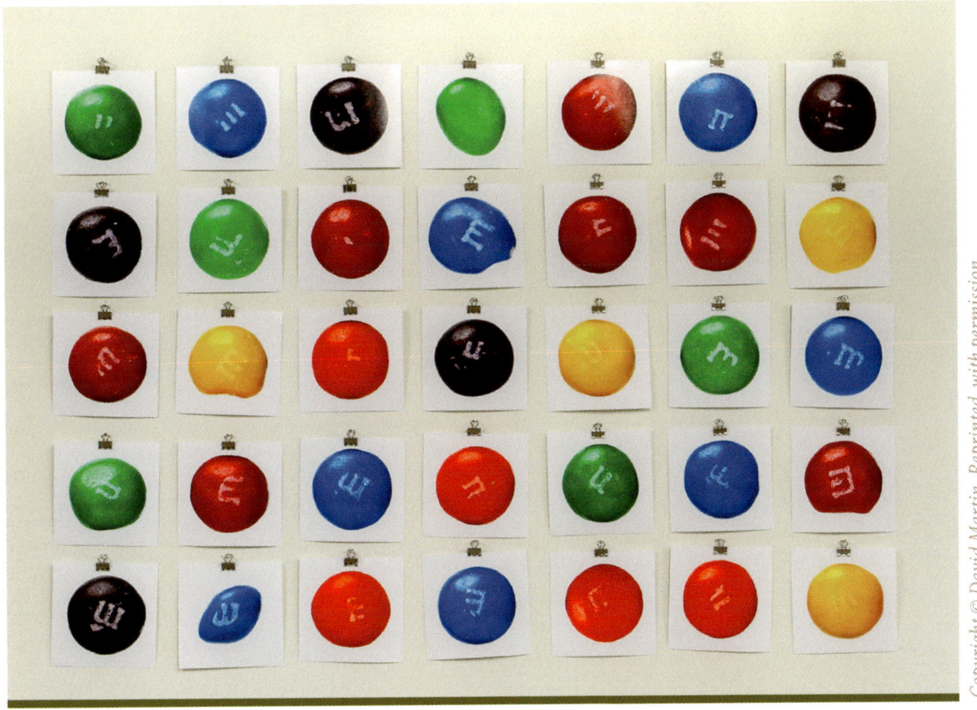

FIGURE 3.34 – Sexuality I, David Martin. 2012. 4 x 4 in. (each). Digital photography (series of 35 images).

part 3

ARCHITECTURE

In Paleolithic Africa (c. 100,000 BC), early man sought shelter in natural rock formations, such as caves. Over the centuries man observed his environment, looked to the past for inspiration and adapted to the materials available to suit his ever-changing needs for shelter. Even today in parts of the world, people look to natural resources and recycled materials from which to build.

NATURAL RESOURCES

Millions of years ago, a volcanic eruption covered what is now Cappadocia, Turkey with a thick blanket of ash that over time formed soft rock. Erosion, created by wind and water, shaped its landscape into a mass of towering lava rock formations. Because of the ease in which the lava rock can be carved, people have used these formations to create their homes. In *Rock Formations* (see Figure 3.35), the image shows multiple openings carved into the face of the rock formations. These rock homes not only provided protection from the elements, but left land open for agriculture and other needs of the community. To this day, the local people are still occupying them.

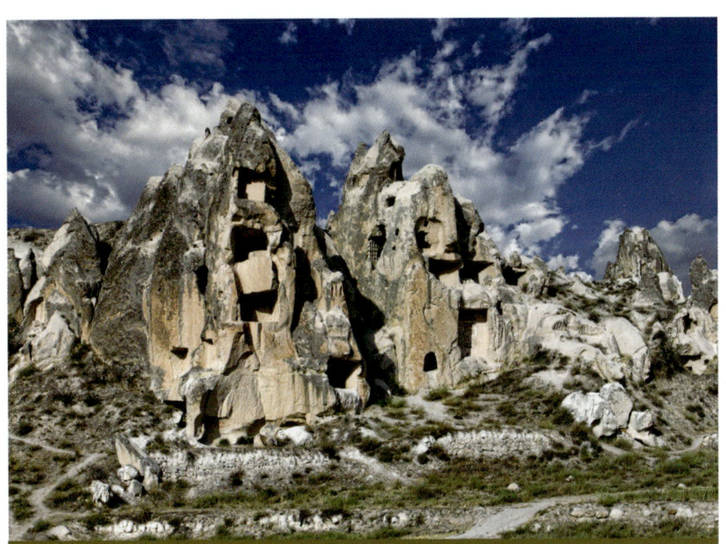

FIGURE 3.35 – Rock Formations. Cappadocia, Turkey. c. 8th–7th century BC.

For centuries, this region of Turkey has been surrounded by conflict. In response to the spikes of violence and political unrest throughout history, people living in Cappadocia created a safe haven in which to survive. Recent discoveries revealed two hundred underground 'cities' spreading across a 100 square mile stretch that have been utilized at various points for shelter. Many of these have been expanded upon over time, connected by a series of tunnels and built to include temples, secret rooms, hidden passageways, areas for livestock, communal rooms, pits for cooking, and water tanks. Built in ventilation shafts allowed for survival underground for long periods of time.

Derinkuyu is one of the largest underground cities. It extends eleven levels deep, with hundreds of entrances and the capacity to support thousands of people. In times of invasion, people quietly and unseen left their homes through tunnels directly connected to the underground city. In the interior of *Derinkuyu Cave City* (see Figure 3.36), the image shows the layout of a section of this underground city. Multiple rooms can be seen extending off the larger one, all of which are carved out of solid lava rock. Traps were laid throughout the corridors to prevent those unfamiliar with them from successful passage. Stones were rolled across doorways and secured in place. In strategic locations, openings were carved into the ceilings so spears could be dropped down on invaders. These cities were extended and added upon over the centuries to serve the needs of a growing population when a tumultuous situation arose.

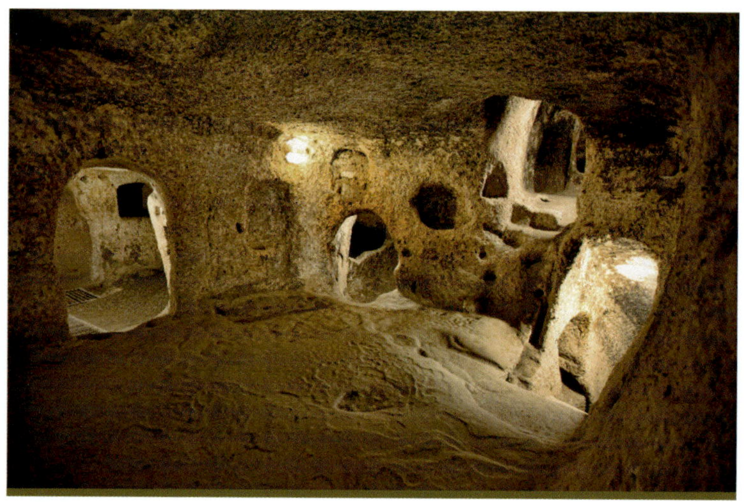

FIGURE 3.36 – Derinkuyu Cave City (interior of city). Capadocia, Turkey. c. 4th century.

In some of the Native American cultures of Alaska and Canada, the people refer to themselves as *Inuit*, meaning 'the people.' At times the construction of homes out of snow was a direct result of the severe climatic conditions in the region. Dense snow was carved into blocks that were stacked upon one another creating a circular wall. With each layer the blocks began to change slightly in shape and/or size resulting in a domed structure or *igloo* (see Figure 3.37) with a small opening carved in the top for ventilation. Typically, a long tunnel that was low to the ground was created as the entrance way and then covered with animal skins. This helped to trap the cold air from entering into the central room. The inside of an igloo was large enough for a couple of men to stand upright, to spread out to sleep at night and with a fire to keep warm. The dense snow trapped the heat of their bodies and the fire which warmed the air of the interior. This caused the inside walls to gradually start to melt. The cold exterior air, however, quickly freezes the melted water. By turning the moisture into ice, the slight gaps between the blocks were sealed, creating a more insulated structure.

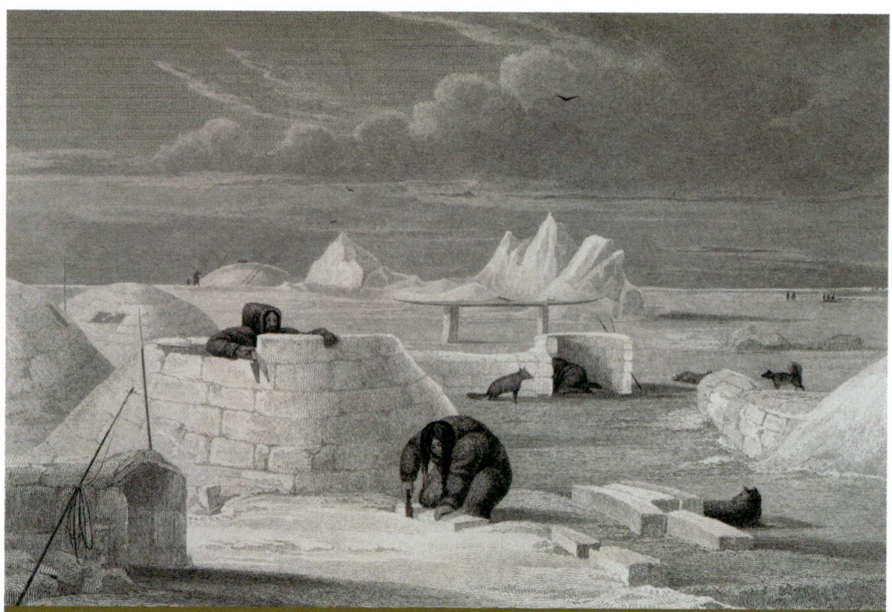

FIGURE 3.37 – Eskimo (Inuit) Building a Snow-Hut, William Edward Parry. 1824. Engraving.

Historically, families lived in igloos during the winter months. Igloos are now mostly constructed by men on hunting and fishing expeditions. These are environmental structures, since they are made out of the resources readily available in the environment. They are easy to maintain or reconstruct, if necessary, and easily recyclable as they simply melt away when warmer weather arrives. Over the years in these remote locations, the combination of commercial whaling and global warming has led to the diminishing of the Inuit's natural food sources. In addition, there is no longer as much of a need for these amazing structures, nor snow dense enough with which to build them.

The Hopi Indians of the American Southwest have utilized natural resources for centuries when building their homes. Since they are a matrilineal culture, which traces its descent through the female line, houses belong to the women. While men will assist with the heavier aspects of construction, it is the Hopi women who are responsible for the majority of the work. The process is rich in tradition and can still be seen today in the construction of homes on reservations.

Before beginning construction, the chief provided a woman with four small eagle feathers, eventually to be placed underneath the four cornerstones of the home. Bowls of food were then placed on either side of where the door would be located. Particles of food were sprinkled in lines to delineate where walls were to be built. The women collected water, clay, and earth to make the mortar, to be placed in between each layer of stone creating the walls. Once the walls were constructed, rafters created from wood limbs were crisscrossed to create the ceiling, which were then covered with layers of reeds and grass. At this point, the women covered the roof and walls of the house with plaster. The interior of a house usually contained a fireplace and chimney, along with minimal furnishings. The final step was to dedicate the home by hanging additional eagle feathers from a roof beam in the central part of the house. Once finished and dedicated, the owner of the house hosted a feast for all her clan members who had helped in its construction.

On the Housetop (see Figure 3.38) shows the Hopi method of building one home on top of another. Historically, this was used as a way to conserve space and provide protection in larger communities. Ladders were used to access the upper levels and could be pulled up to offer more protection during times of invasion. The flat roof of one house became the balcony of another. This outdoor space was used for cooking and sleeping during the summer months. While new architectural materials have been used in more recent times on reservations, there are areas where traditional techniques are still being utillized.

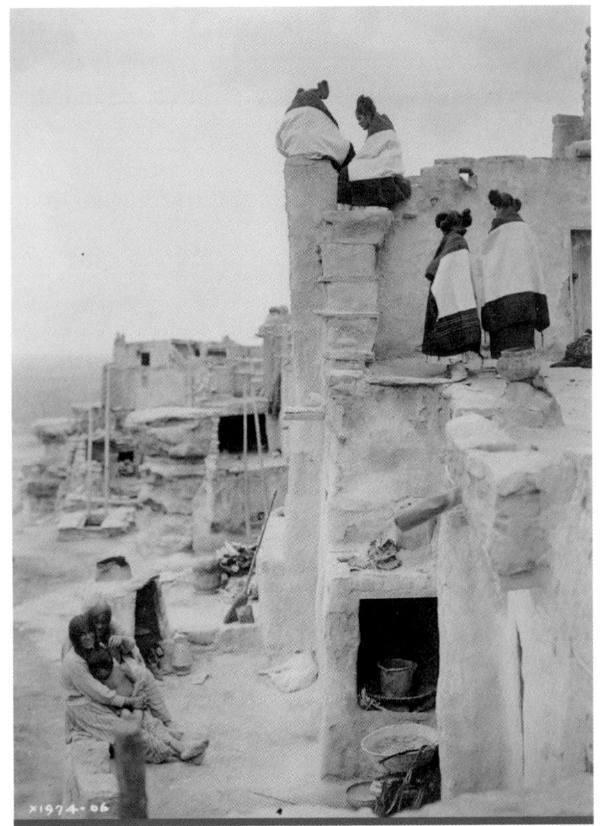

Courtesy of the Library of Congress

FIGURE 3.38 – On the Housetop—Hopi, Hopi Indians. Southwestern, United States.

RECYCLED MATERIALS

Revolutionary construction techniques and materials are being used in architecture today. Founder of Earthship Biotecture, Michael Reynolds (1940–), is one of the pioneers in this area. With the increasing amount of waste (plastic, metal, etc.) produced by the human population and its dependency upon utilities, there is an ever-greater need for recycling and a change to the way that people live. In response, architects have created a new way to construct homes that are self-sustainable and independent of all utilities supplied by outside companies. Thus creating a way of life referred to as living 'off the grid.' This type of housing became known as 'Earthships.'

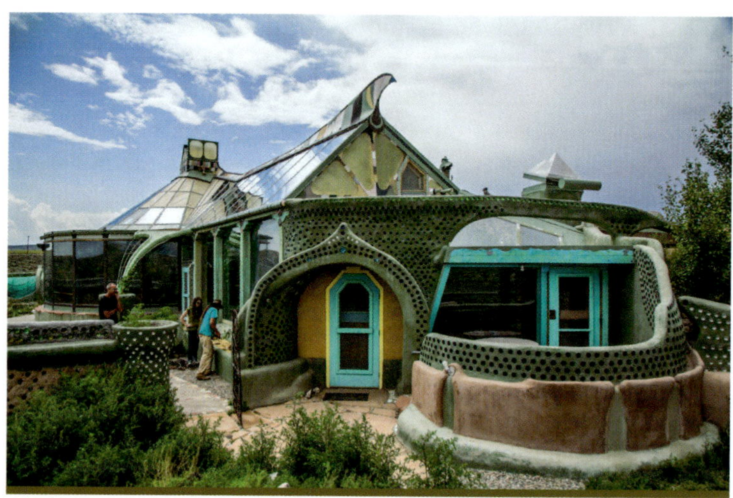
Ricardo DeAratanha/Los Angeles Times/Getty Images

FIGURE 3.39 – Phoenix Earthship, Michael Reynolds. Taos, New Mexico. c. 2004. 5300 ft^2. Recycled materials.

The *Phoenix Earthship* (see Figure 3.39) was built in the Greater World Community in Taos, New Mexico. This particular structure, since its construction, has served as a home to artists, writers, hippies, bikers, and nature lovers. The walls of Earthships are created out of old tires, bottles, and tin cans mixed with concrete. The sewage created by the owners is recycled through both indoor and outdoor treatment cells for landscaping and food production. Any leftover 'gray' water is used to flush toilets. Heating and cooling of these homes are created by using the 'stack effect' design within the building's construction. By creating openings in strategic places within the architecture, a natural ventilation system is created. The density of the air inside and outside the structure regulates the direction of airflow through those openings and its internal temperature.

These 'Earthships' have been built through the United States, and are now being constructed in Europe. Relief projects in Haiti, the Philippines, and other parts of the world are now using these construction techniques and recycled materials. Their ability to allow one to live off the grid, also means that these can be successfully created to provide homes in many third world countries and remote locations lacking resources, such as electricity and an abundance of building materials.

CEREMONIAL

Architecture has not only provided shelter for individuals historically, but has been used to create facilities for large groups to gather for religious, educational or entertainment purposes. Monumental structures have been built for ceremonial purpose, as well. These constructions have been created for centuries without the assistance of beasts of burden, metal tools, or with the help of modern technology.

In the mid-1960s, an ancient site, dating thousands of years earlier than either Stonehenge or the Great Pyramid of Giza, was discovered in the southeastern part of modern day Turkey. Official excavations began in the late 1990s by a team of archaeologists, led by a German named Klaus Schmidt (1953–2014). What they unearthed were a series of ceremonial structures that were created at various times throughout the history of the culture that built them. As more were unearthed and studied, it became evident that a structure, still in good condition, would be buried and then another immediately built nearby. The purpose this served to the people of Gobekli Tepe is unclear.

Globally, people were still living nomadic lifestyles. No permanent architectural structures were built as no one stayed in any one area for an extended period. Historically, it has been believed that large-scale civilizations developed much later in Mesopotamia because of the domestication of plants and animals, allowing for the support of larger numbers of people over longer periods of time. Eventually, this led to permanent architecture, social structures, governments, and written languages. However, in this part of the world, it appears that the need for religion led to this evolution. The construction of Gobekli Tepe was approximately

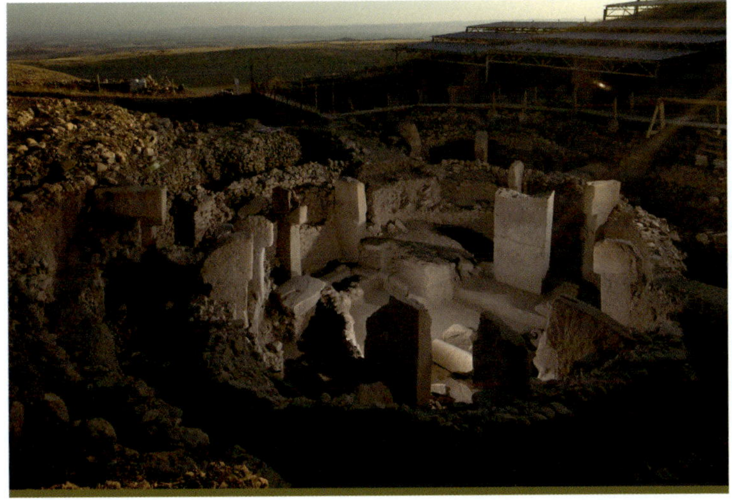

FIGURE 3.40 – Gobekli Tepe, a Religious Sanctuary Built by Hunter. Turkey. c. 9000 BC.

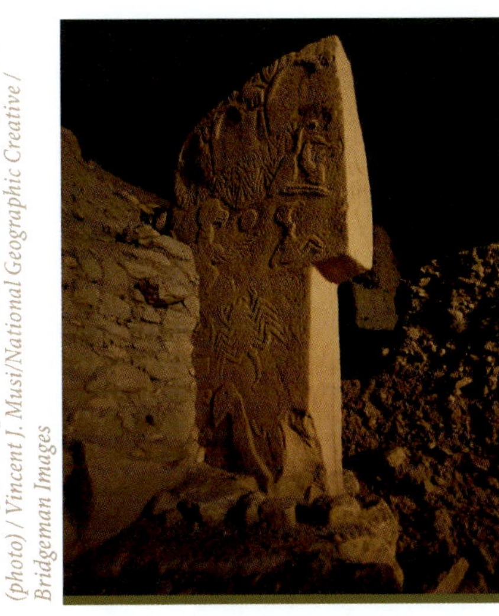

FIGURE 3.41 – A Pillar with a Vulture, Scorpion and a Headless Suman at Gobekli. Turkey. c. 9000 BC. Stone.

three miles from a water source and twenty miles from the nearest village, which seems to have arisen as a means to support those constructing the site. The only living quarters near Gobekli Tepe were for the builders. The stones used for construction came from a hundred yards away. The builders lacked the aid of horses or mules to move them, requiring ingenuity and sheer man power on their part. What led them to pick this location remains a mystery since there are no written records left behind, but to them it clearly possessed a sense of sacredness.

The basic construction of Gobekli Tepe (see Figure 3.40) was circular, enclosed with a stone wall. The inside consists of large T-shaped stones and a series of carvings of animals, insects, and birds, many of which were not believed to be indigenous to that region. Perhaps these were animals (see Figure 3.41) they encountered during their more nomadic ways or were mystical creatures somehow associated with their religious beliefs. Many theories exist as to why the people incorporated the animals into the structure. This ranged from animals that they feared and from which they needed protection to animals they needed to protect to their representations of their many deities.

More recent observations suggest a potential connection to the observation of the star constellations and the layout of the animal images on the stones. Each time one construction was buried and another built, the scale of the structures remained monumental. However, the overall construction and carvings became less refined with each new structure. This suggests, that while religion remained important to the people, there may have been outside forces—environmental or human—that prevented them from taking their time to create a new structure.

In Prehistoric England, located near the modern day city of Salisbury, a monumental architectural form was created. *Stonehenge* (see Figure 3.42) appears to be built in several phases beginning around 3000 BC. Over the span of a thousand years, its construction has changed, been added to and perhaps even been partially knocked down to its current state. Stonehenge started out as a circular ditch with an opening in the northeastern direction, carved with the aid of antler picks. The next phase included the addition of fifty-six

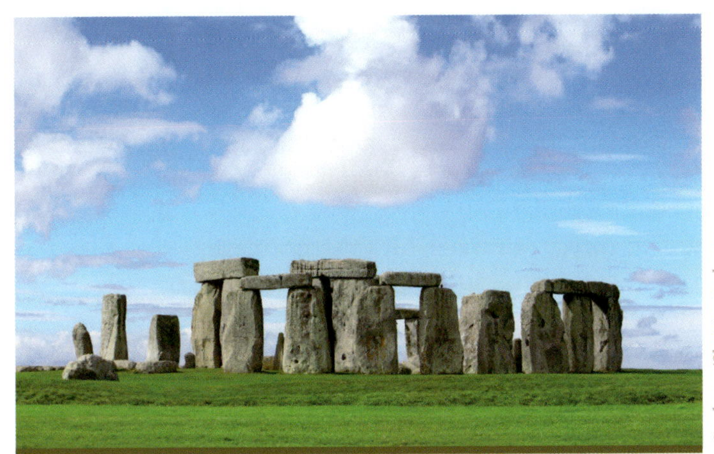

FIGURE 3.42 – Stonehenge an Ancient Prehistoric Stone Monument. Salisbury, UK. 3100–2500 BC. Stone.

wooden posts in a circle inside of the ditch. A grave of a sacrificed child was found located inside this construction, suggesting the purpose of the site may have also changed for its people at that time. Several hundred years later, brought from quarries approximately one hundred and fifty miles away. The people transported eighty bluestones, named for their bluish color. Eventually fifty large sarsen stones, using dolmen architecture, were placed in a circular fashion around the bluestones. Throughout the ages, the bluestones were reconfigured several times, ending in the horseshoe shape seen today. While the true purpose of the various phases of Stonehenge's construction remain a mystery, there seems to be evidence that connects the position of its final state to the passage of the sun and moon during the summer solstice. Today, people still gather to witness the spectacular site that occurs during that time.

Recent discoveries through satellite imaging have revealed the 'missing' stones of the final phase of Stonehenge are still on site. Perhaps knocked down by natural forces or later cultures, these stones were eventually overtaken by nature and remained unknown to the world until 2015.

COMMERCIAL

Throughout the ages, architects have designed the layouts of cities and the massive buildings within. Whether for administrative, business, or entertainment purposes, commercial architects strive to create designs that provide the most desirable space for each structure's intended use.

The Minoans (3650–1450 BC) became a thriving seafaring culture, controlling commerce throughout the Aegean region. Its ports were located in key locations around the Mediterranean Sea and led to large, complex capitals like Knossos. *The Minoan Palace of Knossos* (see Figure 3.43) sat on top of a hill on the Island of Crete overlooking the sea. Knossos was a complex of multi-storied buildings, which served as bathhouses, artisan studios, ceremonial halls, administrative offices, living spaces, and storage facilities. Being central to trade in the region, storage facilities were filled with food, pottery, jewelry, and art objects for trade. Due to the significant number of people who occupied and utilized this capital, architects designed bathrooms, plumbing, and drainage systems to continually provide better amenities and water to support its inhabitants and help prevent health issues. Roofs were slanted towards drains to direct rainwater into the drainage canals and to assist in directing sewage to septic pits outside the complex's walls.

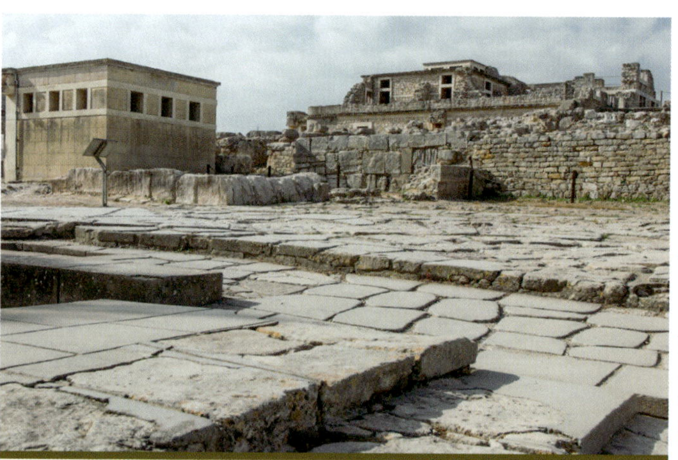

FIGURE 3.43 – The Minoan Palace of Knossos, Minoan. Crete, Greece. c. 1900 BC. Approximately 4 mi^2.

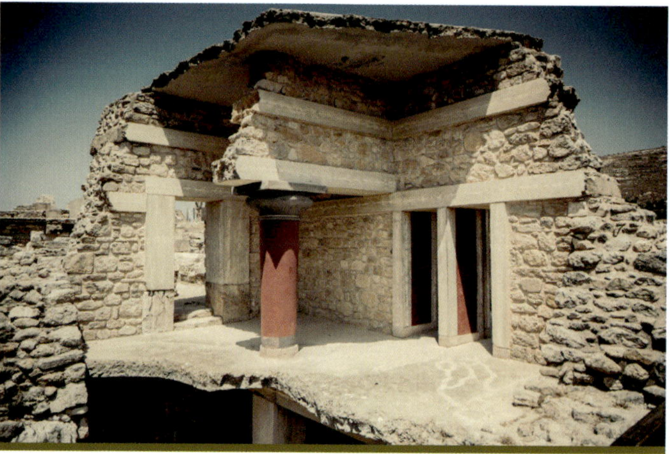

FIGURE 3.44 – Knossos Palace (detail), Minoan. Crete, Greece.

This region was known for being impacted by earthquakes throughout its history. After a major earthquake resulted in devastating damage to the complex, architects devised a technique of incorporating wooden beams above the columns and doorways (see Figure 3.44) into the stone architecture, which allowed for the buildings to flex more easily during an earthquake.

Because of their seafaring ways and love of nature, many of the murals throughout the complex depict images associated with them. Elaborate murals of flora and fauna can be seen, along with murals of aquatic life like the *Dolphin Mural* (see Figure 3.45). This was appropriately placed in a bathhouse within the complex.

Decoration of buildings and pottery found throughout Knossos exhibited their affinity for and awareness of the beauty of the natural world. Images included flora and fauna from sea and land, sea animals, boats, and sources of entertainment, like boxing scenes. The murals and decorative imagery were created with bold, rhythmic patterns, along with curvilinear and undulating forms that create visual movement within the works of art. The fall of the Minoan civilization and destruction of the city of Knossos occurred around 1350 BC. The causes leading to this were believed to be a combination of natural forces (earthquakes and a volcanic eruption) and an invading culture (Mycenaeans). Little was left of Knossos and other community centers on Crete, except for the palace.

CURVILINEAR – a visual element consisting of or alluding to curved lines.

RYTHMN – a visual technique created through the repetition of line, shape, and other formal elements within a work of art.

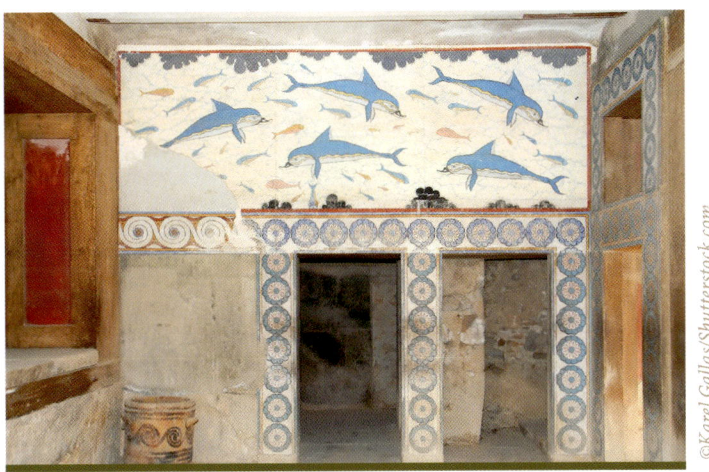

FIGURE 3.45 – Palace Knossos (dolphin mural), Minoan. Crete, Greece. c. 1800–1400 BC. Fresco.

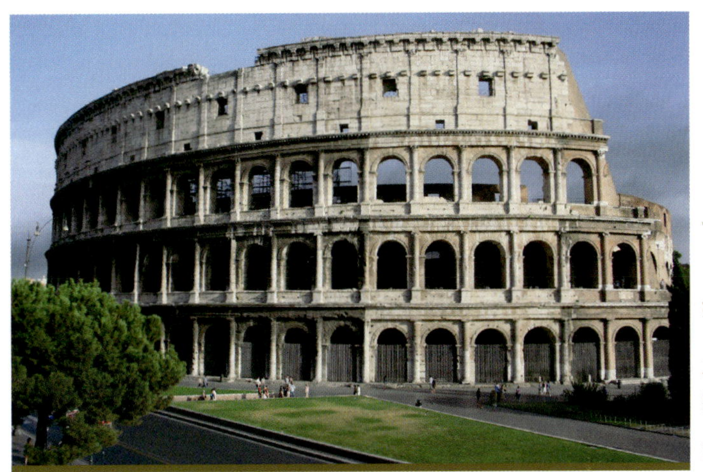

FIGURE 3.46 – The Colosseum (Flavian Amphitheatre). Rome, Italy. 70–80 CE. Covers 6 acres, 157 ft. high.

Throughout the long history of Rome and the impact of its rulers, major architectural strides were made. During the Flavian dynasty, Emperor Vespasian (9–79 CE) wanted to restore Senate authority, promote public welfare, and tone down the excesses of the Roman court, seen previously during Emperor Nero's (37–68 CE) reign. Vespasian commissioned the construction of the Colosseum (see Figure 3.46) in 70 CE as a gesture of his intentions and as a gift to the Roman people. The Colosseum was completed after his death, by his two sons, Titus (39–81 CE) and Domitian (51–96 CE). It officially opened in 80 CE with one hundred days of games, including wild animal fights and gladiatorial combats. However, its final stages of construction would not be finished until Domitian's reign during 81–96 CE.

The Colosseum was one of the first freestanding amphitheaters in the Roman world, seating more than 50,000 spectators. It was constructed out of stone and concrete, stood three stories high, and included underground passageways and rooms to house gladiators and wild animals. In addition, the structure was able to be flooded to re-enact naval battles and had an *valerium*, or awning, that could be extended to provide protection for the audience from the sun and rain. Two hundred and forty wooden beams ran the circumference of the top wall of the Colosseum to support the awning, which consisted of canvas, ropes and netting. When needed, hundreds of sailors from the Roman navy would operate a device to extend the awning.

The overall design of the Colosseum allowed for all spectators to have a clear view of the activities below (see Figure 3.47). There was designated seating based on one's social status. Those of higher rank, like members of the Senate, would be in the lower levels closest to the events, while ordinary citizens would be seated in the higher levels. A system of numbered entrances and staircases allowed rapid entry and exit from the Colosseum, much in the way as present-day athletic stadiums are designed.

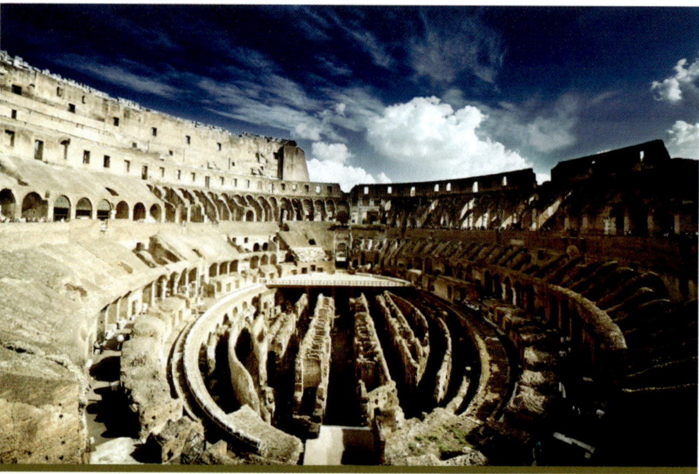

©Jakov Kalinin/Shutterstock.com

FIGURE 3.47 – Inside of Colosseum. Rome, Italy. 70–80 CE.

After four centuries of use, it was estimated that more than 500,000 people and over a million animals died for the entertainment of the Roman people. Struggles within the Roman Empire and the gradual change in the public's taste led to the Colosseum falling into ruin by the sixth century CE. A combination of natural disasters, such as earthquakes, neglect, and acts of vandalism over time had destroyed nearly two thirds of the original structure. By the 1990s, restoration efforts began to restore 85% of the Colosseum.

Another incredible Roman architectural feat was created under Emperor Trajan's (53–117 CE) rule. It was a large-scale commercial structure, known as Trajan's Market, built in 107 CE. It consisted of small shops, a covered market, and a residential apartment block. The three levels of Trajan's market were built into the terraced hillside behind it. The first two levels consisted of shops and businesses, while the upper level was used for apartments. The architecture was primarily constructed out of concrete, a material allowing more flexibility in overall design than carved stone. This is one of many structures historically that laid the groundwork for the design of shopping centers and apartment complexes one sees today.

Born in Denmark, Jørn Utzon (1918–2008) grew up under the influence of his father, who was a naval architect and engineer and director of a local shipyard. He spent a great deal of time sailing and intended on becoming a naval engineer like his father. However, within eight years of graduating and having worked in that field, Utzon changed his professional direction and opened his own architectural firm in 1950.

In 1956, an international design competition was held for the creation of an opera house with two performance halls to be built along the shores of Sydney Harbor in Australia. As the story goes, all but one member of the jury committee arrived on time and began dividing the submissions into two piles—potentials and rejects. When the last member of the committee, American architect Eero Saarinen (1910–1961), finally arrived, he glanced down at the discarded submissions. Seeing Jørn Utzon's design, he rescued and presented it to the committee, declaring it a bold and visionary design. The design called for two halls (one for instrumental music and the other for opera) arranged side by side, with their long axes running north-south. The auditoria were facing south, away from the harbor, with their stages located between the audience and the city. The vaulted roofs,

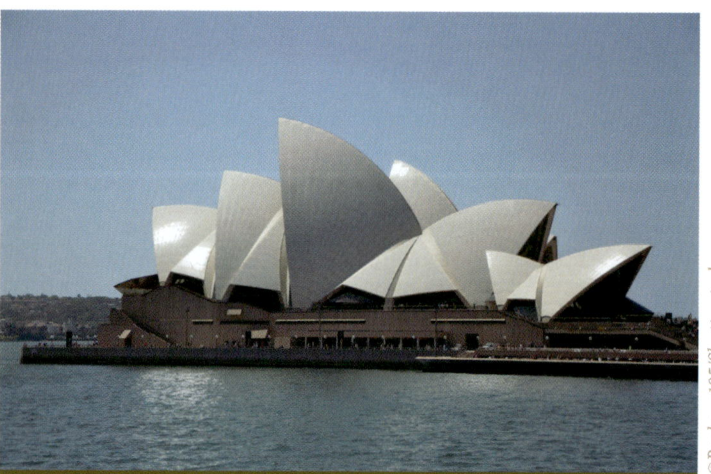

©Barbara185/Shutterstock.com

FIGURE 3.48 – Sydney Opera House. Australia. 1958–1973. 4.4 acres, 600 x 213 x 394 ft.

referred to as 'sails', were shaped like shells, each faced with glazed off-white tiles. These tiles reflected the color of the sun and were used to project colors, images, and designs for various events. Ultimately, Utzon's design was chosen and he was commissioned as the sole architect for the project.

Jørn Utzon's life and travels influenced his design for the *Sydney Opera House* (See Figure 3.48). Having never visited the project site, he used his maritime knowledge to study the naval charts of the harbor. Utzon's childhood exposure to shipbuilding served as inspiration for the opera house's sails and helped him solve construction challenges that arose along the way. Inspiration from his travels to Mexico led to his placing the building on a wide horizontal platform. Since nothing like the sail roof of his design had been done before, Utzon worked with several of the world's best construction engineers and craftsmen to create new building techniques to accomplish his vision. Although there was no budget restriction in the original proposal, in 1965 the leader of the new Liberal government eventually stopped payments to Utzon because of the extraordinary expense involved tackling these unique design challenges. This forced Utzon to resign and the public to protest. Ultimately, Australian architect, Peter Hall (1931–1995), was brought in to complete the opera house's construction.

Although, he was not in attendance for the opening of the Sydney Opera House, Jørn Utzon was awarded the Gold Medal from the Royal Australian Institute of Architects by Queen Elizabeth II (1926–) on October 20, 1973. Over twenty years later, at the request of the government and the Sydney Opera House Trust members, he agreed to create the 'Design Principles', a reference guide for all future changes to the building. Utzon said, "I like to think of the Sydney Opera House like a musical instrument, and like any fine instrument, it needs a little maintenance and fine tuning, from time to time, if it is to keep on performing at the highest level."

CORRUGATED – a material shaped to give its surface ridges and grooves.

Canadian-born Frank Gehry (1929–) was creative from an early age. From items he found in his grandfather's hardware store, he would build imaginary homes and cities. This early exploration led to his interest in using unconventional building materials throughout his career. In 1949, Gehry moved to the Unites States to pursue his education in architecture. He began establishing a name for himself with the creation of 'Easy Edges'—furniture created from layers of corrugated cardboard. Although achieving success with his furniture design, Gehry was more interested in architecture. He remodeled his family home, splitting the structure open with an angled skylight and surrounding the existing building with corrugated steel and chain-link fence. The avant-garde design caught the attention of the architectural world. As he grew in status, Gehry began pushing the scale of his buildings, as well as their unique shapes and designs, often appearing chaotic or unfinished. He is best known for the Walt Disney Concert Hall in the United States and the Guggenheim Museum in Spain.

AVANT GARDE – a term applied to artists from the late nineteenth-century to twentieth-century using experimental or unorthodox methods to create new directions or develop new concepts in their art.

For years, Frank Gehry refused to design a building in Las Vegas, Nevada. After meeting and forming a bond with Larry Ruvo (1946–), a Las Vegas liquor distributor, he had a change of heart. Ruvo impacted by his father's struggle with Alzheimer's, was compelled to open a neurological research facility. It would support current research

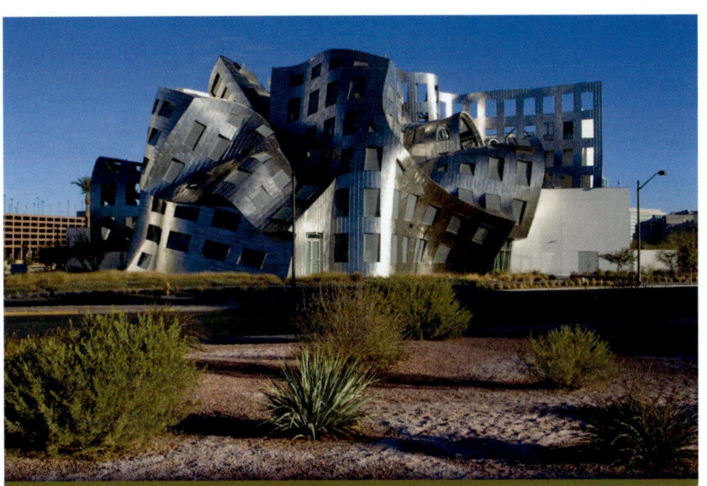

George Rose/Getty Image News/Getty Images

FIGURE 3.49 – Cleveland Clinic Lou Ruvo Center for Brain Health, Frank Gehry. Las Vegas, Nevada. 2010.

and scientific studies for the treatment of Alzheimer's, Parkinson's, Multiple Sclerosis and ALS (Lou Gehrig's Disease), as well as focus on prevention, early detection, and education. A longtime friend of Gehry's experienced the loss of his wife and three sister-in-laws to Huntington's disease. The impact of that on his friend left a lasting impression on the architect. Gehry agreed to design the building for Ruvo, as long as he added Huntington's disease to the list that the new facility would treat and study. In 2010, the Cleveland Clinic Lou Ruvo Center for Brain Health opened in Las Vegas.

STAINLESS STEEL – a type of metal which is virtually rust-free and is silver in appearance.

The exterior of the *Cleveland Clinic Lou Ruvo Center for Brain Health* (see Figure 3.49) was designed to reflect the depths and ultimately the limits of the human mind. The main building is made of curving and folding pieces of stainless steel with multiple windows throughout. It has misaligned openings and the appearance of jumbled forms thrown together, creating a destabilizing visual effect. The energy or liveliness of the exterior's design reflects the spirit of the mind—its creative and intellectual abilities. In contrast, the interior is calming, with its wide-open space, curved hallways, and abundance of natural light pouring in through windows. Interior lighting is directed upward to create a soft glow further transforming the facility into something more friendly than a traditional hospital setting.

A great piece of architecture—like an artwork—will often create controversy or debate. Since the release of Frank Gehry's design for the center in 2006, there have been mixed reviews and debates. Discussions ensued about the beauty—or lack thereof—in its design and whether it was appropriate for Alzheimer's patients. In its chaos, critics claimed the building's appearance would increase the anxiety within and lead to further disorientation of the people it was meant to help.

part 4

EARTHWORKS

HISTORICAL

Historically cultures have created earthworks—manmade structures created from earth, stone, and elements of nature—for burial or ceremonial purposes. These were associated with a wide range of human needs from fertility to survival to entering into the afterlife. These earthworks take on many shapes ranging from circular mounds or enclosures, the human body, and various representations from the animal kingdom.

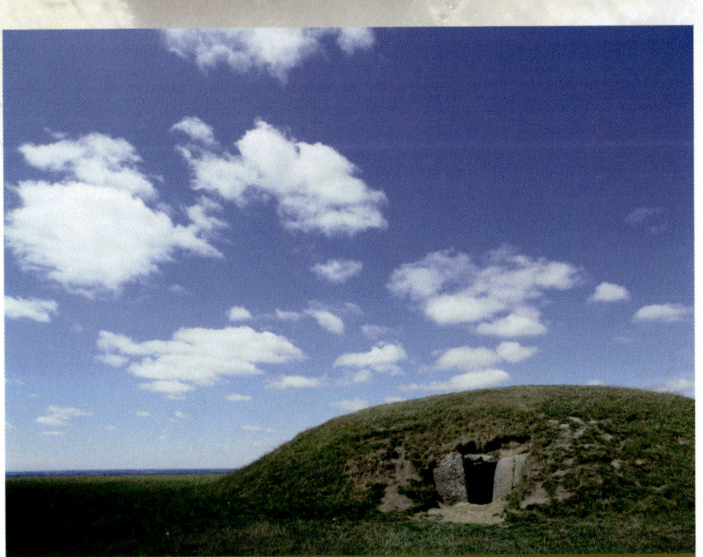
Werner Forman/Universal Images Group/Getty Images

FIGURE 3.50 – The Hostage's Mound at Tara Hill Co. Ireland. 13th century.

In Ireland, the *Hill of Tara* is an example of a *barrow* or earthen circle. This is an extraordinary example of a barrow because of the cursos (ceremonial roadway) that leads to it. The raised embankment of the barrow stands about three feet in height. Although not high enough to provide defense, it is certainly enough to create a sacred space to serve any number of functions from burial to the coronation of kings. While Hill of Tara's original purpose is unknown, during the Neolithic period dating back to 3000 BC, the oldest construction at this site is a passage tomb. Known as the *Hostage's Mound* (see Figure 3.50), the tomb is a small mound that lies north of the two linked enclosures. Legend has it that the mound was named this because of the tradition of Irish kings to retain important personages of nearby kingdoms in the enclosure to ensure their submission. Archaeologists in the 1950s discovered the ashes of over two hundred individuals within the structure.

In later years, new legends associated with the Hill of Tara tell the eighteenth century tale of two Milesian brothers from Spain who divided Ireland between themselves. Eber Finn, who ruled the southern territory and Eremon Finn, who ruled the northern, which included the Hill of Tara. Issues between their wives led to war between the brothers, when Eber's wife wanted the Hill Tara for herself. Tea, the wife of Eremon, was killed during the war. She was buried in the Hill of Tara, which remained tied to her forever. At this point Eremon, who successfully defeated his brother, took sole control of Ireland. He was crowned at Tara, beginning the tradition of this site being the location of the coronation of future Irish kings.

The two mounds inside the barrow were then referred to as the 'Royal Seat' where the coronations occurred. The *Stone of Destiny* (see Figure 3.51) was placed at the center of the mound on the left. It was believed that the man standing before it was a true king if a sound, much like the roar of a lion, emanated from it. Perhaps centuries ago a strong wind blowing through during a king's coronation created an unusual sound that was attributed to this stone and the legend that ensued. Eventually with the rise in power of Christianity, the Hill of Tara no longer was used as a political or religious center. During the eighteenth and nineteenth centuries, it became the site for peaceful protests and violent conflicts. By 2008, the Hill of Tara was placed on UNESCO's list of 100 Most Endangered Sites because of a proposed motorway to be constructed nearby.

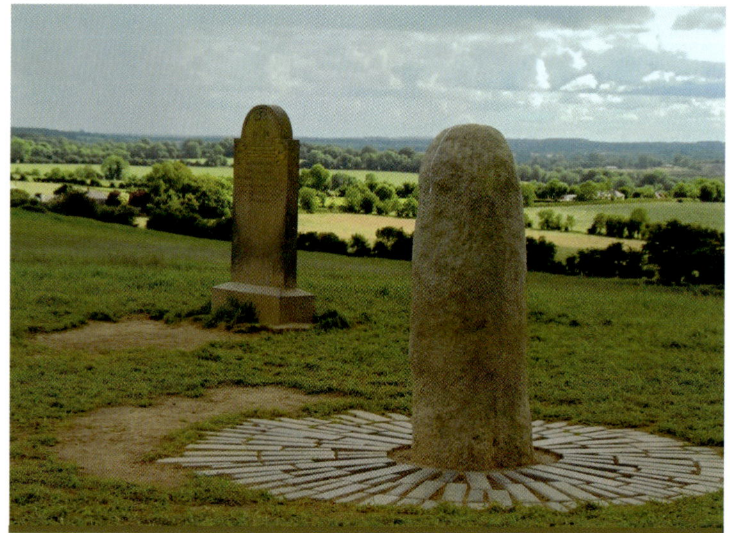

FIGURE 3.51 – The Stone of Destiny at the Hill of Tara. Ireland. 13th century.

In Peru, from 200 BC–700 CE, an indigenous group of people created a series of images, lines and geometric shapes on the desert floor that stretched 50 miles between the towns of Nazca and Palpa. There is considerable mystery behind their creation because of the scale of the images and because their creators left no record of their significance. What are now called the Nazca Lines were unknown to the world until someone flying in an airplane over the desert discovered them. Their sheer scale creates a sense of awe and bewilderment in how people who did not have the means to view these from above could create such symmetrical and sometimes intricate depictions of birds, animals (see Figure 3.52), and insects.

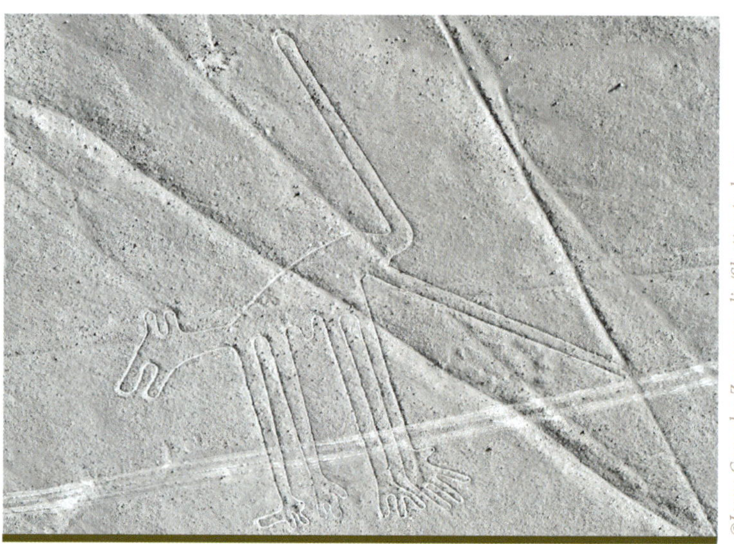

FIGURE 3.52 – Nazca Lines Peruvian Desert (dog). Peru. 200 BC–500 CE.

Through a great deal of exploration, experimentation, and study, some plausible theories have been formed. In 1985, archaeologist Johan Reinhard (1943–) published his findings supporting the theory that the Nazca lines were associated with religious rituals. Further studies over the years have revealed crushed seashells around the edges of the images. The study of the weather and climate changes in that region over the centuries has led to the realization that it was slowly becoming more arid. Eventually around 1000 CE, this area was completely abandoned by the Nazca people. Perhaps the increasing lack of water/precipitation led to the creation of these images as a way to communicate with their gods in

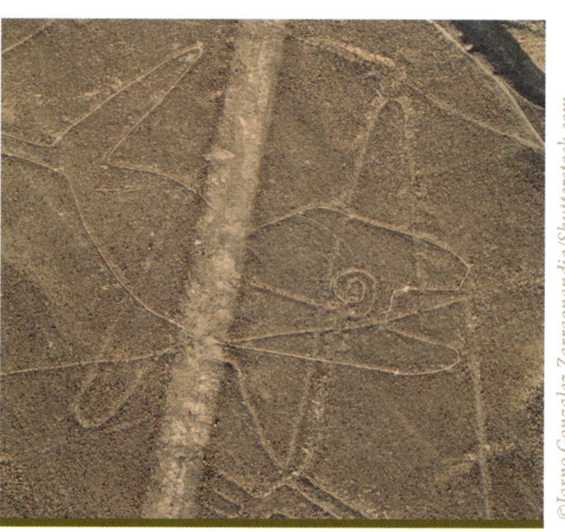

FIGURE 3.53 – Nazca Lines Peruvian Desert (whale). Peru. 200 BC–500 CE.

attempt to bring rain. Images were seen by some archaeologists to potentially be walking temples, where the people would walk the images, praying to their gods, and leaving crushed shell offerings behind.

Among the recognizable images of birds, animals, and anthropomorphic figures, there are images that remain a mystery. For example, there is a carving of a human figure with one four-fingered hand and the other normal. The whale image (see Figure 3.53) is shown with more fins than an actual whale and it is often holding a head. Perhaps these were meant to be visual representations of their gods. Upon closer look of the depiction of the whale, it appears to be fairly realistic overall. Because the image is located in the Nazca desert makes it even more puzzling. However, they were within 30 miles of an ocean where whales are often sighted even today. This would have been a long journey for them, but it is one that could have been made.

Mounds in the shape of serpents are found around the world. However, none are of the scale or as impressive as that of Serpent Mound in Peebles, Ohio in the United States. Believed to have been created by the Adena culture (1000–200 BC), the purpose of the mound is as mysterious as its creators. The mound is located on top of a plateau in a region that is rich with food and water resources. In addition, it is in a location that has a high magnetic anomaly. In areas such as this, some people can feel electricity about the air that might lead them to claim this spot as a sacred one. Perhaps the Adena people once saw, as others in more recent times have witnessed, migratory birds seemingly stuck in a circular flight pattern above the plateau. Due to the magnetic anomaly in this location, these birds cannot get their bearing, much like a compass needle that is unable to determine north from south or east from west. This would certainly seem strange and 'magical' to the Adena people.

Serpent Mound (see Figure 3.54) stretches 1350 feet and stands three feet in height. Like the Hill of Tara, this suggests the purpose of this earthen mound was not for defense. Perhaps it served as some kind of 'walking temple' to the Adena people. Much like the Nazca lines, Serpent Mound can only truly be seen in its entirety from above. Excavations of it found that it is made solely of stone and dirt and not used for burial purposes. As the serpent appears to be slithering its way across the top of the plateau, its jaws are fully open and it appears to be in the process of swallowing an egg or orb. Through extensive studies during the various equinox and solstices, it has been realized that the coils of the serpent's body align directly with the passage of the sun and/or moon during those times. During the summer solstice in particular the setting of the sun is in direct alignment with the orb shape. Perhaps this is meant to represent the sun itself and at this particular time of year, the serpent is preparing to swallow the sun as it disappears into the earth.

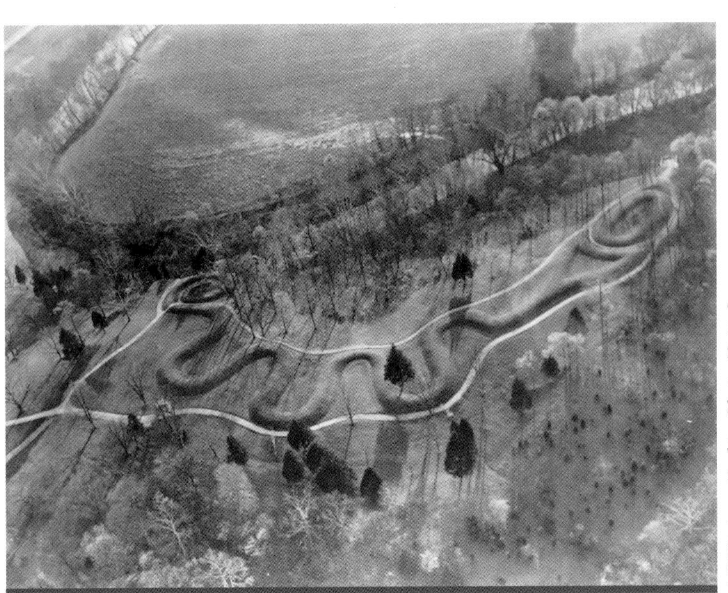

FIGURE 3.54 – Serpent Mound, Adena Culture. United States. c. 800 BC. 1348 ft. long x 3 ft. high.

CONTEMPORARY

In the late 1960s, America was in the midst of a revolution with the civil rights and women's liberation movements, anti-war protests, and the rise of environmental activism occurring. Some artists began rejecting traditional sculptural forms and art venues in their own form of protest. The result was Earth Art—large-scale earthworks created in site-specific locations, where the landscape was the canvas and the earth the artistic medium. The artists were often influenced by ancient cultures and their monumental creations. Earth Art experimented with light, space, time, and perception, and was often ephemeral in nature, existing now only through photography and film.

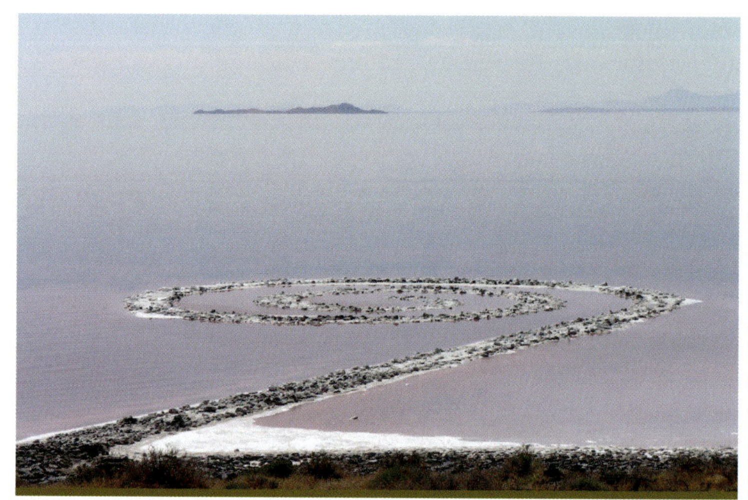

FIGURE 3.55 – View of Spiral Jetty, Robert Smithson. Great Salt Lake, Utah. 1970. Coil 1,500 ft. long x 15 ft. wide. Earthwork (basalt rock, salt crystals, earth and water).

In 1970, American artist Robert Smithson (1938–1973) founded the earthwork art movement. As seen up to this period, earthworks were used for specific cultural purposes rather than being considered a form of art by their creators. In rebellion of museums and galleries, the restrictions of how art was viewed within these settings and an attempt to alter the way people observed their environments, 'earthwork' artists took art out into nature. Smithson coined this movement 'Land Art.'

Land Art was created in a variety of environments and utilized the materials at hand. The range of scale, permanence, and tools with which the artists created varies tremendously throughout the years. One of the most iconic of Smithson's earthworks is the *Spiral Jetty* (see Figure 3.55). This piece is located in the United States at Rozel Point in the Great Salt Lake National Park in Utah. Smithson used over 6000 tons of black basalt rock and earth to create it. The spiral coils 1500 feet long and is approximately 15 feet wide. One of the draws to this location for Smithson was the red color of the water created from algae. As one hiked up over the surrounding hill, a spiral shape seemed to emerge from the lake's surface. Having used the rock and dirt from that location, Smithson built up the spiral shape so that it was a solid mass raised just above the water's surface. Unbeknownst to Smithson at the time, the lake's water level was at its lowest point. Within two weeks of its completion, it was completely submersed under water. It remained that way for thirty years until the water table once again dropped in level to reveal it. At this point the salt in the water had crystalized and altered the *Spiral Jetty*'s appearance. This piece, along with others like *Broken Circle* and *Spiral Hill*, echo ancient sites and cultural symbols used by our ancestors.

Although, the point of land art was to take art off the walls and out of the confines of a museum or gallery setting, many earthwork artists were asked to exhibit within those very spaces. Each took their own approach, some creating actual works of art within the space while others, like Smithson, appeared to rebel in the process. A 'non-site' (or 'indoor earthwork') was a designation created by Smithson to indicate a piece could be shown in a gallery or museum setting. These consisted of displays of materials (see Figure 3.56) from

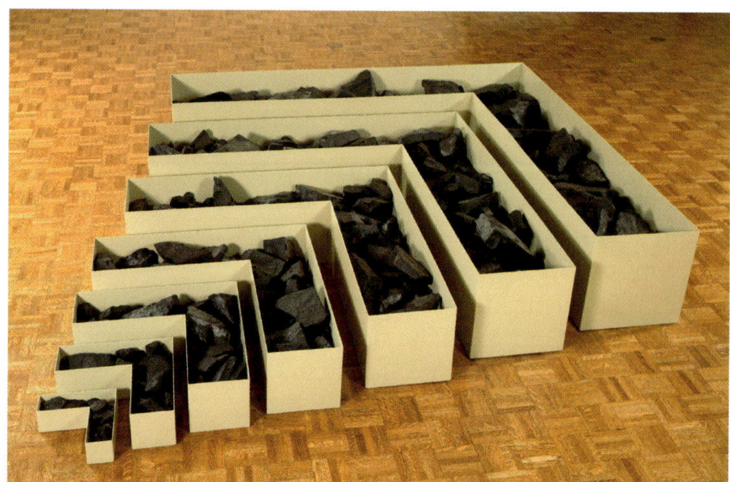

FIGURE 3.56 – Non Site, Robert Smithson. 1968. 38.1 x 228.6 x 228.6 cm. Cannel coal, steel and enamel.

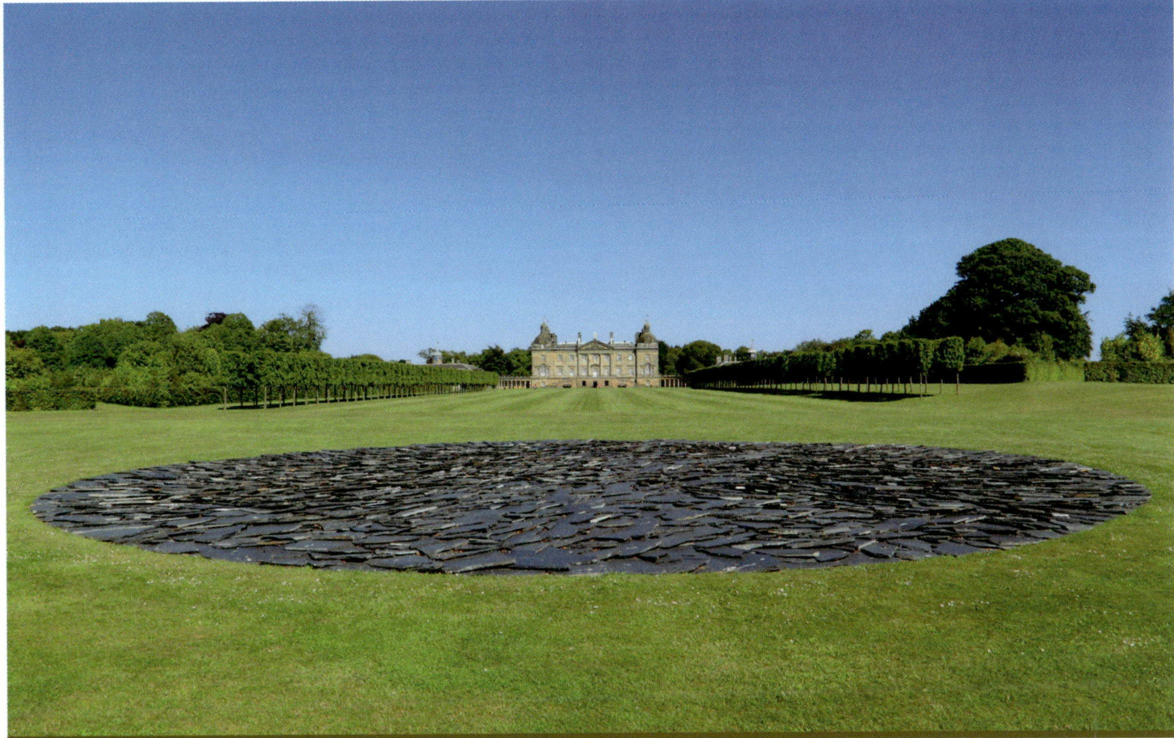

FIGURE 3.57 – Full Moon Circle (Grounds of Houghton Hall), Richard Long. Norfolk, England. 2004. Slate.

a particular site, along with drawings and photographs of the actual earthwork at that site. Like earthworks, this was meant to create an environment that would prompt the viewer to look more closely at the world around them, in this case by looking at the particular material he would use to create.

Richard Long (1945–) is an earthwork artist from Bristol, England. He creates earthworks that speak about man's relationship with nature. In *A Line Made by Walking* (1967), he simply created a line by walking back and forth across the same path. His first piece was done in a field in the English countryside of Wiltshire. Through this repetition, he alters the surface he is walking on, leaving his mark behind. "The work often has all kinds of echoes," Long says, "some accidental. If you undertake a walk, you are echoing the whole history of mankind, from the early migrations out of Africa on foot that took people all over the world." While the mark is minimalistic and ephemeral by nature of its creation, the work reflects the interaction of the journey, marking the earth and making a simple alteration to the landscape. For those same reasons, it now exists only in a photograph.

The use of line and circles are repeated throughout the works that Richard Long creates. For him the line represents movement while the circle tranquility. In *Full Moon Circle* (see Figure 3.57), Long has laid slabs of granite down to create a black circle on top of the grass. To the artist, these pieces are reminiscent of the mysterious ancient rituals of our ancestors. The visual contrast between colors and how the light reflects off each pulls the viewer's eye in. As the viewer stands more closely to the piece, their eye is drawn into the different shapes of stone and the negative space created by each. This draws their mind into a quiet place of exploration where the outer world seems to disappear for however briefly.

English born artist, Andy Goldsworthy (1956–) has a wide-range of approaches to creating earthworks. He often uses his own body as a tool to create, whether it is his teeth, saliva, or hands. His work varies from the monumental and more permanent in nature to the intimate and often easily reclaimed by nature. As is with many of his pieces, Goldsworthy views himself as the creator and nature the 'reclaimer.' An example is *Icicle Star (Scotland, 1985)*, a piece created from icicles found in the environment. Breaking them off from where they formed, Goldsworthy used his teeth to shape the ends of each so they could fit together more securely. Then using his saliva as the binder, the cold air freezes the pieces together. Once the artwork is completed, Goldsworthy always preserves such wonderful ephemeral pieces through photography. Nature as the reclaimer can be seen in *Icicle Star* when the heat of the sun began to warm the cold air, slowly melting the ice. The piece eventually breaks down and the water melts back into the earth.

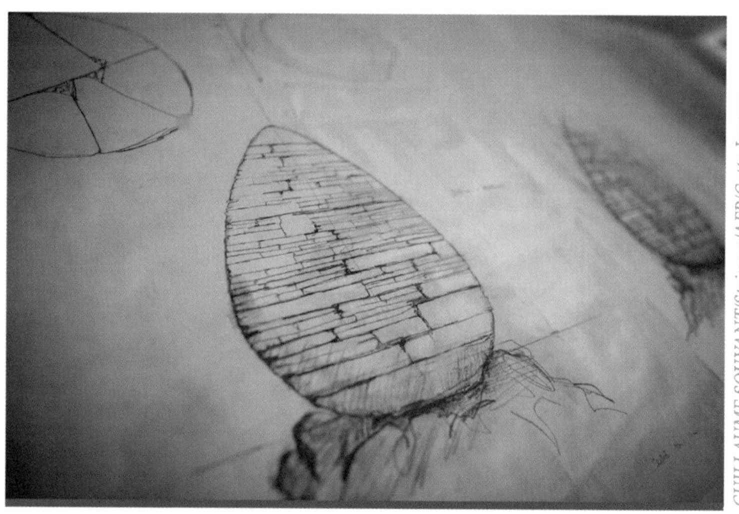

GUILLAUME SOUVANT/Stringer/AFP/Getty Images

FIGURE 3.58 – Egg-shaped Cairn of Slates (drawing), Andy Goldsworthy. Chateau de Chaumont-Sur-Loire, France. 2016. Pencil on paper.

While Andy Goldsworthy documents his finished works through photography, he occasionally works out an idea first through drawing (see Figure 3.58). In *Slate Cairn* (see Figure 3.59), Andy Goldsworthy uses slabs of slate to create the egg-shaped form. Creations such as this reference the cairns made by pre-modern cultures, whose purpose often remains unknown. A sense of mystery is created in Goldsworthy's pieces through his use of abstract forms. While nature can be chaotic and messy, he creates a sense of order from that chaos as he pushes the materials and forms to their limits. In doing so, Goldsworthy's cairns are clearly seen as manmade structures, but allow nature to reveal itself more deeply to the viewer.

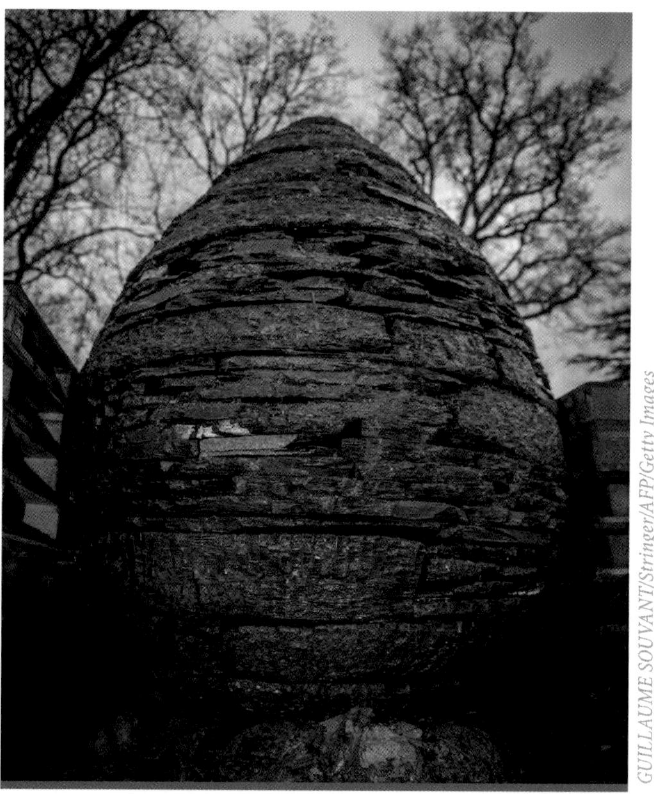

GUILLAUME SOUVANT/Stringer/AFP/Getty Images

FIGURE 3.59 – Slate Cairn (egg-shaped sculpture), Andy Goldsworthy. Chateau de Chaumont-Sur-Loire, France. 2016. Approximately 8.6 ft. in circumference. Slate.

part 5

PUBLIC ART

For centuries artists have been creating larger than life works of art that are displayed publically to memorialize rulers, patriots, and other prominent figures. Eventually artists began to break free of the traditional form of public art to push the boundaries of what one expected to encounter as they moved through their day. The range of what has been and continues to be created pushes the imaginations of all that come in contact with public works of art.

Swedish born artist, Claes Oldenburg (1929–) grew up in Chicago, Illinois in the United States. Three years after graduating from Yale University, he became a naturalized citizen and relocated to New York. Oldenburg started his artistic career by creating drawings and collages of massive ordinary objects placed into public sites. Eventually, he began to create their three-dimensional counterparts out of fabric and other materials, often resulting in something that was playful and whimsical. However, Oldenburg also addressed issues, such as war, gender, and consumerism. His first large-scale public artwork was the 25-foot-high sculpture *Lipstick (Ascending) on Caterpillar Tracks* (1969), a collaborative effort with architectural students from his alma mater. They secretly installed it on Yale's Beinecke Plaza, located in-between the president's office and a World War I memorial. Over the years, this became the backdrop for many student protests, including those against the Vietnam War that coincided with the piece's installation.

Claes Oldenburg is sometimes inspired by other artists' work, along with the history of a location. *Clothespin* (1976), located in Philadelphia, Pennsylvania, was not only inspired by Brancusi's *The Kiss* (1908), but by the city and its history. The shapes of the two pieces of the clothespin resemble the individuals embraced in a kiss in Brancusi's work. The arms that intertwine the two are referenced through the spring of the clothespin. In *Clothespin* (see Figure 3.60), Oldenburg flares the bottom of the clothespin to visually reference the crack in the Liberty Bell, which resides in Philadelphia. The piece was installed in 1976 during the bicentennial anniversary of the Independence of the United States (1776). The spring holding the clothespin is bent into the shape of 76 to reference that historical date.

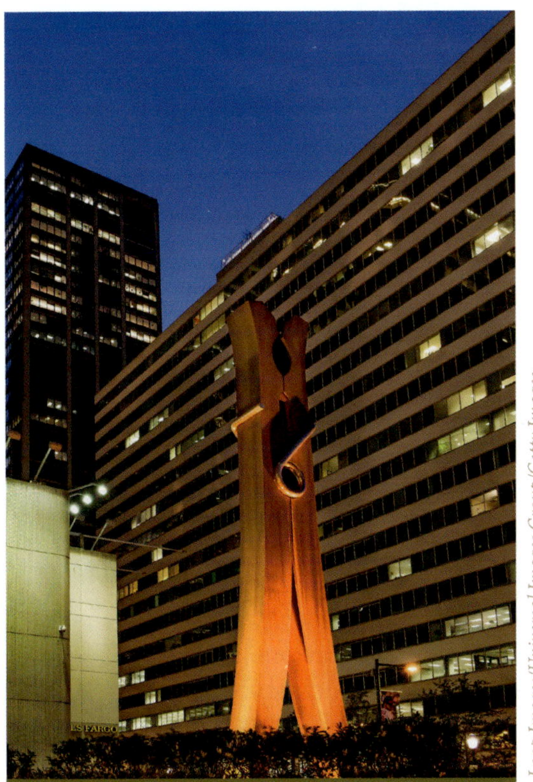

Loop Images/Universal Images Group/Getty Images

FIGURE 3.60 – Clothespin, Claes Oldenburg. Philadelphia, Pennsylvania. 1976. 45 x 12.3 x 21.6 ft. Weathering steel.

In 1977, Claes Oldenburg married a Dutch art historian, Coosje Van Bruggen (1942–2009), who began collaborating with him on his public works. While predominantly handling site logistics and solutions to logistical problems related to his sketches, Coosje contributed to the creative process, as well. In 1991, both were asked to create a large-scale work that would integrate into the setting of the Nelson-Atkins Museum in Kansas City, Missouri. While walking around the galleries in the museum, Coosje was drawn to the Native American headdress, which led to the initial concept of large feathers strewn about the museum's massive lawn, as though having fallen from a huge bird passing overhead. They researched the site and came across an aerial view of the museum grounds. It reminded the artists of a large tennis court in which the museum's building was the net. Large balls could then be placed around the grounds as though deserted by gigantic tennis players. The circular form seemed too repetitive to them, sending them back to the drawing board. Eventually Coosje posed the idea of combining the feathers and balls to create badminton shuttlecocks. The end result was *Shuttlecocks* (see Figure 3.61), where three approximately 18-foot-high sculptures where placed on the front lawn in what appeared to be a random scattering. A fourth shuttlecock was placed on the other side of the building as though it landed in an inverted position. The overall installation created the illusion of an abandoned game of bad mitten in someone's backyard.

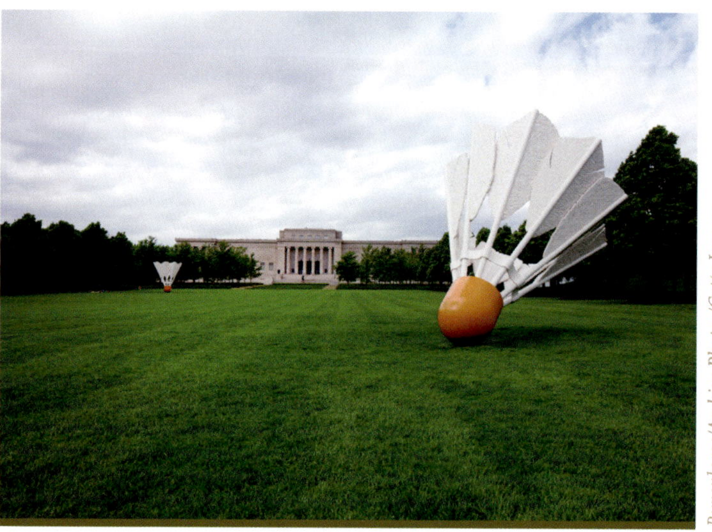
Buyenlarge/Archive Photos/Getty Images

FIGURE 3.61 – Shuttlecocks, Claes Oldenburg and Coosje van Bruggen. Nelson-Atkins Museum, Kansas City, Missouri. 1994. Each is 17 ft. 11 in. high x 15 ft. 1 in. crown diameter x 4 ft. nose diameter. Aluminum and fiber-reinforced plastic, painted with polyurethane enamel.

There was a great deal of controversy surrounding the piece prior to its installation. Some members of the public and the Parks and Recreation Department opposed the use of a mundane object for one of the city's most prestigious sites. The Kansas City Star, the city's newspaper, fueled the fire by posting hostile editorials and cartoons about the piece. Despite this, the museum staff and donors to the project were steadfast in their support and *Shuttlecocks* was installed without incident in 1994.

Dennis Oppenheim (1938–2011), an American artist, created large-scale works of art like Oldenburg—sometimes carrying a message and sometimes not. Created in 1997, *Device to Root Out Evil* (see Figure 3.62) was a proposed piece for a competition held by the Vancouver Park System. It consists of an old-fashioned country church with a large steeple. Rather than being positioned upright as one is accustomed to seeing such architecture, he turned it upside-down so the steeple impaled the earth. The message to the viewer is that a function of religion serves to seek out and destroy evil forces. Here the church

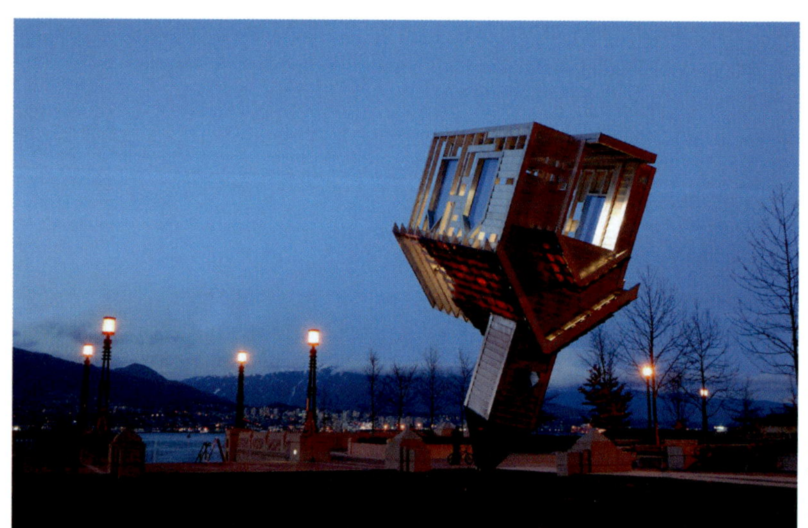
©Xuanlu Wang/Shutterstock.com

FIGURE 3.62 – Device to Root Out Evil in Coal Harbor Park, Dennis Oppenheim. Vancouver, Canada. 1997. 22 x 18 x 9 ft. Galvanized structural steel, anodized perforated aluminum, concrete foundation.

has found a source of evil and is attacking it to draw it out of the earth. Oppenheim visually communicates this idea, as the ground appears to be pulling upward around where the steeple has impaled it.

However, the public viewed this in the opposite way it was intended. They saw the upturned church as being unable to withstand evil forces and being drawn to it. Because of the controversy that it created, the park chose to take it down. The piece found a temporary home for five years at Calgary's Glenbow Museum. Renewed interest and support in the piece eventually led to its installation in downtown Vancouver.

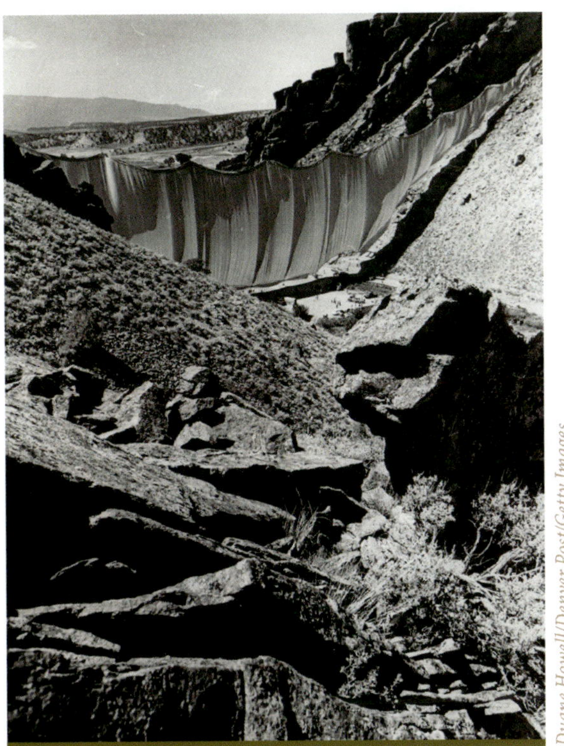

Duane Howell/Denver Post/Getty Images

FIGURE 3.63 – Valley Curtain, Christo and Jeanne Claude. Rifle, Colorado. 1970–1972. 1,250 ft. wide x by 182–365 ft. high. Vivid orange nylon polyamide fabric.

Operating in a similar fashion as Oldenburg and Coosje, Christo (1935–) and Jeanne-Claude (1935–2009) were a husband and wife team who created large-scale public works often involving the use of fabric. Fabric, to these artists, represented the fragility and impermanence of life. Nature often helped to reinforce that during the installation of such pieces like *Valley Curtain* (see Figure 3.63) in Colorado. While the artists were having the work installed, the giant panels of fabric were whipped around and shredded in the strong gusts of wind that blew through the canyon. The panels had to be remade and eventually were successfully installed in that location.

In 1971, German historian Michael Cullen sent the couple a postcard encouraging them to come to his country to wrap the Reichstag (see Figure 3.64), the meeting place of the lower house of Germany's national legislature, in fabric. After almost two decades, Christo and Jeanne-Claude were able to secure the permits to do the piece. The artists worked with 90 professional climbers and 120 workers to install it. Which consisted of 70 tailor-made aluminum colored fabric panels drapped over a 200-ton steel frame structure. As in the *Valley Curtain*, the large panels of fabric were hard to control as the wind turned them into large sails. Eventually, they were able to get the panels under control and complete the installation. The result turned the imposing building into a shimmering form that seems to reveal the 'essence' of the Reichstag. During the two weeks the piece was on display, approximately 5 million tourists came to Berlin to experience it in person.

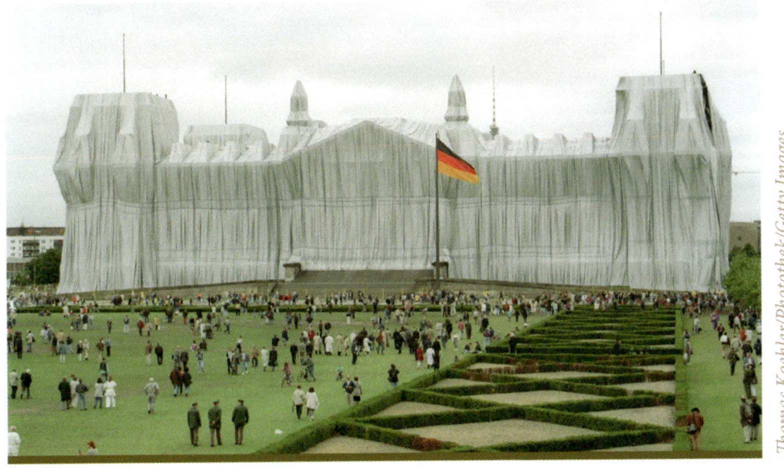

Thomas Koehler/Photothek/Getty Images

FIGURE 3.64 – Wrapped Reichstag, Christo and Jeanne Claude. Berlin, Germany. 1995. 1,076,390 ft^2. Thick, woven polypropylene fabric with aluminum surface, blue polypropylene rope.

part 6

URBAN ART

Graffiti is considered an illegal art form because the 'canvas' on which it is created is property belonging to someone other than the artist. Graffiti artists are often highly creative individuals (see Figure 3.65) who may not believe they can afford to pursue an art education. Abandoned or rundown buildings have become a source of their creative outlet. However, these places are only among the many where a graffiti artist will leave their mark. No surface, whether personal property or newly built structures, is off limits.

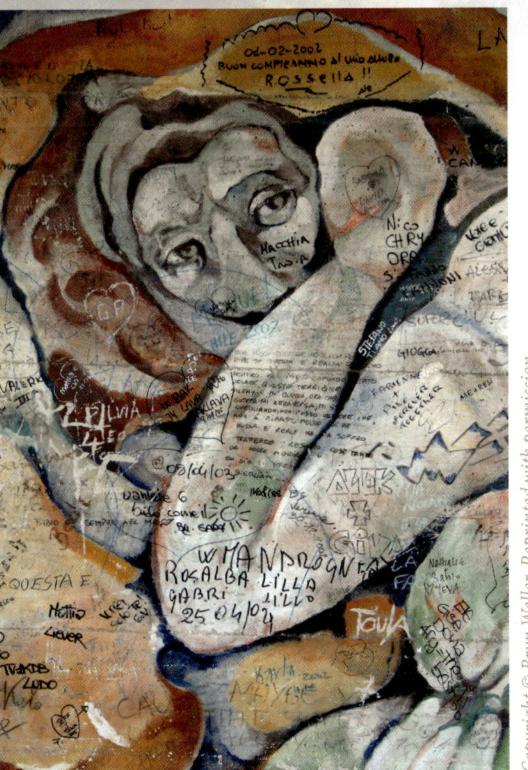

FIGURE 3.65 – Cinque Terre/Graffiti #2, Bryn Weller. Italy. 2006. 13 x 20 in. Digital photography.

In more contemporary times, some graffiti artists have gained international recognition for their style and have entered into the more mainstream art world. Others continue along the path that have led to their fame and continue to create their works illegally.

On the streets of New York City in the 1970s, Jean-Michel Basquiat (1960–1988) began creating graffiti works. Typically, these were in the form of sayings meant to instigate thought about social and other issues he felt people should reflect upon. Towards the late 70s, he and his friend, Al Diaz (ca. 1960–), created the tag (or signature) "SAMO" which was an acronym for 'The Same Old Shit'. They went around the city leaving messages that were anti-politics and anti-religion in nature and signed them with 'SAMO.' Eventually their friendship fell apart and Basquiat left the message about town 'SAMO is Dead' to let the public know there would no longer be messages to view.

Eventually gaining the recognition of key people in the New York art scene, Basquiat was given a studio and materials to pursue his creative process. He collaborated with artists like Andy Warhol (1928–1987) and began showing his works in galleries and museums. Although Basquiat's life was short-lived due to a drug overdose, he left a mark on the art world through his unique imagery and collage-like style. As a child, his mother had given him a copy of *Grey's Anatomy*, which captured his attention. As he created, Basquiat's graffiti past and exposure to the human anatomy through the book appear to have merged creating something extraordinarily unique for the time.

Such influences can be seen in *Untitled* (see Figure 3.66). Often when depicting the human body, his figures appear as though their skin has been removed to expose what lies beneath. The face looks more skull-like and bones or organs are often shown as though the viewer is looking at an x-ray. These visual characteristics speak to his exploration with the tradition of *memento mori*, reminding viewers of the human body's eventual degeneration and for that matter the ephemeral nature of all life.

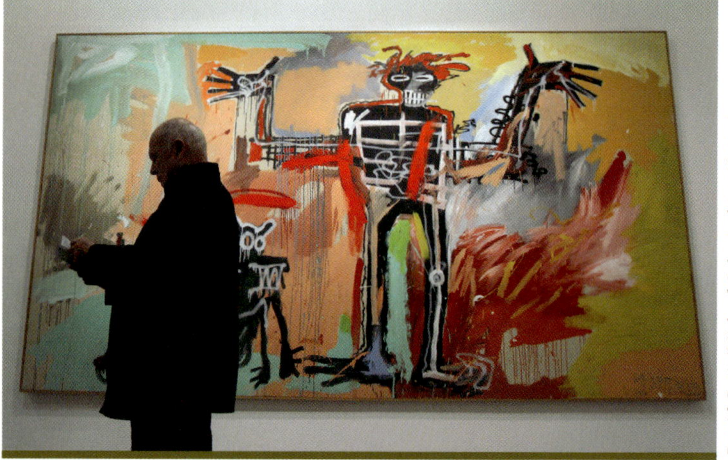

David Corio/Michael Ochs Archives/Getty Images

FIGURE 3.66 – A Man Visits the American Painter Jean-Michel Basquiat. 2010.

English-based graffiti artist, Banksy often creatively incorporates his images into the environment. In pieces like *Thug for Life* (see Figure 3.67), which shows an elderly group of people depicted as a gang, the old man on the right appears to be leaning on the projection of the building's wall. Like Banksy, many graffiti artists gaining recognition artistically find ways to obscure and protect their identity from the authorities that are looking to arrest them for vandalism.

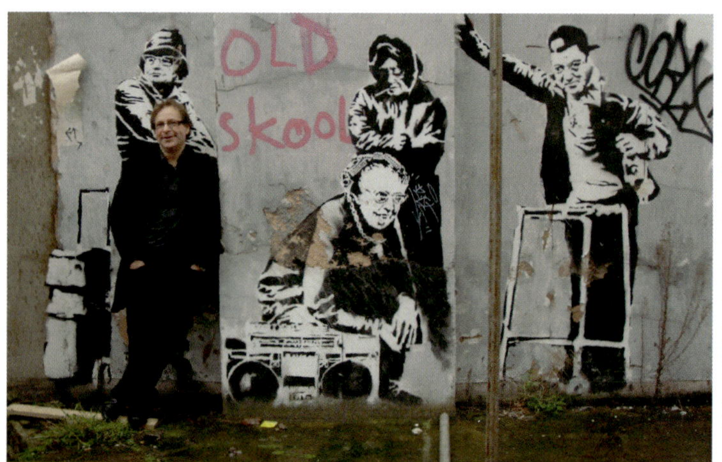

David Corio/Michael Ochs Archives/Getty Images

FIGURE 3.67 – Thug for Life, Banksy. London, UK. c. 2007. Stencil, spray paint.

There was a pivotal point where Banksy's artwork changes from 'acts of vandalism' to highly sought after 'valued art.' Today people are removing his works (see Figure 3.68) and selling or auctioning them off to the highest bidder. In cases like this, there is often greater vandalism or damage done to the structure (or building), since people are removing the wall upon which the graffiti was created.

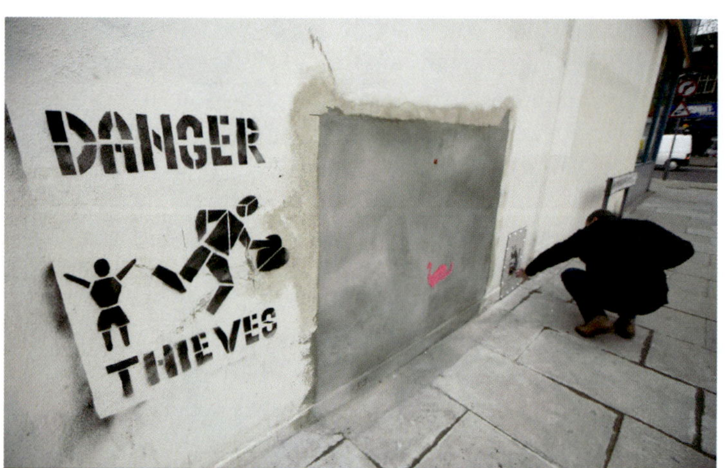

AFP/Stringer/Getty Images

FIGURE 3.68 – Vandalized Image of Banksy's. London, UK. 2013.

Shepard Fairey (1970–) is an American artist based out of Los Angeles, California. In his youth, he was drawn to the stickers of the punk and skateboarding cultures of the mid-1980s. While not participating in either culture, he liked the sense of cultural belonging that the collecting of these stickers created. Soon everything he owned was plastered with them. At first he recreated others' sticker art as a more affordable way to own them. Eventually once he entered art school and realized he was in an environment filled with 'alternative' people, Fairey felt the pull to create his own sticker. He struggled to come up with an idea until what started out as a joke took hold. He did a graphic paper cut stencil of Andre the Giant (1946–1993), a famous French wrestler. The first in the series was the phrase "Andre the Giant has a Posse," which he plastered all over the Providence, Rhode Island, and eventually Boston and New York City. After a local indie paper printed a picture of the sticker and offered a reward to anyone who could reveal its creator and meaning, Fairey found the beginning of his artistic pursuits.

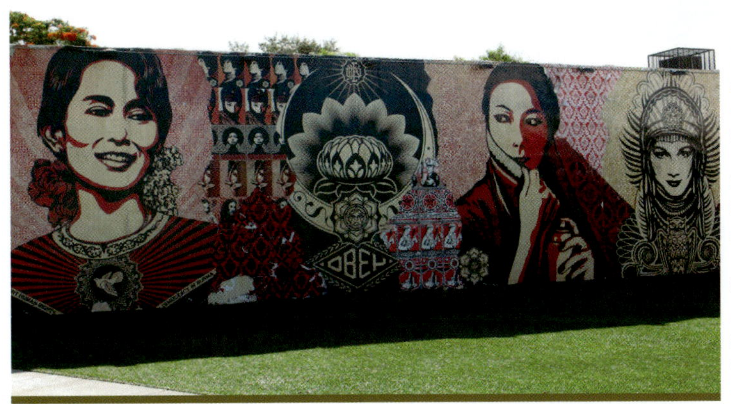

FIGURE 3.69 – Wynwood Arts District Mural, Shepard Fairey. Miami, Florida, USA. 2012. Stencil, spray paint.

Slowly gaining recognition over the years, Shepard Fairey's art is now sought out by cities and property owner's wanting to be a part of the experience. He creates posters and murals addressing a wide range of concerns from capitalism, blind support of war and nationalism, counter culture, and more. Fairey combines the influences of Art Nouveau, revolutionary propaganda, and the hippie culture into a unique visual graphic language. In the *Wynwood Arts District Mural* (see Figure 3.69), the artist is collaging together symbols of peace. The woman depicted on the far left is Aung San Suu Kyi (1945–), who received the Nobel Prize for Peace in 1991 for her continued non-violent initiatives towards democracy and human rights in Burma. One of the images tiled in the background to the right of her image is of Angela Davis (1944–), an activist and writer promoting racial justice and women's rights. Fairey created other symbols of peace that can be seen throughout his work, such as the lotus image and Peace goddess shown in this image.

GRAFFITI MEETS PUBLIC ART

Sometimes graffiti art is embraced by the public as true art. In such cases, these artists are given the opportunity to create their work in a safe environment without threat of being arrested for vandalism.

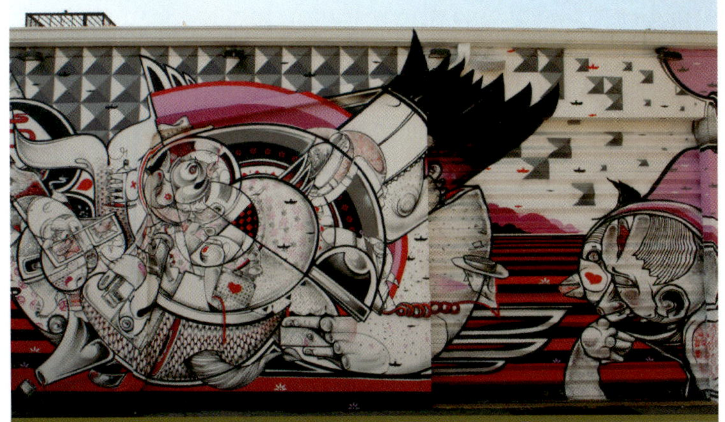

FIGURE 3.70 – Wynwood Arts District Mural. How & Nosm. Miami, Florida, USA. 2012. Spray paint.

In the United States, an abandoned business district in Miami, Florida became the target of local graffiti artists who used the buildings for their art. In 2009, a real estate developer and arts visionary, Tony Goldman (1943–2012) looked at what was before him. Known for revitalizing such areas, he saw these buildings not as vandalized structures but as a potential large-scale outdoor gallery space (see Figure 3.70). After proposing this idea to the city, he was able to put a call out to graffiti artist—not just locally, but nationally and internationally—giving them a safe environment to create their work and in essence to celebrate it. Graffiti artists from all over the world, including Banksy and Fairey, came to Miami to be a part of this project. As the place was transformed, it became a tourist attraction and people traveled there specifically to see what was going on. Over time businesses, restaurants, and other galleries have moved into the area, making it a thriving location once again. Goldman's vision was that every few years this 'outdoor gallery' would have a new body of work for public viewing. Despite initial enthusiasm and his efforts, a current lack of funding threatens his vision from coming to fruition.

REVERSE GRAFFITI

Inspired by dirty vehicles, like semi-trucks, and the 'wash me' message often found on them, reverse graffiti took root. Artists began to see how dirty our world has become due to the result of our actions. Pollution created from the emissions of cars and other vehicles continues to leave behind layers of dirt and soot, as seen all over the places one lives—city's walls, tunnels, and more.

Rather than creating works of art or 'graffiti' through the use of something permanent like spray paint, reverse graffiti is created with cleaning supplies. By cleaning areas that are coated with pollutants, the original structure is slowly revealed and used as the medium to create the image (see Figure 3.71).

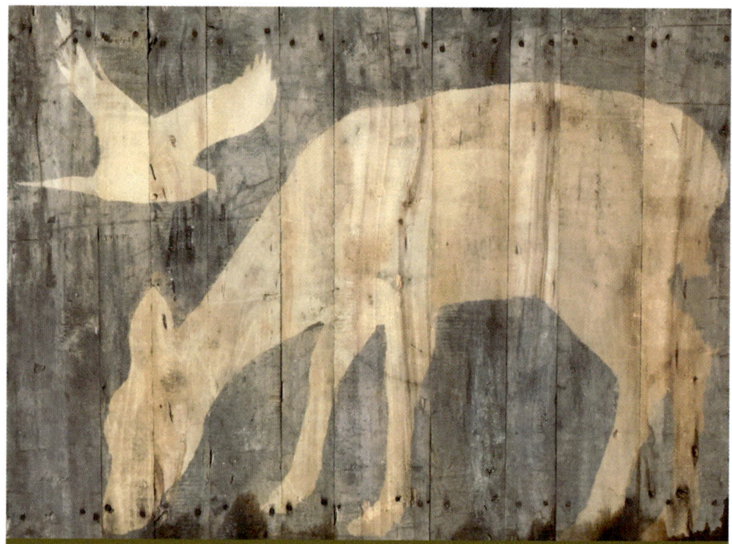

FIGURE 3.71 – Conversation. Celene Hawkins and Paige Wideman. USA. 2016. 60 x 40 in. Wooden palette and power washer.

Many artists have gained recognition recently for their work in this area. British graffiti artist, Paul "Moose" Curtis refers to himself as a 'Green' artist and is one of the pioneers of this technique. His medium is pollution and his tools scrub brushes, power washers, water, and stencils. Creating interesting designs or advertisements on dirty retaining walls or on areas where nature has taken over, Moose is often working illegally on property that he does not own. Over the years when he seeks out the permission of a property owner first, he struggles to find people who will allow him to 'clean' their walls, seeming to prefer the dirt over something creative. The police in his hometown of Leeds are baffled as to what to do with him. While they consider what he is doing to be vandalism, Moose is creating his imagery by cleaning away the effects of urban life. "I'm waiting for the kind of Monty Python court case where exhibit A is a pot of cleaning fluid and exhibit B is a pair of my old socks," he jokes.

The Brazilian graffiti artist, Alexandre Orion (1978–) creates reverse graffiti with a more overtly environmental approach. In the summer of 2007 in Sao Paolo, he began turning the soot-covered walls of a transport tunnel into a striking mural of skulls and messages like 'Go Gently.' The images glowed the bright white of the walls original color. The police were at a loss because while this is considered illegal graffiti, the artist is not leaving behind a permanent mark that is destroying the property. This makes it difficult to arrest the artist since Orion is simply cleaning. In response to this, the authorities power washed the area where his images were. He simply moved to the wall on the other side of the tunnel to continue his work. This led the authorities to take more drastic measures. They cleaned not only the entire tunnel Orion had been working in, but all others in Sao Paulo, as well.

WORKSHEETS

Worksheets are designed to see what your thoughts are on the topics and images addressed and how you support those ideas with visual clues within the related artwork. Do not do any research on the imagery before completing the assignments.

Name ______________________________ Date ______________

WORKSHEET: BODY LANGUAGE

In the projected image, what emotion is being communicated through the position of the figure's body?

What about the figure and/or its posture supports your choice of emotion?

What other elements within the image reinforce that is the emotion being conveyed? And why?

Name ______________________________ Date ______________

WORKSHEET: PRIMORDIAL COUPLE

In the projected images, look closely at the two examples of primordial couples to answer the following questions.

Provide 3 or more similarities between the two works.

Provide 3 or more differences between the two works.

How is the natural world (landscape) represented in each?

Name ______________________ Date ______________

WORKSHEET: CHALLENGING SOCIETAL PERCEPTIONS

David Martin's *Straight Bed/Queer Bed I* helps the viewer to realize that people are people despite their differences in race, gender, and sexuality. Saad Ghosn's *Beds and Beds* is another way an artist uses beds to address equality/inequality. Look closely at the image to answer the questions below.

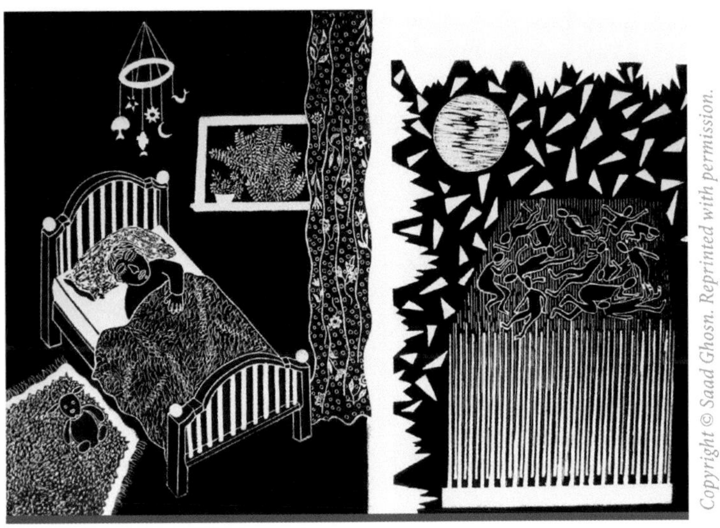

FIGURE 4.1 – Beds and Beds, Saad Ghosn. 2013. 30 x 22 in. Woodcut on Rives BFK paper.

What is the one most significant element depicted in Ghosn's piece that is lacking in Martin's?

What are the differences between the beds besides one being captured through photography and the other through drawing?

What other differences are visible between the two images?

"In our society and world, inequality, unfortunately, often starts in a child's bed. Some children have a bed of comfort, while others a bed of nails." - Saad Ghosn

Knowing the artist's intent with Beds and Beds, what in the image visually communicates his idea besides the difference in the beds?

Which artist do you feel better challenges societal perceptions and why?

Name ____________________ Date __________

WORKSHEET: RESTORATION

Iconoclasm is the destruction of religious or cultural art and architecture often by an outside culture for political purposes. In some cases, people want to give back what has been lost through the restoration of damaged works.

Should outsiders be allowed to do this? Why or why not?

Should the government of such countries have controlling say over what should or shouldn't be done? Why or why not?

Should the citizens of a country be the ones to determine the outcome of such cultural treasures? Why or why not?

Are the rules and regulations imposed by UNESCO helping or hurting in these situations?

Name ______________________________ Date ______________

WORKSHEET: CHANGING PERCEPTIONS

Many societies have not only dealt with issues of racism throughout their history, but still struggle with them today. Artists have used their art as a means of communicating the various viewpoints and perspectives on what is happening around them.

Andy Warhol created *Race Riot* using the silkscreen process and a single photographic image. In this piece, he captured a moment in the United States' history where racism was prevalent.

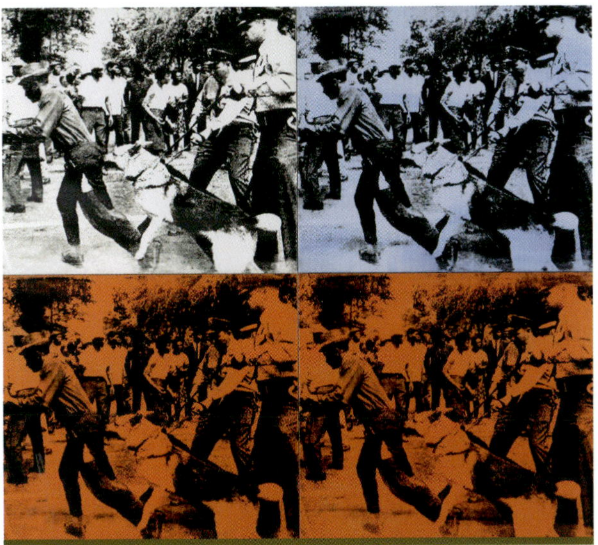

Race Riot, 1964 (silkscreened ink and synthetic polymer on canvas), Warhol, Andy (1928-87) / Private Collection / Photo © Christie's Images / Bridgeman Images

FIGURE 4.4 – Race Riot, Andy Warhol. 1964. 60 x 66 in. Acrylic and silkscreen ink on linen.

Focusing on the black and white panel in the image above, list all of what you see occurring.

In Warhol's *Race Riot* above, the same image is repeated four times.

What might the significance be of having one panel just white and black?

What might the significance be of having one panel just blue and black?

What might the significance of using red in the two panels at the bottom of the image?

What could the use of red, white and blue represent, as a whole, in relation to the image?

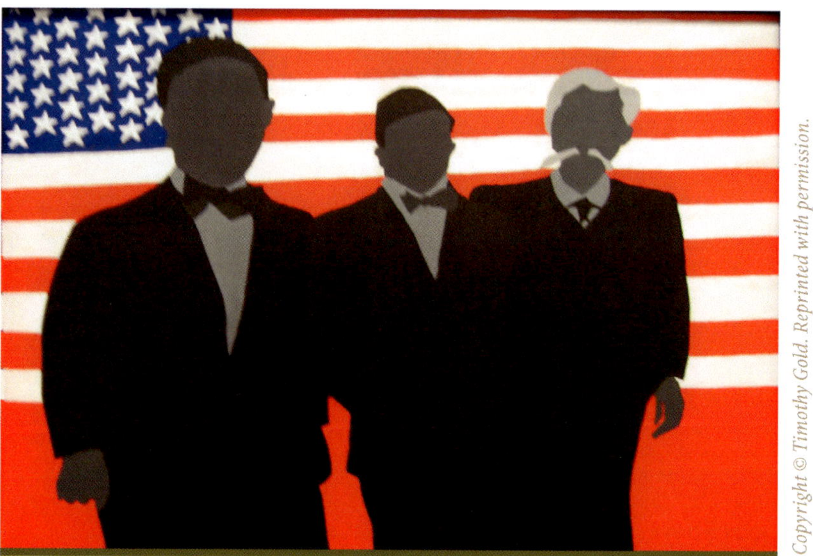

FIGURE 4.5 – With Liberty and Justice for All, Timothy Gold. 2004. 28 x 22 in. Acrylic paint on canvas.

Timothy Gold created *With Liberty and Justice for All.* The artist is making a statement about racial injustice.

There are three African-American men depicted in the image. Why are they lacking facial features?

Why is there an age difference shown among them?

Why are they in suits?

Why are they standing in front of the American flag?

What is the artist trying to communicate by making the bottom portion of the image all red?

Name ______________________________ Date ______________

WORKSHEET: DEGENERATE ART

Now that you have watched the Degenerate Art video, answer the following questions based on a specific work of art.

Artist ______________________________

Title ______________________________

Medium/Date Created ______________________________

In the space below, provide a written description or sketch of the chosen artwork.

In a short paragraph (4–5 sentences), why would this have been considered this degenerate art.

In a short paragraph (4–5 sentences), explain why this artwork should be considered a valued piece of art and why?

Name ______________________________ Date ______________

WORKSHEET: MEMORIAL ART

The *Stumbling Stones* memorial piece by Gunter Demnig was positively received by many people over the years. However, some reacted poorly to having the stones placed in front of their homes or businesses.

How would you feel if you discovered these memorial stones on your property and why?

Name ____ Date ____________________

WORKSHEET: NATURE

After viewing some examples of how artists have created landscapes, look closely at the Chinese landscaping painting provided and the projected image. Answer the questions below.

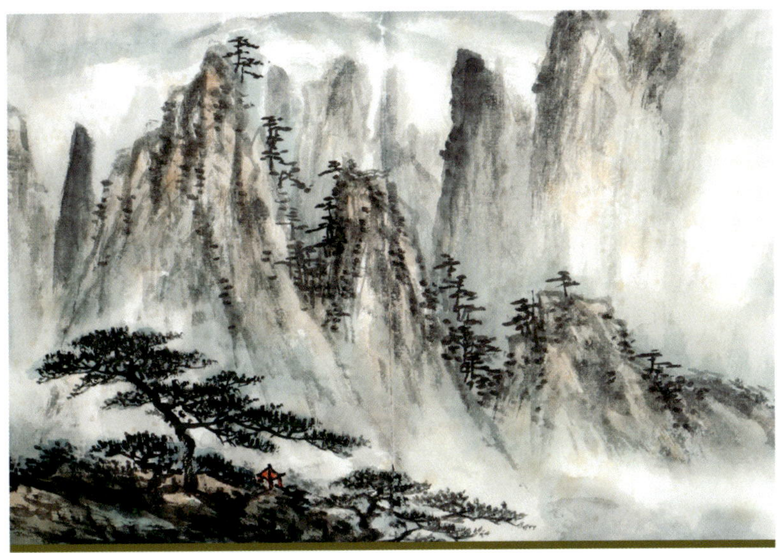

FIGURE 4.6 – Chinese Landscape Painting.

How is this painting different?

What emotion does it evoke in the viewer? Why?

Do you feel this is a successful way of capturing a landscape? Why or why not?

Name ______________________________________ Date ____________________

WORKSHEET: NATURE IN ART

Randel Plowman frequently uses elements of nature in his collages. Look closely at Plowman's *Minotaur* and the projected image of Piercefield's *Memory Map* to answer the questions below.

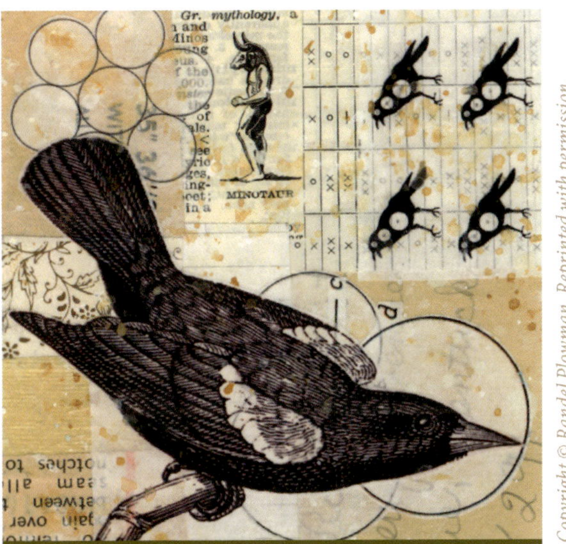

FIGURE 4.7 – Minotaur, Randel Plowman. 2009. 4 x 4 in. Collage on paper.

What is the similarity you notice between the two works?

What is different?

Which piece do you feel uses nature more successfully to tell a visual story and why?

Name ______________________________ Date ______________

WORKSHEET: ILLNESS AND TELLING THE TALE

Alzheimer's disease impacts millions of people around the world. It is a brain disorder that impacts a person's memory, thinking skills, and ability to perform everyday tasks. One way that artists use their creativity is to help them process what they are experiencing in their lives. Liliana Duque Piñero's installation was about her mother's recent diagnosis of Alzheimer's.

Andrea Knarr also experienced the same with her mother. The image below is a result of thinking about how the disease had impacted her mother and what both of them experienced as a result. Look closely at the image to answer the questions below.

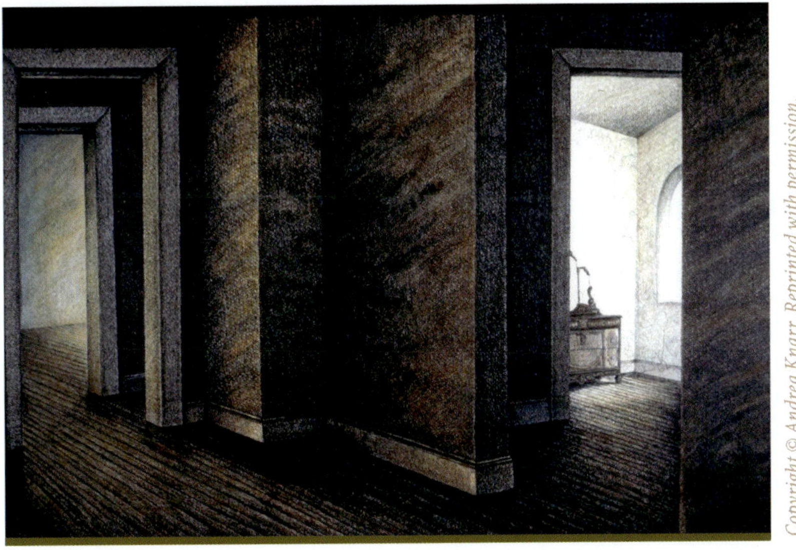

FIGURE 4.8 – Memory, Andrea Knarr. 1990. 33 x 25 in. Ink and Prismacolor pencil.

What does Knarr use to represent the sense of isolation that a person with Alzheimer's experiences?

What within Knarr's image is used to show the loss of memory due to the disease?

What within Knarr's image is used to show that there are temporary flashes of memory that someone with Alzheimer's may experience from time to time?

Look at the projected piece of Piñero's installation. What two things are similar in these artists' works?

Do they deliver the same message? Yes or No (circle one)

Why or why not?

Which do you feel best captures what a person with Alzheimer's experiences? Why?

Name ______________________________ Date ______________

WORKSHEET: FOOD

In the two images below, one is a fossilized fish embedded in rock and the other a fish made out of clay.

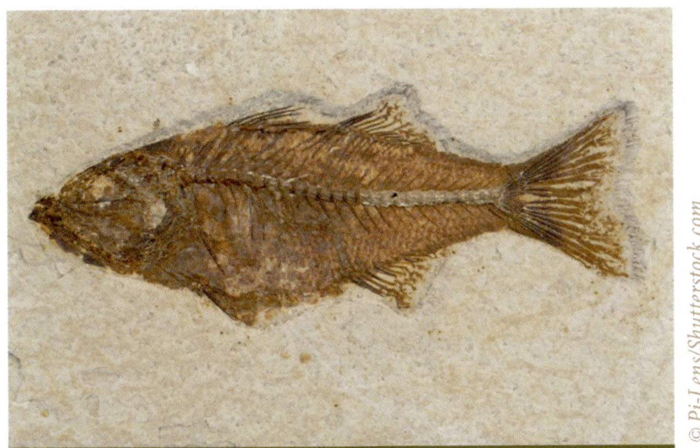

FIGURE 4.9 – Fossilized Skeleton of Prehistoric Fish.

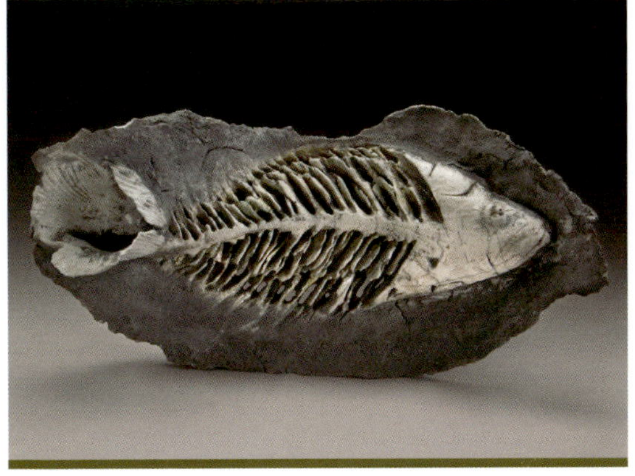

FIGURE 4.10 – Fish in Rock, Lisa Merida-Paytes. 2007. 16 x 26 x 18 in. Clay, raku.

What similarities do you see between the two?

What way may the artist be influenced by the fossilized fish skeleton when creating this piece?

Name ______________________________ Date ______________

WORKSHEET: GENDER IN ARCHITECTURE

Look closely at the two images and answer the questions below.

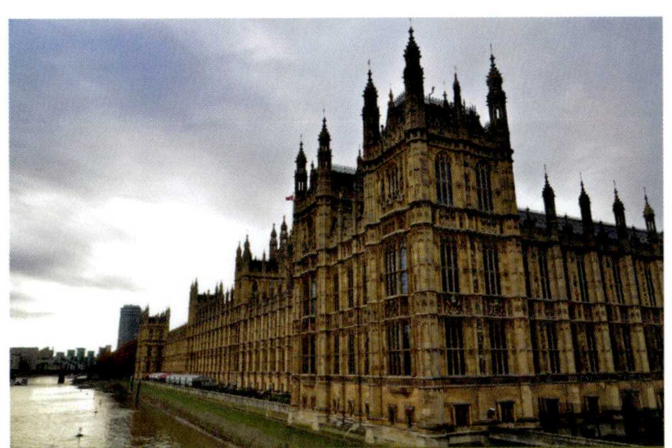

© Honey Cloverz/Shutterstock.com

FIGURE 4.11 – The Palace of Westminster. London, UK. c. 1045–1050. Reconstruction in 1859 designed by Sir Charles Barry.

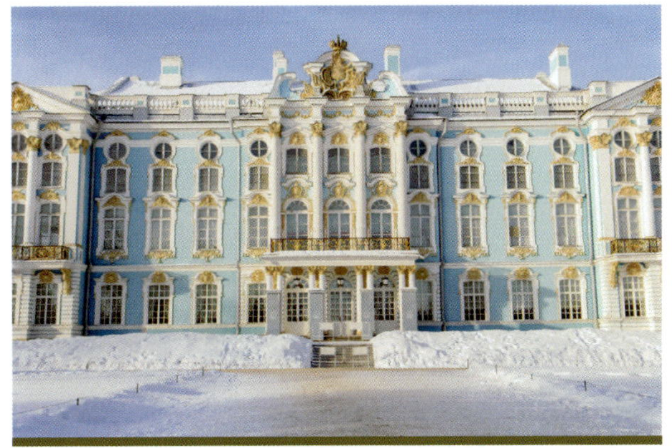

© Natalya RozSova/Shutterstock.com

FIGURE 4.12 – Catherine the Great Palace, German architect Johann-Friedrich Brunstein. Saint Petersburg, Russia. c. 1717.

Which one is more feminine in appearance?

Which one is more masculine in appearance?

What visual and design aspects of the image on the left made you choose that gender?

Are there elements of the image on the left that you feel could reflect the opposite gender? What are they and why?

What visual and design aspects of the image on the right made you choose that gender?

Are there elements of the image on the right that you feel could reflect the opposite gender? What are they and why?

Name ______________________________ Date ______________

WORKSHEET: ART OR VANDALISM

Graffiti art comes in all shapes and sizes. To some, an image may simply be graffiti, while to another it is art.

Do you feel graffiti is art or vandalism? Why?

Imagine that you have just discovered graffiti on something that you own, such as your car or house. Does this change your opinion? Why or why not?

GLOSSARY

abstraction – The act of simplifying or distorting an image or object from nature or art expressed solely through non-objective forms.

altar – A place or structure where religious ceremonies or sacrifices occur.

amphitheater – A circular or oval structure surrounding an open space or stage with tiered seating, allowing for an unobstructed view.

amphora – A vessel used to carry wine or oil by the ancient Romans and Greeks distinguishable by its narrow neck and two-handles.

aquatint – A printmaking process where an image is created through a range of tonal values rather than distinct lines on a surface prior to inking and printing.

architecture – Large structures or buildings. The art and science of designing and constructing buildings.

Art Nouveau – An early twentieth-century Western art movement that included forms based on the natural world.

artifact – An object crafted by a human being, often having cultural or historical significance.

Arts and Crafts – A late nineteenth-century art movement focused on the ideal of craftsmanship during an age of mass production and mechanization.

asymmetry – Creating visual imbalance by positioning more color, line, and other formal elements on one area of the composition.

atheism – The disbelief in the existence of a higher power, such as gods or God.

Avant Garde – A term applied to artists from the late nineteenth-century to twentieth-century using experimental or unorthodox methods to create new directions or develop new concepts in their art.

background – The part of an image or work of art that is furthest from the viewer.

balance – Visual equality within a composition or work of art achieved by the organization of all aspects within an artwork. Types of balance include, but not limited to, symmetrical and asymmetrical.

binder – A liquid substance that holds color pigment and when dries creates of paint layer.

border – The area which creates a clean edge around an image or work of art.

bronze – A metal made from various alloys of copper and tin.

calligraphy – A form of decorative handwriting.

canvas – A heavy, woven material upon which a painting is completed. Any surface upon which an artist creates a work of art, like a building for a graffiti artist.

carving – A sculptural method for creating a work of art by removing material from a source, like a block of clay, wood, or stone.

casting – The process of making a 'positive' or image from a mold out of a range of materials, such as bronze, clay, or plaster.

catacomb – A multi-level subterranean cemetery with recessed areas in the walls for graves.

ceramic – *See* pottery.

church – A building constructed for Christian congregational worship.

collograph – A form of printmaking where materials and objects are applied to a rigid surface, such as wood or artist board, to create an image before inking and printing.

composition – An arrangement of visual elements in a work of art.

concrete – A hard and durable building material made of sand, pebbles, and broken stone.

corrugated – A material shaped to give its surface ridges and grooves.

Cubism – An early twentieth-century art movement where by multiple viewpoints of a single object, space, or landscape is captured simultaneously in a single image. Often breaking forms from the natural world down to simple geometric representations.

curvilinear – A visual element consisting of or alluding to curved lines.

deity – A god or goddess. A being perceived as being divine.

diagram – An outline, plan, or sketch used to explain or clarify something.

digital art – Works of art created with the aid of electronic devices and technology.

dimensional – A measurement of an object or work of art in length, depth, and thickness. May also be the appearance of depth within an artwork created through various techniques, such as carving, modeling, or perspective.

drawing – A process of representing forms or objects through lines on a surface, such as paper.

dry point – A printmaking (etching) process where the image or design is scratched onto a surface prior to inking and printing.

Earth Art – *See* Land Art.

earthenware – A type of low-fired clay that remains slightly porous after being fired in a kiln.

effigy – A sculpture of a human being created for a variety of purposes, such as political, cultural or personal.

emphasis – The part of the composition to which viewer's eye is drawn.

engraving – A printmaking process where an image is created by incising lines on a hard surface, such as a metal plate, prior to inking and printing.

exhibition – A public showing of a body of artwork within a space, such as a gallery or museum.

foreground – The part of an image or work of art which is closest to the viewer.

form – The defined shape of an object or natural element.

formal elements – Line, shape, form, texture, pattern, and color used within an artwork to create the overall image.

fresco – A painting technique where pigment is applied to a plaster surface.

graffiti – Images or text created on a public wall or other surface, usually created without property owner's permission, therefore considered illegal.

genre painting – A form of painting where the subject matter focuses on aspects of everyday life.

geometric – Description of the simple shapes such as circles, squares, triangles, or rectangles in a design.

hand building – An ancient technique to create pottery and other ceramic objects using various methods, such as coiling or slab construction.

hieroglyphic – An ancient form of writing utilizing pictures or symbols rather than letters. Most commonly associated with the Egyptian culture.

icon – An important symbol or a representation of a sacred personage often seen in Christian art.

iconoclasm – The destruction of images created for religious purposes.

illustration – A picture, image, or design used to decorate written text.

Impressionism – A late nineteenth-century Western painting style characterized by capturing subtle light through small brush strokes and strong color.

installation art – A form of art created for a specific location, sometimes incorporating materials or physical aspects of the site.

intangible – Something which cannot be defined, realized, or perceived by the senses or touch.

kiln – A type of furnace or oven used to bake, dry, or harden various materials, such as clay and brick.

Land Art – Usually large-scale outdoor artistic designs or constructions made with local materials from the surrounding environment, such as dirt, wood, or rock.

line – An element with length but variable width used to create an image.

linear perspective – A form of perspective used in two-dimensional art to create the illusion of depth and distance through the convergence of two parallel lines.

lithograph – A printmaking process where an image is drawn on a flat stone surface with a greasy or oily medium, such as a crayon, prior to inking and printing.

mandala – Often a circular design which includes other geometric elements and other shapes representing deities and the cosmos in Hindu and Buddhist traditions.

manuscript – A handwritten document, such as a poem or book.

marble – A type of stone often used in art and architecture.

mausoleum – An above-ground tomb which is majestic or grand in manner.

medium/media – The materials used to create a work of art.

middle ground – The area within an image or work of art that lies between the foreground and background.

mixed media – A work of art created from two or more materials.

monochromatic – Having or being created from one color, using the various tones of it.

monotheism – A religious practice of worshipping a single deity or god.

monotype – A form of printmaking by which an image is created with ink or paint on a flat surface before printing, producing a single, unique print.

mosaic – An image created from combining small pieces of material, such as glass, stone, or tile.

mosque – A building constructed for Islamic worship.

mummification process – A process by which the human body is dried and preserved before burial, commonly practiced by the ancient Egyptians.

mural – Images painted on or covering a wall.

naturalism – Rendering an image or object so it closely resembles as it is seen in the natural world.

niche – A recessed area in a wall, usually designed to display an object, such as a statue.

outline – A line that defines the outer boundaries of an object or figure.

painting – An artistic process by which a picture or image is created by applying paint to a surface, such as canvas.

palette – A range of colors used by an artist with their work. A board used by an artist to hold paint and provide an area for mixing colors during the painting process.

papyrus – A material from the pith of an aquatic sedge used by ancient cultures upon which to write or paint.

pattern – A repeating or decorative element within a composition.

performance art – An art form where by various media are used, such as painting, film, music, or video, resulting in a theatrical presentation.

perspective – Rendering the illusion of a three-dimensional space on a flat, two-dimensional surface.

photography – An artistic process which produces images of objects or the natural world on photosensitive surfaces, providing the ability to print multiples of a single image.

pigment – Color in the form of powder which can be mixed with a binder to create paint.

pilgrimage – Often a personal journey to a sacred place, shrine, or relic.

plaster – A mixture of lime, sand, and water, often used to coat walls or create works of art.

plinth – A base or stone slab on which an object or structure is placed.

potlatch – A ceremonial feast held by some Pacific Northwest Coast Native American people in celebration of significant event like marriage or raising of a totem pole.

polytheism – A religious practice of worshipping multiple deities or gods.

pottery – Objects, such as bowls, plates, pots, or vases, made from clay which becomes hard and durable after firing.

principles of design – Unity, variety, rhythm, balance, emphasis, subordination, scale, and proportion used within an artwork to create the overall image.

prints – An image that is produced through various photography and printmaking techniques.

propaganda – The deliberate spreading of ideas or information to promote or damage a cause, movement, or nation.

proportion – The size relationships between parts of a whole or object.

Realism – A nineteenth-century art style depicting the natural world as it appears, not through distortion or exaggeration.

relief – Form of sculpture, with a partially raised image projected from a flat surface and meant to be viewed from the front.

reliquary – A receptacle designed to store or display a holy relic, such as ashes or bones of a spiritual figure.

restoration – An act of repairing or rebuilding that which has been destroyed, altered, or damaged.

reverse graffiti – Imagery created using cleaning substances to remove grime and pollutants from a surface area.

rhythm – A visual technique created through the repetition of line, shape, and other formal elements within a work of art.

Rococo – An early eighteenth-century Western art form distinguished by its ornate style and light colors.

sarcophagus – A coffin made of stone, typically decorated with images or inscribed with words.

scarification – A process where by a design or pattern is created through shallow cuts made on human flesh. Often a colorant or irritant is rubbed into the wound to enhance the resulting scar tissue.

scale – The size of an image or object in relation to others around it.

sculpture – Three-dimensional (or in-the-round) artwork created through the shaping of material by various processes, such as chiseling, casting, modeling, or carving.

shape – A flat, two-dimensional form or the configuration of a thing or object.

shrine – A holy place, a receptacle for sacred objects, and/or a place devoted to a holy person or deity.

silkscreen – A method of printmaking where by a design is created on a screen using a stencil. Ink is then forced through the mesh of the screen onto a surface, such as paper or fabric.

stainless steel – A type of metal which is virtually rust-free and is silver in appearance.

stencil – A sheet of plastic, wood, or other material in which a design and/or lettering has been cut out. Ink or paint can be applied to the surface of the sheet or through the open areas to transfer an image onto another surface, such as cloth or a building's wall.

still-life – A group of mostly inanimate objects assembled to create a composition used as subject matter in an artwork.

studio – A room or facility where an artist creates works of art.

stupa – A dome-shaped structure used as a commemorative shrine or reliquary in the Buddhist and Jainist philosophies.

style – Specific characteristics that are consistent within a body of work, which can be seen in an historical period, cultural tradition, or an individual artist' body of work.

subject matter – The idea represented in a work of art.

subordination – The areas within a composition that are toned down or made less interesting than the area of focus or emphasis.

symmetry – Creating visual balance through equal distribution of color, shape, line, and other formal elements throughout a composition.

synagogue – A building constructed for Jewish congregational worship and religious instruction.

tangible – Something which can be realized, understood, or is discernible by touch.

tattoo – A permanent design or mark made on the body through the process of puncturing and ingraining indelible ink into the skin.

technique – A method for making a work of art.

temple – A building constructed for religious worship or rituals in Hindu and other religions.

terracotta – A type of low-fired clay that is brownish-orange in color.

texture – The feel or visual appearance of a surface.

totem – An emblem or symbol, such as an animal, plant, or natural form, representing a group of people with family ties or a clan.

ukiyo-e – A Japanese genre painting or print where the subject matter is taken from everyday life.

undulating – A wave-like pattern or appearance.

UNESCO (United Nations Educational, Scientific, and Cultural Organization) – A United Nations agency established to promote education, communication, and the arts.

unity – A sense of order and things belonging together, visually creating a sense of wholeness.

variety – A sense of difference, chaos, or disorder adding visual interest to a work of art without disturbing its unity.

visual texture – The illusion of real texture created through various artistic techniques in two-dimensional formats, such as drawing and painting.

wax – A pliable substance that is heat sensitive and insoluble in water.

weaving – Interlocking of threads or fibers to create cloth or an artwork, often using a loom.

wheel throwing – A technique of creating pottery and other ceramic forms using a spinning wheel.

woodcut (woodblock printing) – A printmaking process where an image is carved onto a wood surface prior to inking and printing.

World Heritage Site – A place, such as a monument, building, city, or natural location, listed by UNESCO as having special cultural or physical significance.

WPA (Works Projects Administration) – A program created in 1935 by the United States government to provide economic relief to artists and others during the Depression years.

REFERENCES

"Abraham Lincoln Life Masks." *Abraham Lincoln Online.* N.p., 2015. Web. 2 Jan. 2016 <http://www.abrahamlincolnonline.org/lincoln/resource/masks.htm>.

"About ReligionFacts.com." *ReligionFacts.com.* 10 Nov. 2015. Web. 1 Nov. 2015. <www.religionfacts.com/about>.

"About the Artist." *PBS.* PBS, 26 Aug. 2006. Web. 12 Mar. 2016.

"A Brief History of Baseball Cards." *A Brief History of Baseball Cards.* N.p., n.d. Web. 04 Mar. 2016. <http://www.cycleback.com/1800s/briefhistory.htm>.

"Afterlife." *Ancient Egypt.* N.p., n.d. Web. 04 Mar. 2016. <http://ccsancientegypt.weebly.com/afterlife.html>.

"Albert Bierstadt: The Complete Works." *Albert Bierstadt Biography.* N.p., 2002. Web. 04 Mar. 2016.

American Museum of Natural History, and Aldona Jonaitis. *From the Land of the Totem Poles: The Northwest Coast Indian Art Collection at the American Museum of Natural History.* New York: The Museum, 1988. Print.

"Ancient Egypt: The Mythology—Anubis." *Ancient Egypt: The Mythology—Anubis.* Egyptian Myths, Aug. 2014. Web. 01 Feb. 2016. <http://egyptianmyths.net/anubis.htm>.

"Ancient Roman Colosseum in Rome." *Romanlife-romeitaly.com.* Marcus Ruhl, 2013. Web. <http://www.romanlife-romeitaly.com/ancient-roman-colosseum.html#colosseum-history>.

Arts, CBC. "Inverted Church Sculpture Moves from Vancouver to Calgary." *CBCnews.* CBC/Radio Canada, 02 June 2008. Web. 21 Apr. 2016.

Art Institute of Chicago. *Impressionism and Post-Impressionism in The Art Institute of Chicago.* Art Institute of Chicago, 2000, p. 128.

Astier, Marie-Bénédicte. "Work Aphrodite, Known as the "Venus De Milo"" *Aphrodite, Known as the "Venus De Milo"* Louvre, n.d. Web. 04 Mar. 2016. <http://www.louvre.fr/en/oeuvre-notices/aphrodite-known-venus-de-milo>.

Barnett, Errol. "Rock Churches of Lalibela, the Jerusalem of Ethiopia—CNN.com." *CNN.* Cable News Network, June 2013. Web. 11 Nov. 2015. <http://www.cnn.com/2013/06/27/travel/rock-churches-lalibela-ethiopia>.

Barolsky, Paul. "BOTTICELLI'S GOLDEN GODDESS". *Source: Notes in the History of Art* 32.2 (2013): 4–5. Web.

"Basquiat Timeline—Basquiat Biography." *Basquiat Biography.* N.p., n.d. Web. 19 Apr. 2016.

"3,000,000–9000 BCE—Paleolithic Art." *Ancient to Medieval Art.* N.p., 05 Sept. 2012. Web. 15 Feb. 2016. <https://klimtlover.wordpress.com/art-before-history/paleolithic-art/>.

Biography.com Editors. "Author Biography." *Bio.com.* A&E Networks Television, n.d. Web. 12 Mar. 2016.

Biography.com Editors. "Chuck Close Biography." *Bio.com.* A&E Networks Television, n.d. Web. 04 Mar. 2016. <http://www.biography.com/people/chuck-close-9251491>.

Biography.com Editors. "Chuck Close Biography." *Bio.com.* A&E Networks Television, n.d. Web. 27 July 2016.

Biography.com Editors. "Diego Rivera Biography." *TheBiography.com.* A&E Televison Network, n.d. Web. 12 Mar. 2016.

Biography.com Editors. "Dorothea Lange Biography." *Bio.com.* A&E Networks Television, n.d. Web. 03 Mar. 2016. <http://www.biography.com/people/dorothea-lange-9372993>.

Biography.com Editors. "Elisabeth Vigée Le Brun Biography." *Bio.com.* A&E Networks Television, n.d. Web. 12 Mar. 2016.

Biography.com Editors. "Karl Marx Biography." *Bio.com.* A&E Networks Television, n.d. Web. 12 Mar. 2016.

Blatty, David. "Gustav Klimt Biography." *The Biography.com.* A&E Television Networks, n.d. Web.

Bobin, Frédéric. "Disputes Damage Hopes of Rebuilding Afghanistan's Bamiyan Buddhas." *The Guardian.* Guardian News and Media, 10 Jan. 2015. Web. 12 Mar. 2016.

Boltanski, Christian. *Autel de Lycée Chases*, 1986–87. Six photographs, six desk lamps, and twenty-two tin boxes, 170.2 × 214.6 × 24.1 cm. Rubell Family Collection, Miami © 2010 Artists Rights Society (ARS), New York/ADAGP, Paris.

Bos, Carole. "CHILDREN of MARIE ANTOINETTE." *AwesomeStories.com*, 01 Oct. 2006. Web.

Bosco, David. "Waking the Buddha". *Archaeology* 58.1 (2005): 18–23. Web.

"Bring "Device to Root Out Evil" Back to Vancouver." *Vancouver Biennale.* N.p., 28 Mar. 2013. Web. 21 Apr. 2016.

Brehmer, Debra. "The Pieta: A Story in Five Parts." *Portrait Society Gallery.* N.p., n.d. Web. 3 Mar. 2016. <https://portraitsocietygallery.com/essays-about-portraiture/the-pieta-a-story-in-five-parts/>.

Brune, Adrian. "Shepard Fairey: 'My Goal Was to Make Art by Any Means Necessary'." *The Guardian.* Guardian News and Media, 16 Oct. 2015. Web. 21 Apr. 2016.

"Buddhism." *ReligionFacts.com.* 10 Nov. 2015. Web. 1 Nov. 2015. <www.religionfacts.com/buddhism>.

Cain, Abagail. "Nine Types of Printmaking You Need to Know." *Lower East Side Printshop.* Artsy, 2016. Web. 12 Mar. 2016.

Campbell, Wendy. "Paul Curtis: Reverse Graffiti—Daily Art Fixx—a Little Art, Every Day." *Daily Art Fixx a Little Art Every Day.* N.p., 30 June 2009. Web. 21 Apr. 2016.

Cartwright, Mark. "Olmec Colossal Stone Heads." *Ancient History Encyclopedia*. N.p., 21 Mar. 2014. Web. 03 Mar. 2016. <http://www.ancient.eu/article/672/>.

Cartwright, Mark. "Roman Sculpture." *Ancient History Encyclopedia*. N.p., 25 Aug. 2013. Web. 03 Mar. 2016. <http://www.ancient.eu/Roman_Sculpture/>.

Cartwright, Mark. "Trajan's Market." *Ancient History Encyclopedia*. N.p., 08 Oct. 2013. Web. 19 Mar. 2016.

"Chinese Ceramics." *New World Encyclopedia*. N.p., 09 June 2008. Web. 05 Mar. 2016.

"Christianity." *ReligionFacts.com*. 10 Nov. 2015. Web. 1 Dec. 2015. <www.religionfacts.com/christianity>.

"Chuck Close." *Artsy*. N.p., 2016. 19 Jan. 2016 Web. <https://www.artsy.net/artist/chuck-close>.

"Chuck Close Biography, Art, and Analysis of Works." *The Art Story*. N.p., n.d. Web. 27 July 2016.

Ciarla, Roberto. *The Eternal Army: The Terracotta Soldiers of the First Chinese Emperor*. Vercelli: White Star, 2005. Print.

Circle of Enlightenment: Tibetan Buddhist Sand Mandala. Canton, NY: St. Lawrence U, 1999. 10-24. Print.

Clark, Darci. "Viking Religion and Burial Rituals." *SemiramisSpeakscom*. N.p., 15 July 2014. Web. 04 Mar. 2016. <http://semiramis-speaks.com/viking-religion-and-burial-rituals/>.

Close, Chuck, Kim Levin, and Pace Gallery. *Chuck Close, Recent Work: [exhibition] October 26–24 November, 1979, the Pace Gallery*. New York: The Gallery, 1979. Print.

Coen, Jon. "Shepard Fairey—Painting Ashbury Park with the Obey Founder." *Huck Magazine*. N.p., 21 Dec. 2011. Web. 21 Apr. 2016.

Constantelos, Stephen. "Bob Bescher." *Society for American Baseball Research*. N.p., n.d. Web. 4 Mar. 2016. <http://sabr.org/bioproj/person/a0fba611>.

Coomaraswamy, Ananda K. *Hinduism and Buddhism*. New York: Philosophical Library, 1943. 3–45. Print.

Cormack, Robin. *Icons*. Cambridge, MA: Harvard UP, 2007. 7–63. Print.

Cortissoz, Royal. *Personalities in Art*. Freeport, N.Y.: Books for Libraries Press, 1968. Print. Essay index reprint series.

Coughlan, Robert, and Time-Life Books. *The World of Michelangelo, 1475–1564*. New York: Time, 1966. Print. Time-Life library of art.

"Cuevas De Las Manos, Argentina—The Cave of the Hands." *Bradshaw Foundation*. N.p., n.d. Web. 03 Mar. 2016. <http://www.bradshawfoundation.com/south_america/cueva_de_los_manos/index.php>.

Danti, Michael D. "Ground-based Observations of Cultural Heritage Incidents in Syria and Iraq". *Near Eastern Archaeology* 78.3 (2015): 132–141. Web.

Das, Subhamoy. "About Hinduism: Hindu Beliefs, Practices, and Culture." *About.com Religion & Spirituality*. N.p., Dec. 2014. Web. 01 Feb. 2016. <http://hinduism.about.com/>.

Davis, William. "Consuming Ancient Egypt." *Ure Museum*. N.p., 2003. The University of Reading. Web. 4 Mar. 2016. <http://www.reading.ac.uk/Ure/leaflets/Ure_modelboats.pdf>.

"Deepwater Horizon oil spill of 2010". *Encyclopædia Britannica*. Encyclopædia Britannica Online. Encyclopedia Britannica Inc., 2016. Web. 12 Mar. 2016. <https://www.britannica.com/event/Deepwater-Horizon-oil-spill-of-2010>.

Delman, Edward. "Afghanistan's Buddhas Rise Again." *The Atlantic.* Atlantic Media Company, 10 June 2015. Web. 12 Mar. 2016.

Delors, Catherine. "Versailles and More." *Versailles and More.* N.p., 2008. Web. 12 Mar. 2016.

Demaline, Jackie. "NKU's New School of the Arts Prepares to Open First Artistic Collaboration." *The River City News.* N.p., 2015. Web. 15 Mar. 2016.

Demato, Richard J. "Kevin Muente." *RJD Gallery.* N.p., 2015. Web. 03 Feb. 2016.

Department of Asian Art. "Woodblock Prints in the Ukiyo-e Style." In *Heilbrunn Timeline of Art History.* New York: The Metropolitan Museum of Art, 2000–. http://www.metmuseum.org/toah/hd/ukiy/hd_ukiy.htm (October 2003)

"Diego Rivera Biography." *www.diegorivera.org.* N.p., 2010. Web.

"Diego Rivera Biography, Art, and Analysis of Works." *The Art Story.* The Arts Story Foundation, n.d. Web. 12 Mar. 2016.

"Diego Rivera, His Life and Art." *Diego Rivera.* N.p., 2010. Web. 12 Mar. 2016.

Dint. "Sweden Road Ways Two on the Loose TRAVEL HUMANITIES PHOTOS: Anundshog Viking Burial Mound at Vasteras." *Sweden Road Ways Two on the Loose TRAVEL HUMANITIES PHOTOS: Anundshog Viking Burial Mound at Vasteras.* N.p., 8 Feb. 2011. Web. 04 Mar. 2016. <http://swedenroadways.blogspot.com/2011/02/anundshog-viking-burial-mound-at.html>.

"Dolmens Homepage." *Dolmens Homepage.* N.p., n.d. Web.

"Drakensberg Rock Art." *South Africa: Inspiring New Ways.* South African Tourism, 2016. Web. 9 Feb. 2016 <http://www.southafrica.net/za/en/articles/entry/article-southafrica.net-drakensberg-rock-art>.

Dunham, Chris. "Life and Death in Tana Toraja, Indonesia." *Transitions Abroad.* N.p., 1995. Web. 18 Jan. 2016 <http://www.transitionsabroad.com/listings/travel/narrative_travel_writing/life_and_death_in_tana_toraja_indonesia.shtml>.

Donati, Jessica. "Afghanistan Halts Suspected Reconstruction of Ancient Buddhas." *Reuters.* Thomson Reuters, 12 Feb. 2014. Web. 12 Jan. 2016. <http://www.reuters.com/article/us-afghanistan-buddhas-idUSBREA1B13J20140212>.

Donati, Jessica. "Afghanistan Halts Suspected Reconstruction of Ancient Buddhas." *Reuters.* Thomson Reuters, 12 Feb. 2014. Web. 12 Mar. 2016.

Editorial, Artsy. "Nine Types of Printmaking You Need to Know." *Artsy.* N.p., 29 Oct. 2013. Web. 12 Mar. 2016.

"Egyptian Gods: Ptah." *Egyptian Gods and Goddesses* RSS. N.p., n.d. Web. 11 Jan. 2016. <http://egyptian-gods.org/egyptian-gods-ptah/>.

Eliade, Mircea, and Willard R. Trask. *Shamanism: Archaic Techniques of Ecstasy.* [Rev. and enl.]. New York: Bollingen Foundation; distributed by Pantheon Books, 1964. Print. Bollingen series, 76; Bollingen series, 76.

"Elisabeth Louise Vigée Le Brun: Woman Artist in Revolutionary France." *The Met.* MOMA, 2000. Web. 12 Mar. 2016

Ellsworth-Jones, Will. "History, Travel, Arts, Science, People, Places." *History, Travel, Arts, Science, People, Places [Smithsonian].* Smithsonian.com, Feb. 2013. Web. 19 Apr. 2016.

"Ernst Haeckel". *Encyclopædia Britannica.* Encyclopædia Britannica Online. Encyclopædia Britannica Inc., 2016. Web. 01 Jun. 2016 <http://www.britannica.com/biography/Ernst-Haeckel>.

Evans, Arthur, and Joan Evans. T*he Palace of Minos: A Comparative Account of the Successive Stages of the Early Cretan Civilization As Illustrated by the Discoveries at Knossos.* New York: Biblo and Tannen, 1964. Print.

Fernández, G. "Fresco of Dolphin." *The ArtWolf.com—Online Art Magazine.* N.p., n.d. Web. 20 Jan. 2016 <http://www.theartwolf.com/masterworks/knossos.htm>.

Fernández, G. "Paul Cezanne." *The Art Wolf.* N.p., n.d. Web. 02 Jan. 2016.

Forman, Werner, and Stephen Quirke. *Hieroglyphs and the Afterlife in Ancient Egypt.* London: British Museum Press, 1996. Print.

François, Aline. "Work The Wedding Feast at Cana." *The Wedding Feast at Cana.* Louvre, n.d. Web. 16 Feb. 2016. <http://www.louvre.fr/en/oeuvre-notices/wedding-feast-cana>.

"Frank Gehry: "The Cleveland Clinic Lou Ruvo Center for Brain Health." *Designboom.* N.p., 28 May 2010. Web. <http://www.designboom.com/architecture/frank-gehry-the-cleveland-clinic-lou-ruvo-center-for-brain-health/>.

"Frank Smith (1900s Pitcher)." *Wikipedia.* Wikimedia Foundation, 19 Feb. 2016. Web. 04 Mar. 2016. <https://en.wikipedia.org/wiki/Frank_Smith_%281900s_pitcher%29>.

"Fred R. Kline Gallery: George Biddle Biography." *Fred R. Kline Gallery: George Biddle Biography.* N.p., n.d. Web. 03 Mar. 2016. <http://www.klinegallery.com/Biddle01_Bio.html>.

"Fresco painting". *Encyclopædia Britannica.* Encyclopædia Britannica Online. Encyclopædia Britannica Inc., 2016. Web. 15 May. 2016 <http://www.britannica.com/art/fresco-painting>.

FWS. "The 47 Ronin." N.p., n.d. Web. 28 Jan. 2016.

Galvin, John. "ABYDOS: Life and Death at the Dawn of Egyptian Civiization." *National Geographic.* N.p., n.d. Web. 4 Mar. 2016. <http://ngm.nationalgeographic.com/ngm/0504/feature7/index.html>.

Ghosn, Saad. "Farron Allen's Body of Work." *Streetvibes Cincinnatis Alternative News Source.* N.p., 11 Mar. 2010. Web. 15 Jan. 2016.

Gogh, Vincent van, and W. H. Auden. *Van Gogh: A Self-Portrait; Letters Revealing His Life as a Painter.* Greenwich, Conn.: New York Graphic Society, 1961. Print.

"Graffiti". *Encyclopædia Britannica. Encyclopædia Britannica Online.* Encyclopædia Britannica Inc., 2016. Web. 15 May. 2016 <http://www.britannica.com/art/graffiti-art>.

"haka". *Encyclopædia Britannica. Encyclopædia Britannica Online.* Encyclopædia Britannica Inc., 2014. Web. 01 Dec. 2014 <http://www.britannica.com/EBchecked/topic/252091/haka>.

Hale, Nancy. *Mary Cassatt.* Garden City, NY: Doubleday, 1975. Print.

"Hand Paintings and Symbols in Rock Art." *Bradshaw Foundation.* N.p., n.d. Web. 03 Mar. 2016. <http://www.bradshawfoundation.com/hands/index.php>.

Harvey, Ben. "Cézanne, Mont Sainte-Victoire." *Khan Academy.* N.p., n.d. Web. 01 Mar. 2016.

"Haunted: Contemporary Photography/Video/Performance, Christian Boltanski: Documentation and Reiteration." *Arts Curriculum.* The Solomon R. Guggenheim Foundation, n.d. Web. 19 Apr. 2016.

Hawthorne, Christopher. "Architecture Review: Frank Gehry's Cleveland Clinic Lou Ruvo Center for Brain Health in Las Vegas." *Los Angeles Times.* N.p., 19 May 2010. Web.

"Healing the Earth: A Sacred Art by the Tibetan Lamas of Drepung Loseling Monastery." *The Mystical Arts of Tibet.* Drepung Loseling Monastery, n.d. Web. 14 Mar. 2016 <http://www.mysticalartsoftibet.org/>.

Hill, J. "Bull Cults in Ancient Egypt." *Religion in Ancient Egypt: Bull Cults.* N.p., 2010. Web. 01 Feb. 2016. <http://www.ancientegyptonline.co.uk/bullcult.html>.

"Hinduism." *ReligionFacts.com.* 10 Nov. 2015. Web. 1 Nov. 2015. <www.religionfacts.com/hinduism>.

Hirst, K. Kris. "Maya Lady Xoc." *About.com Education.* N.p., Dec. 2014. Web. 01 Feb. 2016. <http://archaeology.about.com/od/northamerica/ig/Ancient-Americas-/Maya-Lady-Xok.htm>.

"History a Look Back." *Hill of Tara.* Maguire's Hill of Tara, n.d. Web. 21 Apr. 2016.

History.com Staff. "Colosseum." *History.com.* A&E Television Networks, 2009. Web. 08 Mar. 2016.

History.com Staff. "Colosseum." *History.com.* A+E Networks, 2009. Web. 03 Mar. 2016 <http://www.history.com/topics/ancient-history/colosseum>.

History.com Staff. "Dust Bowl." *History.com.* A&E Television Networks, 2009. Web. 03 Mar. 2016. <http://www.history.com/topics/dust-bowl>.

History.com Staff. "Nefertiti." *History.com.* A&E Television Networks, 2010. Web. 03 Mar. 2016. <http://www.history.com/topics/ancient-history/nefertiti>.

Holloway, April. "The Incredible Rock Houses and Underground Cities of Cappadocia." *Ancient Origins.* N.p., 28 Feb. 2014. Web. 16 Feb. 2016. <http://www.ancient-origins.net/ancient-places-europe/incredible-rock-houses-and-underground-cities-cappadocia-001394?nopaging=1>.

Holloway, April. "The Toraja People and the Most Complex Funeral Rituals in the World —See More At: Http://www.ancient-origins.net/ancient-places-asia/toraja-people-and-most-complex-funeral-rituals-world-001268?nopaging=1#sthash.j0lStn8U.dpuf." *Ancient Origins.* N.p., 24 Jan. 2014. Web. <http://www.ancient-origins.net/ancient-places-asia/toraja-people-and-most-complex-funeral-rituals-world-001268?nopaging=1>.

"Courtesans and the Licensed Pleasure Quarters in Edo Japan." *Asian Art Museum.* N.p., 2012. Web. 05 Mar. 2016.

Huang, Alice. "Totem Poles." *Indigenous Foundations Arts.* UBC, CA: The University of British Columbia, 2009. Web. 02 Feb. 2016 <http://indigenousfoundations.arts.ubc.ca/home/culture/totem-poles.html>.

Huda. "What Is the Ka'aba, and How Do Muslims Use It in Worship?" *About.com Religion & Spirituality.* N.p., Mar. 2015. Web. Jan. 2016. <http://islam.about.com/od/mecca/p/kaaba.htm>.

Hutchison, Jane Campbell. *Albrecht Dürer: A Biography.* Princeton, NJ: Princeton UP, 1990. Print.

"Hyper Realistic Portrait Paintings by Chuck Close with Fingerprints Read More Http://prafulla.net/graphics/art-graphics/hyper-realistic-portrait-paintings-by-chuck-close-with-fingerprints/." *Parfulla.net.* N.p., 01 Jan. 2011. Web.

"Icon of the Archangel Michael." *Byzantine and Christian Museum*. N.p., n.d. Web. Jan. 2016. <http://www.byzantinemuseum.gr/en/permanentexhibition/byzantine_world/the_final_flowering/?bxm=1353>.

"In the Omnibus." *In the Omnibus*. National Gallery of Art, 2016. Web. 15 Jan. 2016.

Inuit Hunting and Fishing Implements. Columbia: University of Missouri-Columbia, Museum of Anthropology, n.d. PDF.

"Irish Megalithic Portal Dolmens." By Martin Byrne. *Sacred Island Guided Tours*. N.p., n.d. Web.

"Islam." *ReligionFacts.com*. 13 Nov. 2015. Web. 1 Dec. 2015. <www.religionfacts.com/islam>.

Ivanova, Natasha. "Knossos—Palace Frescoes." *Greek Art/Knossos-Palace Frescoes*. PBWorks, 2009. Web. 17 Feb. 2016. <http://sasgreekart.pbworks.com/w/page/10150010/Knossos%E2%80%94Palace%20Frescoes>.

James, Laura. "A Kind of Science: Ana England Has Her Own Ideas about Nature." *City Beat* [Cincinnati] N. p., n.d. Print.

Jones, Chad. "Liliana Duque Piñeiro." *Quarterline Design Management*. N.p., n.d. Web. 14 Mar. 2016.

Jones, Gwyn. *A History of the Vikings*. London: Oxford UP, 1968. Print.

Jones, J. Sydney. "Inuit." *Gale Encyclopedia of Multicultural America*. 2000. Encyclopedia.com. 16 Feb. 2016 <http://www.encyclopedia.com>.

"Judaism." *ReligionFacts.com*. 10 Nov. 2015. Web. 1 Dec. 2015. <www.religionfacts.com/judaism>.

"Kathe Kollwitz". *Encyclopædia Britannica. Encyclopædia Britannica Online*. Encyclopædia Britannica Inc., 2016. Web. 15 May. 2016 <http://www.britannica.com/biography/Kathe-Kollwitz>.

Kim, Chongsuh. "The Concept of 'Korean Religion' and Religious Studies in Korea". *Journal of Korean Religions* 1 (2010): 23–41.

"King Menkaura (Mycerinus) and Queen." *Museum of Fine Arts, Boston*. N.p., n.d. Web. 04 Mar. 2016. <http://www.mfa.org/collections/object/king-menkaura-mycerinus-and-queen-230>.

"Knossos." *Knossos*. Ancient Greece.org, 2002. Web. 16 Feb. 2016. <http://ancient-greece.org/archaeology/knossos.html>.

Koda, Harold. "The Chiton, Peplos, and Himation in Modern Dress [Essay] Heilbrunn Timeline of Art History | The Metropolitan Museum of Art." *The Met's Heilbrunn Timeline of Art History*. N.p., Oct. 2003. Web. 11 Jan. 2016. <http://www.metmuseum.org/TOAH/hd/god3/hd_god3.htm>.

Koerner, Joseph Leo. *The Moment of Self-Portraiture in German Renaissance Art*. Chicago: University of Chicago Press, 1993. Print.

Kozlowski, Jaime. "The Etruscans: Obsession with Death." *The Etruscans: Mystery People of Italy*. N.p., 2014. Web. <http://www.domspe.org/etruscans/obsession.html>.

Kucharz, Christel. "The Real Story Behind Van Gogh's Severed Ear." *ABC News*. N.p., 5 May 2009. Web. <http://abcnews.go.com/International/story?id=7506786&page=1>.

Kuchmak, Nick. "Life and Death on Sulawesi." *Matador Network*. N.p., 12 July 2010. Web. 04 Mar. 2016. <http://matadornetwork.com/trips/photo-essay-life-and-death-on-sulawesi/>.

"Labors of the Months from the Très Riches Heures." *The Public Domain Review*. N.p., n.d. Web. 17 Feb. 2016.

La Cueva De Los Sueños Olvidados Cave of Forgotten Dreams. Dir. Werner Herzog. Cameo, 2012. Film.

Lacaille, Frédéric. *Napoleon.org.* Bonaparte Crossing the Great St Bernard Pass, 2013. Web. 02 Feb. 2016 <http://www.napoleon.org/en/essential_napoleon/key_painting/files/482581.asp>.

Lawler, Andrew. "From the Trenches—Back to Bamiyan, Afghanistan, Ten Years Later—Archaeology Magazine Archive." *From the Trenches—Back to Bamiyan, Afghanistan, Ten Years Later—Archaeology Magazine Archive.* Archaeology Magazine, July-Aug. 2011. Web. 12 Mar. 2016.

Lawler, Andrew. "Global Support Grows for Afghan Restoration". *Science* 295.5554 (2002): 419–419.

Lawler, Andrew. "Remains of Bamiyan Buddhas Yield Additional Details about Statues' Origins." Washington Post. *The Washington Post,* 06 Mar. 2011. Web. 12 Mar. 2016.

Lazzari, Margaret R., and Dona Schlesier. *Exploring Art: A Global, Thematic Approach.* South Melbourne, Victoria, Australia: Wadsworth, Thomson Learning, 2002. Print.

"Les Très Riches Heures Du Duc De Berry." *Les Très Riches Heures Du Duc De Berry.* N.p., n.d. Web. 15 Feb. 2016. <http://www.christusrex.org/www2/berry/limbourg.html>.

"Life in A Medieval Castle Medieval Food." *Castle Life.* Castles and Manor Houses, 2010. Web. 15 Feb. 2016. <http://www.castlesandmanorhouses.com/life_04_food.htm>.

Lightbown, R. W. *Sandro Botticelli: Life and Work.* 2nd ed. New York: Abbeville Press, 1989. Print.

"Limbourg brothers". *Encyclopædia Britannica. Encyclopædia Britannica Online.* Encyclopædia Britannica Inc., 2016. Web. 15 Feb. 2016 <http://www.britannica.com/biography/Limbourg-brothers>.

Lloyd, Seton. *The Archaeology of Mesopotamia: From the Old Stone Age to the Persian Conquest.* London: Thames and Hud, 1978.

Long, Richard. "Richard Long Official Website." *Richard Long Official Website.* N.p., n.d. Web. 19 Apr. 2016.

Lyon, William S. *Encyclopedia of Native American Shamanism: Sacred Ceremonies.* ABC-CLIO, 1998.

"Māori Chief's Pātaka." *AMNH.* American Museum of Natural History, n.d. Web. 19 Apr. 2016.

"Maori Pataka (storehouse)." *Te Papa Our Place.* Museum of New Zealand, 2007. Web. 05 Feb. 2016 <http://collections.tepapa.govt.nz/topic/1539>.

"Maori Tattoo: The Definitive Guide to Ta Moko." *Tattoo History—Maori / New Zealand Tattoos—History of Tattoos and Tattooing Worldwide.* ZealandTattoo, n.d. Web. 4 Mar. 2016. <http://www.zealandtattoo.co.nz/tattoo-styles/maori-tattoos/>.

Mark, Joshua J. "Akhenaten." *Ancient History Encyclopedia.* N.p., 17 Apr. 2014. Web. 03 Mar. 2016. <http://www.ancient.eu/Akhenaten/>.

Mark, Joshua J. "Akhenaten." *Ancient History Encyclopedia.* N.p., 17 Apr. 2014. Web. 15 Jan. 2016.

Mark, Joshua J. "Knossos." *Ancient History Encyclopedia.* N.p., 15 Oct. 2010. Web. 25 Mar. 2016.

Mark, Joshua J. "The Egyptian Afterlife and The Feather of Truth." *Ancient History Encyclopedia.* N.p., 2008. Web. 04 Mar. 2016. <http://www.ancient.eu/article/42/>.

Mancoff, Debra N. "Vincent Van Gogh Final Paintings." *HowStuffWorks.* N.p., 21 Aug. 2007. Web. 04 Mar. 2016. <http://entertainment.howstuffworks.com/arts/artwork/vincent-van-gogh-final-paintings7.htm>.

"Maori of New Zealand." Manaia in Maori Carving in New Zealand. N.p., 2001. Web. 24 Apr. 2016.

"Marie Antoinette and Her Children: The Mystery and the History of Louis Charles in the Tower. Part 2." *Culture & Stuff.* N.p., 4 May 2010. Web.

"Marie Antoinette and Her Children: The Queen's Adopted Family." *Culture & Stuff.* N.p., 22 Feb. 2010. Web.

Metrick, Lenore. "Disjunctions in Nature and Culture: Andy Goldsworthy." *Sculpture.* May 2003: N. p. Web. 08 Mar. 2016.

Meyer, Karl E. "The Sack of Mesopotamia". *World Policy Journal* 21.4 (2004): 91–93. Web.

Meyer, Susan E. *Mary Cassatt.* New York: Abrams, 1990. Print. First impressions; First impressions (New York, NY).

Miller, Jay. "Alaskan Tlingit and Tsimshian." *American Indians of the Pacific Northwest Collection.* University of Washington Libraries, n.d. Web. 21 Apr. 2016.

Millmore, Mark. "Akhenaten." *Discovering Ancient Egypt.* N.p., 1997. Web. 03 Mar. 2016. <http://discoveringegypt.com/ancient-egyptian-kings-queens/akhenaten/>.

"Minoan Art Pottery." *Ceramics and Pottery Arts and Resources.* N.p., 25 Sept. 2013. Web. 07 Mar. 2016 <http://www.veniceclayartists.com/minoan-art-pottery/>.

"Minoan Pottery." *Minoan Pottery.* N.p., July 2005. Web. 24 Apr. 2016.

Minster, Christopher. "Why Did the Ancient Olmec Carve Colossal Heads?" *About.com Education.* N.p., 15 Jan. 2016. Web. 03 Mar. 2016. <http://latinamericanhistory.about.com/od/ancientlatinamerica/p/The-Colossal-Heads-Of-The-Olmec.htm>.

Moffat, Charles. "Elisabeth Vigee-Lebrun: Biography & Art—The Art History Archive." *Elisabeth Vigee-Lebrun: Biography & Art—The Art History Archive.* N.p., 2007. Web. 12 Mar. 2016.

"Moose Curtis—Reverse Graffiti Munich." *YouTube.* Kammermedia, n.d. Web. 19 Apr. 2016.

Morgan, Tiernan. "The Praise and Prejudices Vigée Le Brun Faced in Her Exceptional 18th-Century Career." *Hyperallergic RSS.* Biography.com, 12 May 2016. Web. 12 Mar. 2016.

"Mount Meru." *Summit Post.* N.p., n.d. Web. Jan. 2016. <http://www.summitpost.org/mount-meru/150789>.

"Mural". *Encyclopædia Britannica. Encyclopædia Britannica Online.* Encyclopædia Britannica Inc., 2016. Web. 15 May. 2016 <http://www.britannica.com/art/mural-painting>.

"Museo Altamira." *Chronology.* N.p., n.d. Web. 15 Feb. 2016. <http://en.museodealtamira.mcu.es/Prehistoria_y_Arte/cronologia.html>.

Nance, James J. "Abraham Lincoln Art Gallery. Com." *Masks.* Abraham Lincoln Art Gallery, 2003. Web.

"National Museum of Women in the Arts." *Käthe Kollwitz.* National Museum of Women in the Arts, 2014. Web. 27 12 Mar. 2016.

"Native American Ghost Dance." *Native American Online.* N.p., n.d. Web. 15 Jan. 2016.

"Native Halibut Hooks." *Exclusive Alaska.* N.p., n.d. Web. 15 Feb. 2016. <http://www.exclusivealaska.com/halibut/halibutHooks.cfm>.

"National Museum of Women in the Arts." *Élisabeth Louise Vigée-LeBrun.* National Museum of Women in the Arts, 2014. Web.

Oldenburg, Claes, and Coosje van. Bruggen. *Claes Oldenburg, Coosje Van Bruggen: Large-Scale Projects.* New York: Monacelli Press, 1994. Print.

"Pacific Northwest Coast Stories-Tlingit Frog Story" *Alaskan and Pacific Northwest Legends.* N.p., n.d. Web. Jan. 2016. <http://www.northwest-art.com/NorthwestArt/WebPages/StoriesTlingitFrogStory.htm>.

Park, George K. "animism". *Encyclopædia Britannica. Encyclopædia Britannica Online.* Encyclopædia Britannica Inc., 2016. Web. 01 Feb. 2016 <http://www.britannica.com/topic/animism>.

Patterson, Michael Robert. "James Brewerton Ricketts, Major General, United States Army." *James Brewerton Ricketts, Major General, United States Army.* Arlingtonton National Cemetery, 2011. Web. 04 Mar. 2016. <http://www.arlingtoncemetery.net/jbricketts.htm>.

"Paul Cézanne." *Philadelphia Museum of Art.* N.p., n.d. Web. 07 Mar. 2016.

Phipp, Simon E. "Home Page." *Simon Phipp.* N.p., 1999. Web. 01 Jan. 2016. <http://www.soltakss.com/indexsoltakss.html>.

"Pieter Claesz (1597-1660)." Pieter Claesz: Still Life Painter. *Encyclopedia of Old Master Painters,* n.d. Web. 21 Apr. 2016.

"Pieter Claesz.—Artists—Explore the Collection—Rijksmuseum." *Rijks Museum.* N.p., n.d. Web. 21 Apr. 2016.

"Pieter Claesz". *Encyclopædia Britannica. Encyclopædia Britannica Online.* Encyclopædia Britannica Inc., 2016. Web. 21 Apr. 2016 <http://www.britannica.com/biography/Pieter-Claesz>.

Pitt Rivers Museum—Animals and Belief—Ancient Egypt. Ollie Douglas DCF Court Project, 2003. Web. 01 Feb. 2016. <http://www.prm.ox.ac.uk/AnimalMummification.html>.

"Places of Peace and Power: Angkor Wat Facts." *SacredSites.* N.p., n.d. Web. 11 Nov. 2015 <http://sacredsites.com/asia/cambodia/angkor_wat_facts.html>.

Pollitt, Ben. "David, Napoleon Crossing the Alps." *Khan Academy.* N.p., n.d. Web. 4 Mar. 2016. <https://www.khanacademy.org/humanities/monarchy-enlightenment/neo-classicism/a/david-napoleon-crossing-the-alps>.

Popova, Maria. "Shepard Fairey on Capitalism, Freedom, Selling Out, and What Makes Great Art." *Brain Pickings.* Amazon Services LLC Associates Program, 11 June 2014. Web. 21 Apr. 2016.

"Preston Singletary: Raven and the Box of Daylight." *Museum of Glass.* N.p., n.d. Web. 21 Apr. 2016.

"Projects | Wrapped Reichstag." *Christo and Jeanne-Claude.* N.p., n.d. Web. 21 Apr. 2016.

Proulx, Donald A. "The Nasca Culture: An Introduction." *The Nasca Culture: An Introduction* (n.d.): 1–25. University of Massachusetts. Web.

Rama, Lauren. "Definition of Shamanic Practice." *Shamanic Practice.* Soul Restore, n.d. Web. 15 Dec. 2015 <http://www.eaglespiritministry.com/teaching/texts/shamanicp.htm>.

Richardson, Milda Bakšys. "Reverence and Resistance in Lithuanian Wayside Shrines". *Perspectives in Vernacular Architecture* 10 (2005): 249–267. Web.

"Reichstag." *Encyclopedia Britannica Online.* Encyclopedia Britannica, 26 Nov. 2014. Web. 03 Mar. 2016.

"Reincarnation." *New World Encyclopedia.* N.p., n.d. Web. 05 Dec. 2015. <http://www.newworldencyclopedia.org/entry/Reincarnation>.

Reliquary Guardian Figures." *A Personal Journey: Central African Art. Lawrence Gussman Collection,* n.d. Web. 4 Mar. 2016. <http://africa.si.edu/exhibits/journey/guardian.html>.

"Reliquary Guardian Figure (Boumba Bwiti)." *Brooklyn Museum: Arts of Africa:* N.p., n.d. Web. 04 Mar. 2016. <https://www.brooklynmuseum.org/opencollection/objects/100716/Reliquary_Guardian_Figure_Boumba_Bwiti>.

Reynolds, Emma. "Man Who 'buggered up the Opera House' Really Saved It from Disaster." *Nws Act.* N.p., 01 Feb. 2016. Web. 05 Mar. 2016.

Richardson, Geneviève. "The Tlingit People—Tlingit Art." *The Tlingit People.* N.p., n.d. Web. 04 Jan. 2016 <http://thetlingitpeople.weebly.com/art.html>.

"Robert H. Bescher, Cincinnati Reds, National League." *The Metropolitan Museum of Art, I.e. The Met Museum.* Art League, 2000. Web. 04 Mar. 2016. <http://www.metmuseum.org/art/collection/search/624828>.

Roehrig, Catharine H., et al. *Hatshepsut, from Queen to Pharaoh.* New York: The Metropolitan Museum of Art, 2005. Print.

"Ronin (masterless Samurai)." *Nakasendo Way: A Journey to the Heart of Japan.* N.p., 20 Dec. 2010. Web. 03 Mar. 2016. <http://www.nakasendoway.com/ronin-masterless-samurai/>.

Rosemary's Blog. "Hiking in France 3: Goldsworthy Refuges D'Art." *Rosemarys Blog.* N.p., 28 May 2013. Web. 21 Apr. 2016.

"Sand Mandalas: Creating A Perfectly Harmonious World." *YoWangdu.* YoWangdu, 07 Oct. 2012. Web. 01 Feb. 2016. <http://www.yowangdu.com/tibetan-buddhism/sand-mandalas.html>.

"Sand painting". *Encyclopædia Britannica. Encyclopædia Britannica Online.* Encyclopædia Britannica Inc., 2016. Web. 15 May. 2016 <http://www.britannica.com/art/sand-painting>.

"Scared-destinations.com." *Scared-destinations.com.* N.p., n.d. Web. 24 Nov. 2015. <http://www.scared-destinations.com/nepal/kathmandu-boudhanath-stupa>.

Schiele, Egon, and Erwin Mitsch. *The Art of Egon Schiele.* London: Phaidon, 1975. Print.

Schiele, Egon, Klaus Albrecht Schröder, and Graphische Sammlung Albertina. *Egon Schiele.* Vienna: Albertina, 2005. Print.

"Sculpture". *Encyclopædia Britannica. Encyclopædia Britannica Online.* Encyclopædia Britannica Inc., 2016. Web. 15 May. 2016 <http://www.britannica.com/art/sculpture/Methods-and-techniques>.

Senthilingam, Meera. "Earthships, the Sustainable Homes Made with Old Junk—CNN.com." *CNN.* Cable News Network, 19 Nov. 2015. Web. 16 Feb. 2016. http://www.cnn.com/2014/09/26/living/earthships-new-mexico/index.html.

"Shepard FaireyE Pluribus Venom—Jonathan Levine Gallery." *Jonathan Levine Gallery.* N.p., 2007. Web. 21 Apr. 2016.

Smilgys, Hubertas. *Kryžiu Kalnas.* Vilnius: Saulės Delta, 1999. Print.

"Sofia Synagogue and Its History Museum—Sofia City." *Bulgaria—Official Tourism Portal of Bulgaria.* N.p., n.d. Web. 14 Dec. 2015. <http://bulgariatravel.org/en/object/254/Sofiiska_sinagoga_i_muzej_Sofia>

Stewart, Hilary. *Looking at Totem Poles.* Vancouver: Douglas & McIntyre, 1993. Print.

Strain, Eric. "Lou Ruvo Center Design Defines Purpose of Facility." *LasVegasSun.com.* N.p., 04 Apr. 2010. Web. 06 Feb. 2016.

Strieder, Peter. *Albrecht Dürer, Paintings, Prints, Drawings.* 1st ed. New York: Abaris Books, 1982. Print.

Sullivan, Mary Ann. "Mural: Class Struggle, Palacio Nacional De Mexico." *Mexico City, Mexico.* N.p., 2010. Web.

Styles, Ruth. "Are These the World's Most Painful Tattoos? Ethiopian and Sudanese Tribes Show off Their Intricate Raised Patterns Created Using THORNS." *Mail Online. Associated Newspapers,* 18 Feb. 2014. Web. 04 Mar. 2016. <http://www.dailymail.co.uk/femail/article-2561949/Ethiopian-Sudanese-tribes-intricate-raised-patterns-created-using-THORNS.html>.

Sujato, Bhikkhu. "Thedeathandresurectionofthebuddha–Santipada." *Thedeathandresurection-ofthebuddha—Santipada.* N.p., n.d. Web. 15 Nov. 2015. <https://sites.google.com/site/santipada/thedeathandresurectionofthebuddha>.

"Sydney Opera House—the Architect." *Samsung.* Sydney Opera House, 2016. Web. 09 Mar. 2016 <http://www.sydneyoperahouse.com/about/the_architect.aspx>.

Szczepanski, Kallie. "What Was a Ronin in Feudal Japan?" *About.com Education.* N.p., 31 Dec. 2015. Web. 03 Mar. 2016. <http://asianhistory.about.com/od/glossaryps/g/GlosRonin.htm>.

"Tantra." *Merriam-Webster.com.* Merriam-Webster, n.d. Web. 11 Feb. 2016.

"Tattoo History—Maori / New Zealand Tattoos—History of Tattoos and Tattooing Worldwide." *Tattoo History—Maori / New Zealand Tattoos—History of Tattoos and Tattooing Worldwide.* N.p., 2013. Web. 04 Mar. 2016. <http://www.vanishingtattoo.com/tattoo_museum/maori_tattoos.html>.

"TE AO HOU THE MAORI MAGAZINE [electronic Resource]." *TE AO HOU THE MAORI MAGAZINE [electronic Resource].* National Library of New Zealand, n.d. Web. 19 Apr. 2016.

Taylor, Nick. *American-Made: The Enduring Legacy of the WPA: When FDR Put the Nation to Work.* New York: Bantam Book, 2008.Print.

"The Actor Nakamura Utaemon in the Role of Kato Masakiyo." *WDL RSS.* Library of Congress, 18 Sept. 2015. Web. 04 Mar. 2016. <https://www.wdl.org/en/item/9/>.

The Biography.com Editors. "Banksy." *Bio.com.* A&E Networks Television, n.d. Web. 19 Apr. 2016.

"The Haka—Dance of War—Maori Haka—New Zealand | Tourism NZ." *The Haka—Dance of War—Maori Haka—New Zealand | Tourism NZ.* 100% Pure New Zealand, n.d. Web. 04 Mar. 2016. <http://www.newzealand.com/us/feature/haka/>.

"The Hill of Tara, Meath." *The Hill of Tara, Meath.* N.p., n.d. Web. 19 Apr. 2016.

"The History Place—Dorothea Lange Photo Gallery: Migrant Farm Families." *The History Place—Dorothea Lange Photo Gallery: Migrant Farm Families.* N.p., 2012. Web. 03 Mar. 2016. <http://www.historyplace.com/unitedstates/lange/>.

"The Faith of a Heretic." *The Faith of a Heretic.* WordPress, n.d. Web. 21 Apr. 2016.

"The Life, Paintings & Sculptures of Paul Gauguin." *The Art History Archive.* N.p., n.d. Web. 15 Feb. 2016.

"The Maori - Settlement - New Zealand in History." *The Maori—Settlement—New Zealand in History.* N.p., n.d. Web. 19 Apr. 2016.

"The Sculpture Non-Violence." *The Sculpture.* N.p., n.d. Web.

"Thought". *Dictionary.com Unabridged.* Random House, Inc. 15 May. 2016. <Dictionary.com http://www.dictionary.com/browse/thought>.

"Tobacco Baseball Cards." *Baseball Almanac.* N.p., 2000. Web. 15 Mar. 2016 <http://www.baseball-almanac.com/treasure/autont005.shtm>.

"Toreador Frescoes at Knossos." *Toreador Frescoes at Knossos.* McGraw-Hill Higher Education, n.d. Web. 03 Mar. 2016. <http://www.mhhe.com/socscience/art/timelines/the_aegean/html/frescoes.html>.

"Totem Pole Carver Ellen Neel (1916-1966)." *Totem Pole Carver Ellen Neel (1916–1966).* Goldi Productions Ltd., 2005. Web. 15 Jan. 2016.

Trentinella, Rosemarie. "Roman Portrait Sculpture: Republican through Constantinian." (Essay) Heilbrunn Timeline of Art History, The Metropolitan Museum of Art. *The Met's Heilbrunn Timeline of Art History.* N.p., Oct. 2003. Web. 03 Mar. 2016. <http://www.metmuseum.org/toah/hd/ropo/hd_ropo.htm>.

Trentinella, Rosemarie. "Roman Portrait Sculpture: The Stylistic Cycle." (Essay) Heilbrunn Timeline of Art History, The Metropolitan Museum of Art. *The Met's Heilbrunn Timeline of Art History.* Heilbrunn Timeline of Art History., Oct. 2003. Web. 03 Mar. 2016. <http://www.metmuseum.org/toah/hd/ropo2/hd_ropo2.htm>.

"Tsogho Reliquary Figure." *Tsogho Reliquary Figure.* ABeNA Tribal Art Gallery, 2006. Web. 04 Mar. 2016. <http://www.abenatribalart.com/item/3076-mbumba-bwete-tsogho-reliquary-figure>.

Turton, David. *Mursi Online.* University of Oxford, 2013. Web. 21 Mar. 2016 <http://mursi.org/>.

Ullrich, Madeline. "The Art of Contradiction: Nazi Reception of Käthe Kollwitz." *Broad Strokes The National Museum of Women in the Arts Blog.* N.p., 16 May 2014. Web.

"UNRV Ancient Roman Empire History." *UNRV.* N.p., n.d. Web. Jan. 2016. <http://www.unrv.com/>.

Vinnicombe, Patricia. *People of the Eland: Rock Paintings of the Drakensberg Bushmen as a Reflection of Their Life and Thought.* Pietermaritzburg: University of Natal Press, 1976. Print.

"Vincent Van Gogh Gallery." *Vincent Van Gogh Gallery.* N.p., 2002. Web. 04 Mar. 2016. <http://www.van-goghgallery.com/misc/van-goghs-ear.html>.

"Vishnu." *ReligionFacts.com.* 10 Nov. 2015. Web. 1 Feb. 2016. <www.religionfacts.com/vishnu>.

Voorhies, James. "Paul Cézanne (1839–1906)." *Heilbrunn Timeline of Art History. New York: The Metropolitan Museum of Art, 2000–.* http://www.metmuseum.org/toah/hd/pcez/hd_pcez.htm (October 2004)

Wallace, Robert. "Off the Beaten Track in Northern Kentucky." *Aeqai.* N.p., 04 Oct. 2014. Web. 02 Feb. 2016.

"War Dance of the Polynesian Islands." *War Dance of the Polynesian Islands.* N.p., n.d. Web. 04 Mar. 2016. <http://polynesianwardances.tumblr.com/?soc_src=mail&soc_trk=ma>.

Whitt, Stephen. "A House of Snow and Ice." *Beyond Penguins and Polar Bears.* The Ohio State University, n.d. Web. 18 Mar. 2016 <http://beyondpeng uins.nsdl.org/>.

"Who's Who in the New Deal." *Who's Who in the New Deal.* N.p., n.d. Web. 03 Mar. 2016. <http://www.wpamurals.org/whoswho.html>.

Witcombe, Christopher L.C.E. "Menkaure and His Queen: 2. Description." *Menkaure and His Queen: 2. Description*. Art History Resources, 1995. Web. 04 Mar. 2016. <http://arthistoryresources.net/menkaure/menkauredescription.html>.

Wolf, Justin. "The Art Story.org—Your Guide to Modern Art." *The Art Story: Works Progress Administration (WPA).* The Art Story Foundation, n.d. Web. 03 Mar. 2016. <http://www.theartstory.org/org-wpa.htm>.

"WPA Federal Art Project". *Encyclopædia Britannica. Encyclopædia Britannica Online*. Encyclopædia Britannica Inc., 2016. Web. 19 May. 2016 <http://www.britannica.com/topic/WPA-Federal-Art-Project>.